PARIS AWAITS YOU!

An enchanting glimpse of Paris which conjures up a vision of the living city, whose charming manners and customs can only be fully appreciated through knowledge of its vivacious language. Several well-known landmarks, including the Eiffel Tower and the Cathedral of Notre Dame, can be found in this panoramic view.

FRENCH

HOW TO SPEAK
AND WRITE IT

An informal conversational method
for self study with 400 illustrations

by Joseph Lemaître

DOVER PUBLICATIONS, INC.
New York

This new Dover edition, first published in 1962, is a slightly revised version of the work first published by Odhams Press Limited. The revision consists of minor editing to adapt the book for the American audience.

This edition is published by special arrangement with Odhams Press Limited.

International Standard Book Number: 0-486-20268-2
Library of Congress Catalog Card Number: 63-357

Manufactured in the United States of America

Dover Publications, Inc.
31 East 2nd Street
Mineola, N.Y. 11501

CONTENTS

*A DETAILED ALPHABETICAL GUIDE TO THE
CONTENTS IS GIVEN ON PAGE 403*

TUNISIAN STREET SCENE

French is spoken throughout a large part of the African continent, which also forms the background of many French literary works. This scene recalls the delightful travel memoirs of Eugène Fromentin, the nineteenth-century painter-writer.

HOW TO USE THE COURSE

THE purpose of the present French Course is to lead students easily and naturally into a real working knowledge of the French language, and also to afford them an opportunity of appreciating French literature.

This course deals more thoroughly with the elementary stage and the grading of progress is less steep than is usual in language courses. It is so designed that any intelligent person can start as an absolute beginner and finish with a practical working knowledge of French. The text must be thoroughly mastered and its correct pronunciation acquired with the aid of the translation and the imitated pronunciation. A good plan would be to study together with friends. If you know someone whose native tongue is French, so much the better, for he can check your pronunciation.

Grammar is conveyed throughout by practical examples which should be memorised as far as possible. This method is preferred to the mere learning of rules by rote which tends to produce a type of student who has mastered the most abstruse niceties of grammar yet is unable correctly to ask his way to a station or order a meal in a restaurant.

FRENCH PRONUNCIATION

No doubt you have heard Frenchmen speaking their language on the radio, in the cinema or elsewhere. You will have noticed that it sounds quite different from English; you may even have called it a "gabble." How are you going to learn to understand that gabble, and speak the same

Note.—In the case of certain prices quoted in the Course for meals, the reader must make allowances for varying conditions.

language yourself in a way a Frenchman will understand? It is not enough to know what a French word means and how it is spelt; you must know how to pronounce it, too, and, with that, how to recognise it when spoken.

Neither this book nor any other can teach you the correct pronunciation of French. It can help you to acquire it, and can explain the difficulties, but it cannot speak French to you.

Luckily, there are other ways—the wireless, for example. Listening-in, even if you

don't at first understand, will gradually attune your ears to French sounds and intonation.

Suppose you switch on the radio and hear the French announcer introduce a programme. You don't understand him, but he says: **Programme National,** etc.

You recognise the words now that you

see them. Why did you fail to recognise the words as the announcer uttered them? We use the words in English, too, but the French pronounce them differently. If you listen very carefully you may come to the conclusion that what the announcer said was not *programme* but *brogramme*. You may have this idea too when you first hear a Frenchman say **pardon!** where we say "sorry!" or **une seconde** where we say "one moment, please!" It may sound like *bardon, s'gonde*. To discover the reason for this, hold a lighted match in front of your mouth and say the English word "programme." The match will probably go out, or certainly flicker, because so much breath is expelled before you actually make the first sound. In pronouncing the French *p* you must let out as little breath as possible before the sound; try to say *programme* in such a way that the flame of the match is disturbed as little as possible.

National. This is pronounced with the sounds "nah-syo-nahl," the first syllable as in "not" and the last like the "al" in "pal." But this is still not enough to tell us what the word sounds like. Take again the corresponding English word "National." It is easy to say what sound the vowel in the first syllable is, because it bears a very heavy stress, but with the other two it is more difficult, because we pronounce them quickly and rather indistinctly. In rapid speech we may even say *nashnl*. The French will have none of this mumbling, and every syllable in the word must be pronounced equally clearly, with an equal stress on all three.

Now we know that the announcer said: *pro-grahm nah-syo-nahl.*

To explain the remaining sounds of French we will take some words that are common to both French and English. The reader is almost certainly familiar with the words **charlotte russe, hors d'œuvre, restaurant, liqueur, Camembert,** etc. They are all French words which are often used in English, and they all have to do with eating. In the mouths of the English people these words have either an English pronunciation or a compromise between the

English and the French; in either case the pronunciation of them would puzzle a Frenchman.

Charlotte russe: The first part of the name of this sweet is pronounced *shahr-lot*, just as in English, except that the *r* is pronounced more strongly and that we must beware of stressing the first syllable at the expense of the second. Both must have equal attention. The vowel of the second word, *russe*, meaning Russian, has no English equivalent. If you say *ee* with your lips right out, as though you were going to whistle, you will get the sound. This we represent in our imitated pronunciation by ẹẹ.

Hors d'œuvre: The first part of the word is pronounced like the underlined part of the word <u>lor</u>d, and *œu* is pronounced like *ea* in <u>ear</u>th. This sound is rendered as ầy in our system of simplified pronunciation (the combination *œu* is rather unusual) so that we can render the pronunciation of *hors d'œuvre* by *or-dầyvr.*

Restaurant: The first part is pronounced like "rest." The vowel *au* is the pure "oh." The only difficulty will be the sound of the last syllable. In French it is a nasal sound, and to get it right you will have to practise it a little. The term "nasal" indicates that the sound is made through the nose. That is to say, it will bear a resemblance to the sounds a Cockney or an American makes if he has a twang. Begin by humming a long *m* on one note. Do this hard enough and you will feel a slight vibration inside the nose. Still keeping up the humming sound, suddenly open your mouth and say *ah*. The result will be the French nasal *a*, represented in the word restaurant by *an*. The *n* is not sounded; it only serves to show that the *a* is to be nasalised in the way described. Naturally you will not need to hum every time you make this sound; that is only a way the beginner may acquire it. In our system of imitated pronunciation we shall show this sound by a capital N to mark the difference between an ordinary *n* and a nasal. It is not a consonant, but merely an indication that the preceding vowel is a nasal one.

In actual French spelling the sound aN is rendered by either an, am, en or em.

tante	gant	ambassade
taNt	gaN	aN-bah-sahd
aunt	*glove*	*embassy*
enfant	vente	embrasser
aN-faN	vaNt	aN-brah-say
child	*sale*	*to embrace*

The French word for *long* is spelt the same as in English. To pronounce it correctly you have to let as much air as possible pass through the nose and to clip off the suspicion of *g* you can hear in the English pronunciation of the word. You also have to round your lips slightly. Now say, pronouncing *oN* in the same way:

crayon	bon	réponse
kray-yoN	boN	ray-poNs
pencil	*good*	*reply*
pont	son	tombeau
poN	soN	toN-boh
bridge	*sound*	*tomb*

Now say *bang* without sounding the *g*, allowing part of the air to escape through the nose. This is the way to pronounce the French word for "bath," which is spelt *bain*. In our imitated pronunciation we give it as biN, rendering the nasal by iN. In ordinary French spelling it usually appears as either in (im), ain (aim), or ein (eim).

vin	pain	Américain
viN	piN	ah-may-ree-kiN
wine	*bread*	*American*
fin	impoli	teint
fiN	iN-po-lee	tiN
end	*impolite*	*complexion*

If you pronounce *i* as in "sir" with slightly rounded lips and allow part of the air to pass through the nose you will be able to pronounce *un* or *um* and to say:

parfum	Verdun
pahr-fuN	vair-duN
perfume	*Verdun*
un	brun	lundi
uN	bruN	luN-dee
one	*brown*	*Monday*

The four nasal sounds are aN (as in *restaurant*), oN (as in *long*), iN (as in *vin*), and uN (as in *Verdun*). All the four nasals are to be found in

un bon vin blanc (*a good white wine*)
uN boN viN blaN.

DIFFERENCE BETWEEN ENGLISH AND FRENCH PRONUNCIATION

1. *French sounds are always pure*
    When you say "me" or "fee" in English the sound "ee" always remains the same, and so does the position of your lips. In other words: this "ee" is a pure vowel. But if you say "home," watching your lips, you will notice that they gradually close, and that what you actually say is a kind of double sound (called diphthong), rather like "ho-oom."
    Now, in French, the vowels sound invariably pure, and the sound remains the same from beginning to end: "a" is pure *ah*, "ô" is pure *oh* and "é" pure *eh*, and so on.
    When you say "Paris" in English, if you hold a lighted match in front of your mouth and try to say the "p" in such a way that the flame remains undisturbed, you will say the pure French *p*. The same applies to *b*, *m*, *f* and *v* which, like the *p*, are produced by separating the lips. In French, therefore, when making these sounds, you must try to let as little air as possible come out of your mouth.

2. *The syllables of a French word are evenly pronounced*
    In English it is just the opposite. There is a strong stress on one syllable—usually the first—whereas the others are muttered more or less indistinctly, and often com-

pletely slurred together. Compare the rapid English pronunciation of "national"—*nashnl*—with the French pronunciation, *nah-syo-nahl.*

While English speech can be likened to a string of beads where some big beads alternate with some small ones, French

speech, on the contrary, may be likened to a string of pearls in which all are of the same size, thus:

From this we must learn that every syllable in French is to be pronounced evenly. There should be no drawling, or mumbling, as in English. This rule holds good for all words except those which end in *e* without an accent sign over it, which *e* is always silent, e.g., **table, téléphone, dame**—pronounced: "tahbl," "tay-lay-fon," "dahm."

3. *Greater mobility of the speech organs necessary in speaking French*

The lips and the tongue must be more mobile in French, and the mouth must frequently be opened wider than in English:

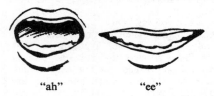

       "ah"   "ee"

e.g., when saying "pah-tees-ree" (**pâtisserie**), the mouth must be wide open for the "ah," and for the "ee" the corners of the lips have to be wide apart.

4. *When silent letters cease to be silent*

Many words are joined together in speech. Just as the English words "ham and eggs" are often pronounced as if they were one word, "hamaneggs," so, in

French, words are often similarly joined together. This linking together is called liaison.

As a rule, the final consonant of a word is not pronounced in French. When, however, a word ending in a consonant is followed by a word beginning with a vowel, the final consonant is often linked with the vowel of the following word. This linking occurs especially with words which are closely connected in sense.

EXAMPLES:

Ils (which means "they" and is pronounced "eel") and **ont** (which means "have" and is pronounced "oN"), when occurring together become "eel-zoN."

Trois (which means "three" and is pronounced "trwah") and **amis** (which means "friends" and is pronounced "ah-mee"), when coming together are said as "trwah-zah-mee."

En (which means "in" and is pronounced "aN") and **été** (which means "summer" and is pronounced "ay-tay") are said together as "aN-nay-tay."

Note from the last example that in liaison the *n* of a nasal sound is pronounced: among some French-speakers the nasal quality of the vowel is less marked as a result.

The ãy Sound in Imitated Pronunciation

The sound of *eu* (sometimes *œu*) in French is represented in our imitated pronunciation by ãy, this special type indicating the sound of those letters in English, when spoken with rounded lips. There is actually a difference between the pronunciation of *eu* in French when final as in *feu* (fire) or when followed by a silent consonant as in *deux* (two); and when followed by a hard consonant, as in *fleur* (flower). In order to avoid multiplication of special characters, we indicate both by the same symbol, but students should keep their ears attuned to mark the difference in French as spoken by Frenchmen.

et and *est*

Our representation of both these words by "ay." in the imitated pronunciation, is only an approximation, though it should enable you to make yourself understood by a Frenchman. But if you wish to speak correctly, you will listen carefully for the way in which these sounds really differ in French as spoken by educated persons. **Est-ce** we have indicated as "ais."

Pronunciation of -lle and -gn-

The letters *-lle* coming after *i* in French with certain exceptions such as *ville* (town) which is pronounced "veel," are reproduced by a sound like the "y" in "yes." Examples are **fille** (fee*y*) daughter, and **tilleul** (tee-yāyl) linden-tree.

We print this *y* in italics when it comes at the end of a word, so as to avoid confusion.

We also use this italicised *y* in similar cases when representing the -gn- sounds in French, which are reproduced by a sound resembling the "ny" in "canyon."

Thus, students cannot easily fall into the error of pronouncing veen*y* (**vigne,** vine) in our imitated pronunciation, to rhyme with "Sweeney" or kaN-pahn*y* (**campagne,** countryside) to rhyme with "canny."

PRONUNCIATION AND SPELLING

In English the same letter may be pronounced in various ways, e.g., the letter "a" is pronounced differently in the words "far," "ball," "gate," "at," "general." On the other hand, the same sound may be represented by several different spellings, as when in writing "keen," "machine," "lean," and "scene."

French has a less irregular spelling than English in so far as each letter and each combination of letters usually corresponds to one sound only. On the other hand, the same sound may be represented by several different spellings, although not quite to the same extent as in English. For instance, the sound *k*, which is usually represented by *c*, is in some words rendered by *k* or *qu*. The nasal sound "aN" will be found represented variously by *an, am, en* or *em*.

This, I fear, is rather confusing to the beginner, so in order to avoid confusion,

we have adopted a system of simplified spelling, i.e., one in which each letter and each combination of letters corresponds to one sound only. As far as possible we have rendered French sounds by their English equivalents, but in those instances where there is no English equivalent, we have rendered the French sound by the *nearest* English equivalent, together with a sign indicating how the French sound differs from the English.

As the two ways in which French vowels differ from their nearest English equivalents are either in rounding of the lips or nasalisation, we have indicated by ⌒ that the lips have to be rounded whilst producing the corresponding sound, and by "N" that the preceding vowel has to be nasalised in the manner described in the preceding pages.

SOUNDS OF SPOKEN FRENCH

Tabulating the sounds of French, as represented in our system of imitated pronunciation, we have:—

ah	like "ar" in "car" cut short and without pronouncing the "r"; but when spelt "â," and in some other words, long and open as in the exclamation "bah!"
ai	as in "fair" (mouth open a little wider).
aN	nasal "ah."
ay	like the "a" in "gate" (corners of the lips wide apart).
āy	the same with rounded lips—no English equivalent, but somewhat like the "ea" in "earth."
e	as in "wonder."
ee	as in "feet" (corners of the lips wide apart).
ēē	the same with closely rounded lips—no English equivalent.
iN	nasal "ai" (like "an" in "bang").
o	like "aw" in "lawyer" (lips pushed out, slightly rounded).
oh	as in "note" (lips further advanced and more rounded).
oo	as in "boot."

oN   nasal "o" (nearly as "on" in "long").
uN   like the "u" in "fur," but nasalised.
g   as in "go."
l   as in "lamp" (never as in "ball").
r   unlike English r, French r is produced
     by vibration of the soft palate at
     the back of the mouth; it resembles
     the sound of gargling.
s   as in "so."
sh   as in "shop."
zh   like the "s" in "measure."
w   as in "wise."
ẅ   the same with closely rounded lips
     (in position for pronouncing eē).
ny or ny as in "canyon."

THE ALPHABET AS PRONOUNCED IN FRANCE

A	ah	J	zhee	S	ais
B	bay	K	kah	T	tay
C	say	L	ail	U	eē
D	day	M	aim	V	vay
E	e	N	ain	W	doobl-vay
F	aif	O	oh	X	eeks
G	zhay	P	pay	Y	ee-graik
H	ahsh	Q	keē	Z	zaid
I	ee	R	air		

SIGNS AND ACCENTS

(ˊ) accent aigu (ahk-saN-tay-geē) gives to
the "e" the sound (ay): été (ay-tay) =
summer.

(ˋ) accent grave (ahk-saN grahv) gives to
the "e" the sound of (ai) as in "fair":
père (pair) = father.
Over a and u it does not affect the
sound, but distinguishes words, e.g.,
la=the là=there; a=has; à=to;
ou (oo)=or où=where.

(ˆ) accent circonflexe (ahk-saN seer-koN-
flaiks) lengthens the vowel on which
it is placed; on the e it sounds as in
the English word "there." tête (tait)
=head; pâte (paht)=paste.

(ç) la cédille (say-deey) gives the c the
sound of s: leçon (le-soN)=lesson.

(¨) le tréma (tray-mah) indicates that the
vowel bearing it is pronounced
separately from the preceding vowel:
Noël (noh-ail)=Christmas.

(ˈ) l'apostrophe (ah-pos-trof) indicates
omission of a vowel: l'hôtel (loh-tail)
=the hotel.

THE NUMBERS (0-20)

0	zéro	zay-roh
1	un	uN
2	deux	daȳ
3	trois	trwah
4	quatre	kahtr
5	cinq	siNk
6	six	sees
7	sept	sait
8	huit	ẅeet
9	neuf	naȳf
10	dix	dees
11	onze	oNz
12	douze	dooz
13	treize	traiz
14	quatorze	kah-torz
15	quinze	kiNz
16	seize	saiz
17	dix-sept	dees-sait
18	dix-huit	deez-ẅeet
19	dix-neuf	deez-naȳf
20	vingt	viN

VOCABULARY-BUILDING DIAGRAMS AND TEXT UNDER PHOTOGRAPHS

The most important aim of the Course is that you should complete it in possession of a proper groundwork from which you can proceed to widen your knowledge of French.

The additional vocabularies provided in the vocabulary-building diagrams, in the matter introduced for general information, and in the text under photographs contain certain words useful for background knowledge and for reading, but not necessarily heard in everyday colloquial speech.

There is no need for you to memorise all these words before working through the rest of the Course, unless you find them especially useful for your particular purpose in learning the language. You can return to them as your knowledge and vocabulary increase.

PREMIÈRE LEÇON—*FIRST LESSON*

Madame Roberts   **Monsieur Roberts**
(la mère)   (le père)

The Roberts and Lesage Families

These are the people whose adventures in Paris and in the country, at home and in public, through the myriad incidents of daily life in France, you will follow during the present Course.

The families consist of:

Mr. Roberts (English) and his wife (French); her father and mother, M. and Mme Georges Lesage; her children Charles and Madeleine; the Paul Lesages and their children, Georges and Lucie.

They are nice people, and we hope you will like them.

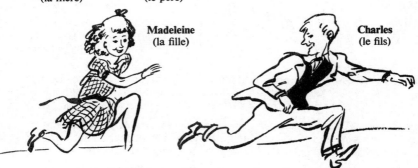

Madeleine
(la fille)

Charles
(le fils)

Monsieur Roberts est le père.   Mme Roberts est la mère.   Charles est le
m's-y@y[1] ro-bairts ay le pair.   mah-dahm ro-bairts ay lah mair.   shahrl ay le
Mr. Roberts is the father.   Mrs. Roberts is the mother.   Charles is the

fils de Monsieur et de Madame Roberts.   Madeleine est la fille de Monsieur
fees de m's-y@y ay de mah-dahm ro-bairts.   mahd-lain ay lah feey de m's-y@y
son of Mr. and (of) Mrs. Roberts.   Madeleine is the daughter of Mr.

et de Madame Roberts.   Monsieur et Madame Roberts sont les parents
ay de mah-dahm ro-bairts.   m's-y@y ay mah-dahm ro-bairts soN lay pah-raN
and (of) Mrs. Roberts.   Mr. and Mrs. Roberts are the parents

---

[1] This is the pronunciation of "monsieur" in rapid speech.   Spoken slowly it is pronounced "me-sy@y"; *me* to be sounded like *le* or *de* with slightly rounded lips.

de Charles et de Madeleine. Charles et Madeleine sont les enfants de Monsieur et
de shahrl ay de mahd-lain. shahrl et mahd-lain soN lay-zaN-faN de m's-yãy ay
of Charles and (of) Madeleine. Charles and Madeleine are the children of Mr. and

de Madame Roberts. Monsieur Georges Lesage est le père de Madame
de mah-dahm ro-bairts. m's-yãy zhorzh le-sahzh ay le pair de mah-dahm
(of) Mrs. Roberts. M. Georges Lesage is the father of Mrs.

Mme Paul Lesage   Paul Lesage
(la tante)   (l'oncle)

Monsieur Lesage   Madame Lesage
(le grand-père)   (la grand'mère)

Roberts. Il est le grand-père de Charles et de Madeleine. Madame Lesage
ro-bairts. ee-lay le graN-pair de shahrl ay de mahd-lain. mah-dahm le-sahzh
Roberts. He is the grandfather of Charles and (of) Madeleine. Mme Lesage

est leur grand'mère. Monsieur Paul Lesage est le frère de Mme Roberts.
ay lãyr graN-mair. m's-yãy pol le-sahzh ay le frair de mah-dahm ro-bairts.
is their grandmother. M. Paul Lesage is the brother of Mrs. Roberts.

Il est l'oncle de Charles et de Madeleine. Mme Paul Lesage est leur tante.
ee-lay loNkl de shahrl ay de mahd-lain. mah-dahm pol le-sahzh ay lãyr taNt.
He is the uncle of Charles and (of) Madeleine. Mme Paul Lesage is their aunt.

Monsieur et Madame Paul Lesage sont les parents de Georges et de Lucie
m's-yãy ay mah-dahm pol le-sahzh soN lay pah-raN de zhorzh ay de lẽe-see
M. and Mme Paul Lesage are the parents of Georges and (of) Lucie

Lesage. Georges est le frère de Lucie. Ils sont le
le-sahzh. zhorzh ay le frair de lẽe-see. eel soN le
Lesage. Georges is the brother of Lucie. They are the

cousin et la cousine de Charles et de Madeleine. Madeleine est la
koo-ziN ay lah koo-zeen de shahrl ay de mahd-lain. mahd-lain ay lah
(masculine and feminine) cousins of Charles and (of) Madeleine. Madeleine is the

sœur de Charles. Monsieur et Madame Roberts sont grands. Madame Roberts
sǣr de shahrl.   m's-yāy ay mah-dahm ro-bairts soN graN.   mah-dahm ro-bairts
sister of Charles.   Mr. and Mrs. Roberts are tall.   Mrs. Roberts

et Mademoiselle Lesage sont grandes.
ay mahd-mwah-zail le-sahzh soN graNd.
and Mlle Lesage are tall.

Monsieur et Madame Roberts sont blonds.
m's-yāy ay mah-dahm ro-bairts soN bloN.
Mr. and Mrs. Roberts are fair.

Madame Roberts et Madeleine sont
mah-dahm ro-bairts ay mahd-lain soN
Mrs. Roberts and Madeleine are

blondes. Charles et Madeleine
bloNd.   shahrl ay mahd-lain
fair.   Charles and Madeleine

sont-ils petits?   Oui, ils sont petits.
soN-teel p'tee?   w̄ee eel soN p'tee.
are they small?   Yes, they are small.

Lucie   Georges
(la cousine)   (le cousin)

HOW TO TRANSLATE "THEY"

There are two French words for the English "they": **ils** the plural of **il** (he), and **elles** of **elle** (she). Use **ils** for masculines and **elles** for feminines. When referring to both masculines and feminines, **ils** is used.

Examples:—
le père (the father) **il** (he).
les pères (the fathers) **ils** (they).
la mère (the mother) **elle** (she).

les mères (the mothers) **elles** (they).
les parents (the parents) **ils** (they).
les enfants (the children), **ils** when referring to boys or boys and girls.
elles (they) when referring to women or girls only.

In the plural both nouns and adjectives add **s**; this s is silent. **Le petit garçon** (the little boy). **Les petits garçons** (the little boys). **La petite fille** (the little girl). **Le͏s petites filles** (the little girls).

ils sont grands
eel soN graN
they (masc.) are tall

ils sont petits
eel soN p'tee
they (masc.) are small

elles sont grandes
ail soN graNd
they (fem.) are tall

elles sont petites
ail soN p'teet
they (fem.) are small

Anglais (Britannique)[1]
aN-glai (bree-tah-neek)
English (British)

Français
fraN-sai
French

Américain
ah-may-ree-kiN
American

Russe
rêes
Russian

Chinois
shee-nwah
Chinese

Monsieur Roberts est Anglais.[2]
m's-yãy ro-bairts ay-taN-glai.
Mr. Roberts is English.

Madame Vanderbilt est Américaine.
mah-dahm vaN-dair-beelt ay-tah-may-ree-kain.
Mrs. Vanderbilt is American.

Madame Roberts est Anglaise.
mah-dahm ro-bairts ay-taN-glaiz.
Mrs. Roberts is English.

   M. Ivanovich est-il Russe?
   m's-yãy ee-vaN-noh-veesh ay-teel rêes?
   M. Ivanovich is he Russian?

Monsieur Lesage est Français.
m's-yãy le-sahzh ay fraN-sai.
M. Lesage is French.

Madame Ivanovich est-elle Russe?
mah-dahm ee-vaN-noh-veesh ay-tail rêes?
Mme. Ivanovich is she Russian?

Madame Lesage est Française.
mah-dahm le-sahzh ay fraN-saiz.
Mme. Lesage is French.

   Monsieur Soong est-il Chinois?
   m's-yãy soong ay-teel shee-nwah?
   Mr. Soong is he Chinese?

Monsieur Vanderbilt est Américain.
m's-yãy VaN-dair-beelt ay-tah-may-ree-kiN.
Mr. Vanderbilt is American.

   Madame Soong est-elle Chinoise?
mah-dahm soong ay-tail shee-nwahz?
   Mrs. Soong is she Chinese?

Madame Roberts et Madeleine sont-elles Françaises ou Anglaises?
mah-dahm ro-bairts ay mahd-lain soN-tail fraN-saiz oo aN-glaiz?
Mrs. Roberts and Madeleine are they French or English?

Elles sont Anglaises
ail soN-taN-glaiz
They are English

Écossaises
ay-kos-saiz
Scottish

Irlandaises
eer-laN-daiz
Irish

Galloises
gah-lwahz
Welsh

Australiennes
oh-strah-lyain
Australian

All the above are the feminine plural versions of the adjectives meaning English, etc.

[1] The word **Anglais** is more frequently used in France than **Britannique** to denote the inhabitants of any part of the United Kingdom.

[2] A capital letter is used at the commencement of such a word in French only when the sense involved is "a Frenchman," "an Englishman," etc., but a small letter if the sense is merely "French" or "English," used adjectively: **un auteur français, la cuisine française.**

LA CATHÉDRALE DE NOTRE-DAME

Cette belle étude photographique montre la rose vitrée de la nef centrale, les contreforts et les tours encore inachevées de la Cathédrale de Paris.

Étude (f.)   **rose** (f.)   **vitré-e** (adj.)   **nef** (f.)   **contrefort** (m.)   **tour** (f.)   **inachevé-e** (adj.)
Study   rose-window   glass (glazed)   nave   buttress   tower   unfinished

N'est-elle pas jolie?
nay-tail pah zho-lee?
Isn't she pretty?

Il n'est pas riche
eel nay pah reesh
He is not rich

HOW TO TRANSLATE "NOT"

(1) Not is expressed by two words **ne** and **pas**. Before a vowel **ne** becomes **n'** e.g., **il n'est pas riche**=he is not rich. Note the position of the two words.

Adjectives ending in -e

(2) When an adjective ends in e without any accent sign in the masculine, the feminine remains the same: **Il est riche**=he is rich; **elle est riche**=she is rich.

MEN, WOMEN AND CHILDREN

1. **le bébé (le petit enfant)**
   bay-bay (p'tee-taN-faN)
   baby

2. **le petit garçon**
   p'tee gahr-soN
   small boy

3. **la petite fille (fillette)**
   p'teet feey (fee-yait)
   little girl

4. **le jeune homme**
   zhay-nom
   young man

5. **la jeune fille (la demoiselle)**
   zhayn feey (d'mwah-zail)
   girl (young lady)

6. **l'homme (le monsieur)**
   om (m's-yay)
   man

7. **la femme (la dame)**
   fahm (dahm)
   woman (lady)

8. **un homme âgé (le grand-père)**
   omm ah-zhay (graN-pair)
   old man (grandfather)

9. **une femme âgée (la grand'mère)**
   fahm ah-zhay (graN-mair)
   old woman (grandmother)

10. **grand**
    graN
    tall (masc.)

11. **grande**
    graNd
    tall (fem.)

12. **petit**
    p'tee
    short, small (masc.)

13. **petite**
    p'teet
    short, small (fem.)

14. **fort**
    for
    strong (masc.)

15. **forte**
    fort
    strong (fem.)

16. **mince**
    miNs
    slim (masc. and fem.)

MORE ABOUT THE ROBERTS FAMILY

(Sentences using adjectives are given on pages 19 and 20)

Monsieur Roberts est-il riche?   Non, il n'est pas riche.   Il est très
m's-yay ro-bairts ay-teel reesh?   noN eel nay pah reesh.   eel ay tray-
Mr. Roberts is he rich?   No, he is not rich.   He is very

intelligent et Madame Roberts est très charmante.   Charles et
ziN-tai-lee-zhaN ay mah-dahm ro-bairts ay tray shahr-maNt.   shahrl ay
intelligent and Mrs. Roberts is very charming.   Charles and

Madeleine sont-ils intelligents? **Madeleine est intelligente, mais Charles**
mahd-lain soN-teel iN-tai-lee-zhaN? mahd-lain ay-tiN-tai-lee-zhaNt mai shahrl
Madeleine are they intelligent? *Madeleine is intelligent, but Charles*

n'est pas très intelligent. **Mais il est beau et charmant.** **Madame**
nay pah trai-ziN-tai-lee-zhaN. mai ee-lay boh ay shahr-maN mah-dahm
is not very intelligent. *But he is good-looking and charming.* *Mrs.*

Roberts et Mademoiselle Lesage sont-elles petites? **Non, monsieur,**
ro-bairts ay mahd-mwa-zail le-sahzh soN-tail p'teet? noN, m's-yay,
Roberts and Mlle. Lesage are they small? *No, sir,*

elles sont grandes. **Elles sont aussi toutes les deux intelligentes.**
ail soN graNd. ail soN-toh-see toot lay day-ziN-tai-lee-zhaNt.
they are tall. *They are also both (lit. "all the two") intelligent.*

SENTENCE BUILDING. TABLES SUMMARISING THE FIRST LESSON

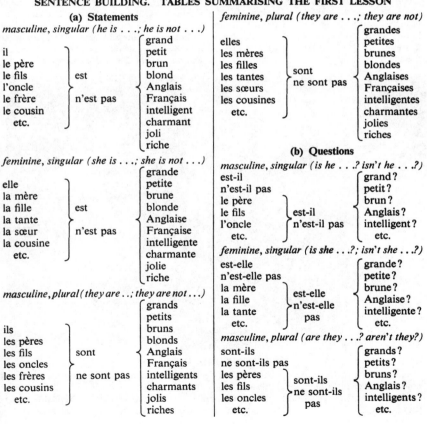

(a) Statements

masculine, singular (he is . . .; he is not . . .)

il, le père, le fils, l'oncle, le frère, le cousin, etc.	est / n'est pas	grand, petit, brun, blond, Anglais, Français, intelligent, charmant, joli, riche

feminine, singular (she is . . .; she is not . . .)

elle, la mère, la fille, la tante, la sœur, la cousine, etc.	est / n'est pas	grande, petite, brune, blonde, Anglaise, Française, intelligente, charmante, jolie, riche

masculine, plural (they are . .; they are not . . .)

ils, les pères, les fils, les oncles, les frères, les cousins, etc.	sont / ne sont pas	grands, petits, bruns, blonds, Anglais, Français, intelligents, charmants, jolis, riches

feminine, plural (they are . . .; they are not)

elles, les mères, les filles, les tantes, les sœurs, les cousines, etc.	sont / ne sont pas	grandes, petites, brunes, blondes, Anglaises, Françaises, intelligentes, charmantes, jolies, riches

(b) Questions

masculine, singular (is he . . .? isn't he . . .?)

est-il, n'est-il pas, le père, le fils, l'oncle, etc.	est-il / n'est-il pas	grand? petit? brun? Anglais? intelligent? etc.

feminine, singular (is she . . .?; isn't she . . .?)

est-elle, n'est-elle pas, la mère, la fille, la tante, etc.	est-elle / n'est-elle pas	grande? petite? brune? Anglaise? intelligente? etc.

masculine, plural (are they . . .? aren't they?)

sont-ils, ne sont-ils pas, les pères, les fils, les oncles, etc.	sont-ils / ne sont-ils pas	grands? petits? bruns? Anglais? intelligents? etc.

feminine, plural (are they . . .? aren't they . . .?)

sont-elles		grandes?
ne sont-elles pas		petites?
les mères		brunes?
les filles	sont-elles	Anglaises?
les tantes	ne sont-elles pas	intelligentes?
etc.		etc.

(c) Exclamations

masculine, singular (isn't he . . .!)

n'est-il pas		grand!
le père		petit!
le fils	n'est-il pas	charmant!
le frère		joli!
etc.		etc.

feminine, singular (isn't she . . .!)

n'est-elle pas		grande!
la mère		petite!
la fille	n'est-elle pas	charmante!
la sœur		jolie!
etc.		etc.

masculine, plural (aren't they . . .!)

ne sont-ils pas		grands!
les pères		petits!
les fils	ne sont-ils pas	charmants!
les frères		jolis!
etc.		etc.

feminine, plural (aren't they . . .!)

ne sont-elles pas		grandes!
les mères		petites!
les filles	ne sont-elles pas	charmantes!
les sœurs		jolies!

TEST IT YOURSELF.—It would be a good idea, at this stage, to practise these questions and exclamations, and so to check how many you yourself have actually learned since you started the Course.

You now know 55 words. You can make over 800 statements, ask over 400 questions and make over 200 exclamations.

CHIFFONNIERS DE PARIS

Tous les matins à l'aube, les chiffonniers de Paris farfouillent dans toutes les poubelles pour y trouver des objets vendables.

| **Chiffonnier-ère** (m.f.) | **aube** (f.) | **farfouiller** | **poubelle** (f.) | **vendable** (adj.) |
| Rag-picker | dawn | to rummage | dustbin | saleable |

DEUXIÈME LEÇON—*SECOND LESSON*

This picture shows the Roberts family packing for Paris. First read the vocabulary, then cover over the text and see if you can make a list of the objects in the picture in French. Next cover over all but the French text of the sentences below, and try to find the mistakes which the artist has deliberately introduced into the picture.

le chapeau	la malle	le parapluie	le pardessus	les chaussures
shah-poh	mahl	pah-rah-plw̄ee	pahr-de-sēē	shoh-sēēr
hat	*trunk*	*umbrella*	*overcoat*	*footwear*

	la valise	la chaise	le sac	la table	les gants
	vah-leez	shaiz	sahk	tahbl	gaN
	suitcase	*chair*	*bag*	*table*	*gloves*

Le chapeau est sur la chaise.   Le sac est sous la chaise.   Les chaussures sont sur la
le shah-poh ay sēēr lah shaiz.   le sahk ay soo lah shaiz.   lay shoh-sēēr soN sēēr lah
The hat is on the chair.   *The bag is under the chair.*   *The shoes are on the*

table.   Les gants sont dans le chapeau.   Le chapeau est-il sur la table?   Non,
tahbl.   lay gaN soN daN le shah-poh.   le shah-poh ay-teel sēēr lah tahbl?   noN
table.   *The gloves are in the hat.*   *The hat is it on the table?*   *No,*

il n'est pas sur la table.   Où est le chapeau?   Il est sur la chaise.   Où est la
eel nay pah sēēr lah tahbl.   oo ay le shah-poh?   ee-lay sēēr lah shaiz.   oo ay lah
it is not on the table.   *Where is the hat?*   *It is on the chair.*   *Where is the*

valise?   Elle est sous la table.   Les gants sont-ils dans la valise?   Ils ne sont pas
vah-leez?   ai-lay soo lah tahbl.   lay gaN soN-teel daN lah vah-leez?   eel ne soN pah
suitcase?   *It is under the table.*   *The gloves are they in the suitcase?*   *They are not*

dans la valise.   Où sont-ils?   Ils sont dans le chapeau.   Le chapeau est sur la table.
daN lah vah-leez. oo soN-teel? eel soN daN le shah-poh. le shah-poh ay se͞er lah tahbl.
in the suitcase.   Where are they?   They are in the hat.   The hat is on the table.

GENDER

In French every noun is either masculine or feminine[1]. From the examples given above you can see that **le chapeau, le parapluie, le manteau, le gant,** etc., are masculine, whereas **la malle, la table, la chaise, la chaussure,** etc., are feminine. Now it seems absurd to speak of a chair as feminine or of a hat as masculine. In grammar, however, the term masculine or feminine is used in an unusual sense. All French nouns are divided into two groups according to the word they use for the translation of "the." All the words which translate "the" by **le** are called masculine, because all the male beings are in this group, and all the words which translate "the" by **la** are called feminine, because all the female beings are in that group. If we say **la table** is feminine, then we use the word feminine not in the same sense as if we would speak of feminine charm or feminine beauty; we simply mean that this word belongs to one of the two groups into which all French nouns are divided.

HOW TO TRANSLATE "IT"

Special care must be taken with the translation of the words "it" and "they." Use **il** when it stands for a masculine noun in the singular. Use **elle** when it stands for a feminine noun in the singular. Use **ils** when it stands for a masculine noun in the plural. Use **elles** when it stands for a feminine noun in the plural.

For example, when translating "it is brown," "it" referring to **le chapeau,** i.e., masculine in French, you have to use the word **il**=he for the translation of "it": **il est brun.** But when the "it" refers to **la chaise,** you have to use the word for she= **elle** and so the French for this is: **elle est brune.**

---

[1] With the exception of such words as **enfant** =child, which is masculine when meaning a boy and feminine when meaning a girl.

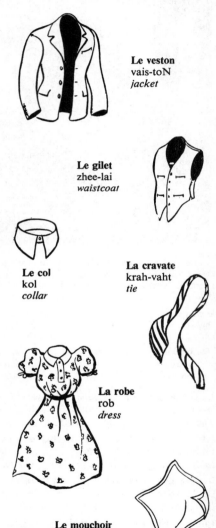

Le veston
vais-toN
jacket

Le gilet
zhee-lai
waistcoat

Le col
kol
collar

La cravate
krah-vaht
tie

La robe
rob
dress

Le mouchoir
moosh-wahr
handkerchief

La dame à gauche: Pour voyager je préfère les valises.
Lady on the left: poor vwah-yah-zhay zhe pray-fair lay vah-leez.
For travelling, I prefer suitcases.

La dame à droite: J'aime mieux les malles.
Lady on the right: zhaim myay lay mal.
I like trunks better.

le pantalon	**la chemise**	**la pantoufle**	**le manteau**	**le soulier**	**la lingerie**
paN-tah-loN	sh'meez	paN-toofl	maN-toh	sool-yay	liNzh-ree
trousers	*shirt*	*slipper*	*coat*	*shoe*	*underwear*

la blouse	**la bottine**	**la jaquette**	**la jupe**	**les bretelles** (f.)	**les jarretelles** (f.)
blooz	bo-teen	zhah-kait	zhẽep	lay bre-tail	lay zhahr-tail
blouse	*boot*	*jacket*	*skirt*	*braces*	*sock suspenders*
		(ladies' or boys')			

COULEURS (koo-lа̄yr)

masculine:			*feminine:*	
le . . . (il) est			la . . . (elle) est	
rouge	roozh	*red*	**rouge**	roozh
bleu	blа̄y	*blue*	**bleue**	blа̄y
vert	vair	*green*	**verte**	vairt
jaune	zhohn	*yellow*	**jaune**	zhohn
gris	gree	*grey*	**grise**	greez
noir	nwahr	*black*	**noire**	nwahr
blanc	blaN	*white*	**blanche**	blaNsh

Note from the opposite column (1) that the adjectives ending in -e remain the same in feminine as in masculine. (2) The irregular feminine of **blanc**=white; **blanche**. (3) That **le pantalon** the (pair) of trousers is singular in French, so that you have to say **le pantalon est gris**, when you say in English "the trousers *are* grey." (On the other hand, "furniture"=**les meubles** is plural in French.)

TALKING OF COLOURS

Le chapeau est brun. Le manteau est noir. Le parapluie est vert. La table est
le shah-poh ay bruN. le maN-toh ay nwahr. le pah-rah-plẁee ay vair. lah tahbl ay
The hat is brown. The coat is black. The umbrella is green. The table is

brune. La valise est jaune. La malle est noire. Le col est blanc. La cravate est
brẽen. lah vah-leez ay zhohn. lah mal ay nwahr. le kol ay blaN. lah krah-vaht ay
brown. The suitcase is yellow. The trunk is black. The collar is white. The tie is

rouge. Le veston est bleu. La robe est blanche. Le pantalon est gris. Les gants
roozh. le vais-toN ay blа̄y. lah rob ay blaNsh. le paN-tah-lon ay gree. lay gaN
red. The jacket is blue. The dress is white. The trousers are grey. The gloves

sont bruns.   Le mouchoir est-il blanc?   Oui, il est blanc.   La cravate est-elle
soN bruN.   le moosh-wahr ay-teel blaN?   wee ee-lay blaN.   lah krah-vaht ay-tail
are brown.   The handkerchief is it white?   Yes, it is white.   The tie is it

blanche?   Non, elle n'est pas blanche.   De quelle couleur est la cravate?   Elle est
blaNsh?   noN ail nay pah blaNsh.   de kail koo-lāyr ay lah krah-vaht?   ai-lay
white?   No, it is not white.   (Of) what colour is the tie?   It is

rouge.   De quelle couleur sont les gants?   Ils sont bruns.
roozh.   de kail koo-lāyr soN lay gaN?   eel soN bruN.
red.   (Of) what colour are the gloves?   They are brown.

SOME QUESTIONS AND ANSWERS

Qu'est-ce que c'est? or **Qu'est-ce?**   **Ceci est** or **c'est**   **Cela est** or **c'est**
kais ke say   kai-se   se-see ay, say   se-lah ay,   say
What is — this? — that?   *this is*   *that is*

uN   ẽn   **Ceci est la porte**
un chapeau *a hat*   **une cravate** *a tie*   se-see ay lah port
un veston *a jacket*   **une robe** *a dress*   *This is the door*
un sac *a bag*   **une valise** *a suitcase*
un parapluie *an umbrella* **une chaise** *a chair*

Ce sont les valises   **Ce sont les malles**
se soN lay vah-leez   se soN lay mal
These are the suitcases   *Those are the trunks*

Qu'est-ce que c'est?   **Ce sont**
kais-ke-say?   se soN
What are these?   *These are . . .; those are*

lay
les fenêtres   **les portes**   **les mouchoirs**
the windows   *the doors*   *the handkerchiefs*

les chaussures   **les cols**   **les gants**
the footwear   *the collars*   *the gloves*

1) **un** and **une** are the French equivalents for *a* or *an*.
Use **un** with masculine nouns, **une** with feminine.
2) **ce** (c' before a vowel) is the short form for both
ceci and **cela**. 3) **qu'est-ce que c'est?** (kais-ke-say)
can mean (1) what is it? (2) what is this? (3) what
is that? (4) what are they? (5) what are these?
(6) what are those?

Qu'est-ce que c'est?   **Est-ce une valise?**
kais ke say?   ais ẽn vah-leez?   **Cela est la fenêtre**
                                                              se-lah ay lah fe-naitr
Oui, c'est une valise.   **Est-ce un sac?**   *That is the window*
wee say-tẽn vah-leez.   ais uN sak?

Mais non, monsieur, ce n'est pas un sac.
mai noN m's-yāy se nay pah-zuN sak.

The Roberts family off to the station. The objects they are carrying are words you have learned. Cover over the text and see if you can name them in French.

Monsieur Roberts a deux valises, Madame Roberts a un sac et une
m's-yāy ro-bairts ah dāy vah-leez, mah-dahm ro-bairts ah uN sak ay ēēn
Mr. Roberts has two suitcases, Mrs. Roberts has a bag and a

couverture, Charles a une petite valise, Madeleine a un carton à chapeaux.
koo-vair-tēēr, shahrl ah ēēn p'teet vah-leez, mahd-lain ah uN kahr-toN ah shah-poh.
rug, Charles has a small suitcase, Madeleine has a hat-box.

SUMMARY OF SECOND LESSON
(a) Statements

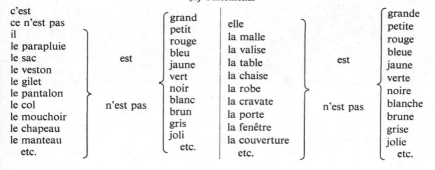

| c'est
ce n'est pas
il
le parapluie
le sac
le veston
le gilet
le pantalon
le col
le mouchoir
le chapeau
le manteau
etc. | est

n'est pas | grand
petit
rouge
bleu
jaune
vert
noir
blanc
brun
gris
joli
etc. | elle
la malle
la valise
la table
la chaise
la robe
la cravate
la porte
la fenêtre
la couverture
etc. | est

n'est pas | grande
petite
rouge
bleue
jaune
verte
noire
blanche
brune
grise
jolie
etc. |

PARIS VU DE NOTRE-DAME

Une des chimères grimaçantes de Notre-Dame dans ce ciel d'orage semble menacer la Capitale encore ensoleillée. Au loin, la silhouette blanche de la Basilique du Sacré-Cœur s'élève en acropole moderne au-dessus du panorama.

Chimère (f.)	**grimaçant-e** (adj.)	**ciel** (m.) **d'orage** (m.)	**ensoleillé-e** (adj.)
Chimera	frowning, grimacing	stormy sky	sunlit

ils les parapluies les sacs les vestons les gilets les pantalons les cols les mouchoirs les chapeaux les manteaux etc.	sont ne sont pas	grands petits rouges bleus jaunes verts noirs blancs bruns gris jolis etc.
elles les malles les valises les tables les chaises les robes les cravates les portes les fenêtres les couvertures etc.	sont ne sont pas	grandes petites rouges bleues jaunes vertes noires blanches brunes grises jolies etc.

(b) Questions

est-il est-ce le parapluie le sac le veston etc.	est-il n'est-il pas	grand? petit? rouge? bleu? jaune?
est-elle la malle la valise la table etc.	est-elle n'est-elle pas	grande? petite? rouge? bleue? jaune? etc.
sont-ils les parapluies les sacs les vestons etc.	sont-ils ne sont-ils pas	grands? petits? rouges? bleus? jaunes? etc.
sont-elles les malles les valises les tables etc.	sont-elles ne sont-elles pas	grandes? petites? rouges? bleues? jaunes? etc.

(c) Exclamations

n'est-il pas n'est-ce pas le parapluie le sac etc.	n'est-il pas	grand! petit! joli! etc.
n'est-elle pas la table la fenêtre etc.	n'est-elle pas	grande! petite! jolie! etc.
ne sont-ils pas les parapluies les sacs etc.	ne sont-ils pas	grands! petits! jolis! etc.
ne sont-elles pas les tables les fenêtres etc.	ne sont-elles pas	grandes! petites! jolies! etc.

You now know 100 words. You can make over 980 statements, ask over 800 questions, and make over 400 exclamations.

EXERCISES

1 Answer in French

1. Qu'est-ce que c'est?

2. Le sac est-il joli?

3. Est-ce Mademoiselle Lesage?

4. Mademoiselle Lesage est-elle jolie?

5. Qui est le cousin de Mademoiselle Lesage?

6. Le veston est-il joli?

7. Qu'est-ce que c'est?

8. Charles est-il grand?

9. Qui est la sœur de Charles?

10. Qui sont les parents de Charles?

11. La robe est-elle élégante?

12. La chaise est-elle grande?

13. Le libre est-il sur la table?

14. Où (oo = where) est le livre?

15. Le livre est-il sur la chaise?

16. Qu'est-ce que c'est?

17. Qu'est-ce que c'est?

18. De quelle couleur sont les chaussures?

(For Key see page 51)

II   **Translate into French**

1. The tie is white and blue. 2. The jacket is brown. 3. The dress is green. 4. The hat is not green, it is brown. 5. Is the overcoat black? 6. No, sir, it is grey. 7. Is the table large? 8. Yes, it is large. 9. Is the window large? 10. No, it is small. 11. Is the handkerchief red and blue? 12. No, it is white. 13. Are the gloves brown? 14. No, madam, they are yellow. 15. Are the trunks yellow? 16. No, they are brown. 17. What is it? 18. Is it the book? 19. Yes, sir, it is the book. 20. No, sir, it is not the book, it is the bag. 21. What colour is the bag? 22. It is blue. 23. Isn't it pretty! 24. Isn't the suitcase brown? 25. Isn't the child charming! 26. Where are the children? 27. Where is George's father? 28. Where is he? 29. Where is she? 30. Where are they (the parents)?

III   **Replace the nouns by il, elle, ils or elles**

1. Le mouchoir est blanc. 2. La porte est blanche. 3. La malle n'est pas grande. 4. Les livres sont rouges. 5. Les chaussures sont noires. 6. Monsieur et Madame Roberts sont les parents de Charles et de Madeleine. 7. Madame Roberts et Madeleine sont blondes. 8. De quelle couleur est le veston? 9. De quelle couleur est la porte? 10. Où est Charles? 11. Où est Madeleine? 12. Où sont les enfants? 13. Où sont les livres? 14. Où sont les valises?

(For Key see page 52)

Où sont les enfants?

TROISIÈME LEÇON—*THIRD LESSON*

When you have read the text below, cover it over and see if you can describe in French what the Roberts family are doing on the ship.

La famille Roberts est sur le bateau.   Monsieur Roberts est fatigué.
lah fah-mee*y* ro-bairts ay s*ē̆*r le bah-toh.   m's-y*āy* ro-bairts ay fah-tee-gay.
The Roberts family is on the boat.   Mr. Roberts is tired.

Il lit un roman amusant et fume sa courte pipe anglaise.   Madame
eel lee uN rom-aN ah-m*ē̆*-zaN ay f*ē̆*m sah koort peep aN-glaiz.   mah-dahm
He reads an amusing novel and smokes his short English pipe.   Mrs.

Roberts n'est pas fatiguée, elle parle avec une autre dame.   Charles est
ro-bairts nay pah fah-tee-gay, ail pahrl ah-vek *ē̆*n ohtr dahm.   shahrl ay
Roberts is not tired, she is speaking with another lady.   Charles is

malade.   Le jour est beau mais Charles n'aime pas la mer.   Madeleine n'est pas
mah-lahd.   le zhoor ay boh mai shahrl naim pah lah mair.   mahd-lain nay pah
ill.   The day is fine but Charles does not like the sea.   Madeleine is not

malade.   Elle parle avec une autre jeune fille anglaise.   La mer est assez
mah-lahd.   ail pahrl ah-vek *ē̆*n ohtr zh*āy*n fee*y* aN-glaiz.   lah mair ay-tah-sa*y*
ill.   She is talking with another young English girl.   The sea is fairly

calme.   Les autres passagers sont très contents.
kahlm.   lay-zohtr pah-sah-zhay soN trai koN-taN.
calm.   The other passengers are very happy.

Ces messieurs sont sur un bateau français.
say mais-yay soN seer uN bah-toh fraN-sai.
These gentlemen are on a French boat.

Cette dame est petite et mince.
sait dahm ay p'teet ay miNs.
This lady is small and slim.

Cette enfant est méchante.
sait-aN-faN ay may-shaNt.
This child is naughty.

Ce monsieur est grand et fort.
se m's-yay ay graN tay for.
This man is big and strong.

THIS, THAT, THESE, THOSE

Note from the above that there are three French equivalents for English "this" when used in connection with nouns; **ce**, **cette** and **cet**; **ce** is used in connection with masculine nouns.

ce livre = this book; **cette** is used in connection with feminine nouns, e.g., **cette table** = this table; **cet** is used with masculine nouns when they begin with a vowel or mute *h*, e.g., **cet enfant** = this child, **cet hôtel** = this hotel.

ces (say) is the plural of **ce**, **cette** or **cet**: **ces livres** = these books; **ces tables** = these tables; **ces enfants** = these children.

As we have already seen in the previous lesson the difference between "this" and

NOTE:

un monsieur
m's-yay
a gentleman

Monsieur Roberts
Mr. Roberts

une dame
dahm
a lady

Madame Roberts
Mrs. Roberts

la fille
feey
the daughter

une jeune fille
zhayn feey
a girl

une petite fille
p'teet feey
a little girl or

une fillette
fee-yait

"that" or "these" and "those" is not so clearly marked in French as it is in English; **ce livre** can also mean "that book," **cette table**=that table, **ces enfants**=those children, etc.

If, however, the Frenchman wishes to make a clear distinction between the two he adds two little words to the nouns: **-ci** (pronounced see) for "this" and "these," **-là** for "that" and "those":

THIS AND THAT

ce livre-ci	*this book*
ce livre-là	*that book*
cette table-ci	*this table*
cette table-là	*that table*
cet enfant-ci	*this child*
cet enfant-là	*that child*
ces livres-ci	*these books*
ces livres-là	*those books*
ces tables-ci	*these tables*
ces tables-là	*those tables*
ces enfants-ci	*these children*
ces enfants-là . . .	*those children*

-ci is the contraction of **ici**=here, of which the opposite is **là**=there.

Cette tasse-là est pour vous.
sait tahs-lah ay poor voo.
That cup (there) is for you.

Cette tasse-ci est pour moi.
sait tahs-see ay poor mwa.
This cup (here) is for me.

Voici une tasse de thé.
vwah-see ën tahs de tay.
Here is a cup of tea.

Voilà un verre de vin.
vwah-lah uN vair de viN.
There is a glass of wine.

Voici les tasses.   **Voilà les verres.**
vwah-see lay tahs.   vwah-lah lay vair.
Here are the cups.   *There are the glasses.*

Le café est-il bon? Oui, il est bon.   **La bière est-elle bonne? Oui, elle est bonne.**

This picture illustrates two simple sentences which you can translate for yourself. Try to make up descriptive sentences from the vocabulary you have now acquired.

The feminine of **bon** (boN)=good is **bonne** (bon). Note that when the n is doubled the o loses its nasal quality, and the n is now pronounced.

Ces verres-ci sont
say vair-see soN
These glasses are

pour les messieurs.
poor lay mais-yãy.
for the gentlemen.

Ces verres-là sont
say vair lah soN
Those glasses are

pour les dames.
poor lay dahm.
for the ladies.

VOICI—VOILÀ

Note that **voici** can mean both "here is" and "here are," **voilà** = "there is" or "there are."

voici la petite fille = *here is the little girl*
voilà la petite fille = *there is the little girl*
voici les petites filles = *here are the little girls*
voilà les petites filles = *there are the little girls*

voici and **voilà** are two very useful little words; **voici** is also used in the meanings

of "here it is," "here they are" and **voilà** with the meanings of "there it is," "there they are."

Où est la valise? = *Where is the suitcase?*
La voici = *here it is*
La voilà = *there it is*
Où sont les enfants? = *Where are the children?*
Les voici = *here they are*
Les voilà = *there they are*

MRS. ROBERTS TALKS WITH A LADY ABOARD

La Dame: **Nous avons une bonne traversée, n'est-ce pas, madame?**
noo-zah-voN-zẽen ton trah-vair-say nais-pah mah-dahm?
We have (are having) a good crossing, haven't we, madam?

Mme Roberts: **Notre traversée n'est pas mauvaise. Le ciel est pur, la mer est**
notr trah-vair-say nay pah mo-vaiz.   le syail ay pẽer lah mair ay
Our crossing is not bad.   The sky is bright, the sea is

   calme, et le bateau est très confortable.
kahlm, ay le bah-toh ay trai koN-for-tahbl.
calm, and the ship is very comfortable.

La Dame: **Êtes-vous fatiguée, madame?**
ait-voo fah-tee-gay mah-dahm?
Are you tired, madam?

Mme Roberts: **Non, madame, je ne suis pas fatiguée.   Et vous, madame?**
noN mah-dahm zhe ne sỹee pah fah-tee-gay.   ay voo mah-dahm?
No, madam, I am not tired.   And you, madam?

La Dame: **Je suis un peu fatiguée.   J'ai mal dormi cette nuit.**
zhe sỹee-zuN pãy fah-tee-gay.   zhay mal dor-mee sait nỹee.
I am a little tired.   I slept badly this (last) night.

Mme Roberts: **Prenez un transatlantique, madame.   Charles, apportez un**
prenay-zuN traNs-aht-laN-teek, mah-dahm, shahrl ah-por-tay-zuN
Have a deck-chair, madam.   Charles, bring a

   transatlantique pour madame.
traNs-aht-laN-teek poor mah-dahm.
deck-chair for madam.

Charles (qui apporte un transatlantique): Voilà, madame.
(kee ah-port uN traNs-aht-laN-teek): vwah-lah mah-dahm.
(who brings a deck-chair): There you are, madam.

La Dame: **Merci bien. Vous êtes bien aimable. (à Madame R.) Votre**
mair-see byiN. voo-zait byiN-nai-mahbl. (ah mah-dahm airr.) votr
Thanks very much. You are very kind. (to Mrs. R.) Your

fils est charmant, madame. Quel âge a-t-il?
fees ay shahr-maN, mah-dahm. kail ahzh ah-teel?
son is charming, madam. How old is he? (lit. What age has he?)

Mme Roberts: **Il a dix ans.**
ee-lah dee-zaN.
He is (lit. has) ten years.

La Dame: **Et la charmante petite fille, est-elle votre fille?**
ay lah shahr-maNt p'teet feey ay-tail votr feey?
And the charming little girl, is she your daughter?

Mme Roberts: **Oui, c'est ma fille.**
wee say mah feey.
Yes, it's my daughter.

La Dame: **Quel âge a-t-elle?**
kai-lahzh ah-tail?
How old is she?

Mme Roberts: **Elle a douze ans.**
ai-lah doo-zaN.
She is twelve.

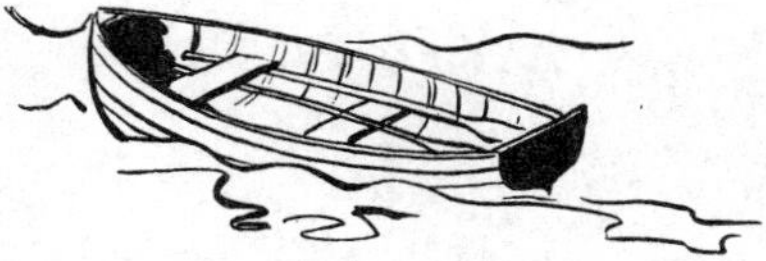

Un bateau à rames
uN bah-toh ah rahm
A rowing-boat

La Dame: **Vous allez à Paris, madame?**
voo-zah-lay ah pah-ree mah-dahm?
You are going to Paris, madam?

Mme Roberts: **Oui, madame, nous allons à Paris pour voir mes parents.**
wee mah-dahm noo-zah-loN-zah pah-ree poor vwahr may pah-raN.
Yes, madam, we are going to Paris to see my parents.

La Dame: **Vos parents sont-ils Français?**
voh pah-raN soN-teel fraN-sai?
Are your parents French?

Mme Roberts: **Oui, madame, ils sont Français.**
wee mah-dahm eel soN fraN-sai.
Yes, madam, they are French.

La Dame: **Et vous, madame, êtes-vous Française?**
ay voo mah-dahm ait voo fraN-saiz?
And you, madam, are you a Frenchwoman?

This and other diagrams are provided to extend your vocabulary in a simple and interesting way. First compare the English words and their French equivalents, then

THE MAIL STEAMER

English

1. Anchor and anchor-chain; 2. Look-out; 3. Deck-hand; 4. Railing; 5. Forecastle; 6. Sailing boat; 7. Gangway; 8. Hatches; 9. Derricks; 10. Lifebelts; 11. Port light; 12. Mast; 13. Masthead light; 14. Halyards; 15. Bridge; 16. Captain; 17. Compass; 18. Steering-gear; 19. Engine-room telegraph; 20. Wireless cabin; 21. Siren; 22. Funnel; 23. Engine-room ventilator; 24. The ship herself (mail steamer); 25. Tarpaulin; 26. Davits; 27. Lifeboats; 28. Signal halyards; 29. Boat deck; 30. Upper deck; 31. Rafts; 32. Ship's colours; 33. Wake; 34. Stern and aft; 35. Propeller and p.-shaft; 36. Upper and lower berths; 37. Private cabin; 38. Steerage; 39. Drinking-water tank; 40. Cabins; 41. Turbines; 42. Amidships; 43. Dining-room steward; 44. 1st class dining saloon; 45. Main Boilers; 46. Saloon drawing room; 47. Starboard light; 48. Stoker; 49. Galley; 50. Freshwater tanks; 51. Galley steward; 52. Fuel tanks; 53. Officers' quarters; 54. 1st class smoking room; 55. Cargo hold; 56. Crew's quarters; 57. Portholes; 58. Bow-wave; 59. Fore and forrad; 60. Cutwater.

French

1. Ancre (f.) et chaîne (f.) d'ancre; 2. Vigie (f.); 3. Matelot (m.) de pont; 4. Bastingages (m.pl.); 5. Gaillard (m.) d'avant; 6. Bateau (m.) à voiles (f.pl.);

cover over the letterpress and see how many French words you can attach to the numbers on the diagram. Turn back to the diagrams when you have advanced in the course.

LE PAQUEBOT

7. Passerelle (f.); 8. Panneaux (m.pl.); 9. Mâts (m.pl.) de charge; 10. Ceintures (f.pl.) de sauvetage; 11. Feu de bâbord; 12. Mât (m.); 13. Feu (m.) de tête de mât; 14. Drisses (f.pl.); 15. Pont; 16. Capitaine; 17. Boussole (f.), compas (m.); 18. Mécanisme (m.) à gouverner; 19. Cadran (m.) de transmission d'ordres; 20. Cabine (f.) de T.S.F. (télégraphie sans fil); 21. Sirène (f.); 22. Cheminée (f.); 23. Manche (f.) à ventilation; 24. Paquebot (m.); 25. Prélart (m.); 26. Bossoirs (m.pl.); 27. Baleinières (f.pl.) de sauvetage; 28. Drisses des signaux; 29. Pont des embarcations; 30. Pont supérieur; 31. Radeaux (m.pl.); 32. Pavillon (m.); 33. Sillon, sillage (m.); 34. (De l') arrière (m.);

35. Hélice (f.) et arbre (m.) de l'hélice; 36. Couchettes (f.pl.) supérieures, inférieures; 37. Cabine privée; 38. Entrepont (m.); 39. Cales (f.pl.) à eau potable; 40. Cabines; 41. Turbines (f.pl.); 42. Par le travers; 43. Garçon de salon; 44. Salon-restaurant de 1re classe; 45. Grandes chaudières (f.pl.); 46. Salon de 1re classe; 47. Feu de tribord; 48. Chauffeur; 49. Cuisine (f.); 50. Cales à eau douce; 51. Garçon de cuisine; 52. Réservoirs (m.pl.) à essence; 53. Poste (m.) des officiers; 54. Fumoir (m.) de 1re classe; 55. Soute (f.) à marchandises; 56. Poste (m.) des matelots; 57. Sabords, hublots (m.pl.); 58. Lame (f.) d'étrave; 59. (De l') avant (m.); 60. Étrave (f.).

Mme Roberts: je suis née Française, mais mon mari est Anglais.
zhe swee nay fraN-saiz mai moN mah-ree ay-taN-glai.
I was (lit. am) born a Frenchwoman, but my husband is an English-man.

La Dame: Vous parlez anglais comme une Anglaise.
voo pahr-lay-zaN-glai ko-meen aN-glaiz.
You speak English like an Englishwoman.

Mme Roberts: Merci, madame, vous êtes très aimable.
mair-see, mah-dahm, voo-zait tray zai-mahbl.
Thank you, madam, you are very kind.

Êtes-vous fatigués, mes enfants?
ait-voo fah-tee-gay may-zaN-faN?
Are you tired, my children?

Charles et Madeleine: Non, maman, nous ne sommes pas fatigués.
noN, mah-maN, noo ne som pah fah-tee-gay.
No, mummy, we are not tired.

Nous ne sommes pas malades. Nous avons
noo ne som pah mah-lahd. noo-zah-voN-
    une bonne traversée.
    zeen bon trah-vair-say.
We are not ill. We have[1] a good crossing.

Ils sont malades. Ils ont une mauvaise
eel-soN mah-lahd. eel-zoN-teen mo-vaiz
    traversée.
    trah-vair-say.
They are ill. They have a bad crossing.

---

[1] It will be noted that, in early Lessons, we frequently make a literal translation of the French text, in cases where the corresponding expression in normal idiomatic English is easily guessed, as in the present case, where "we are having" would be more usual. This is in order to accustom readers to the French construction.

Ces dames sont contentes. Elles ont une
say dahm soN koN-taNt.   ail-zoN-tᴈᴈn
conversation intéressante.
koN-vair-sahs-yoN iN-tay-rai-saNt.
These ladies are happy. They are having an
interesting talk.

N'EST-CE PAS?

Vous êtes le capitaine, n'est-ce pas?
voo-zait le kah-pee-tain nais-pah?
You are the captain, aren't you?

Vous avez la valise, n'est-ce pas?
voo-zah-vay lah vah-leez nais-pah?
You have the suitcase, haven't you?

Le capitaine est content. Il a un joli bateau.
le kah-pee-tain ay koN-taN. ee-lah uN zho-
lee bah-toh.
The captain is happy. He has a beautiful
ship.

Elle est jolie, n'est-ce pas?
ail-ay zho-lee nais-pah?
She is pretty, isn't she?

Vous parlez français, n'est-ce pas?
voo pahr-lay fraN-sai nais-pah?
You speak French, don't you?

You will hear French people throw in
n'est-ce pas? after many sentences; it
corresponds to the English "isn't he?"
"isn't she?" "isn't it?" "aren't they?"
"aren't you?" "don't you?" "doesn't he?"
"haven't you?" etc. **N'est-ce pas** means
all these expressions rolled into one; it is
actually an abbreviation of **n'est-ce pas**
vrai? "is it not true?"

---

1. **Il a** means "he has," and you would
expect **a-il** for "has he?" But this does not
sound pleasant to a Frenchman so **"t"** is
put in: **a-t-il** which makes the sound
pleasanter. The same applies to **a-t-elle?**
meaning "has she?" **parle-t-il?** "does he
speak?" **parle-t-elle?** "does she speak?" etc.
2. The French do not say "do you?"
when asking questions. "Do you speak?"
must be translated **parlez-vous?**=speak
you? "Does he speak?" is **parle-t-il?**=
"speaks he?" "Do they come?" must be
turned into "come they?" "do we start?"
into "start we?" etc.
3. There is no difference in French
between "I speak" and "I am speaking";
both are translated by **je parle.**

ÊTRE=*to be*

je suis (zhe sᴡee)	**je ne suis pas**
I am	*I am not*
vous êtes (voo-zait)	**vous n'êtes pas**
you are	*you are not*
nous sommes	**nous ne sommes pas**
(noo som)	*we are not*
we are	
il est (ee-lay)	**il n'est pas**
he is	*he is not*
elle est (ai-lay)	**elle n'est pas**
she is	*she is not*
ils sont (eel soN)	**ils ne sont pas**
they are (masc.)	*they are not* (masc.)
elles sont (ail soN)	**elles ne sont pas**
they are (fem.)	*they are not* (fem.)

suis-je?	ne suis-je pas?
am I?	*am I not?*
êtes-vous?	n'êtes-vous pas?
are you?	*are you not?*
sommes-nous?	ne sommes-nous pas?
are we?	*are we not?*

AVOIR = *to have*

j'ai (zhay)	je n'ai pas
I have	*I have not*
vous avez	vous n'avez pas
(voo-zah-vay)	*you have not*
you have	
nous avons	nous n'avons pas
(noo-zah-voN)	*we have not*
we have	
il a (ee-lah)	il n'a pas
he has	*he has not*
elle a (ai-lah)	elle n'a pas
she has	*she has not*
ils ont (eel-zoN)	ils n'ont pas
they have (masc.)	*they have not* (masc.)
elles ont (ail-zoN)	elles n'ont pas
they have (fem.)	*they have not* (fem.)
avez-vous (ah-vay-voo)	n'avez-vous pas?
have you?	*haven't you?*
a-t-il? (ah-teel)	n'a-t-il pas?
has he?	*hasn't he?*
a-t-elle? (ah-tail)	n'a-t-elle pas?
has she?	*hasn't she?*
ont-ils? (oN-teel)	n'ont-ils pas?
have they?	*haven't they?*
ont-elles? (oN-tail)	n'ont-elles pas?
have they?	*haven't they?*

POSSESSIVE ADJECTIVES

mon père	ma mère
moN pair	mah mair
my father	*my mother*

mes parents
may pah-raN
my parents

son père	sa mère
soN pair	sah mair
his or her father	*his or her mother*

ses parents
say pah-raN
his or her parents

notre père	notre mère
notr pair	notr mair
our father	*our mother*

nos parents
noh pah-raN
our parents

votre père	votre mère
votr pair	votr mair
your father	*your mother*

vos parents
voh pah-raN
your parents

leur père	leur mère
lâyr pair	lâyr mair
their father	*their mother*

leurs parents
lâyr pah-raN
their parents

SINGULAR		PLURAL
Masc.	*Fem.*	*(both genders)*
mon (moN)	ma (mah)	mes (may) *my*
son (soN)	sa (sah)	ses (say) *his, her, its*
notre (notr)		nos (noh) *our*
votre (votr)		vos (voh) *your*
leur (lâyr)		leurs (lâyr) *their*

The possessive adjectives (my, your, his, her, our, their), like any other adjectives in French, agree in gender with the thing possessed. **Sa chaise** is both "his chair" and "her chair" because **chaise** is feminine in French; **son livre** is both "his" and "her book" because **livre** is masculine. When translating "his" or "her" you must keep in mind that the French **son** and **sa** are not determined by the sex of the possessor.

EXERCISES

I Answer in French

1. La famille R. a-t-elle une bonne traversée? 2. La mer est-elle calme? 3. M. Roberts est-il fatigué? 4. Est-il malade? 5. Qui est malade? 6. Madeleine est-elle malade? 7. Quel âge a-t-elle? 8. Mme R. est-elle Anglaise? 9. Ses parents sont-ils Français? 10. Êtes-vous Français? 11. Êtes-vous fatigué? 12. Vos parents sont-ils Anglais?

II Translate into English

1. Ce verre-ci est pour moi, ce verre-là est pour vous. 2. C'est une tasse de thé.

3. Ceci est un verre de bière, cela est un verre de vin. 4. Voici un joli bateau français. 5. Le capitaine est grand et mince. 6. Voici un transatlantique pour vous. 7. Merci, monsieur, vous êtes bien aimable. 8. Avez-vous mon sac? 9. Voilà votre sac. 10. Votre mari est-il Français? 11. Non, madame, il est Écossais. 12. N'êtes-vous pas fatigués? 13. Nous ne sommes pas fatigués. 14. Ses enfants sont charmant(e)s, n'est-ce pas? 15. Sa fille parle français, n'est-ce pas? 16. Les Françaises sont charmantes, n'est-ce pas? 17. Son fils apporte un transatlantique, n'est-ce pas?

III Translate into French

1. My mother is French, my father is English. 2. They have three children. 3. We are on a French boat. 4. We are not tired. 5. We are having a good (bad) crossing. 6. Is this cup for me? 7. What is this? 8. Is it a cup of tea? 9. This cup is not big. 10. Haven't you got a deck-chair? 11. Aren't you pleased? 12. You are tired, aren't you? 13. Your brother is tired, isn't he? 14. Their children are charming, aren't they? 15. Where is his hat? 16. Here is his hat. 17. Where is her bag? 18. There is her bag. 19. Have you got my gloves? 20. There are your gloves on the chair. 21. Are they brown or yellow? 22. They are not yellow. 23. They are having a good crossing, aren't they? 24. The coffee is good, isn't it? 25. Is this glass for me?

(Key to I, II and III on page 52.)

DANS LE WAGON-RESTAURANT

Assis dans le wagon-restaurant d'un express continental les voyageurs attendent le déjeuner.

| **Assis-e** (adj.)
Seated | **wagon-restaurant** (m.)
restaurant-car | **voyageurs** (m.), **voyageuses** (f.)
passengers | **attendre**
to await |

PARIS: LA PLACE ET LA COLONNE VENDÔME

Coulée dans le bronze des canons pris à l'ennemi, la colonne Vendôme est surmontée de la statue de Napoléon 1er, ce lieutenant corse devenu Empereur des Français.

Place (f.)	**coulé-e** (m.f.)	**prendre à (quelq'un)**	**surmonté-e** (m.f.)
Square	cast	to take from (someone)	crowned, surmounted

QUATRIÈME LEÇON—*FOURTH LESSON*

In this picture are shown the notices which correspond to the English "No Smoking", "Exit", "Customs". Can you find them? Also try to make a list in French of the other objects shown in this picture of a French customs scene.

M. Roberts: **(À sa famille.) Maintenant nous sommes en France. Parlez français,**
ah sah fah-mee*y*. miNt-naN noo som-zaN fraNs. pahr-lay fraN-sai,
(To his family). *Now we are in France.* *Speak French,*

mes enfants. Où est la douane? La voilà à gauche (droite).
may-zaN-faN. oo ay lah dwahn? lah vwa-lah ah gohsh (drwaht).
my children. *Where is the customs?* *There to (the) left (right).*

M. Roberts: **(Au porteur.) Porteur, êtes-vous libre? Prenez nos bagages,**
oh por-tãyr. por-tãyr ait voo leebr? pren-ay noh bah-gahzh
(To the porter.) *Porter, are you free?* *Take our luggage,*

s'il vous plaît. Nous avons quatre colis. Portez-les à
seel-voo-plai. noo-zah-voN kahtr ko-lee. por-tay lay ah
please. *We have four articles (of luggage).* *Carry them to*

la douane, s'il vous plaît.
lah dwahn seel-voo-plai.
the customs, please.

Le douanier: **Avez-vous quelque chose à déclarer? Tabac, cigarettes?**
ah-vay voo kail-ke shohz ah day-klah-ray? tah-bah see-gah-rait?
Have you anything to declare? *Tobacco, cigarettes?*

M. Roberts: Rien, monsieur, à l'exception du tabac dans ma blague.
ryiN m's-yãy ah laiks-aip-syoN dẽ tah-bah daN mah blahg.
Nothing, sir, with the exception of the tobacco in my pouch.

Le douanier: Ouvrez, s'il vous plaît.   Ces bas sont-ils neufs?
oov-ray seel-voo-plai.   say bah soN-teel nãyf?
Open, please.   These stockings are they new?

M. Roberts: Non, monsieur, ils ne sont pas neufs.   **Douanier:** Vous pouvez fermer.
noN m's-yãy eel ne soN pah nãyf.   voo poo-vay fair-may.
No, sir, they are not new.   *You can close (it).*

Le sac est fermé.
le sahk ay fair-may.
The bag is shut.

Le sac est ouvert.
le sahk ay-too-vair.
The bag is open.

CONVERSATION AT THE STATION

M. Roberts: (au porteur) Trouvez-nous un compartiment pour fumeurs,
oh port-ãyr troo-vay-noo uN koN-pahr-tee-maN poor fẽ-mãyr,
(to the porter) Find us a smoking compartment,

deuxième classe.   À quelle heure part le train pour Paris?
dãy-zyaim klahs.   ah kai-lãyr pahr le triN poor pah-ree?
second class.   At what time leaves the train for Paris?

Le porteur: À trois heures vingt, monsieur.   Il est trois heures maintenant.
ah trwa-zãyr viN, m's-yãy.   eel ay trwa-zãyr miNt-naN.
At three (hours) twenty, sir.   It is three (hours) now.

M. Roberts: (à sa famille) Voulez-vous manger quelque chose?
(ah sah fa-mee*y*) voo-lay-voo maN-zhay kailk-shohz?
(to his family)   Do you want to eat something?

Voici le buffet.
vwah-see le bẽ-fay.
Here is the buffet.

La famille R.: Je n'ai pas faim, mais j'ai soif..................Une tasse de café
zhe nay pah fiN mai zhay swahf............ẽn tahs de kah-fay
I have not hunger, but I have thirst................A cup of coffee

pour moi. . . . . **Je préfère une limonade.**
poor mwah . . . . zhe pray-fair ën lee-mo-nahd.
for me . . . . *I prefer a lemonade.*

M. Roberts: **Garçon, deux cafés, une limonade et un demi**
gahr-soN dāy kah-fay ën lee-mo-nahd ay uN de-mee
Waiter, two coffees, a lemonade and a half (-litre)

de bière blonde pour moi. Le garçon: Café nature ou au lait?
de byair bloNd poor mwah. kay-fay nah-tër oo oh lai?
of light ale for me. Natural (black) or with milk?

Mme R. **Café nature pour moi** . . . . **Café crème, s'il vous plaît.**
et Charles: kah-fay nah-tër poor mwah . . . . . . kah-fay kraim seel voo-plai.
Black for me . . . . *Coffee with cream, please.*

La porte est fermée.
lah port ay fairmay.
The door is closed.

La porte est ouverte.
lah port ay-too-vairt.
The door is open.

Je ferme la porte.
zhe fairm lah port.
I shut the door.

J'ouvre la porte.
zhoovr lah port.
I open the door.

Le garçon: **Voilà les deux cafés et le sucre, la limonade et la bière.**
vwah-lah lay dãy kah-fay ay le sẽ̃kr la lee-mo-nahd ay lah byair.
Here are the two coffees and the sugar, the lemonade and the beer.

Charles: **Mais le café est dans un verre.   C'est drôle, n'est-ce pas?**
mai le kah-fay ay daN-zuN vair.   say drohl nais-pah?
But the coffee is in a glass.   That is funny, isn't it?

Le garçon: **Autre pays, autre mœurs.   Évidemment, c'est votre première**
ohtr pai-ee ohtr mãyrs.   ay-vee-dah-maN say votr prem-yair
Other country, other habits.   Evidently this is your first

               visite en France.   Mais vous parlez français assez bien.
vee-zeet aN fraNs.   mai voo pahr-lay fraN-sai ah-say byiN.
visit to France.   But you speak French rather well.

Charles: **Je parle un peu seulement; mais je comprends, si on ne**
zhe pahrl uN pãy sãyl-maN mai zhe coN-praN see oN ne
I speak a little only; but I understand if one does not

               parle pas trop vite.   Ma mère est Française.
pahrl pah troh veet.   mah mair ay fraN-saiz.
speak too fast.   My mother is French.

Le garçon: **Alors, je comprends.**
ah-lor zhe coN-praN.
Then, I understand.

Mme Roberts: **Le café est bon en France.   Et la bière, aimez-vous**
le kah-fay ay boN aN fraNs.   ay lah byair ai-may voo
The coffee is good in France.   And the beer, do you like

               la bière française, mon mari?
lah byair fraN-saiz moN mah-ree?
the French beer, my husband?

M. Roberts: **Elle n'est pas mauvaise.   Mais je préfère mon pale ale anglais.**
ail nay pah mo-vaiz.   mai zhe pray-fair moN pail-ail aN-glai.
It is not bad.   But I prefer my English pale ale.

               Garçon, l'addition, s'il vous plaît.   Le garçon: Cent trente francs.
gahr-soN lah-dees-yoN seel-voo plai.   saN traNt fraN.
Waiter, the bill, please.   Hundred and thirty francs.

M. Roberts: **Voilà deux cents francs.   Gardez la monnaie.**
vwah-lah dãy saN fraN.   gahr-day lah mo-nai.
Here's two hundred francs.   Keep the change.

Le garçon: **Merci bien, monsieur.   Je vous souhaite bon voyage.**
mair-see byiN m's-yãy.   Zhe voo-swait boN vwah-yahzh.
Thanks very much, sir.   I wish you a good journey.

This picture shows a somewhat unenthusiastic porter with the Roberts' luggage. In the list below only four of the words, which we translate, are unknown to you. Can you recognise the others from their French names?

Le ıourreau	l'étiquette (f.)	la courroie	la canne
foo-roh	ay-tee-kait	koo-rwah	kahn
Case, sheath	*luggage tag*	*strap*	*(walking) stick*

La valise	la malle	le carton à chapeaux	le sac de voyage
Le parapluie	la couverture de voyage		le porteur	les bagages

USEFUL EXPRESSIONS AT THE STATION

De quel quai part le train pour Paris?
de kail kai pahr le triN poor pah-ree?
From which platform leaves the train for Paris?

Quai numéro deux.   **Les billets, s'il vous plaît.**
kai nē̃-may-roh dāȳ.   lay bee-yay seel-voo-plai.
Platform number two.   *(The) tickets please.*

Est-ce le train pour Paris? **Est-ce un fumeur?**
ais le triN poor pah-ree? ais uN fē̃-māȳr?
Is this the train for Paris? *Is this a smoker?*

(un non-fumeur)   **Cette place est-elle libre?**
uN noN fē̃-māȳr   sait plahs ay-tail leebr?
(a non-smoker)   *Is this seat disengaged?*

Est-ce que vous avez nos bagages?
ais-ke voo-zah-vay noh bah-gahzh?
Have you got our luggage?

En voiture, mesdames, messieurs!
aN vwah-tē̃r may-dahm mais-yāȳ!
Take your seats, ladies and gentlemen!

Mettez ceci dans le filet.
mai-tay se-see daN le fee-lay.
Put this into the (luggage) net (=rack).

Mettez cette boîte à cette place.
mai-tay sait bwaht ah sait plahs.
Put this box on that seat.

Cela fait combien?
se-lah fai koN-byiN?
That makes how much?
How much is that?

Cinquante francs, monsieur, c'est notre tarif[1].
siN-kaNt fraN m's-yāȳ say notr tah-reef.
Fifty francs, sir, that's our tariff.

[1] French railway-porters have a fixed list of charges.

A TALK IN THE TRAIN

Mme Roberts: **L'air est assez mauvais.** **Vous permettez que je baisse la glace?**
lair ay-tah-say mo-vay. voo pair-mai-tay ke zhe bais lah glahs?
The air is rather bad. *You allow that I lower the window?*

Le monsieur: **Permettez-moi, madame.** **Cette glace-là peut-être?**
pair-mai-tay mwa mah-dahm. sait glahs lah pāȳ-taitr?
Allow me, madam. *That window there, perhaps?*

Mme Roberts: **Merci bien, monsieur, vous êtes bien aimable.**
mair-see byiN m's-yāȳ voo-zait byiN-nai-mahbl.
Thanks very much, sir. *You are very kind.*

Le monsieur: **Vous permettez que je fume?**
voo pair-mai-tay ke zhe fē̃m?
You allow that I smoke?

Mme Roberts: **Certainement, monsieur.** **Ça ne nous dérange pas.**
sair-tain-maN m's-yāȳ. sah ne noo day-raNzh pah.
Certainly, sir. *That disturbs us not.*

Le monsieur (à M. Roberts):   **Cigarette, monsieur?**
see-gah-rait m's-yǣy?
Cigarette, sir?

M. Roberts: **Merci bien, monsieur. Mais je préfère ma pipe.**
mair-see byiN m's-yǣy.   mai zhe pray-fair mah peep.
Thank you very much, sir. But I prefer my pipe.

Le monsieur: **Est-ce que vous fumez, madame?**
ais-ke voo fǣ-may mah-dahm?
Do you smoke, madam?

Mme Roberts: **Merci, monsieur, je ne fume pas. Mon mari fume pour moi!**
mair-see m's-yǣy zhe ne fǣm pah. moN mah-ree fǣm poor mwah!
Thank you, sir, I don't smoke. My husband smokes for me!

HOW TO ASK QUESTIONS.   **Est-ce que** literally means "is it that"; placed before an ordinary statement it turns the statement into a question:

Vous allez à Paris.		**Le chapeau est brun.**
You are going to Paris.	**EXAMPLES**	*The hat is brown.*
Est-ce que vous allez à Paris?		**Est-ce que le chapeau est brun?**
Are you going to Paris?		*Is the hat brown?*

POSITIVE FORM
je fume   (zhe fǣm)   *I smoke, I am smoking, I do smoke*
il ⎫ **fume** (eel ⎫ fǣm)   *he (it)* ⎫ *smokes, is smoking, does smoke*
elle ⎭ (ail ⎭   *she (it)* ⎭
nous fumons (noo fǣ-moN)   *we smoke, are smoking, do smoke*
vous fumez (voo fǣ-may)   *you smoke, are smoking, do smoke*
ils ⎫ **fument** (eel ⎫ fǣm)   *they smoke, are smoking, do smoke*
elles ⎭ (ail ⎭

AS QUESTIONS
fumé-je or **est-ce que je fume?**   *am I smoking? do I smoke?*
fume-t-il? or **est-ce qu'il fume?**   *is he smoking? does he smoke?*
fume-t-elle? or **est-ce qu'elle fume?**   *is she smoking? does she smoke?*
fumons-nous? or **est-ce que nous fumons?**   *are we smoking? do we smoke?*
fumez-vous? or **est-ce que vous fumez?**   *are you smoking? do you smoke?*
fument-ils (elles)? or **est-ce qu'ils (elles) fument?**   *are they smoking? do they smoke?*

NEGATIVE FORM
je ne fume pas   *I am not smoking, I don't smoke*
il ne fume pas   *he is not smoking, he does not smoke*
elle ne fume pas   *she is not smoking, she does not smoke*
nous ne fumons pas   *we are not smoking, we do not smoke*
vous ne fumez pas   *you are not smoking, you don't smoke*
ils (elles) ne fument pas   *they are not smoking, they don't smoke*

AS QUESTIONS
ne fume-t-il pas? or **est-ce qu'il ne fume pas?**   *is he not smoking? doesn't he smoke?*
ne fume-t-elle pas? or **est-ce qu'elle ne fume pas?**   *is she not smoking? doesn't she smoke?*
ne fumez-vous pas? or **est-ce que vous ne fumez pas?**   *are you not smoking? don't you smoke?*
ne fument-ils (elles) pas? or **est-ce qu'ils (elles) ne fument pas?**   *are they not smoking? don't they smoke?*

This and other diagrams are provided to extend your vocabulary in a simple and interesting way. First compare the English words and their French equivalents, then

English

1. Platform; 2. Engine; 3. Tender; 4. Luggage van; 5. Funnel (smoke-stack); 6. Coach (carriage); 7. Compartment; 8. Smokers' (compartment); 9. Non-smokers' (compartment); 10. Permanent way; 11. Local train (2nd and 3rd cl.); 12. Express trains (1st and 2nd cl.); 13. Station-master; 14. Buffers; 15. Engine-driver; 16. Fireman; 17. Guard; 18. Platform barrier;

THE RAILWAY STATION

19. Ticket-collector; 20. Male traveller; 21. Female traveller; 22. Porter; 23. Newspaper trolley; 24. Rug and pillow trolley; 25. Luggage trolley; 26. (Carriage) window; 27. Advertisement; 28. Hanging lights; 29. Trunks; 30. Suitcases; 31. Ventilators; 32. Coal fuel; 33. Whistle; 34. Safety-valve; 35. Headlight; 36. Train-indicator.

French

1. Quai (m.); 2. Locomotive (f.);

cover over the letterpress and see how many French words you can attach to the numbers on the diagram. Turn back to the diagrams when you have advanced in the course.

LA GARE DE CHEMIN DE FER

3. Tender (m.); 4. Fourgon (m.) à bagages; 5. Cheminée (f.); 6. Voiture (f.); 7. Compartiment (f.); 8. (Compartiment de) fumeurs (m.pl.); 9. (Compartiment de) non-fumeurs; 10. Voie ferrée (f.); 11. Train (m.) d'intérêt local, 2me et 3me cl.; 12. Trains-express; rapides (m.pl.) 1re et 2me cl.; 13. Chef (m.) de gare; 14. Heurtoirs; butoirs (m.pl.); 15. Mécanicien; 16. Chauffeur (m.); 17. Chef de train; 18. Contrôle (m.); 19. Contrôleur (m.); 20 & 21. Voyageur-euse; 22. Porteur; 23. Poussette (f.) à journaux; 24. Poussette à oreillers et couvertures; 25. Chariot (m.) à bagages; 26. Glace (f.); 27. Annonce (f.); 28. Éclairage (m.) suspendu; 29. Malles (f.pl.); 30. Valises (f.pl.); 31. Ventilateurs (m.pl.); 32. Charbon; combustible (m.); 33. Sifflet (m.) à vapeur; 34. Soupape (f.) de sûreté; 35. Phare; projecteur (m.); 36. Tableau (m.) indicateur.

If you look up "to smoke" in a dictionary you will find **fumer** (f@̄-may); to speak is **parler** (pahr-lay); to carry is **porter** (por-tay). The form of a verb[1] which you find in the dictionary is called the Infinitive.[2] The Infinitives of most French verbs end in **-er**, pronounced ay.

All verbs ending in **-er** with the exception of **aller**=to go, have the same endings as shown above for **fumer**, i.e., they end in **-e** (which is silent) in connection with **je, il** or **elle**, in **-ez** (ay), when used with **vous**, in **-ons** (oN) with **nous** and in **-ent** (silent) when used in connection with **ils** or **elles**.

If we call the part of a verb that does not change, the stem; and the part that does, the ending, then **fum-, parl-, port-** are the stems of the verbs **fumer, parler** and **porter**. To say "I speak" or "I am speaking" you don't have to add anything to the stem, but in writing **-e** is added; thus you say zhe pahrl and you write **je parle**. "He (she) speaks (or: is speaking)"=**il (elle) parle** (the e remains silent). To say "you speak" or "you are speaking" you add **-ez** to the stem: **vous parlez** (voo pahr-lay); "you carry" or "you are carrying" is **vous portez**; to ask "do you smoke?" or "are you smoking?" you just reverse the order and say "smoke you?"=**fumez-vous** or

est-ce que vous fumez? "Do you speak English?" is: **parlez-vous anglais?** or **est-ce que vous parlez anglais?** "Are you carrying my luggage?"=**portez-vous mes bagages?** or **est-ce que vous portez mes bagages?** etc.

Study carefully the forms of the verb **fumer**, not forgetting its negative and question forms as given on page 47. If you replace the stem **fum-** by the stem of any other verbs ending in **-er** (and there are over 4,000 of them) you will be able to make hundreds and hundreds of other statements and questions. Other verbs in **-er** having occurred in this lesson besides **fumer, parler** and **porter** are **déclarer**=to declare, **fermer**=to close, **débarquer**=to land, **trouver**=to find, **apporter**=to bring and **déranger**=to disturb.

We shall deal with the verb **aller** in the following lessons, and in later lessons with those verbs which do not end in **-er**.

---

[1] A "verb" is a word used for asserting something about a person or thing.

[2] The "infinitive" is that part of a verb which names the action with no reference to who is doing it or when it takes place.

It is the part usually cited: thus one does not speak of "the verb **je fume**," but of "the verb **fumer, parler, porter**," etc.

SUMMARY

Affirmative

je ⎫		I------------,	I am------ing,	I do--------
il ⎬--------*e*[1]	⎧ he (it)-------s,	is---------ing,	does-------
elle ⎭	⎨ she (it)-------s,	is---------ing,	does-------
vous----------*ez*[2]	you-----------,	are-------ing,	do----------
nous---------*ons*[3]	we-----------,	are-------ing,	do----------
ils-----------*ent*[1] ⎫	they----------,	are-------ing,	do----------
elles ⎭			

Interrogative

-------------- *é-je?*	am I----------------ing?	do I-------------?
------------- *e-t-il?*	is he---------------ing?	does he----------?
----------- *e-t-elle?*	is she--------------ing?	does she---------?
----------- *ez-vous?*	are you-------------ing?	do you-----------?
----------- *ons-nous?*	are we--------------ing?	do we-----------?
----------- *ent-ils?*[4] ⎫	are they------------ing?	do they----------?
ent-elles?[4] ⎭		

or: put **est-ce que** (ais-ke) in front of the affirmative form.

Negative

je ne- - - - - - - - -e[1] *pas*	I am not- - - - - - - - - - - - -ing,	I don't- - - - - - - - - - -
il ne- - - - - - - - -e[1] *pas*	he is not- - - - - - - - - - - - -ing,	he does not- - - - - - -
elle ne- - - - - - -e[1] *pas*	she is not- - - - - - - - - - - - -ing,	she does not- - - - - - -
vous ne- - - - - -ez[2] *pas*	you are not- - - - - - - - - - -ing,	you don't- - - - - - - - -
nous ne- - - - -ons[3] *pas*	we are not- - - - - - - - - - -ing,	we don't- - - - - - - - -
ils (elles) ne-ent[1] *pas*	they are not- - - - - - - - - -ing,	they don't- - - - - - - -

Negative and Interrogative

ne- - - - - - - - -é-je *pas?*	am I not- - - - - - - - - - - - -ing?	don't I- - - - - - - - - - -?
ne- - - - - - - -e-t-il *pas?*	is he not- - - - - - - - - - - - -ing?	doesn't he- - - - - - - -?
ne- - - - - -e-t-elle *pas?*	is she not- - - - - - - - - - - -ing?	doesn't she- - - - - - -?
ne- - - - - -ez-vous *pas?*	are you not- - - - - - - - - - -ing?	don't you- - - - - - - -?
ne- - - - -ons-nous *pas?*	are we not- - - - - - - - - - -ing?	don't we- - - - - - - - -?
ne-ent[4]-ils(elles) *pas?*	are they not- - - - - - - - - -ing?	don't they- - - - - - - -?

or: put **est-ce que** in front of the negative form.

[1] this ending is silent.   [2] pronounced **ay**.   [3] pronounced **oN**.   [4] the t is sounded.

EXERCISES

I   Translate into French

1. Do you smoke? 2. Is she smoking? 3. He does not smoke. 4. We are landing. 5. They keep the change. 6. I don't shut the door. 7. Haven't you got the luggage? 8. Is he not carrying our luggage? 9. We speak English. 10. We don't speak French. 11. Are we now in France? 12. Can't you find (say: find you not) your ticket? 13. Waiter, three coffees, please. 14. The bill, please. 15. Is this the train for Paris? 16. Are these stockings new? 17. You are disturbing that lady. 18. Do you mind my smoking? (translated: Do you allow that I smoke *or* does it disturb you that I smoke?) 19. Porter, are you not free? 20. Is it to the right or to the left?

II   Answer in French

1. Parlez-vous français? 2. Est-ce que nous sommes en France? 3. Les bas de Mme Roberts sont-ils neufs? 4. Qui porte les bagages? 5. À quelle heure part le train de la famille Roberts? 6. Qui apporte les consommations? 7. Charles a-t-il faim? 8. Est-ce que la famille Roberts va à Marseille? 9. Charles a-t-il un café nature? 10. Qu'est-ce qu'il a? 11. Le café est-il bon? 12. Est-ce que Monsieur R. fume une cigarette? 13.

Qu'est-ce qu'il préfère? 14. Est-ce que vous avez une allumette? 15. Est-ce que Madame R. fume?

III   Give the correct ending and translate into English

1. Je *ferm-* la porte. 2. Il *trouv-* un billet. 3. Elles ne *fum-* pas. 4. Ne *débarqu-* -vous pas? 5. Ne *dérang-* -t-elle pas? 6. Vous *parl-* assez bien. 7. Nous *apport-* les bagages. 8. Ils ne *trouv-* pas le porteur. 9. Le garçon *n'apport-* -t-il pas l'addition? 10. Est-ce qu'elles ne *ferm-* pas la porte? *(Key to I, II and III on pages 52 and 53.)*

KEY TO THE EXERCISES
Lesson Two
I

1. C'est un gant. 2. Oui, il est joli (non, il n'est pas joli). 3. Non, ce n'est pas Mlle Lesage. 4. Oui, elle est jolie. 5. Charles est le cousin de Mlle Lesage. 6. Oui, il est joli (non, il n'est pas joli). 7. Ce sont des gants. 8. Non, il n'est pas grand. 9. Madeleine est la sœur de Charles. 10. M. et Mme Roberts. 11. Oui, elle est élégante. 12. Non, elle n'est pas grande. 13. Non, il n'est pas sur la table. 14. Il est sur la chaise. 15. Oui. 16. C'est un gilet. 17. Ce sont des chaussures. 18. Elles sont noires et blanches.

II

1. La cravate est blanche et bleue. 2. Le veston est brun. 3. La robe est verte. 4. Le chapeau n'est pas vert, il est brun. 5. Le pardessus est-il noir? 6. Non, monsieur, il est gris. 7. La table est-elle grande? 8. Oui, elle est grande. 9. La fenêtre est-elle grande? 10. Non, elle est petite. 11. Le mouchoir est-il rouge et bleu? 12. Non, il est blanc. 13. Les gants sont-ils bruns? 14. Non, madame, ils sont jaunes. 15. Les malles sont-elles jaunes? 16. Non, elles sont brunes. 17. Qu'est ce que c'est? 18. Est-ce le livre? 19. Oui, monsieur, c'est le livre. 20. Non, monsieur, ce n'est pas le livre, c'est le sac. 21. De quelle couleur est le sac? 22. Il est bleu. 23. N'est-il pas joli! 24. La valise, n'est-elle pas brune? 25. L'enfant[1] n'est-il pas charmant! 26. Où sont les enfants? 27. Où est le père de Georges? 28. Où est-il? 29. Où est-elle? 30. Où sont-ils?

III

1. Il est blanc. 2. Elle... 3. Elle... 4. Ils... 5. Elles... 6. Ils... 7. Elles... 8. ... est-il? 9. ... est-elle? 10. ... est-il? 11. ... est-elle? 12. ... sont-ils? 13. ... sont-ils? 14. ... sont-elles?

Lesson Three

I

1. Oui, elle a une bonne traversée. 2. Oui, elle est calme. 3. Oui, il est fatigué. 4. Non, il n'est pas malade. 5. Charles est malade. 6. Non, elle n'est pas malade. 7. Elle a douze ans. 8. Non, elle n'est pas Anglaise. 9. Oui, ils sont Français. 10. Non je ne suis pas Français. 11. Non, je ne suis pas fatigué. 12. Oui, ils sont Anglais (Non, ils ne sont pas Anglais).

II

1. This glass is for me, that glass is for you. 2. It's a cup of tea. 3. This is a glass of beer, that is a glass of wine. 4. Here is a nice French boat. 5. The captain is tall and thin. 6. Here is a deck-chair for you. 7. Thank you, sir, you are very kind. 8. Have you got my bag? 9. There is your bag. 10. Is your husband French? 11.

No, madam, he is Scottish. 42. Aren't you tired? 13. We are not tired. 14. His (or her) children are charming, aren't they? 15. His (or her) daughter speaks French, doesn't she? 16. Frenchwomen are charming, aren't they? 17. His (or her) son is bringing a deck-chair, isn't he?

III

1. Ma mère est Française, mon père est Anglais. 2. Ils ont trois enfants. 3. Nous sommes sur un bateau français. 4. Nous ne sommes pas fatigués. 5. Cette tasse est-elle pour moi? 6. Cette tasse est-elle pour moi? 7. Qu'est-ce que c'est? 8. Est-ce une tasse de thé? 9. Cette tasse n'est pas grande. 10. N'avez-vous pas un transatlantique? 11. N'êtes-vous pas content(e)? 12. Vous êtes fatigué(e), n'est-ce pas? 13. Votre frère est fatigué, n'est-ce pas? 14. Leurs enfants sont charmants[2], n'est-ce pas? 15. Ou est son chapeau? 16. Voici son chapeau. 17. Où est son sac? 18. Voilà son sac. 19. Avez-vous mes gants? 20. Voilà vos gants sur la chaise. 21. Est-ce qu'ils sont bruns ou jaunes? 22. Ils ne sont pas jaunes. 23. Ils (elles) ont une bonne traversée, n'est-ce pas? 24. Le café est bon, n'est-ce pas? 25. Ce verre est-il pour moi?

Lesson Four

I

1. Fumez-vous? *or* Est-ce que vous fumez? 2. Fume-t-elle *or* est-ce qu'elle fume? 3. Il ne fume pas. 4. Nous débarquons. 5. Ils (elles) gardent la monnaie. 6. Je ne ferme pas la porte. 7. N'avez-vous pas les bagages? 8. Ne porte-t-il pas nos bagages? 9. Nous parlons anglais. 10. Nous ne parlons pas français. 11. Est-ce que nous sommes (*or* sommes-nous) maintenant en France? 12. Ne trouvez-vous pas (est-ce que vous ne trouvez pas) votre billet? 13. Garçon, trois cafés, s'il vous plaît. 14. L'addition, s'il vous plaît. 15. Est-ce le train pour Paris? 16. Ces bas

---

[1] As mentioned in footnote to p. 22, **enfant** is masculine when meaning a boy and feminine when a girl is indicated. In this case for a girl child one would say "elle" and **charmante**.

[2] **Charmantes**, if girls are referred to.

sont-ils neufs? 17. Vous dérangez cette dame. 18. Permettez-vous que je fume? *or* Est-ce que ça vous dérange que je fume? 19. Porteur, n'êtes-vous pas libre? 20. Est-ce à droite ou à gauche?

II

1. Je parle français (je ne parle pas français) *or*: un peu seulement. 2. Nous ne sommes pas en France. 3. Non, ils ne sont pas neufs. 4. Le porteur porte les bagages. 5. Le train part à trois heures vingt. 6. Le garçon apporte les consommations. 7. Non, il n'a pas faim. 8. Elle ne va pas à Marseille. 9 and 10. Non, il a un café crème. 11. Oui, il est bon.

12. Non, il ne fume pas une cigarette. 13. Une pipe. 14. Oui, j'ai une allumette. 15. Non, elle ne fume pas.

III

1. *ferme*: I close the door. 2. *trouve*: He finds a ticket. 3. *fument*: They don't smoke *or* they are not smoking. 4. *débarquez*: Are you not going on land? 5. *dérange-t-elle*: Is she not disturbing? *or* Doesn't she disturb? 6. *parlez*: You speak quite well. 7. *apportons*: We bring (are bringing) the luggage. 8. *trouvent*: They don't find the porter. 9. *n'apporte-t-il pas*: Doesn't the waiter bring the bill? 10. *ferment*: Don't they shut the door?

The Roberts family are now in France. Are you also in France? If you have studied the Lessons and listened in to French on the wireless, you should be setting your foot there already.

DEVANT LES BOUQUINISTES

C'est une scène familière—des passants qui s'attardent à feuilleter les livres aux étalages des bouquinistes de la rive gauche, quartier des étudiants et des professeurs.

Bouquiniste (m.f.)	**s'attarder à**	**feuilleter**	**étalage** (m.)
(Second-hand) bookseller	dally over	glance through (book)	stall

LA SORBONNE (UNIVERSITÉ DE PARIS)

Héritiers d'une grande tradition, ces étudiants profitent d'un moment de liberté dans la cour d'honneur pour respirer l'air et philosopher.

Héritier-ère (m.f.)	**étudiant-e** (m.f.)	**profiter de**	**cour** (f.) **d'honneur**
Heir, inheritor	student	take advantage of	grand quadrangle

CINQUIÈME LEÇON—*FIFTH LESSON*

Cover over the English lines of the text below, and, with the help of the picture, see if you can follow how the Roberts family are passing the time in the train.

Il est six heures du soir.   Le train n'est plus loin de Paris.   La famille
ee-lay see-zâyr dée swahr.   le triN nay plée lwiN de pah-ree.   lah fah-mee*y*
It is six o'clock of the evening.   The train is no longer far from Paris.   The Roberts

Roberts ne dort plus.   Charles lit un livre.   M. Roberts lit un journal.
ro-bairts ne dor plée.   shahrl lee uN leevr.   m's-yây ro-bairts lee uN zhoor-nahl.
family sleeps no more.   Charles is reading a book.   Mr. Roberts is reading a paper.

Mme R. regarde par la fenêtre.   Madeleine parle avec le monsieur.
mah-dahm R. re-gahrd pahr lah fe-naitr.   mahd-lain pahrlah-vaik le m's-yây.
Mrs. R. looks out of the window.   Madeleine is talking to the gentleman.

Madeleine: **Est-ce que nous sommes encore loin de Paris?**
ais-ke noo som-zaN-kor lwiN de pah-ree?
Are we still far from Paris?

Le monsieur: **Encore une demi-heure.   Nous arrivons à six heures trente.**
aN-kor éen demee âyr.   noo-zah-ree-voN ah see-zâyr traNt.
Still half an hour.   We arrive at six thirty.

Madeleine: **Est-ce que vous allez aussi à Paris, monsieur?**
ais-ke voo-zah-lay oh-see ah pah-ree m's-yây?
Are you going also to Paris, sir?

Le monsieur: **Non, mademoiselle. Je ne reste à Paris que deux heures.**
noN mahd-mwah-zail. zhe ne raist ah pah-ree ke dāy-zāyr.
No, miss. I am staying in Paris only for two hours.

Puis je vais en Italie. Ma femme y est déjà.
pw̃ee zhe vai-zaN-nee-tah-lee.   mah fahm ee ay day-zhah.
Then I am going to Italy. My wife is already there.

Madeleine: **Vraiment! Vous allez en Italie.**
vrai-maN! voo-zah-lay-zaN-nee-tah-lee.
Really! You are going to Italy.

Le monsieur: **Et vous, mademoiselle, est-ce que vous restez à Paris?**
ay voo mahd-mwah-zail ais-ke voo rais-tay ah pah-ree?
And you, miss, are you going to stay in Paris?

Madeleine: **J'y reste plusieurs semaines. Puis je vais au bord de la**
zhee raist plēēz-yāyr se-main.   pwee zhe vai zoh bor de lah
I stay there several weeks.   Then I am going either to the

mer ou à la campagne.
mair oo ah lah kaN-pany.
seaside or to the country.

Le monsieur: **Et votre frère, où va-t-il?**
ay votr frair oo vah-teel?
And your brother, where is he going?

Madeleine: **Il va où je vais, naturellement.**
eel vah oo zhe vai nah-tēē-rail-maN.
He goes where I go, naturally.

Charles: **Non, je ne vais pas avec vous. Je reste à Paris.**
noN zhe ne vai pah-zah-vaik voo.   zhe raist ah pah-ree.
No, I am not going with you.   I stay in Paris.

Le monsieur: **Et vos parents, est-ce qu'ils vont aussi à la campagne?**
ay voh pah-raN aisk-eel voN-toh-see ah lah kaN-pany?
And your parents, are they going also to the country?

Madeleine: **Oui, probablement, mais mon père va bientôt retourner**
w̃ee prob-ahbl-maN mai moN pair vah byiN-toh re-toor-nay
Yes, probably, but my father will soon return

pour quelque temps en Angleterre.
poor kail-ke taN aN-naN-gle-tair.
for some time to England.

Charles (après quelques minutes): J'ai faim, maman.
(ah-prai kail-ke mee-nēēt): zhay fiN mah-maN.
(after a few minutes): I am hungry, mummy.

THE VERB ALLER=TO GO

je vais zhe vai I go, I am going

il ⎫ va **eel** ⎫ vah he (it) ⎫ goes,
elle ⎭ **ail** ⎭ she (it) ⎭ is going

nous allons noo-zah-loN we go, are going
vous allez voo-zah-lay you go, are going

ils ⎫ vont **eel** ⎫ voN they go,
elles ⎭ **ail** ⎭ are going

NO MORE OR NO LONGER

il ne parle plus=he is no longer speaking
le train n'est plus loin de Paris=the train is no longer far from Paris
ils ne restent plus à Londres=they are no longer staying in London

Note that **ne** precedes the verb and **plus** follows it, the same as **ne . . . pas**

ONLY

il ne reste que deux heures=he stays only (for) two hours
Elle n'a que trois ans=She is only three years (old)
Qui retourne en Angleterre? Mon père seulement=who returns to England? Only my father

Note that **ne** precedes the verb and **que** follows it, in the same way as **ne . . . pas,** or **ne . . . plus.** But if "only" is used apart from a verb, it must be translated by **seulement** (sâyl-maN).

Mme R.: **Voici une pomme. Donnez-en la moitié à Madeleine.**
vwah-see ễn pom. do-nay-zaN lah mwaht-yay ah mahd-lain.
Here's an apple. Give (of it the) half to Madeleine.

Madeleine: **Non, merci, je n'ai pas faim.**
noN mair-see zhe nay pah fiN.
No, thank you, I am not hungry.

Charles: **Papa, donnez-moi votre canif, s'il vous plaît.**
Pah-pah do-nay mwah votr kah-neef seel-voo-plai.
Father, give me your (pocket-) knife, please.

Monsieur R.: **(donnant son canif à Charles):**
(do-naN soN kah-neef ah shahrl)
(giving his knife to Charles):
Voilà, mon fils.
vwah-lah moN fees.
There you are, my son.

Charles: **Merci, papa. Voulez-vous l'autre moitié?**
mair-see pah-pah. voo-lay voo lohtr mwaht-yay?
Thank you, father. Do you want the other half?

Monsieur R.: **Non, mon petit, pas pour moi. Mais donnez-la à Monsieur.**
noN moN p'tee pah poor mwah. mai do-nay lah ah m's-yâŷ.
No, my little one, not for me. But give it to (the) gentleman.

Charles: **Pardon, monsieur, est-ce que vous voulez la moitié de ma pomme?**
pahr-doN m's-yâŷ ais-ke voo voo-lay lah mwaht-yay de mah pom?
Excuse me, sir, would you like (the) half of my apple?

Le monsieur: **Merci bien, mon ami. Vous êtes bien aimable, mais**
mair-see byiN moN-nah-mee. voo-zait byiN-nai-mahbl mai
Thank you very much, (my friend). You are very kind, but
je ne mange jamais avant le repas.
zhe ne maNzh zhah-mai ah-vaN le re-pah.
I eat never before the meal (meals).

AT A FRENCH AIRPORT

For instructions on the method of using these

English

1. Wing(s); 2. Engine; 3. Three-bladed airscrew; 4. Non-smoking cabin; 5. Smoking cabin; 6. Aerial; 7. Steward's galley; 8. Direction-finder; 9. Navigator; 10. Mast head light; 11. Radio cabin; 12. Pilot; 13. Second pilot; 14. Landing lights; 15. Electrically-heated speed indicator; 16. Control tower; 17. Wind-sock; 18. French flag; 19. Body of plane; 20. Rear landing-wheel; 21. Baggage compartment and extra passenger accommodation; 22. Steward; 23. Tail-plane; 24. Rudder fin (port); 25. Stabiliser; 26. Retractable under-carriage.

French

1. Aile(s) (f.); 2. Moteur (m.); 3. Hélice

DANS UN AÉROPORT FRANÇAIS
vocabulary building diagrams, see pages 34 *and* 35.

(f.) à trois pales; 4. Cabine (f.) de non-fumeurs; 5. Cabine de fumeurs; 6. Antenne (f.); 7. Cuisine (f.); 8. Radiogoniomètre (m.); 9. Navigateur (m.); 10. Feu (m.) de tête de mât; 11. Cabine de T.S.F.; 12. Pilote (m.); 13. Pilote en second; 14. Feu d'atterrissage (m.); 15. Indicateur (m.) de vitesse chauffé à l'électricité; 16. Tour (f.) de contrôle; 17. Sac (m.) à vent; 18. Pavillon (m.) national; 19. Fuselage (m.); 20. Roue (f.) de la dérive; 21. Soute (f.) à bagages et place supplémentaire pour passagers; 22. Garçon de cabine, steward (m.); 23. Plan (m.) fixé; 24. Gouvernail (m.) de direction de bâbord; 25. Stabilisateur (m.); 26. Châssis (m.) d'atterrissage relevable.

Lui: Embrassez-moi!
lⱳee aN-brah-say mwah!
He: Kiss me!

Elle: Jamais!
ail zhah-mai!
She: Never!

NEVER

je ne mange jamais . . . I never eat
il ne parle jamais . . . He never speaks
  ne precedes the verb and **jamais** follows
it, in the same way as **ne . . . pas, ne . . .
que**, or **ne . . . plus.** If "never" is used
without a verb **jamais** only is said.

HOW TO ASK FOR SOMETHING
donnez! = give! **mangez!** = eat! **parlez!** =
speak! The imperative of a verb ends in
-ez (pronounced ay).

HOW TO TRANSLATE *DON'T*
ne parlez pas . . . don't speak
ne mangez pas . . . don't eat
ne parlez plus . . . don't speak any more
ne mangez plus . . . don't eat any more
ne parlez jamais . . . don't ever speak,
                        never speak

Charles: **Alors je mange l'autre moitié aussi.**
ah-lor zhe maNzh lohtr mwaht-yay oh-see.
Then I eat the other half too.

Mme R.:   **Ne mangez pas si avidement, mon enfant!**
ne maN-zhay pah see ah-veed-maN moN-naN-faN!
Don't eat so greedily, my child!

Charles: **Quel long voyage!**
kail loN vwah-yahzh!
What a long journey!

Le monsieur: **N'aimez-vous pas voyager?   Regardez le beau village.**
nai-may voo pah vwah-yah-zhay?   re-gahr-day le boh vee-lahzh.
Don't you like to travel?   Look at the beautiful village.

Charles: **J'aime bien voyager.   Mais je n'aime pas les longs voyages**
zhaim byiN vwah-yah-zhay. mai zhe naim pah lay loN vwa-yahzh
I like very much to travel.   But I don't like the long journeys

en train.   J'aime mieux aller en auto.
aN triN.   zhaim myaⱳ ah-lay aN-noh-toh.
by train.   I like better to go by car.

Le monsieur: **Ou en avion?   On évite tous les changements**
oo aN-nahv-yoN?   oN-nay-veet too lay shaNzh-maN
Or by aeroplane?   One avoids all the changing

de bateau en train.
de bah-toh aN triN.
from boat to train.

Charles: **C'est ça, monsieur.**
say sah m's-yay.
That's right, sir (literally: That's it).

Madeleine: **Quelles jolies petites maisons! Regardez, maman!**
kail zho-lee p'teet mai-zoN! re-gahr-day mah-maN!
What pretty little houses! Look, mother!

Mme R.:   **Oui, elles sont très belles, ma fille.**
wee ail soN trai bail mah feey.
Yes, they are very beautiful, my daughter.

Charles: **Quelle heure est-il maintenant?**
kai-layr ay-teel miNt-naN?

Le monsieur: **Il est six heures et quart. Encore un quart d'heure et**
ee-lay see-zayr ay kahr. aN-kor uN kahr dayr ay
It is six o'clock and quarter. Another quarter of an hour and

nous sommes à Paris si nous arrivons à l'heure.
noo-som-zah pah-ree see noo-zah-ree-voN zah layr.
we are in Paris if we arrive on time (literally: "to the hour").

HOW TO TRANSLATE "LET US ..."

Allons! *Let us go!...* **Parlons français!** *Let us speak French!*

Note that the ending -ons (pronounced oN) gives to a verb the meaning of "let us. ..."

HOW TO TRANSLATE "BEAUTIFUL"

Le chapeau est beau ..... *The hat is beautiful*
La maison est belle ..... *The house is beautiful*
Les chapeaux sont beaux ..... *The hats are beautiful*
Les maisons sont belles ..... *The houses are beautiful*

Note (1) That the plural of words in -eau ends in -x (which is silent except in liaison, when it is sounded like z).
(2) The irregular feminine of beau: belle.

HOW TO TRANSLATE WHAT A .... WHAT .... WHICH ...

Quel beau chapeau! ..... *What a beautiful hat!*
Quelle belle maison! ..... *What a beautiful house!*
Quels beaux chapeaux! ..... *What beautiful hats!*
Quelles belles maisons! ..... *What beautiful houses!*
Quel livre avez-vous? ..... *Which book have you (got)?*
Quelle valise prenez-vous? ..... *Which suitcase are you taking?*
Quels livres avez-vous? ..... *Which books have you (got)?*
Quelles valises prenez-vous? ..... *Which suitcases are you taking?*

Note: (1) That there is no difference in French between "what a ..., what ..., which ...," when used in connection with nouns, i.e., like adjectives.
(2) Like all other adjectives there is a special form for the feminine, **quelle,** and in the plural -s is added.
(3) **quel, quelle, quels, quelles** are all pronounced the same (kail).

WHAT TIME IS IT?—IN HOURS

De midi à minuit
de mee-dee ah mee-nŵee
From midday to midnight

A ..	..	**il est une heure** ..	.. ēen-âyr
B ..	..	**il est deux heures** ..	.. dâÿ-zâyr
C ..	..	**il est trois heures** ..	.. trwah-zâyr
D ..	..	**il est quatre heures** ..	.. kaht-râyr
E ..	..	**il est cinq heures** ..	.. siN-kâyr
F ..	..	**il est six heures** ..	.. see-zâyr
G ..	..	**il est sept heures** ..	.. sai-tâyr
H ..	..	**il est huit heures** ..	.. ŵee-tâyr
I ..	..	**il est neuf heures** ..	.. nâÿ-vâyr
J ..	..	**il est dix heures** ..	.. dee-zâyr
K ..	..	**il est onze heures** ..	.. oN-zâyr
L ..	..	**il est midi (minuit)** ..	.. mee-dee (mee-nŵee)

Note.—As the twenty-four hour clock is practically universal in France, especially in railway guides, it is wise to start now thinking in terms of **treize, quatorze heures** (1 and 2 p.m.), etc.

WHAT TIME IS IT?—IN MINUTES

De midi à une heure
de mee-dee ah ēēn-āÿr
From midday to one o'clock

A	..	..	**il est midi cinq**	mee-dee siNk
B	..	..	**il est midi dix**	mee-dee dees
C	..	..	**il est midi et quart**	mee-dee ay kahr
D	..	..	**il est midi vingt**	mee-dee viN
E	..	..	**il est midi vingt cinq**	mee-dee viNt siNk
F	..	..	**il est midi et demi**	mee-dee ay de-mee
G	..	..	**il est une heure moins vingt-cinq**	ēēnāÿr mwiN viNt siNk
H	..	..	**il est une heure moins vingt** ..	mwiN viN
I	..	..	**il est une heure moins le quart** ..	mwiN le kahr
J	..	..	**il est une heure moins dix** ..	mwiN dees
K	..	..	**il est une heure moins cinq** ..	mwiN siNk
L	..	..	**il est une heure précise**	pray-seez

Note.—When indicating time with precision in hours and minutes, one may also use, *e.g.*, 12·51, **midi cinquante-et-un**; 3·17, **trois heures dix-sept**, etc. After **midi** and **minuit** (both m.) you use **demi**. After **une heure** (f.), etc., you use **demie**.

EXERCISES

I   Translate into English

1. Aimez-vous les livres? 2. J'aime bien les livres. 3. Mon livre est très intéressant. 4. Je n'aime pas les livres de mon père; ils ne sont pas intéressants. 5. Regardez cette jolie petite fille; n'est-elle pas belle? 6. Est-ce que vous allez en France? 7. Non, monsieur, je vais en Angleterre. 8. Mes enfants y vont aussi. 9. Mon père ne va pas à la campagne. 10. Ils vont au bord de la mer.

II   Replace the dashes by quel, quelle, quels or quelles

1. — fenêtre est ouverte? 2. — portes sont fermées? 3. — livre est rouge? 4. — valises sont jaunes? 5. — monsieur est votre père? 6. — dame est votre tante? 7. Dans — train est-il? 8. Dans — valise sont les pommes? 9. — sont vos chapeaux? 10. — heure est-il?

III   Translate into French

1. What's the time, please? 2. It is four o'clock. 3. It is two-thirty. 4. It is six minutes past five. 5. It is a quarter past eleven. 6. It is twenty-five minutes past nine. 7. It is a quarter to eight. 8. It is twenty to seven. 9. It is five minutes before midnight. 10. How old is your sister? 11. She is only twelve years old. 12. Where are you going? I am going to Paris. 13. We are going to the seaside. 14. Are you going to the countryside? 15. Is your wife also there? 16. Are your children going to Italy? 17. Is your son still hungry? 18. Thank you, madam; he is no longer hungry. 19. I never speak to my brother. 20. What a beautiful bridge! 21. What a beautiful house they have! 22. What pretty girls they are! 23. Let us look at the bridge. 24. Let us get our luggage ready. 25. Please give me the half of your apple. 26. Don't speak so quickly.

(Key to I, II and III on page 101)

PARIS AU PRINTEMPS

Au coin du Boulevard Montmartre, un beau jour de printemps. Mais malgré le soleil, on garde toujours le pardessus. "En avril ne quitte pas un fil."

malgré	garder	fil (m.)	"En avril ne quitte pas un fil"
in spite of	to keep (on)	thread	"Ne'er cast a clout till May be out"

SIXIÈME LEÇON—*SIXTH LESSON*

In this picture of the Robertses' arrival in Paris, there are at least fifteen objects you should be able to name in French. Can you do so? For the key, see page 92.

M. Roberts: **Nous avons trois gros bagages.   Voici le bulletin.**
noo-zah-voN trwah groh bah-gahzh.   vwah-see le bẽẽl-tiN.
We have three articles of big luggage.   Here is the receipt.

Laissez les bagages à main, je les prendrai moi-même.
lai-say lay bah-gahzh ah miN zhe lay praN-dray mwah-maim.
Leave the hand luggage, I'll take it (them) myself.

Mme R.:   **Voici l'oncle Lesage.   Bonjour, Paul!**
vwah-see loNkl le-sahzh.   boN-zhoor pol!
Here is uncle Lesage.   Hallo, Paul!

M. Lesage: **Bonjour,[1] ma chérie!   Bonjour, Roberts!**
boN-zhoor mah shay-ree!   boN-zhoor Ro-bairts!
Good morning, my dear!   Good morning, Roberts!

---

[1] **Bonjour** literally means *good day*. Note that it is also said in the morning and afternoon, as there are no French equivalents for our *good morning* and *good afternoon*. In the evening they say **bon soir** (boN swahr), even late in the night, when we would say *good night*. **Bonne nuit** (bon-nŵee) the French for *good night*, is said only to someone going to bed.

A droite: la Gare St. Lazare, terminus des lignes de Dieppe et du Havre; également la plus importante des gares de banlieue desservant Paris.

On the right: the Gare St. Lazare, terminus of the lines from Dieppe and Le Havre; also the most important of the stations serving the suburbs of Paris.

———

En bas: la Gare du Nord, dont la construction évoque une architecture d'ordre ionique d'un ensemble heureux.

Below: the Gare du Nord, the construction of which calls to mind the pleasing effect of architecture of the Ionic order.

PARIS: LES GRANDES GARES D'ARRIVÉE EN VENANT DE LONDRES

Bonjour, Madeleine! Bonjour, Charles! Qu'il est grand,
boN-zhoor mahd-lain! boN-zhoor shahrl! kee-lay graN
Good morning, Madeleine! Good morning, Charles! How big he is,

ce fripon! (il les embrasse tous à l'exception de Charles!)
se free-poN! (eel-lay-zaN-brahs toos ah laik-saip-syoN de shahrl!)
this rascal! (he kisses them all with the exception of Charles!)

Charles (évitant d'être embrassé): Bonjour, mon oncle.
(ay-vee-taN daitr aN-brah-say): boN-zhoor moN-noNkl.
(avoiding to be kissed): Good day, (my) uncle.

M. Roberts: Comment allez-vous?
              ko-maN-tah-lay-voo?
              How are you?

M. Lesage: Très bien, merci. Et vous?
              trai byiN mair-see. ay voo?
              Very well, thanks. And you?

M. Roberts: Pas mal non plus.
              pah mahl noN plēē.
              Not bad either.

M. Lesage: Vous avez bonne mine, Roberts. Alors, venez chez nous prendre
              voo-zah-vay bon meen ro-bairts. ah-lor ve-nay shay noo preNdr
              You are looking well, Roberts. Now then, come to us to have

              le petit déjeuner. Ah, voilà ma fille avec notre voiture.
              le p'tee day-zhāy-nay. Ah vwah-lah mah feey ah-vaik notr vwah-tēēr.
              breakfast. Oh, there is my daughter with our car.

              Vous connaissez ma fille?
              Voo ko-nai-say mah feey?
              You know my daughter?

M. Roberts: Mais oui, je connais Mademoiselle Lucie. Excusez-moi,
              mai wee zhe ko-nai mahd-mwah-zail lēē-see. aiks-kēē-zay mwah
              But yes, I know Miss Lucie. Excuse me,

              je vais chercher mon porteur. (Il trouve le porteur
              zhe vai shair-shay moN por-tāyr. (eel troov le por-tāyr
              I am going to look for my porter. (He finds the porter

              aux bagages.) Ah, vous voilà! Portez les bagages
              oh bah-gahzh.) ah voo vwah-lah! por-tay lay bah-gahzh
              at the luggage office.) Ah, there you are! Take the luggage

              à une voiture, s'il vous plaît. Venez avec moi.
              ah ēēn vwah-tēēr seel-voo-plai. ve-nay ah-vaik mwah.
              to a car, please. Come with me.

Le porteur: Je viens, monsieur.
              zhe vyiN m's-yāy.
              I am coming, sir.

M. Lesage (au porteur): **Mettez les malles là-dessus, s'il vous plaît.**
(oh por-tāyr): mai-tay lay mahl lah de-sēē seel-voo-plai.
(To the porter): Put the trunks on there, please.

Mme Roberts: **Est-ce que les malles sont en sûreté là?**
ais-ke lay mahl soN-taN sēēr-tay lah?
Are the trunks safe (literally: in safety) there?

M. Lesage: **Certainement, ma chérie.** **M. Roberts: Cela fait combien?**
sair-tain-maN mah shay-ree. se-lah fai koN-byiN?
Certainly, my dear. *That makes how much?*

Le porteur: **Quatre-vingt-dix francs, monsieur.** **Trente francs par colis.**
kahtr-viN-dee fraN m's-yāy. traNt fraN pahr ko-lee.
Ninety francs, sir. *Thirty francs per piece of luggage.*

M. Lesage: **Montez, s'il vous plaît, et partons.**
moN-tay seel-voo-plai ay pahr-toN.
Get in, please, and let's start.

SALUTATIONS

Comment allez-vous? . . . How are you?
(Literally: How are you going?)
Je vais bien . . . I am well
Vous allez bien . . . You are well
Il (elle) va bien . . . He (she) is well
Nous allons bien . . . We are well
Ils (elles) vont bien . . . They are well

Alternative forms of the
colloquial language are:
Comment ça va? . . . How are things?
(Literally: How goes it?)
Ça va bien. . . . I am all right.
(Literally: It goes well.)
Ça va bien? . . . You are all right?
You are getting on well?

ROUND THE TOWN

Un Conseil pour les Gens Avisés

Si vous voulez vraiment connaître Paris par vous-même, vous ne pouvez mieux faire que de vous mettre entre les mains d'un chauffeur parisien, en lui disant de vous prendre chaque jour à votre gîte. Dites-lui: "Chauffeur, on voudrait connaître les restaurants où l'on mange bien, et tous les bons coins du vieux Paris." La plupart des chauffeurs sont de bons types, et à cause de leur occupation ils connaissent la ville à fond. Il leur est facile de choisir leur restaurant dans n'importe quel quartier et s'ils montrent une préférence pour un certain établissement, celui-ci est presque toujours un restaurant où l'on mange bien et à bon marché. Naturellement, si votre chauffeur a des velléités de vous jouer "le truc des étrangers," arrêtez les frais—et choisissez-en un autre.

A Tip for the Wise

If you wish really to get to know Paris well on your own, you cannot do better than to put yourself in the hands of a Paris chauffeur, and arrange that he fetches you every day where you're staying. Say to him: "Chauffeur, we'd like to know the restaurants where one eats well, and all the interesting corners of old Paris." The majority of the chauffeurs are "good scouts," and on account of their occupation they know the city thoroughly. It is easy for them to choose their restaurant in no matter what district, and if they show a preference for a certain establishment, this is nearly always a restaurant where one eats well and cheaply. Naturally, if your driver shows a disposition to play the "stranger act" on you, cut your losses—and choose another driver.

L'ÉGLISE DE LA MADELEINE ET LA RUE ROYALE

Inspiré du Parthénon, cet édifice est un des plus beaux réalisés dans le style néo-classique. Il fut commencé sous Louis XVI en 1764, pour servir d'église paroissiale. La Révolution en fit un temple païen à la "Déesse Raison". Aujourd'hui cet édifice a été rendu à sa designation originelle: une église paroissiale de Paris.

| **paroissial-e** (adj.) | **église** (f.) | **païen-ne** (adj.) | **déesse** (f.) | **raison** (f.) |
| parish | church | pagan | goddess | reason |

The following list is from the buffet of a French railway station. Owing to fluctuations of the franc, the prices are omitted.

TARIF	tah-reef	TARIFF
*	*	*
BIÈRES	byair	*beer*
Bock.............	bock........,...........	*small glass (of beer)*
Demi.............	de-mee...............	*large glass (of beer)*
Pilsen............	peel-sain.............	*Pilsen*
Pale Ale, Bouteille....	pail-ail, boo-tai*y*........	*pale ale, bottle*
et Demi-Bouteille..	de-mee boo-tai*y*.........	*and half-bottle*
Stout, Quart........	kahr...................*stout, mug (quarter of a litre)*

CAFÉ—INFUSIONS	kah-fay iN-fẽẽz-yoN	*coffee, infusions*
Café nature..........	kah-fay nah-tẽẽr........	*coffee, black*
Café filtre...........	kah-fay feeltr...........	*coffee, percolated*
Café glacé...........	kah-fay glah-say........	*coffee, iced*
Café au lait..........	kah-fay oh lai...........	*coffee with milk*
Lait froid...........	lai frwa...............	*milk, cold*
Lait chaud..........	lai shoh...............	*milk, hot*
Chocolat............	sho-ko-lah.............	*chocolate*
Chocolat glacé.......	sho-ko-lah glah-say......	*chocolate, iced*
Thé................	tay...................	*tea*
Infusions............	iN-fẽẽz-yoN...........	*infusions*

DIVERS	dee-vair	*miscellaneous*
Citron pressé........	seet-roN prai-say........	*lemon squash*
Citronnade glacée.....	seet-ro-nahd glah-say....	*lemonade, iced*
Orange pressée.......	oh-raNzh prai-say.......	*orange squash*
Orangeade glacée.....	oh-raN-zhahd glah-say...	*orangeade, iced*
Glaces..............	glahs.................	*ices*
Champagne, la coupe..	shaN-pan*y* la koop......	*champagne, the glass*
Bordeaux Blanc, le verre	bor-doh blaN le vair.....	*white Bordeaux wine, the glass*
Bordeaux Rouge, le verre	bor-doh roozh le vair....	*red Bordeaux wine, the glass*
Vin chaud, le verre....	viN shoh le vair........	*mulled wine, the glass*

CASSE-CROÛTE	kahs-kroot	*snacks*
Sandwich Jambon....	sahnd-veech zhaN-boN..	*ham sandwich*
Sandwich Veau.......	sahnd-veech voh........	*veal sandwich*
Sandwich Rosbif.....	sahnd-veech roz-beef....	*beef sandwich*
Brioches...........	bree-osh...............	*rolls (kind of)*
Gâteaux............	gah-toh...............	*cakes*
Tartes.............	tahrt.................	*pastries*

APÉRITIFS	ah-pay-ree-teef	
Vermouth Chambéry..	vair-moot shaN-bay-ree..	*French (dry) Vermouth*
Turin Martini........	tẽẽ-riN mahr-tee-nee.....	*Italian Vermouth*

Turin Cinzano*	tẽe-riN siN-zah-noh	*Vermouth*
Dubonnet*	dẽe-bo-nay	*cordial wine*
Raphaël*	rah-fah-ail	*do.*
Amer Picon*	ah-mair pee-koN	*bitters*
Amer Campari*	ah-mair kaN-pah-ree	*do.*
Anis divers	ah-nee dee-vair	*aniseed*
Pernod Fils*	pair-noh fees	*(resembles) absinthe**

VINS DE LIQUEUR	viN de lee-kãyr	*dessert wines*
Porto	por-toh	*port*
Madère	mah-dair	*Madeira*
Malaga	mah-lah-gah	*Malaga*
Xérès	kay-rais	*sherry*
Frontignan	froN-teen-yaN	*Frontignan*

LIQUEURS & SIROPS	lee-kãyr ay see-ro	*liqueurs and syrups*
Menthe Verte	maNt vairt	*spearmint*
Cassis-Curaçao	kah-sees kẽe-rah-soh	*blackcurrant and Curaçao*
Guignolet-Menthe	geen-yo-lay maNt	*cherry brandy and mint*
Sirop nature	see-ro nah-tẽer	*plain syrup*
Sirop alcoolisé	see-ro ahl-ko-lee-zay	*alcoholic syrup*
Crème de Cassis	kraim de kah-sees	*blackcurrant*
Cerises à l'eau de vie	s'reez ah loh d'vee	*brandied cherries*

ALCOOLS, LIQUEURS	ahl-kol lee-kãyr	*strong liqueurs*
Marc de Bourgogne	mahr de boor-gony	*white brandy*
Rhum Vieux	rom vyãy	*old rum*
Kirsch	keersh	*Kirsch*
Mirabelle	mee-rah-bail	*mirabelle-plum*
Framboise	fraN-bwahz	*raspberry*
Calvados	kahl-vah-doss	*cider-brandy*
Fine Champagne	feen shaN-pany	*liqueur brandy (from the Champagne de Saintonge adjoining the Bordeaux district) flavoured with caraway seed, aniseed, etc.*
Cherry Brandy	shai-ree brahn-dee	
Bénédictine	bay-nay-deek-teen	
Kummel	kẽe-mail	

EAUX MINÉRALES	oh mee-nay-rahl	*mineral waters*
Saint-Galmier*	siN gahlm-yay	* *Proprietary brands*
Vittel, Vichy*	vee-tail vee-shee	*Note: Absinthe is nowadays forbidden in France. Pernod is a substitute.*
Évian*	ayv-yaN	
Perrier-Carola*	pair-yay kah-roh-lah	
Soda	soh-dah	

This list of refreshments in railway buffets is fairly representative of what you will usually find in the average French café. The café is the Frenchman's club, where he reads, writes and meets his friends. There you will find most of the day's newspapers, and it is quite usual to ask the waiter for writing materials (de quoi écrire).

A STREET IN PARIS

Cover over the text from the start, and see how many of the objects in the drawing you can name in French from your existing vocabulary. Consult the key only when

une rue barrée	**le magasin**	**la devanture**	**le cinéma**	**un agent de police**[1]
street closed to traffic	shop	shop-window	cinema	policeman

une affiche	**une bicyclette de livreur**	**un étudiant**	**un arrêt obligatoire**	**une midinette**
poster	carrier-bicycle	student	compulsory (bus) stop	milliner's girl

[1] The word **gendarmes,** often erroneously used for Paris policemen, really applies only to a

UNE RUE DE PARIS

necessary. Repeat until you are satisfied that you know the French for everything which is shown in the picture, whether living or inanimate.

un arrêt facultatif request (bus) stop	**un homme-sandwich** sandwich man	**le trottoir** pavement	**le bord du trottoir** kerb	**la chaussée** roadway
un autobus bus	**une auto** car	**le mendiant** beggar	**une église** church	**le refuge** refuge (island)	**une horloge** clock

semi-military body of constabulary who are to be found only in the country parts of France.

ENTERING PARIS

Charles: **Quelle est cette rue-ci, mon oncle?**
kai-lay sait rêe-see moN-noNkl?
What street is this, (my) uncle?

M. Lesage: **C'est la rue La Fayette, une grande voie de communication.**
say la rêe lah-fah-yait êen graNd vwah de kom-mêe-nee-kah-syoN.
It's rue La Fayette, a main artery (of communication).

Charles: **Vous habitez loin d'ici?**
voo-zah-bee-tay lwiN dee-see?
You live far from here?

M. Lesage: **Encore un quart d'heure, mon petit.**
aN-kor uN kahr dâyr moN p'tee.
Another quarter of an hour, my little (friend).

Mlle Lucie: **Quel âge avez-vous, ma chérie?**
(à Madeleine) kai-lahzh ah-vay voo mah shay-ree?
How old are you, my dear?

Madeleine: **J'ai douze ans, ma cousine.**
zhay doo-zaN mah koo-zeen.
I am twelve, (my) cousin.

Mlle L.:   **Vous parlez bien le français. Trouvez-vous le français difficile?**
voo pahr-lay byiN le fraN-sai. troo-vay voo le fraN-sai dee-fee-seel?
You speak well French. Do you find French difficult?

Madeleine: **Pas trop, ma cousine.**
pah troh mah koo-zeen.
Not too much, (my) cousin.

THREE IRREGULAR VERBS

Three irregular verbs occur in the above conversations:
venir = to come; **connaître** = to know (a person or place);
savoir = to know (something).

I come, am coming, etc.	*I know (a person or thing), etc.*	*I know (about), etc.*
je **viens** (vyiN)	je **connais** (ko-nai)	je **sais** (sai)
il ⎱ **vient** elle ⎰ (vyiN)	il ⎱ **connaît** elle ⎰ (ko-nai)	il ⎱ **sait** elle ⎰ (sai)
nous **venons** (ve-noN)	nous **connaissons** (ko-nai-soN)	nous **savons** (sah-voN)
vous **venez** (ve-nay)	vous **connaissez** (ko-nai-say)	vous **savez** (sah-vay)
ils ⎱ **viennent** elles ⎰ (vyain)	ils ⎱ **connaissent** elles ⎰ (ko-nais)	ils ⎱ **savent** elles ⎰ (sahv)

Les deux enfants viennent de l'hôtel et vont à l'école

Charles: Qu'ils sont petits, les autobus de Paris!
keel soN p'tee lay-zoh-toh-bées de pah-ree!
How small they are, the buses of Paris!

Et voilà un agent de police!
ay vwah-lah uN nah-zhaN de po-lees!
And there is a policeman!

M. Lesage: C'est l'agent de la circulation, mon ami.
say lah-zhaN de lah seer-kée-lahs-yoN moN-nah-mee.
It's the traffic policeman, my friend.

Madeleine: Quelles belles maisons et quels beaux magasins!
kail bail mai-zoN ay kail boh mah-gah-ziN!
What beautiful houses and what fine shops!

Mlle L.: C'est le centre de Paris et le quartier le plus riche.
say le saNtr de pah-ree ay le kahr-tyay le plée reesh
It's the centre of Paris and the district the most rich.

Madeleine: Ah, quelle belle devanture! Regardez, maman! N'allez pas
ah kail bail de-vantéer! re-gahr-day mah-maN! nah-lay pah
Oh, what a beautiful shopwindow! Look, mother! Don't go

si vite, mon oncle, s'il vous plaît.
see veet moN-noNkl seel-voo-plaı.
so fast, (my) uncle, please.

M. Lesage: Eh bien, si vous voulez.   **Charles: Quel est ce bâtiment-là?**
ay byiN see voo voo-lay.   kai-lay se bah-tee-maN lah?
All right, if you want.   *What is that building there?*

La dame vient du magasin et va au café

Les petits garçons viennent de la maison et
vont au cinéma

L'OPÉRA DE PARIS UNE NUIT DE FÊTE NATIONALE

Une foule immense se bouscule pour ne pas manquer un spectacle gratuit. L'Opéra, pris au cours de la soirée populaire d'un jour férié, fut fondé sous Louis XIV, en 1669, sous le nom d'"Académie Nationale de Musique" qui figure d'ailleurs encore aujourd'hui

bousculer	**gratuit-e** (adj.)	**jour férié** (m.)	**fonder**
to bustle, jostle	free, gratuitous	(public) holiday	to found

THE PARIS OPERA HOUSE ON A NATIONAL FESTIVAL NIGHT
au frontispice du monument. Le bâtiment actuel, un des plus beaux d'Europe, fut
commencé sous Napoléon III et achevé en 1875. Deux constructions précédentes
avaient été détruites par des incendies, pendant et après la Revolution Française de 1789.

bâtiment (m.)	précédent-e (adj.)	détruire	incendie (m.)
building	former	to destroy	fire, conflagration

Mlle L.:   C'est l'Opéra, mon petit cousin.
say lo-pay-rah moN p'tee koo-ziN.
It's the Opera, my little cousin.

Charles: Merci bien, ma grande cousine.
mair-see byiN mah graNd koo-zeen.
Thank you very much, my big cousin

Mlle L.:   Il est rigolo, votre petit frère, n'est-ce pas?
(à Madeleine) ee-lay ree-goh-loh votr p'tee frair nais pah?
He is funny, your little brother, isn't he?

Madeleine: C'est un grand fripon, vous savez.
say tuN graN free-poN voo sah-vay.
He is a great rascal, you know.

Mme R.:   Quelle est cette maison-là en face?
kai-lay sait mai-zoN lah aN fahs?
What is that building there opposite (in face)?

Mlle L.:   C'est un immeuble de rapport.   Il doit avoir quinze étages.
say-tuN-nee-maybl de rah-port   eel dwat av-wahr kiNz ay-tazh
It's a block of flats.   It must have fifteen storeys.

Mme R.:   Quel immense bâtiment!
kai-lee-maNs bah-tee-maN!
What an enormous building !

Charles: C'est un gratte-ciel, vous savez.
say-tuN graht syail voo sah-vay.
It's a sky-scraper, you know.

M. Lesage: À gauche est la Madeleine.   C'est une belle église,
ah gohsh ay la mahd-lain.   say-tēn bai-lay-gleez,
To (the) left is the Madeleine.   It's a beautiful church.

n'est-ce pas?   À droite est la rue Royale.
nais-pah?   ah drwaht ay lah rēe rwah-yahl.
isn't it?   To the right is the rue Royale.

Mlle L.:   Prenons la rue Royale, mon père.
pre-noN lah rēe rwah-yal moN pair.
Let's take the rue Royale, (my) father.

M. Lesage: Bon, si vous voulez.
boN see voo voo-lay.
Good, if you want to.

M. Roberts: Quel est le nom de cette belle rue?
kai-lay le noN de sait bail rēe?
What is the name of that beautiful street?

M. Lesage: La rue St. Honoré, mon vieux.
la rēe siN-to-no-ray moN vyāy.
The rue St. Honoré, my old (man).

M. Lesage: **Devant nous, c'est la Place de la Concorde.**
de-vaN noo say lah plahs de-lah koN-kord.
Before us, that's the Place de la Concorde.

Madeleine: **Quel beau monument!**
kail boh mo-nẽẽ-maN!
What a beautiful monument !

Mlle L.:   **Approchons pour voir les statues.**
ah-proh-shoN poor vwahr lay stah-tẽẽ.
Let us go near to see the statues.

Mme R.:   **Ah, qu'il est beau, mon Paris!**
ah kee-lay boh moN pah-ree!
Oh, how it is beautiful, my Paris !

CONTRACTIONS

When **de** or **à** immediately precede the definite article **le** or **les,** contracted forms are used:

    du (dẽẽ) instead of de le
    des (day)   ,,   ,, de les
    au (oh)   ,,   ,, à le
    aux (oh)   ,,   ,, à les

Note. (1) that no contractions are used for **de la** and **de l'.**

(2) You cannot say "the lady's hat" in French. You must turn it into "the hat of the lady"; "my father's house" is "the house of my father"=**la maison de mon père**; "this boy's parents"=**les parents de ce garçon**, etc.

le chapeau de
la dame

le parapluie du monsieur
(**du**=de le)

les enfants de l'oncle

les bagages des enfants
(**des**=de les)

Il donne le livre au petit garçon
(au=à le)

Il donne des fleurs à la dame

Note.—(1) There are no contractions of à **la** and à **l'**. (2) Whereas in English the "to" is omitted in sentences like "He gives the boy the book," it must be translated in French, either by **à** or by **au** (for à le) or by **aux** (for à les).

	Masculine	Feminine	Plural
Of (or from) the:	DU (de l')	DE LA (de l')	DES
To (or at) the:	AU (à l')	À LA (à l')	AUX

The forms in brackets are used before nouns beginning with a vowel or mute h (**le nom de l'hôtel**=the name of the hotel; **à l'église**=to the church).

CONCERNING ACCENTS

Strictly speaking, accents in French should appear over capital letters, thus:

$$\text{À} \quad \text{É} \quad \text{Û, etc.}$$

In practice, however, they are sometimes omitted over capitals. It will be noted that accents are placed over capital letters throughout this book.

Never forget to put accents where necessary over small letters, because to write **a** instead of **à** or **e** instead of **é**, is just as bad a spelling mistake as to write **chapot** instead of **chapeau**.

Le professeur donne une pomme
à l'élève

Il parle aux élèves
(aux=à les)

SENTENCE-BUILDING

I

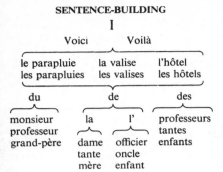

Voici		Voilà
le parapluie	la valise	l'hôtel
les parapluies	les valises	les hôtels

du	de	des
monsieur	la	l'	professeurs
professeur			tantes
grand-père	dame	officier	enfants
	tante	oncle	
	mère	enfant	

II

je parle	il	nous	vous	ils
	elle	parlons	parlez	elles
	parle			parlent

au	à	aux
machiniste	la	l'	professeurs
professeur			petites
contrôleur	grand'mère	oncle	filles
	petite fille	élève	enfants
	dame	enfant	

EXERCISES

I

Turn back to the pictures on pages 74, 75 and answer the following questions: 1. Qui vient de l'hôtel? 2. Qui va au cinéma? 3. D'où viennent les deux enfants? 4. Où vont-ils? 5. Qui vient du magasin? 6. Où va la dame? 7. D'où viennent les petits garçons? 8. Où vont-ils? 9. D'où vient la famille Roberts? 10. Où va-t-elle?

II

Answer the following questions in French, using pronouns instead of the proper nouns:
1. Est-ce que M. Roberts descend du train?
2. „ „ M. Lesage „ „ „
3. „ „ Madeleine „ „ „
4. „ „ Mlle Lesage „ „ „
5. Est-ce que la famille Roberts descend du train?
6. „ „ M. et Mme R. descendent du train?
7. „ „ Mme R. et Madeleine „ „ „

III

Translate into English

1. La sixième leçon n'est pas trop difficile. 2. Le petit garçon n'aime pas être embrassé. 3. Ils vont très bien. 4. Elle ne va pas bien. 5. Il ne connaît pas vos enfants. 6. Mon frère ne vient pas avec vous. 7. Quel est le nom de ce monument? 8. Cette devanture n'est pas belle. 9. Je ne sais pas quelle heure il est. 10. Savez-vous quelle heure il est? 11. Nous venons de l'église. 12. Ils ne connaissent pas cette rue.

IV

Translate into French

1. How are you? 2. I am very well, thank you. 3. How is your little daughter? 4. How are your parents? 5. They are ill. 6. Where are they now? 7. I don't know your little sister. 8. Do you know my uncle? 9. He is going to the cinema. 10. We are coming from the station. 11. We are going to the station. 12. I am going to the café. 13. I am coming from the hotel. 14. Where are you coming from? 15. I am coming from (the) school. 16. Where are you going? 17. I am going to the cinema. 18. They are going to the station. 19. What a beautiful hat you have got! 20. What an intelligent son they have! 21. What beautiful houses are in front of us! 22. What is the name of that beautiful street? 23. My father's house is not far from here. 24. Please give these books to your teacher. 25. These are the teachers' overcoats.

(Key to I, II, III and IV on page 101.)

ARE YOU LISTENING IN EVERY DAY TO BROADCASTING IN FRENCH?

LA PLACE DE LA CONCORDE (AUTREFOIS PLACE LOUIS XV)

De jour, dans une ambiance somptueuse, même les réverbères ont pris un air aristo-cratique. De nuit, l'éclairage diffusé fait ressortir en féerie le jeu des fontaines.

Réverbère (m.)	**éclairage (m.) diffusé**	**faire ressortir**	**jeu (m.)**
Street-lamp	floodlighting	throw up, outline	playing, game

SEPTIÈME LEÇON—*SEVENTH LESSON*

Most of the words connected with the hotel lounge, which Mr. Roberts is now entering, are new to you. Practise, as in other cases, with and without the text.

le bureau de réception	**le gérant**	**la case**	**le tableau aux clefs**
bée-roh de ray-saips-yoN	zhay-raN	kahz	tahb-loh oh klay
office	*booking clerk (manager)*	*pigeon hole*	*board with keys*
le casier du courrier	**le nouvel arrivant**	**le portier**	**le domestique (valet)**
kahz-yay dée koor-yay	noo-vai-lah-ree-vaN	port-yay	do-mais-teek (vah-lay)
letter rack	*new guest*	*hall porter*	*bellboy*
le liftier	**un ascenseur**	**le hall**	**le fauteuil**	**le bar**	**le tabouret**
leeft-yay	ah-saN-sâyr	ahl	foh-tâyy	bahr	tah-boo-ray
lift-boy	*lift*	*entrance hall*	*easy chair*	*bar*	*stool*

How many of these objects can you now name from the picture without the text?

MR. ROBERTS CHOOSES HIS HOTEL

M. Roberts: **Pouvez-vous me recommander un hôtel, pas trop cher?**
poo-vay voo me re-ko-maN-day uN-noh-tail pah troh shair?
Can you recommend me an hotel, not too dear?

M. Lesage: **Le Bienvenu: c'est un excellent hôtel, près d'ici.**
le byiN-ve-née: say-tuN-naik-se-laN-toh-tail prai dee-see.
The Bienvenu: it's an excellent hotel, near here.

M. Roberts: **Allons-y prendre des chambres et laisser nos bagages.**
ah-loN-zee praNdr day shaNbr ay lai-say noh bah-gahzh.
Let us go there (to) take rooms and leave our luggage.

M. Roberts (au gérant de l'hôtel): Avez-vous des chambres libres?
(oh zhay-raN de loh-tail): ah-vay voo day shaNbr leebr?
(to the manager of the hotel): Have you any rooms vacant?

Le gérant: **Il y a trois chambres au deuxième étage.**
eel-yah trwah shaNbr oh dȳz-yaim ay-tahzh.
There are three rooms on the second floor.

Une autre chambre au premier sera libre ce soir.
ȇ-nohtr shaNbr oh prem-yay serah leebr se swahr.
Another room on the first (floor) will be free tonight.

M. Roberts: **Est-ce que vous avez deux chambres à deux lits?**
ais-ke voo-zah-vay dȳ shaNbr ah dȳ lee?
Have you got two double rooms?

Le gérant: **Seulement au deuxième étage, monsieur.**
sȳl-maN oh dȳz-yaim ay-tahzh m's-yȳ.
Only on the second floor, sir.

M. Roberts: **Et le prix?   Combien est-ce?**
ay le pree?   koN-byiN ais-se?
And the price?   How much is it?

Le gérant: **Cela dépend de la chambre.   Depuis huit cents francs par jour.**
se-lah day-paN de lah shaNbr.   de-pw̑ee w̑ee saN fraN pahr zhoor.
That depends on the room.   From 800 francs per day.

M. Roberts: **Combien par semaine?   Je compte rester quelques mois.**
koN-byiN pahr se-main?   zhe koNt rais-tay kail-ke mwah.
How much per week?   I expect to stay (for) several months.

Le gérant: **Ça c'est différent, monsieur.   Nous avons un**
sah say dee-fay-raN m's-yȳ.   noo-zah-voN uN
That's different, sir.   We have a

tarif spécial pour longs séjours.   C'est cinq mille francs
tah-reef spay-syahl poor loN say-zhoor.   say siN meel fraN
special tariff for long residence.   It's 5,000 francs

pour une chambre par semaine, alors ce sera dix mille
poor ȇn shaNbr pahr se-main ah-lor se se-rah dee meel
for one room per week, so it will be 10,000

pour les deux.
poor lay dȳ.
for the two.

M. Roberts: **Est-ce que le petit déjeuner est compris?**
ais-ke le p'tee day-zhȳ-nay ay coN-pree?
Is breakfast included?

Le gérant: **Mais non, monsieur, c'est à part; 150 francs par jour.   Vous**
mai noN m's-yȳ say-tah pahr saN-siN-kaNt fraN pahr zhoor.   voo
Oh, no, sir, it is extra; 150 francs per day.   You

pouvez avoir pension complète comprenant chambre,
poo-vay zah-vwahr paN-syoN koN-plait koN-pre-naN shaNbr
can have full board comprising room,

petit déjeuner, déjeuner et dîner depuis
p'tee day-zhāy-nay day-zhāynay ay dee-nay de-pw̄ee
breakfast, lunch and dinner from

mille deux cents francs par jour.
meeldāy saN fraN pahr zhoor.
1,200 *francs per day.*

M. Roberts: **Puis-je voir les chambres?**
pw̄ee-zh vwahr lay shaNbr?
Can I see the rooms?

Le gérant: **Avec plaisir, monsieur. Veuillez monter dans l'ascenseur. Cette**
ah-vaik plai-zeer m's-yāy vāy-yay moN-tay daN lah-saN-sāyr. sait
With pleasure, sir. Will you please step into the lift. This

chambre est très agréable. Elle donne sur le jardin.
shaNbr ay trai-zah-gray-ahbl. ail don sēēr le zharh-diN.
room is very pleasant. It gives (looks) on to the garden.

Mr. Roberts chooses a pleasant bedroom which gives a fine view over Paris, looking in the direction of the world-famous Eiffel Tower.

Un édredon	le chauffage central	la table de toilette	une esquisse
Eiderdown	central heating	dressing-table	sketch

M. Roberts: **Où donne cette porte-là?**
oo don sait port lah?
Where does that door lead?

Le gérant: **Dans une autre chambre qui est aussi à deux lits.   Elle sera**
daN zĕen ohtr shaNbr kee ay-toh-see ah dãy lee.   ail se-rah
To another room which is also with two beds.   It will be

libre ce soir.   Vous pouvez la voir si vous voulez.
leebr se swahr.   voo poo-vay lah vwahr see voo voo-lay.
free this evening.   You can see it if you like.

M. Roberts: **S'il vous plaît.   Cette chambre n'est pas claire.**
seel voo plai.   sait shaNbr nay pah klair.
Please.   This room is not bright.

Le gérant: **La fenêtre donne sur une cour.   Vous**
lah fenaitr don sĕer ĕen koor.   voo
The window gives on to a courtyard.   You

pouvez en avoir une autre sur le
poo-vay-zaN-nav-wahr ĕen ohtr sĕer le
can have another at the

devant de la maison.   Veuillez entrer
de-vaN de la mai-zoN.   vãy-yay-zaN-tray
front of the house.   Will you please come

dans cette chambre, monsieur.
daN sait shaNbr m's-yãy.
into this room, sir.

M. Roberts: **J'aime mieux cette chambre-ci.   Bon, je prends**
zhaim myãy sait shaNbr see.   boN zhe praN
I like better this room (here).   Good, I take

ces deux chambres.   Voilà vingt mille francs pour
say dãy shaNbr.   vwah-lah viN meel fraN poor
these two rooms.   There is 20,000 francs for

quinze jours.   Quel jour est-ce?
kiNz zhoor.   kail zhoor ais?
15 days (i.e., a fortnight).   What day is it?

Le gérant: **Aujourd'hui, c'est mardi trois ̣uin.**
oh-zhoor-dw̃ee say mahr-dee trwah zhw̃iN.
To-day, it is Tuesday, the third (of) June.

M. Roberts: **Alors, c'est payé jusqu'au dix-huit.**
ah-lor say pai-yay zhĕes-koh deez-w̃eet.
Then it is paid up to the eighteenth.

Le gérant:	**C'est ça, monsieur. Le valet va**
	say sah m's-yay. le vah-lay vah
	That's right, sir. The boots will
	monter vos bagages.
	moN-tay voh bah-gahzh.
	take up your luggage.

M. Roberts:	**Quels sont les numéros de nos chambres?**
	kail soN lay nẽe-may-roh de noh shaNbr?
	What are the numbers of our rooms?
Le gérant:	**Les numéros onze et dix-neuf, monsieur.**
	lay nẽe-mayroh oNz ay deez-nãyf m's-yay.
	(The) numbers eleven and nineteen, sir.

THERE IS, THERE ARE

Il y a une chambre au premier étage	There is one room on the first floor
Il y a deux chambres au deuxième	There are two rooms on the second
Y a-t-il une chambre au premier?	Is there a room on the first?
Y a-t-il des chambres au deuxième?	Are there any rooms on the second?

Note that **il y a** stands for both "there is" and "there are".

I WILL and I CAN

je veux (vay)=I will   je peux (pay)=I can

il
elle } veut (vay)   il
elle } peut (pay)

nous voulons (voo-loN)   nous pouvons (poo-voN)

vous voulez (voo-lay)   vous pouvez (poo-vay)

ils
elles } veulent (vayl)   ils
elles } peuvent (payv.

Il veut parler français
He wants to speak French
Il va parler français
He is going to speak French

Il ne peut pas le faire
He cannot do it
Veuillez parler français
Will you please speak French

Note.—(1) **Je veux** expresses wish or desire; **je vais** the immediate future (I am going to . . .). For the future tense, see page 161.

(2) The "to" of "I want to" or "I am going to" is left out in French, as it is in both English and French after "I can".

(3) **Veuillez** (vay-yay) corresponds to English "will you please" or "would you be so kind as to . . ." or "do you mind . . ."

ROUND THE TOWN

Paris

Le centre géographique et historique de Paris est l'Île de la Cité, qui se trouve au milieu de la Seine. Là s'élève la cathédrale de Notre-Dame.

Sur la rive droite (au nord) de la Seine sont les quartiers commerçants et la plupart des théâtres. La rive gauche (au sud) comprend le Quartier Latin, l'Université de Paris et les grandes écoles, et plusieurs établissements militaires.

Paris

The geographical and historical centre of Paris is the City Island, which is in the middle of the Seine. There stands Notre-Dame Cathedral.

On the right bank (to the north) of the Seine are the commercial districts and most of the theatres. The left bank (to the south), includes the Latin Quarter, the University of Paris and the great schools (of learning) and several military establishments.

avant-hier c'était: ah-vaN-tyair say-tai *(the day) before yesterday it was:*	}	**DIMANCHE 31 MAÍ**	{	dee-maNsh *Sunday* traN-tay-uN mai
hier c'était: yair say-tai *yesterday it was:*	}	**LUNDI 1er JUIN**	{	luN-dee *Monday* prem-yay zhwiN
aujourd'hui c'est: oh-zhoord-ŵee sai *today it is:*	}	**MARDI 2 JUIN**	{	mahr-dee *Tuesday* dâŷ zhwin
demain ce sera: de-miN se se-rah *to-morrow it will be:*	}	**MERCREDI 3 JUIN**	{	mairk-re-dee *Wednesday* trwah zhwiN
après-demain ce sera: ah-prai de-miN se se-rah *after tomorrow it will be:*	}	**JEUDI 4 JUIN**	{	zhâŷ-dee *Thursday* kahtr zhwiN
dans trois jours ce sera: daN trwah zhoor se se-rah *in three days it will be:*	}	**VENDREDI 5 JUIN**	{	vaNdr-dee *Friday* siNk zhwiN
dans quatre jours ce sera: daN kahtr zhoor se se-rah *in four days it will be:*	}	**SAMEDI 6 JUIN**	{	sahmdee *Saturday* sees zhwiN

Il y a vingt-quatre heures dans un jour.   Sept jours forment une semaine.
eel-yah viNt kaht-râŷr daN-zuN zhoor.   sait zhoor form-têên se-main.
There are 24 hours in one day.   Seven days make a week.

Trente ou trente et un jours sont un mois; les douze mois forment une année.
traNt oo traN-tay uN zhoor soN tuN mwah   lay dooz mwah form-têê-nah-nay.
30 or 31 days are a month; the 12 months make one year.

Dans quel mois sommes-nous?   Nous sommes en juin.   Quel jour est-ce aujourd'hui?
daN kail mwah som noo? noo som aN zhŵiN.   kail zhoor ais oh-zhoord-ŵee?
In which month are we?   We are in June.   What day is it to-day?

UN CALENDRIER: A CALENDAR

	janvier	février	mars	avril
dimanche	.. 7 14 21 28	.. 4 11 18 25	.. 3 10 17 24 31	.. 7 14 21 28
lundi	1 8 15 22 29	.. 5 12 19 26	.. 4 11 18 25 ..	1 8 15 22 29
mardi	2 9 16 23 30	.. 6 13 20 27	.. 5 12 19 26 ..	2 9 16 23 30
mercredi	3 10 17 24 31	.. 7 14 21 28	.. 6 13 20 27 ..	3 10 17 24 ..
jeudi	4 11 18 25 ..	1 8 15 22 29	.. 7 14 21 28 ..	4 11 18 25 ..
vendredi	5 12 19 26 ..	2 9 16 23 ..	1 8 15 22 29 ..	5 12 19 26 ..
samedi	6 13 20 27 ..	3 10 17 24 ..	2 9 16 23 30 ..	6 13 20 27 ..

	mai	juin	juillet	août
dimanche	.. 5 12 19 26	.. 2 9 16 23 30	.. 7 14 21 28	.. 4 11 18 25
lundi	.. 6 13 20 27	.. 3 10 17 24 ..	1 8 15 22 29	.. 5 12 19 26
mardi	.. 7 14 21 28	.. 4 11 18 25 ..	2 9 16 23 30	.. 6 13 20 27
mercredi	1 8 15 22 29	.. 5 12 19 26 ..	3 10 17 24 31	.. 7 14 21 28
jeudi	2 9 16 23 30	.. 6 13 20 27 ..	4 11 18 25 ..	1 8 15 22 29
vendredi	3 10 17 24 31	.. 7 14 21 28 ..	5 12 19 26 ..	2 9 16 23 30
samedi	4 11 18 25 ..	1 8 15 22 29 ..	6 13 20 27 ..	3 10 17 24 31

	septembre	octobre	novembre	décembre
dimanche	1 8 15 22 29	.. 6 13 20 27	.. 3 10 17 24	1 8 15 22 29
lundi	2 9 16 23 30	.. 7 14 21 28	.. 4 11 18 25	2 9 16 23 30
mardi	3 10 17 24 ..	1 8 15 22 29	.. 5 12 19 26	3 10 17 24 31
mercredi	4 11 18 25 ..	2 9 16 23 30	.. 6 13 20 27	4 11 18 25 ..
jeudi	5 12 19 26 ..	3 10 17 24 31	.. 7 14 21 28	5 12 19 26 ..
vendredi	6 13 20 27 ..	4 11 18 25 ..	1 8 15 22 29	6 13 20 27 ..
samedi	7 14 21 28 ..	5 12 19 26 ..	2 9 16 23 30	7 14 21 28 ..

C'est aujourd'hui mardi trois juin.   Ce mois-ci est le mois
say toh-zhoord-ŵee mahr-di trwah zhŵiN.   se mwah see ay le mwah
To-day is Tuesday the third (of) June.   This month is the month

de juin; le mois dernier était le mois de mai.   Le mois prochain
de zhŵiN le mwah dair-nyay ayt-ai le mwah de mai.   le mwah pro-shiN
of June; last month was the month of May.   Next month

sera le mois de juillet.   L'année a trois cent soixante-cinq jours.
se-rah le mwah de zhēē-yay.   lah-nay ah trwah saN swah-saNt siN zhoor.
will be the month of July.   The year has 365 days.

Tous les quatre ans, février a vingt-neuf jours, et l'année est appelée
too lay kaht-raN fayv-ryay ah viNt-nŵy zhoor ay lah-nay ay-tah-play
All the four years (=every fourth year) February has 29 days, and the year is called

bissextile.   L'année bissextile a trois cent soixante-six jours.
bee-saiks-teel.   lah-nay bee-saiks-teel ah trwah saN swah-saNt see zhoor.
leap-year.   (The) leap year has 366 days.

L'année a quatre saisons: le printemps, l'été, l'automne et l'hiver.
lah-nay ah kahtr sai-zoN le priN-taN lay-tay loh-ton ay lee-vair.
The year has four seasons: spring, summer, autumn and winter.

Nous ne sommes plus au printemps.   Nous sommes maintenant en été.   Novembre
noo ne som plễ -zoh priN-taN.   noo som miNt-naN aN-nay-tay.   no-vaNbr
We are no longer in spring.   We are now in summer.   November

est en automne et Noël est en hiver.
ay taN-noh-ton ay noh-ail ay-taN-nee-vair.
is in autumn and Christmas is in winter.

Note.—(1) There are two words for "a year," **un an** and **une année.** They are used more or less indiscriminately, but for giving the age of a person **an** is used: **Il a trois ans**=He is three years old (lit., has three years).

(2) The days, months and seasons are masculine and do not take a capital letter.

(3) "In spring"=**au printemps**; but "in summer"=**en été**, in autumn=**en automne**, in winter=**en hiver**.

4th	le / la	quatrième kahtr-yaim
5th	le / la	cinquième siN-kyaim
6th	le / la	sixième seez-yaim
7th	le / la	septième sait-yaim
8th	le / la	huitième ŵeet-yaim

9th   **neuvième**   nâyv-yaim
10th   **dixième**   deez-yaim
11th   **onzième**   onz-yaim
12th   **douzième**   dooz-yaim
13th   **treizième**   traiz-yaim
14th   **quatorzième**   kah-torz-yaim
15th   **quinzième**   kiNz-yaim
16th   **seizième**   saiz-yaim
17th   **dix-septième**   dees-sait-yaim
18th   **dix-huitième**   deez-ŵeet-yaim
19th   **dix-neuvième**   deez-nâyv-yaim
20th   **vingtième**   viNt-yaim
21st   **vingt et unième**   viN-tay-ễn-yaim
22nd   **vingt-deuxième**   viN-dâyz-yaim
30th   **trentième**   traNt-yaim
31st   **trente et unième**   traN-tay-ễn-yaim
32nd   **trente-deuxième**   traNt-dâyz-yaim
40th   **quarantième**   kah-raNt-yaim
50th   **cinquantième**   siN-kaNt-yaim
60th   **soixantième**   swah-saNt-yaim

NUMBERS 21—60

(Numbers 1—20 have been given on page 12)

21. **vingt et un**   viN-tay uN
22. **vingt-deux**   viNt-dây
23. **vingt-trois**   viNt-trwah
24. **vingt-quatre**   viNt-kahtr
25. **vingt-cinq**   viNt-siNk
26. **vingt-six**   viNt-sees
27. **vingt-sept**   viNt-sait
28. **vingt-huit**   viNt-ŵeet
29. **vingt-neuf**   viNt-nâyf
30. **trente**   traNt
31. **trente et un**   traN-tay uN
32. **trente-deux**   traNt-dây
33. **trente-trois**   traNt-trwah
40. **quarante**   kah-raNt
41. **quarante et un**   kah-raN-tay uN
42. **quarante-deux**   kah-raNt-dây
50. **cinquante**   siN-kaNt
51. **cinquante et un**   siN-kaN-tay uN
52. **cinquante-deux**   siNkaNt-dây
60. **soixante**   swah-saNt

Note that the Ordinal Numbers (which denote order, place or rank) are formed by adding -**ième** to the corresponding cardinal number.

ORDINAL NUMBERS

1st	le premier	prem-yay	
	la première	prem-yair	
2nd	le	second	se-goN
		deuxième	dâyz-yaim
	la	seconde	se-gond
		deuxième	dâyz-yaim
3rd	le / la	troisième	trwahz-yaim

EXCEPTIONS

(*a*) **Premier, première** and **second, seconde,** but the latter is used only when there is no third or more in question, otherwise **deuxième** is used for "second."

(*b*) **Cinquième.** The letter **u** is added.

(*c*) **Neuvième.** The **f** of **neuf** becomes **v**.

(*d*) The final **e** of **quatre, onze, douze,** etc., is omitted before the -**ième**.

Note.—(1) In dates the cardinal numbers are used instead of the ordinal (except **PREMIER,** first).

le premier avril = the first of April
le deux avril = the second of April
le trois avril = the third of April

The same applies to the number following the name of a king or pope:

Napoléon premier = Napoleon the First
but: **Louis quinze** = Louis the Fifteenth.

(2) "on the third of July" is **le trois juillet.** Both "on" and "of" are omitted when expressing the date.

(3) **les premières fraises** = the first strawberries.

Ordinal adjectives, like any other adjectives, agree in gender and number with the noun.

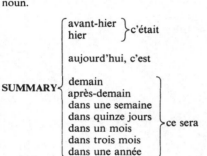

SUMMARY					
avant-hier ⎫ hier ⎬ c'était	dimanche	premier	janvier février
aujourd'hui, c'est	lundi	deux	mars
	mardi	trois	avril mai
demain après-demain dans une semaine dans quinze jours ⎬ ce sera dans un mois dans trois mois dans une année	mercredi	quatre	juin juillet
	jeudi	cinq	août septembre
	vendredi	six	octobre novembre
	samedi	sept, etc.	décembre

EXERCISES

I. Give the following dates in French

2nd of June; 5th of March; 12th of January; 1st of February; 21st of March; 15th of April; 18th of May; 4th of July; 31st of August; Tuesday, the 3rd of December; Sunday, the 22nd of May.

II. Answer the following questions in French

1. Quel hôtel Monsieur Lesage recommande-t-il? 2. Combien (koN-byiN = how many) de chambres sont libres? 3. À quel étage est la chambre qui sera libre ce soir? 4. Est-ce que le prix de 800 francs comprend le petit déjeuner? 5. Est-ce que l'hôtel est cher? 6. Êst-ce que Monsieur Roberts veut avoir des chambres avec pension complète? 7. Est-ce qu'il y a un ascenseur? 8. Où donne la fenêtre de la chambre numéro 11? 9. Est-ce qu'il peut avoir une chambre sur le devant de la maison? 10. Quels sont les numéros de ses chambres? 11. Dans quel mois sommes-nous? 12. Quel jour est-ce aujourd'hui? 13. Combien de semaines y a-t-il dans une année? 14. Quand (kaN = when) commence l'année? 15. Quel est le premier mois de l'année? 16. Quel est le troisième? 17. Quel est le deuxième jour de la semaine? 18. Quel est le sixième? 19. Était-ce hier mardi? 20. Sera-ce le huit lundi? 21. Quel jour sera-ce demain? 22. Dans quelle saison sommes-nous maintenant? 23. Sommes-nous au printemps? 24. Quelle heure est-il maintenant? 25. Est-ce la fin (fiN = the end) de la septième leçon?

III
Translate into French

1. Can you recommend this book? 2. Do you wish to see the monument? 3. Is it far from here? 4. Only five minutes from here. 5. Let us go there. 6. What a nice room! 7. How much is it per week? 8. That is too dear. 9. That's not dear. 10. Would you mind speaking English? 11. Will you please come in. 12. Can't you see the lift? 13. Is there a room on the third floor? 14. Are there any strawberries in spring? 18. You cannot come in now.

(Key to I, II and III on pages 101 and 102.)

La Concierge

Un personnage d'une importance capitale dans la vie de Paris et d'autres villes françaises, c'est la concierge, et si vous désirez que votre séjour en France soit agréable, prenez garde de ne pas froisser ses susceptibilités. Sa loge se trouve au rez-de-chaussée de tous les immeubles de rapport ét de beaucoup d'hôtels. Le système anglais des clefs de maison n'existe guère en France. C'est donc elle qui vous ouvre la porte quand vous rentrez la nuit, et c'est elle qui contrôle toutes vos allées et venues. Surtout, n'oubliez jamais ses "étrennes" au Jour de l'An!

UNE CONCIERGE PARISIENNE

Sa mine renfrognée présage un accueil tumultueux pour les locataires d'habitudes tapageuses.

| **Renfrogné-e** (adj.) | **présager** | **accueil** (m.) | **locataire** (m.f.) |
| Scowling | foretell | welcome | tenant |

The Concierge

A person of capital importance in the life of Paris and of other French cities is the concierge, and if you wish your stay in France to be enjoyable, take care not to hurt her feelings. Her lodge is to be found on the ground floor of all apartment houses and of many hotels. The English latchkey system scarcely exists in France, so it is she who opens the door to you when you return at night, and she who keeps track of all your goings and comings. Above all, never forget her New Year's "box."

Key to picture, p. 65: Une malle, une valise, un porteur, une courroie, un wagon, un compartiment, une glace, un quai, un homme, une femme, un garçon, une jeune fille, un veston, un chapeau, une pipe.

HUITIÈME LEÇON—*EIGHTH LESSON*

À LA TERRASSE DU CAFÉ DE LA PAIX

En se payant ici un apéritif un après-midi d'été, on voit flâner tout un monde cosmopolite.

Se payer (quelque chose)	**flâner**	**cosmopolite** (adj.)
To treat oneself (to something)	to stroll, saunter	cosmopolitan

M. Roberts: **Entrons dans ce café pour le petit déjeuner.**
aN-troN daN se kah-fay poor le p'tee day-zhãy-nay.
Let us go into this café for (the) breakfast.

M. Lesage: **Restons à la terrasse; il fait trop chaud à l'intérieur.**
rais-toN ah lah tai-rahs eel fai troh shoh ah liN-tayr-yãyr.
Let us stay on the terrace; it is (lit., it makes) too hot inside.

              Voilà une table qui est assez grande pour nous tous.
vwah-lah ẽn tahbl kee ay-tah-say graNd poor noo toos.
There is a table which is enough large for us all.

M. Roberts: **Qu'est-ce que vous préférez, du thé ou du café?**
kais-ke voo pray-fay-ray dẽ tay oo dẽ kah-fay?
What do you prefer, (some) tea or (some) coffee?

M. Lesage: **Du café pour moi, s'il vous plaît.**
dẽ kah-fay poor mwah seel-voo-plai.
Coffee for me, please.

Madeleine: Je préfère du chocolat.   **Charles:** Moi aussi.
zhe pray-fair dêê sho-ko-lah.   mwah oh-see.
I prefer chocolate.   *So do I (lit., me too).*

M Roberts: Que voulez-vous boire?   **Mme R.:** Du lait (froid) chaud.
(to Mme R.) ke voo-lay voo bwahr?   dêê lai (frwah) shoh.
What do you want to drink?   *Milk (cold) hot.*

M. Roberts: Garçon—trois cafés, deux chocolats et un lait chaud.
gahr-soN trwah kah-fay dãy sho-ko-lah ay uN lai shoh.
Waiter—three coffees, two chocolates and one hot milk.

Aussi des petits pains, des croissants, et des brioches.
oh-see day p'tee piN day krwah-saN ay day bree-osh.
Also some rolls, some crescent rolls and some buns.

Charles: Je préfère un déjeuner anglais avec du
zhe pray-fair uN day-zhãy-nay aN-glai ah-vaik dêê
I prefer an English breakfast with

pain grillé et des œufs sur le plat avec du jambon.
piN gree-yay ay day-zãy sêêr le plah ah-vaik dêê zhaN-boN.
toasted bread and fried eggs with ham.

Mlle L.: Et du porridge et de la marmelade d'orange, mon petit gourmand.
ay dêê po-reedzh ay de lah mahr-me-lahd do-raNzh moN p'tee
And porridge and marmalade, my little glutton.   [goor-maN.

Charles: Naturellement, ma chère cousine.
nah-têê-rail-maN ma shair koo-zeen.
Naturally, my dear cousin.

Mlle L.: Vous pouvez avoir un œuf à la coque, mon cher.   Mais en
voo poo-vay-zah-vwahr uN nãyf ah lah kok moN shair.   mai aN
You can have a boiled egg, my dear.   But in

France on ne mange pas d'œufs sur le plat pour le petit déjeuner.
fraNs oN ne maNzh pah dãy sêêr le plah poor le p'tee day-zhãy-nay.
France one does not eat fried eggs for (the) breakfast.

Le garçon: Aimez-vous le cacao au lait ou à l'eau?
ai-may voo le kah-kah-oh oh lai oo ah loh?
Do you like (the) cocoa with milk or with water?

M. Lesage: Voici le café.   Prenez-vous du lait?   Prenez-vous du sucre?
vwah-see le kah-fay.   pre-nay voo dêê lai?   pre-nay voo dêê sêêkr?
Here is the coffee.   Do you take milk?   Do you take sugar?

Madeleine: Un peu de lait seulement, mais beaucoup de sucre.
uN pãy de lai sãyl-maN mai boh-koo de sêêkr.
A little (of) milk only, but lots of sugar.

Could you now order yourself a light meal in this typical Paris café? Try first without the text, and afterwards with and without the text alternately.

le garçon	**un siège**	**un verre d'eau**	**une tasse**	**le fauteuil**
waiter	seat	glass of water	cup	armchair

la serveuse	**un croissant**	**le beurre**	**un pot de café**	**le pain**
waitress	crescent roll	butter	a pot of coffee	bread

un petit pain	**le sucrier**	**un verre de citronnade**	**la cuillère**
roll	sugar basin	glass of lemonade	spoon

une soucoupe	**une glace**	**le plateau**
saucer	ice-cream	tray

Je prends trois morceaux de sucre.
zhe praN trwah mor-soh de sẽẽkr.
I take three lumps of sugar.

Mme R.: Je ne prends qu'un morceau de sucre.
zhe ne praN kuN mor-soh de sẽẽkr.
I only take one lump of sugar.

Mlle L.: Je ne prends pas de sucre, mais beaucoup de lait.
zhe ne praN pah de sẽẽkr mai boh-koo de lai.
I don't take sugar, but lots of milk.

SOME, ANY

(1) **Voilà du café** = There is (some) coffee.

(2) **Avec de la crème** = With (some) cream.

(3) **Avez-vous du sucre?** = Have you (any) sugar?

(4) **Avez-vous des oranges?** = Have you (any) oranges?

(5) **Y a-t-il de l'eau dans ce verre?** = Is there (any) water in this glass?

Whereas in English the bracketed words may be omitted, they are essential in French. The noun is rarely used alone in French. In certain cases where in English you would use the noun without any article you have to use the so-called partitive article in French, i.e., **du** before masculine nouns, **de la** before feminines, **des** before plurals, and **de l'** before singular nouns beginning with a vowel or a mute **h.**

The Partitive Article is replaced by **de:**—
(a) After a verb used in the negative:
J'ai du sucre = I have sugar, *but* **Je n'ai pas de sucre** = I have no sugar.

Il veut de la crème = he wants cream, *but* **Il ne veut pas de crème** = he does not want cream.

Nous avons des pommes = We have apples, but **nous n'avons pas de pommes** = we have no apples.

(b) When an adjective precedes the noun:
J'ai du pain = I have got bread. **J'ai de bons gâteaux** = I have some good cakes.

Nous voulons de la confiture = We want jam. **Avez-vous de bonne confiture?** = Have you any good jam?

Ils ont des pommes = They have apples.
Ils ont de petites pommes = They have small apples.

HOW MUCH? HOW MANY? etc.

Combien de tartines avez-vous eues[3]? = How many slices of bread have you had?
Combien d'argent a-t-il? = How much money has he got?
J'ai mangé beaucoup de petits pains = I have eaten many rolls
Il a beaucoup d'argent = He has much money
Elle a mangé peu de pain = She has not eaten much bread (lit., little of bread)
Une bouteille de vin = A bottle of wine
Une douzaine d'œufs = A dozen (of) eggs
Une livre[1] de beurre = A pound of butter
Une boîte d'allumettes = A box of matches
Note that expressions of quantity are followed by **de.**
If you say **du café** you leave it to the waiter how much he shall bring you.
If you want to be more precise, you should say: **un verre de café** or **une tasse de café.**

Note: (1) That **le livre** means "the book" and **la livre** "the pound."
(2) In French "the" is used in respect of the cost of things, where we should say "a." This applies to all kinds of measurements, e.g., **trois francs le mètre** = three francs a metre.
(3) The past participle, when used with the auxiliary verb **avoir,** is invariable unless it is preceded by its direct object, when it agrees in gender and number with the direct object.

Now, without the help of the text, can you name in French all the objects on the table, and order a meal such as the Robertses are enjoying?

La table est mise pour le petit déjeuner.   Sur la table il y a
lah tahbl ay meez poor le p'tee day-zhāy-nay.   sēēr lah tahbl eel-yah
The table is laid for breakfast.   On the table there are

des tasses, des soucoupes, des cuillères, des assiettes, du pain, des
day tahs day soo-koop day kwee-yair day-zahs-yait dēē piN day
cups, saucers, spoons, plates, bread,

petits-pains, des croissants, du beurre, de la marmelade d'orange, un pot de lait,
p'tee piN day krwah-saN dēē bāyr de lah mahr-me-lahd dor-aNzh uN poh de lai
rolls, crescents, butter, marmalade, a milk jug,

un sucrier, un grand couteau pour le pain et de petits couteaux pour
uN sēēkr-yay uN graN koo-toh poor le piN ay de p'tee koo-toh poor
a sugar basin, a large knife for the bread and small knives to

beurrer le pain.   M. Lesage: Encore une tasse de café, Roberts?
bāy-ray le piN.   aN-kor ēēn tahs de kah-fay ro-bairts?
butter the bread.   Another cup of coffee, Roberts?

M. Roberts: Non merci, je n'ai pas fini la mienne.
                noN mair-see zhe nai pah fee-nee lah myain.
                No, thank you, I have not finished mine.

M. Lesage: Encore un peu de cacao, ma chère?
                aN-kor uN pāy de kah-kah-oh mah shair?
                A little more cocoa, my dear?

Madeleine: Volontiers. Je vous remercie, cela suffit.
vo-loNt-yai. zhe voo re-mair-see se-lah sǖe-fee.
Yes, please (lit., willingly). Thank you, that is enough.

Mlle L.:   Voulez-vous que je vous beurre une tartine, mon cousin?
voo-lay voo ke zhe voo bǖyr ǖen tahr-teen moN koo-ziN?
Do you want that I butter you a slice of bread, my cousin?

Charles: Merci, j'ai eu suffisamment.
mair-see zhay ǖ sǖe-fee-zah-maN.
No, thank you, I have had enough.

Mlle L.:   Encore un peu de cette marmelade?
aN-kor uN pǖy de sait mahr-me-lahd?
A little more of that marmalade?

Madeleine: Rien qu'un tout petit peu sur cette tartine de pain bis, s'il vous plaît.
ryiN kuN too p'tee pǖy sǖer sait tahr-teen de piN bee, seel voo plai.
Only a tiny little bit on that slice of brown bread, please.

Mme R.:   Le beurre est excellent. Est-ce qu'il coûte cher à Paris?
le bǖyr ay-taik-sai-laNt. aisk-eel koot shai-rah pah-ree?
The butter is excellent. Does it cost dear in Paris?

Mlle L.:   Nous le payons quatre cents francs la livre.
noo le pay-yoN kahtr saN fraN lah leevr.
We pay 400 francs a pound for it.

M. Lesage: Comment trouvez-vous le café?
ko-maN troo-vay voo le kah-fay?
How do you like (lit., find) the coffee?

M. Roberts: Je trouve le café excellent.
zhe troov le kah-fay aik-sai-laN.
I find the coffee excellent.

Un verre de vin blanc, s'il vous plaît.
uN vair de viN blaN seel voo plai.
A glass of white wine, please.

un verre de vin uN vair de viN *glass of wine (full)*	**un verre à vin** uN vair ah viN *A wine-glass (empty)*

des verres de bière
day vair de byair
glasses of beer

des verres à bière
day vair ah byair
beer glasses

une coupe de champagne
ẽẽn koop de shaN-pany
glass (full) of champagne

une coupe à champagne
ẽẽn koop ah shaN-pany
a champagne glass

des bouteilles de vin
day boo-taiy de viN
bottles of wine

des bouteilles à vin
day boo-taiy ah viN
wine bottles

une tasse de thé
ẽẽn tahs de tay
a cup of tea

une tasse à thé
ẽẽn tahs ah tay
a tea-cup

TO EAT, TO DRINK, TO TAKE

manger = *to eat*

je }
il } **mange** (maNzh)
elle }
nous mangeons (maN-zhoN)
vous mangez (maN-zhay)
ils }
elles } **mangent** (maNzh)

prendre = to take
je prends (praN)
il }
elle } **prend** (praN)
nous prenons (prenoN)
vous prenez (prenay)
ils }
elles } **prennent** (prain)

boire = *to drink*
je bois (bwah)
il }
elle } **boit** (bwah)
nous buvons (bee-voN)
vous buvez (bee-vay)
ils }
elles } **boivent** (bwahv)

Note.—Since g in front of o is pronounced as in "go," an e is inserted between the g and the o in the word **mangeons**, to indicate that the g is to be sounded as zh (i.e., like the s in measure).

SUMMARY

Prenez-vous				pain
	du			vin
Avez-vous				café
				thé
	de la			bière
Donnez-moi				limonade
				crème
Voulez-vous	de l'			eau
				orangeade
j'ai	des			petits pains
je prends				verres
				bouteilles
	un verre			vin
	une tasse			café
	beaucoup	de		thé
	peu			cacao
je veux	assez			lait

EXERCISES

I

Put in **du, de la, des, au,** etc.

1. Je donne—pain—mon cousin. 2. Avez-vous—pommes? 3. Elle donne—lait—enfants. 4. Il prend—bière. 5. Il y a—livres sur la table. 6. Apportez-moi un verre—eau, s'il vous plaît. 7. Il donne—pommes—petit garçon. 8. Elle a—oranges dans sa valise. 9. Ils viennent—gare et vont—hôtel. 10. Ne donnez pas—vin—mon oncle.

II

Answer the following questions in French

1. Avez-vous beaucoup d'amis? 2. Qu'est-ce que vous préférez pour votre petit déjeuner, du thé ou du café? 3. Aimez-vous la bière? 4. Prenez-vous du sucre pour le thé? 5. Combien de morceaux prenez-vous? 6. Qui apporte le café? 7. Que mange-t-on pour le petit déjeuner *(a)* en France, *(b)* en Angleterre? 8. Que mangez-vous? 9. Est-ce que nos amis vont à l'intérieur du café? 10. Où restent-ils? 11. Prenez-vous du lait avec le café? 12. Qu'a-t-on mis sur la table pour le petit déjeuner? 13. Est-ce que Madeleine prend une autre tasse de cacao? 14. Mangez-vous beaucoup de pain? 15. Quel est le prix d'une livre de beurre?

III

Translate into French

1. On Mondays and Thursdays I have breakfast in a café. 2. We drink coffee at 11 o'clock. 3. What do you want to eat? 4. Will you please give me a spoon? 5. Do you like coffee with lots of milk? 6. I take only one lump of sugar. 7. Have you got any apples? 8. We have no oranges today. 9. There are cups on the table. 10. There are no glasses on the chair. 11. Do you want another glass of wine? 12. Yes,

please (say: willingly). 13. Thanks, I
have had enough. 14. There is not
enough butter. 15. How much bread is
there?

(Key to I, II and III on page 102.)

KEY TO THE EXERCISES

Lesson Five

I

1. Are you fond of books? 2. I am very
fond of books. 3. My book is very interesting. 4. I don't like my father's books; they
are not interesting. 5. Look at that pretty
little girl; isn't she beautiful! 6. Are you
going to France? 7. No, sir, I am going to
England. 8. My children are going there
also. 9. My father is not going to the
country. 10. They are going to the
seaside.

II

1. Quelle. 2. Quelles. 3. Quel. 4.
Quelles. 5. Quel. 6. Quelle. 7. Quel.
8. Quelle. 9. Quels. 10. Quelle.

III

1. Quelle heure est-il, s'il vous plaît? 2.
Il est quatre heures. 3. Il est deux heures
et demie. 4. Il est cinq heures six. 5. Il est
onze heures et quart. 6. Il est neuf heures
vingt-cinq. 7. Il est huit heures moins le
quart. 8. Il est sept heures moins vingt.
9. Il est minuit moins cinq. 10. Quel âge
a votre sœur? 11. Elle n'a que douze ans.
12. Où allez-vous? Je vais à Paris. 13.
Nous allons au bord de la mer. 14. Est-ce
que vous allez à la campagne? 15. Votre
femme y est-elle aussi? 16. Est-ce que vos
enfants vont en Italie? 17. Votre fils a-t-il
encore faim? 18. Merci, madame; il n'a
plus faim. 19. Je ne parle jamais à mon
frère. 20. Quel beau pont! 21. Quelle
belle maison ils ont! 22. Quelles jolies
jeunes filles elles sont! 23. Regardons
le pont. 24. Préparons nos bagages.
25. Donnez-moi la moitié de votre pomme,
s'il vous plaît. 26. Ne parlez pas si vite.

Lesson Six

I

1. Les deux enfants. 2. Les deux petits
garçons y vont. 3. Ils viennent de l'hôtel.
4. Ils vont à l'école. 5. La dame. 6. Au
café. 7. De la maison. 8. Au cinéma.
9. De l'Angleterre. 10. Elle va en France.

II

1. Oui, il . . . 2. Non, il ne . . . pas . .
3. Oui, elle . . . 4. Non, elle ne . . . pas . . .
5. Oui, elle . . . 6. Oui, ils . . . 7. Oui,
elles . . .

III

1. The sixth lesson is not too difficult.
2. The little boy does not like to be kissed.
3. They are very well. 4. She is not well.
5. He does not know your children. 6. My
brother is not coming with you. 7. What
is the name of this monument? 8. This
shop-window is not beautiful. 9. I don't
know what time it is. 10. Do you know
what time it is? 11. We come from (the)
church. 12. They don't know that street.

IV

1. Comment allez-vous? 2. Je vais (*or*
Ça va) très bien, merci. 3. Comment va
votre petite fille? 4. Comment vont vos
parents? 5. Ils sont malades. 6. Où sont-
ils maintenant? 7. Je ne connais pas votre
petite sœur. 8. Connaissez-vous mon
oncle? 9. Il va au cinéma. 10. Nous
venons de la gare. 11. Nous allons à la
gare. 12. Je vais au café. 13. Je viens de
l'hôtel. 14. D'où venez-vous? 15. Je viens
de l'école. 16. Où allez-vous? 17. Je vais
au cinéma. 18. Ils vont à la gare. 19. Quel
beau chapeau vous avez! 20. Quel fils
intelligent ils ont! 21. Quelles belles maisons ce sont devant nous! 22. Quel est le
nom de cette belle rue? 23. La maison de
mon père n'est pas loin d'ici. 24. Donnez
ces livres à votre professeur, s'il vous plaît.
25. Ce sont les pardessus des professeurs.

Lesson Seven

I

Le deux juin; le cinq mars; le douze
anvier; le premier février; le vingt et un

mars; le quinze avril; le dix-huit mai; le quatre juillet; le trente et un août; mardi trois décembre; dimanche vingt - deux mai

II

1. Il recommande l'hôtel Bienvenu. 2. Il y a trois chambres qui sont libres. 3. Elle est au premier. 4. Il ne comprend pas le petit déjeuner. 5. Il n'est pas trop cher. 6. Non, il ne veut pas de chambres avec pension complète. 7. Il y a un ascenseur. 8. Elle donne sur le jardin. 9. Oui, il peut . . . 10. Les numéros onze et dix-neuf. 11. Nous sommes en . . . 12. C'est aujourd'hui . . . 13. Il y a cinquante-deux semaines dans une année. 14. Elle commence le premier janvier. 15. Janvier est . . . 16. Mars. 17. Lundi. 18. Vendredi. 19. Oui, c'était (non, ce n'était pas). 20. Oui, ce sera . . . Non, ce ne sera pas . . . 21. Demain, ce sera . . . 22. Nous sommes maintenant en été. 23. Nous ne sommes pas au printemps. 24. Il est . . . heures. 25. Ce n'est pas encore la fin de la leçon.

III

1. Pouvez-vous recommander ce livre? 2. Voulez-vous voir le monument? 3. Est-ce loin d'ici? 4. Seulement à cinq minutes d'ici. 5. Allons-y. 6. Quelle jolie chambre! 7. Combien est-ce par semaine? 8. C'est trop cher. 9. Ce n'est pas cher. 10. Veuillez parler anglais. 11. Veuillez entrer. 12. Ne pouvez-vous pas voir l'ascenseur? 13. Y a-t-il une chambre au troisième étage? 14. Y a-t-il des fraises au printemps? 15. Vous ne pouvez pas entrer maintenant.

Lesson Eight

I

1. du, à. 2. des. 3. du, aux. 4. de la. 5. des. 6. d'. 7. des, au. 8. des. 9. de la. à l'. 10. de, à.

II

1. J'ai beaucoup d'amis (je n'ai pas beaucoup d'amis). 2. Je préfère du . . . 3. J'aime la bière (je n'aime pas la bière). 4. Je prends du sucre (je ne prends pas de sucre). 5. Je prends deux morceaux. 6. Le garçon. 7. (a) En France on mange du pain, des petits pains et des croissants; (b) En Angleterre on mange du pain grillé, des œufs sur le plat, etc. (see page 94). 8. Je mange du pain bis avec du beurre et de la marmelade. 9. Non, monsieur, ils ne vont pas à l'intérieur. 10. Ils restent à la terrasse. 11. Je prends du lait (je ne prends pas de lait). 12. Il y a des tasses, du pain, etc. (see page 97). 13. Oui, elle prend une autre tasse. 14. Je mange (ne mange pas) beaucoup de pain. 15. Quatre cents francs

III

1. Le lundi et le jeudi je prends le petit déjeuner au café. 2. Nous buvons du café à onze heures. 3. Que voulez-vous manger? 4. Veuillez me donner une cuillère. 5. Aimez-vous le café avec beaucoup de lait? 6. Je ne prends qu'un morceau de sucre. 7. Avez-vous des pommes? 8. Nous n'avons pas d'oranges aujourd'hui. 9. Il y a des tasses sur la table. 10. Il n'y a pas de verres sur la chaise. 11. Voulez-vous encore un verre de vin? 12. Volontiers je vous remercie. 13. Merci, j'ai eu assez. 14. Il n'y a pas assez de beurre 15. Combien de pain y a-t-il?

ROUND THE TOWN

L'argot parisien

L'argot est moins en usage entre les gens bien élevés en France, qu'en Angleterre, et l'étudiant doit se garder d'utiliser des expressions qu'il recueille pendant ses excursions. Il vaut mieux se souvenir seulement des expressions qui ont cours entre les Français de votre connaissance personnelle.

Paris Slang

Slang is less current in polite circles in France, than in England, and the learner should be careful about using phrases he may pick up during his wanderings. It is better to remember only those expressions which are current among French people of your own acquaintance.

NEUVIÈME LEÇON—*NINTH LESSON*

Le soleil se lève
le so-lai*y* se laiv
The sun rises

Le soleil à midi
le so-lai*y* ah mee-dee
The sun at noon

Le soleil se couche
le so-lai*y* se koosh
The sun sets

THE WEATHER—LE TEMPS

Le matin;   le lever du soleil.
le mah-tiN   le le-vay dê so-lai*y*
The morning; the rise of the sun.

Le soleil est à l'est; il se lève.
le so-lai*y* ay-tah laist eel se laiv.
The sun is in the east; it is rising.

Midi;   le soleil est au sud.
mee-dee   le so-lai*y* ay-toh sêd
Noon;   the sun is in the south.

Le soir;   le coucher du soleil.
le swahr   le koo-shay dê so-lai*y*.
The evening; the sunset.

Le soleil est à l'ouest;   il se couche.
le so-lai*y* ay-tah lwest   eel se koosh
The sun is in the west;   it is setting.

La nuit;   le soleil n'est pas visible;
lah nŵee   le so-lai*y* nay pah vee-z̄eebl
The night;   the sun is not visible;

il fait noir.   Le jour;   il fait clair.
eel fai nwahr.   le zhoor   eel fai klair.
it is dark.   The day;   it is light.

Le soleil est dans le ciel.
le so-lai*y* ay daN le syail.
The sun is in the sky.

Pendant le jour il fait clair et nous pouvons voir sans allumer le
paN-daN le zhoor eel fai klair ay noo poo-voN vwahr saN-zah-lê-may le
During the day it is light and we can see without lighting the

gaz ou l'électricité.
gahz oo lay-laik-tree-see-tay.
gas or the electricity.

Pendant la nuit le soleil n'est pas visible,
paN-daN lah nŵee le so-lai*y* nay pah vee-zeebl
During the night the sun is not visible,

mais nous pouvons voir la lune et les étoiles.
mai noo poo-voN vwahr la lên ay lay-zay twahl.
but we can see the moon and the stars.

Il fait noir et
eel fai nwahr ay
It is dark and

nous allumons le gaz ou l'électricité.
noo-zah-lêmoN le gahz oo lay-laik-tree-see-tay.
we light the gas or the electric light.

Le soleil se lève le matin;
le so-lai*y* se laiv le mah-tiN
The sun rises in the morning:

il se couche le soir.   **En été le soleil se lève de bonne heure.**   **Il fait jour**
eel se koosh le swahr.   aN-nay-tay le so-lai*y* se laiv de bo-nãÿr.   eel fait zhoor
it sets in the evening.   *In summer the sun rises early.*   *It is light*

à trois heures du matin et les jours sont longs.   **En hiver le**
ah trwah-zãÿr dẽe mah-tiN ay lay zhoor soN loN.   aN-nee-vair le
at three o'clock in the morning and the days are long.   *In winter the*

soleil se lève tard, à sept heures ou encore plus tard.   **Il fait déjà nuit**
so-lai*y* se laiv tahr ah sai-tãÿr oo aN-kor plẽe tahr.   eel fai day-zhah nŵee
sun rises late at seven o'clock or still later (lit., more late).   *It is already night*

à cinq heures du soir, et les jours sont courts.   **Quand le ciel est bleu, il fait du**
ah siN-kãÿr dẽe swahr ay lay zhoor soN koor.   kaN le syail ay blãÿ eel fait dẽe
at five o'clock in the evening, and the days are short.   *When the sky is blue, it makes*

soleil—il fait beau temps.   **Quand le ciel est gris, il est couvert de nuages—**
so-lai*y*   eel fai boh taN.   kaN le syail ay gree ee-lay koo-vair de nẽeahzh
sunshine—it makes fine weather.   *When the sky is grey, it is covered with clouds—*

il fait mauvais temps.   **À Londres il pleut souvent.**   **À Paris il pleut**
eel fai mo-vai taN.   ah IoNdr eel plãÿ soo-vaN.   ah pah-ree eel plãÿ
it makes bad weather.   *In London it rains often.*   *In Paris it rains*

quelquefois.   **À Nice il pleut rarement; il fait généralement beau.**   **Il neige**
kail-ke-fwah.   ah nees eel plãÿ rahr-maN eel fai zhay-nay-rahl-maN boh.   eel naizh
sometimes.   *In Nice it rains rarely; it is generally fine.*   *It snows*

quelquefois à Paris en hiver; en été il ne neige jamais.   **Au**
kail-ke-fwah ah pah-ree aN-nee-vair   aN-nay-tay eel ne naizh zhah-mai.   oh
sometimes in Paris in winter; in summer it snows never.   *At the*

pôle nord il fait toujours froid; il ne fait jamais chaud.
pohl nor eel fai too-zhoor frwah eel ne fai zhah-mai shoh.
North Pole it is always cold; it is never warm.

la nouvelle lune   **la pleine lune**   **la lune à son décours**
lah noo-vail lẽen   lah plain lẽen   lah lẽen ah soN day-koor
new moon   *full moon*   *waning moon*

il fait jour	**il fait nuit**	**le soleil**	**la lune**	**une étoile**	**une étoile filante**
eel fai zhoor	eel fait n͠yee	so-lai*y*	lẽn	ay-twahl	ay-twahl fee-laNt
it is daytime	*it is night*	*sun*	*moon*	*star*	*shooting star*

la pluie (il pleut)	**la neige (il neige)**	**il fait froid**	**il fait chaud**	**la tempête**	
pl͠yee (eel pl͠ay)	naizh (eel naizh)	eel fai frwah	eel fai shoh	taN-pait	
the rain (it is raining)	*the snow (it snows)*	*it is cold*	*it is hot*	*storm*	

il fait du vent	**il fait du brouillard**	**le nuage**	**un orage**	**un éclair**	**la grêle**
eel fai dẽ vaN	broo-yahr	nẽ-ahzh	o-rahzh	ay-klair	grail
it is windy	*it is foggy*	*cloud*	*thunderstorm*	*lightning*	*hail*

COMPARISON OF CENTIGRADE AND ENGLISH (FAHRENHEIT) THERMOMETERS

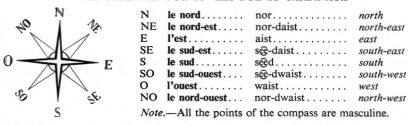

Le Thermomètre (Centigrade)

−20 −10 −5 0 +5 10 15 20 25 30 35 40 45 50 100

↑ point de congélation
pwiN de koN-zhay-lahs-yoN

↑ point s'ébullition
pwiN day-bẽ-lees-yoN

The Thermometer (Fahrenheit)

−4 +14 23 32 41 50 59 68 77 86 95 104 113 122 212

↑ *freezing point*

↑ *boiling point*

To convert Fahrenheit degrees to Centigrade subtract 32 and multiply by $\frac{5}{9}$; for example, 50 degrees F.$=(50-32) \times \frac{5}{9} = 10$ degrees C.

To convert Centigrade degrees to Fahrenheit multiply by $\frac{9}{5}$ and add 32; for example, 5 degrees Centigrade$=(5 \times \frac{9}{5}+32)=41$ degrees F.

THE CARDINAL POINTS—LES POINTS CARDINAUX

N	**le nord**........	nor..............	*north*
NE	**le nord-est**.....	nor-daist.........	*north-east*
E	**l'est**..........	aist..............	*east*
SE	**le sud-est**......	sẽ-daist.........	*south-east*
S	**le sud**.........	sẽd.............	*south*
SO	**le sud-ouest**....	sẽ-dwaist........	*south-west*
O	**l'ouest**........	waist............	*west*
NO	**le nord-ouest**...	nor-dwaist.......	*north-west*

Note.—All the points of the compass are masculine.

FAIRE (fair) *TO MAKE*	je fais (fai) il elle } **fait** (fai) nous faisons (fe-zoN) vous faites (fait) ils elles } **font** (foN)
DIRE (deer) *TO SAY*	je dis (dee) il elle } **dit** (dee) nous disons (dee-zoN) vous dites (deet) ils elles } **disent** (deez)

Note.—There are three verbs only which have the ending **-tes** (only the **t** is pronounced) instead of **-ez**: **vous êtes, vous faites** and **vous dites.**

Mlle LESAGE MAKES A DRESS

In making this frock for her mother, Lucie Lesage is using a sewing machine, scissors, and a dressmaker's dummy. Do you know what the corresponding terms are in French? If not, you will find them on page 401.

Mlle L.:   **Je dois partir maintenant. Je vais travailler.**
zhe dwah pahr-teer miNt-naN.   zhe vai trah-vah-yay.
I must leave now. I am going to work.

Madeleine: **Qu'allez-vous faire?**   **Mlle L.: Une robe pour ma mère.**
kah-lay voo fair?   ēēn rob poor mah mair.
What are you going to make?   *A dress for my mother.*

Madeleine: **Une robe de laine?**   **Mlle L.: Non, une robe de soie pour l'été.**
ēēn rob de lain?   noN ēēn rob de swah poor lay-tay.
A dress of wool (woollen dress)?   *No, a silk dress for the summer.*

Madeleine: **De quelle couleur?**   **Mlle L.: Bleu clair.**
de kail koo-lãȳr?   blãȳ klair.
(of) What colour?   *Light blue.*

Madeleine: **Cela sera bien joli.**   **Mme R.: Mon Dieu,[1] qu'il fait chaud ici!**
se-lah se-rah byiN zho-lee.   moN dyãȳ keel fai shoh ee-see!
That will be very nice.   *Heavens, how hot it is here!*

---

[1] Lit. "My God," but corresponding to "Heavens!" or "Good Gracious!"

M. Lesage: **Oui, il fait chaud aujourd'hui.   C'est le jour le plus chaud de**
ŵee eel fai shoh oh-zhoord-ŵee.   say le zhoor le plẽ shoh de
Yes, it is hot to-day.   It is the hottest day of

l'année.   Trente degrès à l'ombre et trente-cinq au soleil.
lah-nay.   traNt de-gray ah loNbr ay traNt siNk oh so-lai*y*.
the year.   Thirty degrees in the shade and thirty-five in the sun.

Charles: **Combien cela fait-il au thermomètre anglais?**
koN-byiN se-lah fay-teel oh tair-moh-maitr aN-glai?
How much is that on the English thermometer?

M. Roberts: **À peu près quatre-vingt six à l'ombre et exactement**
ah pãy pray kahtr viN sees ah loNbr ay aig-zakt-maN
About 86 in the shade and exactly

quatre-vingt quinze au soleil.
kahtr viN kiNz oh so-lai*y*.
95 in the sun.

Mlle L.: **Il fait lourd.   Je crois qu'il y aura de l'orage.**
eel fai loor.   zhe krwah keel ee oh-rah de lo-rahzh.
It is close.   I think that there will be a storm.

Madeleine: **Croyez-vous, ma chère?   Mme R.: Que dit votre cousine?**
krwah-yay voo mah shair?   ke dee votr koo-zeen?
Do you think so, my dear?   What does your cousin say

Madeleine: **Elle croit qu'il va faire de l'orage.**
ail krwah keel vah fair de lo-rahzh.
She thinks that there will be a storm.

M. Lesage: **Dites, Roberts, l'hiver est-il froid en Angleterre?**
deet ro-bairts lee-vair ay-teel frwah aN-naN-gle-tair?
Tell me, Roberts, is the winter cold in England?

M. Robert: **Il n'est pas très rigoureux.   Il tombe peu de neige,**
eel nay pah trai ree-goo-rãy.   eel toNb pãy de naizh
It is not very severe.   It falls little snow,

excepté dans le nord où il y en a beaucoup.
aik-saip-tay daN le nor oo eel-yaN-nah boh-koo.
except in the north where there is of it a lot.

M. Lesage: **Est-ce qu'il neige en hiver à Londres?**
ais-keel naizh aN-nee-vair ah loNdr?
Does it snow in winter in London?

M. Robert: **Il neige quelquefois à Londres en hiver.**
eel naizh kail-ke fwah ah loNdr aN-nee-vair.
It snows sometimes in London in winter.

PARIS: UN JOUR DE SOLEIL

La brume matinale a fait place à la chaleur accablante d'un après-midi d'été.

Brume (f.)	**matinal-e** (adj.)	**faire place**	**chaleur** (f.)	**accablant-e** (adj.)
Haze, mist	morning	to give place	heat	overpowering

PARIS: UN JOUR DE PLUIE

L'aspect luisant et désert de cette ruelle, laisse deviner qu'à Paris aussi il pleut de temps en temps.

aspect (m.)	**luisant-e** (adj.)	**désert-e** (adj.)	**ruelle** (f.)	**laisser deviner**
appearance	glistening	deserted	by-street	to suggest

NOT A NICE DAY

In this picture some of the weather conditions which you have already learned are illustrated. The others are listed on page 114. Consult that list, then turn back and see if you can describe in French what is happening on this particularly nasty day.

Mlle L.:   **Charles, quelle saison aimez-vous le mieux?**
          shahrl kail sai-soN ai-may voo le myãy?
          Charles, which season do you like (the) best?

Charles: **J'aime bien l'hiver quand on joue au football.**
          zhaim byiN lee-vair kaN-toN zhoo oh foot-bahl.
          I like very much the winter when one plays football.

Mlle L.:   **J'aime mieux l'été, parce qu'il y a de belles fleurs.**
          zhaim myãy lay-tay pahrs keel-yah de bail flãyr.
          I like best the summer, because there are beautiful flowers.

Madeleine: **Moi aussi.   Regardez cette femme qui vend des fleurs.   Elle a de**
          mwah oh-see.   re-gahr-day sait fam kee vaN day flãyr.   ai-lah de
          So do I.   Look (at) that woman who sells flowers.   She has

          jolis bouquets.   Mme R.: Quelles belles fleurs! Qu'est-ce qu'il y a?
          zho-lee boo-kaı.   kail bail flãyr! kais-keel-yah?
          nice bunches.   What beautiful flowers! What is there?

La bouquetière: Il y a des roses, des œillets, des violettes, des pensées, des
la boo-ktyair: eel-yah day rohz day-zãyyay day vyoh-lait day paN-say day
The flower girl: There are roses, carnations, violets, pansies.

AT THE FLORIST'S

After studying the list of flowers given below, cover it over and name in French as many of the flowers shown in the picture as you can recognise.

l'azalée (f.)	**le laurier-rose**	**le coquelicot anglais**		**le pavot**	**le pois de senteur**
ahz-ah-lay	loh-ryay-rohz	kok-lee-ko aN-glai		pah-voh	pwah de saN-tayr
azalea	*oleander*	*Shirley poppy*		*poppy*	*sweet pea*

la clématite	**la primevère**	**la jonquille**	**la glycine**	**le nénuphar**	**le perce-neige**
klay-mah-teet	preem-vair	zhoN-keey	glee-seen	nay-nee-fahr	pairs naizh
clematis	*primrose*	*jonquil*	*wistaria*	*water-lily*	*snowdrop*

la pensée	**l'asphodèle (m.)**	**l'œillet (m.)**	**l'iris (f.)**	**le glaïeul**	**le lis**	**la rose**
paN-say	ahs-foh-dail	ay-yay	ee-rees	glah-yayl	lees	rohz
pansy	*daffodil*	*carnation*	*iris*	*gladiolus*	*lily*	*rose*

le dahlia	**la tulipe**	**le lilas**	**la violette**	**le souci**	**le chrysanthème**	**le bluet**
dahl-yah	tee-leep	lee-lah	vyoh-lait	soo-see	kree-zaN-taim	blee-ai
dahlia	*tulip*	*lilac*	*violet*	*marigold*	*chrysanthemum*	*cornflower*

la marguerite	**le jasmin**	**le muguet**	**le narcisse**	**l'orchidée (f.)**	**la giroflée**
mahr-ge-reet	zhahs-miN	mee-gay	nahr-sees	or-kee-day	zhee-rof-lay
daisy	*jasmine*	*lily of the valley*	*narcissus*	*orchid*	*wallflower*

le fleuriste	**le bouquet**	**le pot de fleurs**	**le panier**	**la couronne**
flay-reest	boo-kai	poh de flayr	pah-nyay	koo-ron
florist	*bunch of flowers*	*pot of flowers*	*basket*	*wreath*

Note.—Flowers play a somewhat greater role in French life than in ours, and are presented on many occasions. A guest dining out, for instance, will very likely bring a bouquet for his hostess.

soucis, des lis et des tulipes.   Mme R.: Prenons un bouquet
soo-see day lees ay day tẽe-leep.   pre-noN uN boo-kay
marigolds, lilies, and tulips.   *Let us take a bunch*

d'œillets pour votre tante.   **Combien coûtent-ils?**
dãy-yay poor votr taNt.   coN-byiN koot-teel?
of carnations for your aunt.   *How much cost they?*

La bouquetière Ils sont à cent francs la pièce, madame.
eel soN-tah saN fraN lah pyais mah-dahm.
They are 100 *francs each, madam.*

Mme R.:   **Veuillez me faire un bouquet d'une douzaine.**
vãy-yay me fair uN boo-kay dẽen doo-zain.
Will you please make me a bunch of a dozen.

Mlle L.:   **Mademoiselle, pouvez-vous me faire une boutonnière de**
mahd-mwah-zail poo-vay voo me fair ẽen boo-ton-yair de
Miss, can you make me a buttonhole of

quelques violettes?   **La bouquetière: À votre service, mesdames.**
kail-ke vyo-lait?   ah votr sair-vees may-dahm.
some violets?   *At your service, my ladies.*

THE NUMBERS FROM 60 (*see also pages* 12 *and* 90)

60	**soixante**	swah-saNt	89	**quatre-vingt-neuf**	kahtr viN nãyf
61	**soixante et un**	swah-saN-tay uN	90	**quatre-vingt-dix**	kahtr viN dees
62	**soixante-deux**	swah-saNt dãy	91	**quatre-vingt-onze**	kahtr viN oNz
63	**soixante-trois**	swah-saNt trwah	92	**quatre-vingt-douze**	kahtr viN dooz
70	**soixante-dix**	swah-saNt dees	93	**quatre-vingt-treize**	kahtr viN traiz
71	**soixante et onze**	swah-saN-tay oNz	94	**quatre-vingt-quatorze**	
72	**soixante-douze**	swah-saNt dooz			kahtr viN kah-torz
73	**soixante-treize**	swah-saNt traiz	99	**quatre-vingt-dix-neuf**	
74	**soixante-quatorze**	swah-saNt kah-torz			kahtr viN deez-nãyf
75	**soixante-quinze**	swah-saNt kiNz	100	**cent**	saN
76	**soixante-seize**	swah-saNt saiz	101	**cent un**	saN uN
77	**soixante-dix-sept**	swah-saNt dees-sait	102	**cent deux**	saN dãy
78.	**soixante-dix-huit**	swah-saN deez-ŵeet	103	**cent trois**	saN trwah
79	**soixante-dix-neuf**		200	**deux cents**	dãy saN
		swah-saNt deez-nãyf	201	**deux cent un**	dãy saN uN
80	**quatre-vingts**	kahtr viN	202	**deux cent deux**	dãy saN dãy
81	**quatre-vingt-un**	kahtr viN uN	300	**trois cents**	trwah saN
82	**quatre-vingt-deux**	kahtr viN dãy	834	**huit cent trente-quatre**	
83	**quatre-vingt-trois**	kahtr viN trwah			ŵee saN traNt kahtr
84	**quatre-vingt-quatre**	kahtr viN kahtr	996	**neuf cent quatre-vingt-seize**	
85	**quatre-vingt-cinq**	kahtr viN siNk			nãyf saN kahtr viN saiz
86	**quatre-vingt-six**	kahtr viN sees	1,000	**mille**	meel
87	**quatre-vingt-sept**	kahtr viN sait	1,001	**mille un**	meel uN
88	**quatre-vingt-huit**	kahtr viN ŵeet	2,000	**deux mille**	dãy meel

AU "BAR DE LA BEAUTÉ"

Quelle idée surprenante, débiter la beauté comme on le ferait d'une boisson! À ce "bar", c'est le souci du velouté de leur peau, et non pas celui d'un vermouth-cassis à déguster, qui attire les femmes du monde au comptoir.

Surprenant-e (adj.)	débiter	souci (m.)	velouté (m.)	attirer
Surprising, astonishing	to sell (retail)	care	softness	to attract

10,000	**dix mille**	dee meel
100,000	**cent mille**	saN meel
1,000,000	**un million**	uN meel-yoN

In the year 1066 = **en mil soixante-six**
aN meel swah-saNt sees

Note.—(1) There are no special words for 70, 80 and 90 (except in Belgian and other dialects, where **septante, octante** and **nonante** are used). 70 is sixty ten, 71 is sixty eleven, etc. 80 is four twenties, 90 is 80+10, 91 is 80+11, etc. (2) **et** is used only in 21, 31, 41, 51, 61 and 71. (3) In dates **mille** is written **mil**. (4) **en** stands for "in the year."

SUMMARY

What is the weather like?   **Quel temps fait-il?**

it is		il fait	
	hot		chaud
	cold		froid
	fine weather		beau (temps)
	bad weather		mauvais (temps)
	nasty weather		un sale temps
	sunny		du soleil
	close		lourd
	cool		frais
	foggy		du brouillard
	windy		du vent
	stormy		un vent furieux
	light		jour
	dark		noir

it		il	
	rains, is raining		pleut
	snows, is snowing		neige
	hails, is hailing		grêle
	freezes, is freezing		gèle
	thaws, is thawing		dégèle
	thunders, is thundering		tonne

there is a thunderstorm (lightning)   il y a de l'orage (des éclairs)

EXERCISES
I Answer in French
1. Où est le soleil? 2. Le soleil est-il visible pendant la nuit? 3. Quand allumons-nous l'électricité, le jour ou la nuit? 4. Quand le soleil se lève-t-il? 5. Quand le soleil se couche-t-il? 6. À quelle heure le soleil se lève-t-il en été? 7. Les jours sont-ils longs en hiver? 8. Les nuits sont-elles courtes en été? 9. Fait-il jour à trois heures du matin en hiver? 10. Que faisons-nous pour voir pendant la nuit? 11. Le soleil se couche-t-il de bonne heure en été? 12. Pouvez-vous voir s'il ne fait pas jour? 13. Fait-il encore jour à six heures du soir en hiver? 14. De quelle couleur sont les nuages? 15. Pleut-il beaucoup à Londres? 16. Neige-t-il en été? 17. Les dames ouvrent-elles leurs parapluies quand il fait du soleil? 18. Fait-il du soleil quand le ciel est gris? 19. Fait-il beau temps aujourd'hui? 20. Fait-il chaud au pôle nord? 21. Neige-t-il quelquefois en juillet? 22. Avez-vous froid? 23. Aimez-vous les fleurs? 24. Quelle saison aimez-vous le mieux? 25. Est-ce qu'il y a des violettes en février?

II Translate into French
1. What is the time, please? 2. It is eleven o'clock in the morning. 3. Is the sun visible now? 4. Is it dark? 5. Will you please light the gas. 6. I am always cold in winter. 7. What is your brother doing? 8. He is making bunches of pansies. 9. Does it rain? 10. It snows sometimes in winter.

III Write in French
4; 6; 11; 56; 78; 87; 91; 95; 99; 106; 234; 354; 456; 692; 1,087; 2,156; 8,967; 13,405.
(Key to I, II and III on pages 150 and 151.)

DIXIÈME LEÇON—*TENTH LESSON*

LETTERS FOR THE LESAGES

See how many of the objects listed on pp. 116–117 you can find in this picture of the postman calling at the Lesages' villa. Then make your own list of them in French.

La famille Lesage habite une jolie petite villa dans un des
lah fah-mee*y* le-sahzh ah-beet ẽen zho-lee p'teet vee-lah daN-zuN day
The Lesage family lives in a nice little villa in one of the

faubourgs de Paris.   Quoique petite, la maison est bien bâtie et
foh-boor de pah-ree.   kwah-ke p'teet lah mai-zoN ay byiN bah-tee ay
suburbs of Paris.   Although small, the house is well built and

contient tout ce qu'il faut pour le confort de la famille.   C'est une maison
koN-tyiN too se keel foh poor le koN-for de lah fah-mee*y*.   say-tẽen mai-zoN
contains all that it needs for the comfort of the family.   It is a house

de douze pièces.   Au rez-de-chaussée il y a la salle-à-manger, la cuisine et un
de dooz pyais.   oh raid-shoh-say eel-yah lah sahl ah maN-shay lah kŵee-zeen ay uN
of twelve rooms.   On the ground floor there is the dining-room, the kitchen and a

petit salon.   Au premier étage il y a le salon, le bureau et du
p'tee sah-loN.   oh prem-yay-ray-tahzh eel yah le sah-loN le bẽe-roh dẽe
small sitting-room.   On the first floor there is the drawing-room, the study of the

maître de la maison et la salle de bain.   Au deuxième étage il y a deux
maitr de lah mai-zoN ay lah sahl de biN.   oh dẽyz-yaim ay-tahzh eel yah dẽy
master of the house and the bathroom   On the second floor there are two

A VILLA: UNE VILLA

English

1. Chimney; 2. Lightning-conductor;
3. Attic; 4. Maid's room; 5. Loft; 6.
Skylight; 7. Aerial; 8. Roof; 9. Shutter;
10. Frieze; 11. Play-pen; 12. Nursery; 13.
Bedroom; 14. 2nd floor; 15. 1st floor; 16.
Diffused lighting; 17. Bathroom; 18.
Grand-father clock; 19. Drawing-room;
20. Rocking chair; 21. Bookcase; 22.
Awning; 23. Balcony; 24. Ground floor;
25. Stove chimney; 26. Door curtain; 27.
Dining-room; 28. Kitchen stove; 29.
Basement; 30. Sawn wood; 31. Sawing-
horse; 32. Central-heating stove; 33.
Stock of coal, coke or anthracite; 34.
Cistern; 35. Wine-barrels; 36. Wine-rack;
37. Staircase; 38. Ladder; 39. Porch; 40.
Door-bell; 41. Steps to House; 42. Lawn;
43. Deck-chair; 44. Garden-railings; 45.
Garden-gate; 46. Roller; 47. Lawn-
mower.

French

1. Cheminée (f.); 2. Paratonnerre (m.);
3. Mansarde (f.); 4. Chambre de domestique; 5. Grenier (m.); 6. Lucarne (f.); 7.
Antenne (f.); 8. Toit (m.); toiture (f.); 9.
Volet (m.); persiennes (f.pl.); 10. Bordure
(f.) (de papier peint); 11. Baby-parc (m.);
12. Chambre des enfants; 13. Chambre à
coucher; 14. Deuxième étage (m.); 15.
Premier étage; 16. Éclairage (m.) diffusé;
17. Salle (f.) de bain(s); 18. Horloge (f.)
comtoise; 19. Salon (m.); salle (f.) de
réception; 20. Fauteuil (m.) à bascule;
21. Bibliothèque (m.); 22. Store (m.); 23.
Balcon (m.); 24. Rez-de-chausée (m.
inv.); 25. Tuyau (m.) de poêle; 26. Portière
(f.); 27. Salle à manger; 28. Fourneau
(m.) de cuisine; 29. Sous-sol (m.); 30. Du
bois scié; 31. Chevalet (m.) de sciage; 32.
Poêle (m.) du chauffage central; 33.
Approvisionnement de charbon, de coke
ou d'anthracite; 34. Citerne (f.); réservoir
(m.) à eau; 35. Fûts (m.pl.) de vin; 36.
Porte-bouteilles; 37. Escalier (m.); 38.
Échelle (f.); 39. Porche (m.); portique
(m.); 40. Timbre (m.); 41. Perron (m.);
42. Pelouse (f.); 43. Transatlantique (m.);
44. Grille, palissade (f.); 45. Grille
d'entrée; 46. Cylindre (m.) compresseur;
47. Tondeuse (f.).

chambres à coucher, la chambre des enfants (aujourd'hui divisée en deux
shaNbr ah koo-shay lah shaNbr day-zaN-faN (oh-zhoor-dw͡ee dee-vee-zay aN da͡y
bedrooms, the bedroom of the children (nowadays divided into two

chambres pour Georges et Lucie).   Au-dessus du deuxième étage il y a
shaNbr poor zhorzh ay lẽ-see).   oh de-sẽ dẽ da͡yz-yaim ay-tahzh eel-yah
rooms for Georges and Lucie).   Above the second floor there is

une mansarde, qui est la chambre à coucher de la bonne.   Au-dessous
ẽn maN-sahrd kee ay lah shaNbr ah koo-shay de lah bon.   oh de-soo
an attic which is the bedroom of the maid.   Under

du rez-de-chaussée est la cave.   Devant la maison il y a un
dẽ rai de shoh-say ay lah kahv.   de-vaN lah mai-zoN eel-yah uN
the ground floor is the cellar.   In front of the house there is a

jardin, qui est bien entretenu.   La pelouse est ornée de
zhahr-diN kee ay byiN-naNtr-te-nẽ.   lah pe-looz ay-tor-nay de
garden, which is well kept.   The lawn is adorned with

parterres de fleurs.   Derrière la maison il y a un plus grand
pahr-tair de fla͡yr.   dair-yair lah mai-zoN eel-yah uN plẽ graN
flower-beds.   Behind the house there is a larger

jardin, qui fournit la famille Lesage en fruits et en légumes.
zhahr-diN kee foor-nee lah fah-meey le-sahzh aN frwee ay aN lay-gẽm.
garden, which supplies the Lesage family with fruit and vegetables.

Au grenier se trouvent les bagages, une vieille chaise cassée, un vieux
oh gren-yay se troov lay bah-gahzh ẽn vyaiy shaiz kah-say uN vya͡y
In the loft are to be found the luggage, an old broken chair, an old

paravent, un cheval à bascule, et une échelle.   La mansarde est la
pah-rah-vaN uN she-vahl ah bahs-kẽl ay ẽnay-shail.   lah maN-sahr-day lah
screen, a rocking horse, and a ladder.   The attic is the

chambre de la bonne.   Dans la salle de bain il y a une grande baignoire
shaNbr de lah bon.   daN la sahl de biN eel-yah ẽn graNd bainy-wahr
room of the maid.   In the bathroom there is a big porcelain

en porcelaine.   On monte et descend l'escalier.   On reçoit les
aN pors-lain.   oN moNt ay dai-saN lais-kahl-yay.   oN re-swah lay
bath.   One goes up and down the stairs.   One receives

visiteurs dans le salon.   Le maître de la maison lit des livres,
vee-zee-ta͡yr daN le sah-loN.   le maitr de lah mai-zoN lee day leevr
visitors in the drawing-room.   The master of the house reads his books,

écrit ses lettres et fume des cigares dans son bureau.
ay-kree say laitr ay fẽm day see-gahr daN soN bẽ-roh.
writes his letters and smokes his cigars in his study.

IN THE HALL AT THE LESAGES'

Your vocabulary is now increasing. Try to name in French ten objects in this picture, without looking at the text below. Check later from the list.

le plafonnier	**l'abat-jour** (m.)	**le tiroir**	**un escalier**	**la rampe**	**la portière**
plah-fo-nyay	abah-zhoor	teer-wahr	ais-kahl-yay	raNp	port-yair
ceiling lamp	*lamp-shade*	*drawer*	*stairs*	*banister*	*door-curtain*

le vestibule	**le portemanteau**	**la glace**	**le porte-parapluies**	**le parapluie**
vais-tee-bǣl	port-maN-toh	glahs	port pah-rah-plw̃ee	pah-rah-plw̃ee
hall	*hall-stand*	*mirror*	*umbrella stand*	*umbrella*

la canne	**le vase à fleurs avec un bouquet**	**le porte-brosses**	**la petite table**
kahn	vahz ah flǣyr ah-vaik uN boo-kai	port-bros	p'teet tahbl
walking stick	*flower vase with cut flowers*	*brush-holder*	*small table*

le tapis-brosse	**le plancher**	**le mur**	**le plafond**	**le compteur électrique**
tah-pee bros	plaN-shay	mǣr	plah-foN	coN-tǟyr ay-laik-treek
mat	*floor*	*wall*	*ceiling*	*meter*

le téléphone	**la lampe**	**il ôte son pardessus**	**elle met son chapeau**
tay-lay-fon	laNp	il oht soN pahr-de-sǣ	ail mai soN shah-poh
telephone	*lamp*	*he takes off his overcoat*	*she is putting on her hat*

Dans le vestibule on ôte son pardessus.   On prend ses repas dans la
daN le vais-tee-bẽl oN-noht soN par-de-sẽ.   oN praN say re-pah daN lah
In the vestibule one takes off one's overcoat.   One takes one's meals in the

salle à manger.   Dans la cuisine il y a un fourneau de cuisine, un
sah-lah-maN-zhay.   daN lah kŵee-zeen eel yah uN foor-noh de kŵee-zeen uN
dining-room.   In the kitchen there is a kitchen stove, a

buffet et une table.   Il y a aussi de la vaisselle, des casseroles et toutes sortes
bẽ-fay ay ẽn tahbl.   eel yah oh-see de lah vai-sail day kahs-rohl ay toot sort
dresser and a table.   There is also crockery, saucepans and all sorts

de choses pour faire la cuisine.   Mme Lesage est une excellente
de shohz poor fair lah kŵee-zeen.   Mah-dahm le-sahzh ai-tẽ-naik-sai-laNt
of things to do the cooking.   Mrs. Lesage is an excellent

cuisinière.   Dans la cave il y a du charbon, du bois, du vin,
kŵee-zeen-yair.   daN lah kahv eel-yah dẽ shahr-boN dẽ bwah dẽ viN
cook.   In the cellar there is coal, wood, wine,

des tonneaux et un sac.   Entrons dans la maison et examinons
day to-noh ay uN sahk.   aN-troN daN lah mai-zoN ay aig-zah-mee-noN
barrels and a sack.   Let us go into the house and look over the

l'intérieur.   Nous entrons dans le vestibule.   À gauche nous
liN-tayr-yẫyr.   noo-zaN-troN daN le vais-tee-bẽl.   ah gohsh noo
interior.   We go into the hall.   On the left we

voyons le portemanteau avec les chapeaux et les manteaux.   À côté
vwah-yoN le port-maN-toh ah-vaik lay shahpoh ay lay maN-toh.   ah koh-tay
see the hall-stand with the hats and coats.   By the side

du porte-parapluies est une grande glace.   De l'autre côté il y a une
dẽ port pah-rah-plŵee ay-tẽn graNd glahs.   de lohtr koh-tay eel-yah ẽn
of the umbrella-stand is a large mirror.   On the other side is a

petite table avec le téléphone.   Un fauteuil est près
p'teet tahbl ah-vaik le tay-lay-fon.   uN foh-tẫyy ay prai
small table with the telephone.   An armchair is near

de la table.   Au milieu du vestibule sur le plancher est un
de lah tahbl.   oh meel-yẫy dẽ vais-tee-bẽl sẽr le plaN-shay ay-tuN
the table.   In the middle of the hall on the floor is a

tapis-brosse.   Au fond nous voyons une porte qui donne dans la
tah-pee bros.   oh foN noo vwa-yoN ẽn port kee don daN la
mat.   At the back we see a door which leads into the

salle à manger.   Cette porte est à demi ouverte.   À droite est une autre
sah-lah maN-zhay.   sait port ay-tah de-mee oo-vairt.   ah drwaht ay-tẽ-nohtr
dining-room.   This door is half open   To the right is another

porte, qui donne dans un petit salon.   Elle est fermée.   Au fond
port kee don daN-zuN p'tee sah-loN.   elle ay fair-may.   oh foN
door which leads into a small sitting-room.   It is shut.   At the back

à droite nous voyons l'escalier qui mène au premier étage.
ah drwaht noo vwah-yoN lais-kahl-yay kee mai-noh prem-yay-ray-tahzh.
to the right we see a staircase which leads to the first floor.

Dans le vestibule il y a deux personnes, un visiteur
daN le vais-tee-bẽl eel-yah dãy pair-son, uN vee-zee-tãyr
In the hall there are two persons, a visitor

qui ôte son pardessus et une jeune dame qui met son chapeau.
kee oht soN par-de-sẽ ay ẽn zhãyn dahm kee mai soN shah-poh.
who is taking off his overcoat and a young lady who is putting on her hat.

C'est une Anglaise qui donne des leçons d'anglais à Georges Lesage
say-tẽ-naN-glaiz kee don day lesoN daN-glai ah zhorzh le-sahzh
It is an Englishwoman who gives lessons in English to Georges Lesage

deux fois par semaine.
dãy fwah pahr semain.
twice a week.

LES JARDINS ET PALAIS DU LUXEMBOURG

Pour les jeunes amateurs de yachts en miniature, les bassins du Luxembourg parmi les pelouses fleuries des jardins constituent un paradis terrestre à deux pas de chez eux.

Amateur-trice (m.f.)	**yacht** (m.) **en miniature**	**bassin** (m.)	**paradis** (m.) **terrestre**
Lover, amateur	model yacht	pond	earthly paradise

"OLD" AND "NEW"

le vieux monsieur (vyay̆)	*the old gentleman*
la vieille dame (vyaiy)	*the old lady*
le vieil oncle (vyaiy)	*the old uncle*
le nouveau fauteuil (noo-voh)	*the new armchair*
la nouvelle saison (noo-vail)	*the new season*
le nouvel an (noo-vail)	*the new year*

These two adjectives, besides having an irregular feminine, have a special form when used before masculine singular nouns beginning with a vowel or mute **h**. This special liaison form is similar to the feminine form of these two adjectives.

There are a few other adjectives which also have a special masculine singular liaison form: **beau** (*fem.* **belle**)=beautiful becomes **bel** before a masculine noun beginning with a vowel or mute **h**; **un bel hôtel**=a beautiful hotel.

Ce (*fem.* **cette**) meaning "this" or "that" becomes **cet** before a masculine noun beginning with a vowel or mute **h**; **cet enfant**=this (or that) child; **cet hôtel**=this (or that) hotel.

TO PLAY, TO TAKE OFF, TO GO DOWN, TO GO UP, TO SLEEP, TO PUT (ON)

jouer=*to play*, **ôter**=*to take off*, **monter**=*to go up*, are regular verbs and their forms can be ascertained by examining the construction of other regular verbs (*see* page 50).

descendre=*to go down*	**mettre**=*to put*	**dormir**=*to sleep*
je descends (dais-saN)	je mets (mai)	je dors (dor)
il ⎱ descend (dais-saN) elle ⎰	il ⎱ met (mai) elle ⎰	il ⎱ dort (dor) elle ⎰
nous descendons (dais-saN-doN)	nous mettons (mai-toN)	nous dormons (dor-moN)
vous descendez (dais-saN-day)	vous mettez (mai-tay)	vous dormez (dor-may)
ils ⎱ descendent (dais-saNd) elles ⎰	ils ⎱ mettent (mait) elles ⎰	ils ⎱ dorment (dorm) elles ⎰

Note.—**mettre** means both *to put* and *to put on* (*clothes*): **Mettez les fleurs dans ce vase**=*Put the flowers into that vase;* **Mettez vos gants**=*Put on your gloves.*

EXERCISES

I   Answer in French

1. Où est la villa de la famille Lesage? 2. Combien de pièces a-t-elle? 3. Où est la salle à manger? 4. Quelles pièces sont au premier étage? 5. Où est la salle de bain? 6. Qu'est-ce qu'il y a au-dessus du deuxième étage? 7. Qu'y a-t-il au-dessous du rez-de-chaussée? 8. Qu'est-ce qui est devant la maison? 9. Où y a-t-il des légumes et des fruits? 10. Où dorment les enfants? 11. Où le maître de la maison écrit-il ses lettres? 12. Où met-on le charbon? 13. Où est le téléphone? 14. Quelle porte est ouverte? 15. Qui est dans le vestibule? 16. Que fait le monsieur? 17. Que fait la vieille dame? 18. Qui est-elle? 19. Prenez-vous des eçons de français? 20. Où est l'escalier?

II   Add the correct ending

1. Je ne parl- pas. 2. Ne dorm- -vous pas? 3. Il ôt- son chapeau. 4. Nous ne descend- pas. 5. Ils dorm-. 6. Que dit--vous? 7. Elles ne vienn- pas. 8. Ne fait-pas cela. 9. Je dor- 10. Elle arriv-.

III   Translate into French

1. Where do you live? 2. Is it far from here? 3. How many rooms has your house? 4. Is there a bathroom in his house? 5. On what floor is the nursery? 6. It is on the second floor. 7. Your trunks are in the loft. 8. You have beautiful flower-beds in your garden, haven't you? 9. Have you got vegetables in your garden? 10. We have only a few flowers. 11. Is this child asleep? 12. Let us go down into the cellar. 13. The kitchen is near the dining room. 14. The dining room is to the left. 15. The telephone is on the left by the side of the hall-stand.

(*Key to I, II and III on page* 151.)

ONZIÈME LEÇON—*ELEVENTH LESSON*

IN THE LESAGES' SITTING ROOM

It all *looks* quite straightforward, but our artist has again introduced several deliberate errors as compared with the text below. How many can you find after reading the French text only? For the answer, see the bottom of page 138.

Nous voici dans le salon de la famille Lesage. À gauche nous
noo vwah-see daN le sah-loN de lah fah-mee*y* le-sahzh. ah gohsh noo
We are here in the sitting room of the Lesage family. On the left we

voyons le foyer et au-dessus de la cheminée une grande glace. Sur
vwah-yoN le fwah-yay ay oh de-sẽ de la shmee-nay ẽn graNd glahs. sẽr
see the fireplace and over the mantelpiece a large mirror. On

la cheminée est une pendule. Elle est en marbre. Devant
la shmee-nay ay-tẽn paN-dẽl. ai-lay-taN mahrbr. de-vaN
the mantelpiece is a clock. It is (made) of marble. In front of

le foyer est un fauteuil. Le grand-père est assis; il fume. À côté de
le fwah-yay ay-tuN foh-tãyy. le graN pair ay tah-see eel fẽm. ah koh-tay de
the fireplace is an easy chair. Grandfather is sitting; he is smoking. By the side of

la cheminée est un secrétaire. Mme Lesage est assise devant.
lah shmee-nay ay-tuN se-kray-tair. mah-dahm le-sahzh ay-tah-seez de-vaN.
the fireplace is a bureau. Mrs. Lesage is sitting in front (of it).

Elle écrit une lettre à sa sœur qui est en Amérique. **Au fond**
ai-lay-kree-tẽn laitr ah sah sãyr kee ay-taN-nah-may-reek.   oh foN
She is writing a letter to her sister who is in America.   *At the back*

du salon est une porte-fenêtre. **C'est la porte du balcon.** **À droite nous**
dẽ sah-loN ay-tẽn port-fe-naitr.   say lah port dẽ bahl-koN.   ah drwaht noo
of the sitting-room is a French window.   *It is the balcony door.*   *On the right we*

voyons la bibliothèque. **M. Lesage est debout devant la**
vwah-yoN lah beeb-lyoh-taik.   m'syãy le-sahzh ay de-boo de-vaN lah
see the bookcase.   *M. Lesage is standing in front of the*

bibliothèque, lisant un livre. **À côté de la bibliothèque dans**
beeb-lyoh-taik leezaN-tuN leevr.   ah koh-tay de lah beeb-lyoh-taik daN-
bookcase, reading a book.   *By the side of the bookcase in*

un coin est une niche. **Il y a un canapé.** **Georges est assis dessus.**
zuN kwiN ay-tẽn neesh.   eel-yah uN kah-nah-pay.   zhorzh ay-tahsee des-sẽe.
a corner is a recess.   *There is a sofa.*   *George is sitting on it.*

De l'autre côté de la bibliothèque est une table à ouvrage,
de lohtr koh-tay de lah beeb-lyoh-taik ay-tẽn tahb-lah oov-rahzh
On the other side of the bookcase is a work table,

devant laquelle la grand'mère est assise; elle reprise. **Au milieu de la**
de-vaN lah-kail lah graN mair ay tah-seez ail repreez.   oh meel-yãy de
in front of which the grand-mother is sitting; she is darning.   *In the middle of*

chambre est une table ronde, sur laquelle sont un album de photos,
lah shaNbr ay-tẽn tahbl roNd sẽr lah-kail soN-tuN ahl-bom de fo-toh
the room is a round table on which are an album of photos,

un vase de fleurs et un portrait. **Devant cette table est un piano.**
uN vahz de flãyr ay uN por-trai.   de-vaN sait tahbl ay-tuN pyah-noh.
a vase of flowers and a portrait.   *In front of that table is a piano.*

Mlle Lucie est assise sur un tabouret; elle joue du piano. **Dans le coin**
Mlle Lẽe-see ay-tah-seez sẽr uN tah-boo-ray ail zhoo dẽ pyah-noh.   daN le kwiN
Miss Lucie is sitting on a stool; she is playing the piano.   *In the corner*

à gauche de la porte est un guéridon sur lequel il y a un appareil
ah gohsh de lah port ay-tuN gay-ree-doN sẽr le-kail eel-yah uN ah-pah-raiy
to the left of the door is a small table on which there is a wireless

de T.S.F. **La famille écoute souvent, surtout de la musique de Londres.**
de tay ais aif.   lah fah-meey ay-koot soo-vaN sẽr-too de lah mẽe-zeek de loNdr.
set.   *The family listens in often, especially to music from London.*

Sur le plancher du salon est un tapis et au plafond au dessus du
sẽr le plaN-shay dẽ sah-loN ay-tuN tah-pee ay oh plah-foN oh de-sẽe dẽ
On the floor of the sitting-room is a carpet and on the ceiling over the

piano il y a un lustre. Le chien est couché devant le foyer. Il
pyah-noh eel-yah uN lêestr. le shyiN ay koo-shay de-vaN le fwah-yay.   eel
piano there is a chandelier.   The dog is lying in front of the fireplace.   He is
dort. Sur les murs du salon il y a plusieurs tableaux.
dor. sêer lay mêer dêe sah-loN eel-yah plêez-yâyr tahb-loh.
asleep.   On the walls of the sitting-room there are several pictures.

OBJECTS IN THE SITTING ROOM

le guéridon	un appareil de T.S.F.[1]	la cheminée	la pendule
gay-ree-doN	ah-pah-raiy de tay ais aif	shmee-nay	paN-dêel
small round table	*wireless set*	*fire-place*	*clock*

le fauteuil	le secrétaire	la porte-fenêtre	la fenêtre	le rideau
foh-tâyy	se-kray-tair	port fe-naitr	fe-naitr	ree-doh
easy chair	*bureau*	*French window*	*window*	*curtain*

le store	la niche	la bibliothèque	la table à ouvrage	une table ronde
stor	neesh	beeb-lyoh-taik	tahbl ah oov-rahzh	tahbl roNd
window-blind	*recess*	*book-case*	*work-table*	*round table*

un album à photos	le vase de fleurs	le piano	le tabouret	un album de musique
ahl-bom ah fo-toh	vahz de flâyr	pyah-noh	tah-boo-ray	ahl-bom de mêe-zeek
photo-album	*vase with flowers*	*piano*	*stool*	*book of music*

le tapis	le tableau	le canapé	le coussin	le lustre
tah-pee	tahb-loh	kah-nah-pay	koo-siN	lêestr
carpet	*picture*	*sofa*	*cushion*	*chandelier*

[1]**Télégraphie sans fil**=telegraphy without wire

SEPT PONTS DE PARIS

Une vue panoramique du Paris fluvial, prise des toitures de l'Hôtel de Ville.   En arrière-plan, cette Tour Eiffel célèbre, symbole de Paris, s'estompe à l'horizon.

Fluvial-e (adj.)	**toiture (f.)**	**en arrière-plan**	**s'estomper**
Riverside	roof	in the background	to loom up

Cover over the English lines below and see if with the help of the picture you can translate the French sentences. Later you can check the number of errors made.

REST AND MOVEMENT

1. **il est assis**	ay-tah-see	*he is sitting*
2. **elle est assise**	ay-tah-seez	*she is sitting*
3. **il est debout**	ay de-boo	*he is standing*
4. **elle est debout**	ay de-boo	*she is standing*
5. **le chien est couché**	shyiN ay koo-shay	*the dog is lying*
6. **la petite fille est couchée**	p'teet feey ay koo-shay	*the little girl is lying*
7. **il entre**	aNtr	*he is coming in*
8. **elle sort**	sor	*she is going out*
9. **il est à genoux**	ay-tah zhe-noo	*he is on his knees*
10. **elle marche**	mahrsh	*she is walking*
11. **il court**	koor	*he is running*

(N.B.—The word **debout** is an adverb, so it has no feminine form.)

CLOCKS AND WATCHES

Une pendule est plus grande qu'une montre. Un bracelet-montre est plus petit
ēēn paN-dēēl ay plēē graNd kēēn moNtr. uN brahs-lai moNtr ay plēē p'tee
A clock is bigger than a watch.   A wrist-watch is smaller

qu'une montre que nous portons dans la poche. Une montre est en or,
kēēn moNtr ke noo portoN daN lah posh. ēēn moNtr ay-taN-nor
than a watch which we carry in the pocket.   A watch is (made) of gold,

en argent, en nickel ou en acier. Une pendule est en bois, en marbre
aN-nahr-zhaN aN nee-kail oo aN-nahs-yay. ēēn paN-dēēl ay-taN bwah aN mahrbr
of silver, of nickel or of steel.   A clock is (made) of wood, marble

| **une montre** | **un bracelet-montre** | **une pendule** | **un réveil** |
| moNtr | brahs-lai moNtr | paN-dẽl | uN ray-vaiy |

ou en bronze. Un réveil n'est pas aussi grand qu'une pendule, que nous
oo aN broNz.   uN ray-vaiy nay pah-zo-see graN kẽn paN-dẽl ke noo
or of bronze.   An alarm clock is not as big as a clock which we

mettons sur la cheminée ou contre le mur. Ma montre va très bien.   Elle
mai-toN sẽr lah shmee-nay oo koNtr le mẽr.   mah moNtr vah trai byiN.   ail
put on the mantelpiece or against the wall.   My watch goes very well.   It

n'avance ni ne retarde.   Dans notre salon il y a une pendule qui ne marche
nah-vaNs nee ne re-tahrd.   daN notr sah-loN eel-yah ẽn paN-dẽl kee ne
is neither fast nor slow.   In our sitting-room there is a clock which does

pas.   Elle est arrêtée, parce qu'elle n'est pas remontée.
mahrsh pah.   ai-lay-tah-rai-tay pahrs kail nay pah re-moN-tay.
not go.   It has stopped, because it is not wound up.

Voici la clef pour la remonter.
vwah-see lah klay poor lah re-moN-tay.
Here is the key to wind it up.

| **trois heures précises** | **trois heures moins dix** | **trois heures cinq** |
| trwah-zãyr pray-seez | trwah-zãyr mwiN dees | trwah-zãyr siNk |

l'heure exacte	**la montre retarde**	**la montre avance**
lãyr aig-zahkt	lah moNtr re-tahrd	lah moNtr ah-vaN
the right time	*the watch is slow*	*the watch is fast*

INSIDE A FRENCH KITCHEN
(*See page* 12 *for notes*

English

1. Saucepan; 2. Frying-pan; 3. Grid-iron; 4. Stove-pipe; 5. Plates; 6. Plate-rack; 7. Cutlery: spoons, forks, knives; 8. Carving-knife; 9. Tin-opener; 10. Gas-stove; 11. Kitchen range; 12. Ingredients (rice, sugar, cloves, pepper, salt, raisins, olive oil, yeast, etc.); 13. Kitchen-sink; 14. Refrigerator; 15. Gas-oven; 16. Kettle; 17. Serving-hatch; 18. Tray; 19. Flour-bin; 20. Bread-bin; 21. Coffee-mill; 22. Coffee-pot; 23. Kitchen-table; 24. Gas-tap; 25. Corkscrew; 26. Steamer; 27. Double-saucepan; 28. Chef, male cook; 29. Stock-pot; 30. Dresser; 31. Rolling-pin; 32. Female cook; apron; 33. Fish-slice; 34. Dish-cloth; 35. Overalls; (chef's cap); 36. Tap-water.

French

1. Casserole (f.); 2. Poêle (f.) à frire; 3. Gril (m.); 4. Tuyau (m.) de poêle; 5. Assiettes (f.pl.); 6. Porte-assiettes; 7. Couvert (m.):

Further Useful Expressions	mijoter to simmer	œufs (m.pl.) sur le plat fried eggs	moudre le café to grind coffee

DANS UNE CUISINE FRANÇAISE
on how to use this picture).

cuillères (f.pl.), fourchettes (f.pl.) couteaux (m.pl.); 8. Couteau à découper; 9. Ouvre-boîtes (m.inv.); 10. Fourneau (m.) à gaz; 11. Fourneau de cuisine; 12. Ingrédients: riz (m.); sucre (m.); clous (m.pl.) de girofle; poivre (m.); sel (m.); raisins (m.pl.) secs; huile (f.) d'olive; levure (f.) etc.; 13. Évier (m.) de cuisine; 14. Appareil (m.) frigorifique (*fam. "frigo"*); 15. Four (m.) à gaz; 16. Bouilloire (f.); 17. Passe-plats (m.inv.); 18. Plateau (m.); 19. Farinière (f.); 20. Huche (f.) au pain; 21. Moulin (m.) à café; 22. Cafetière (f.); 23. Table (f.) de cuisine; 24. Robinet (m.) à gaz; 25. Tirebouchon (m.); 26. Marmite (f.) à vapeur; 27. Bain-marie (m.) (pl. bains-marie); 28. Chef de cuisine (cuisinier); 29. Pot-au-feu (m.); 30. Armoire (f.); 31. Rouleau (m.); 32. Cuisinière (f.); tablier (m.); 33. Truelle (f.) à poisson; 34. Torchon (m.); 35. Blouse (f.); (bonnet, m.); 36. Eau (f.) de la ville.

faire la vaiselle	rôtir; cuire au four	bouillir	griller	assaisonner
to wash up	to roast	to boil	to grill	to season

TO SEE, TO LISTEN, TO READ, TO WRITE, TO ENTER, TO GO OUT

écouter= *to listen* and **entrer**= *to enter* are regular verbs.

voir= *to see*	**lire**= *to read*	**écrire**= *to write*	**sortir**= *to go out*
je vois vwah	**lis** lee	**j'écris** ay-kree	**sors** sor
il **elle** } **voit** vwah	**lit** lee	**écrit** ay-kree	**sort** sor
nous voyons vwahyoN	**lisons** lee-zoN	**écrivons** ay-kree-voN	**sortons** sor-toN
vous voyez vwah-yay	**lisez** lee-zay	**écrivez** ay-kree-vay	**sortez** sor-tay
ils **elles** } **voient** vwah	**lisent** leez	**écrivent** ay-kreev	**sortent** sort

COMPARISONS

Ce chien est grand

Ce chien est plus grand

Ce chien est le plus grand

Ce chien est petit

Ce chien est plus petit

Ce chien est le plus petit

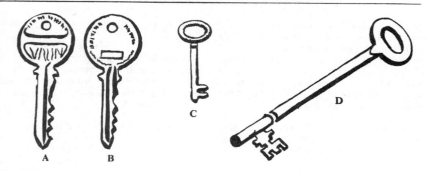

1. **La clef** (klay) **A est aussi grande que la clef B.**
2. **La clef C n'est pas si grande que les clefs A et B.**
   La clef C est moins (mwiN) **grande que les clefs A et B.**
3. **La clef D est plus grande que les clefs A et B.**
   La clef D est la plus grande de ces clefs.
4. **La clef C est la moins grande (la plus petite) de ces clefs.**

Note.—(1) Whereas in English there are two ways of expressing the Comparative degree of Adjectives, i.e., either by adding "-er" or by the use of "more," in French only the latter method is used; **Il est plus grand que vous**=He is taller than you.

(2) With a negative **aussi** becomes **si**:
Il est aussi grand que vous=He is as tall as you.

Il n'est pas si grand que vous=He is not so tall as you.

EITHER . . . OR; NEITHER . . . NOR
1. **Ou vous entrez ou vous sortez**=You either come in or go out.
2. **Il ne mange ni ne boit**=He neither eats nor drinks.
3. **Nous allons ou au bord de la mer ou à la campagne**=We go either to the seaside or to the country.
4. **Ils ne sont ni à la maison ni au jardin**= They are neither in the house nor in the garden.
5. **Il n'est ni trop intelligent ni trop stupide** = He is neither too intelligent nor too stupid.

Note (1) Either . . . or . . . =**ou . . . ou . . .**
(2) Neither . . . nor . . . is **ne . . . ni ne . . .** in connection with verbs (Example 2) and **ne . . . ni . . . ni . . .** in connection with nouns or adjectives (Examples 4 and 5).

EXERCISES

I   Answer these Questions in French
1. Quelles personnes sont dans le salon?
2. Que fait M. Lesage? 3. Que fait Mme Lesage? 4. Qui joue du piano? 5. Combien de personnes y a-t-il dans le salon? 6. Que font le grand-père et la grand'mère? 7. Qu'y a-t-il sur la cheminée? 8. Où est le canapé? 9. Georges est-il debout? 10. Qui n'est pas assis? 11. Qu'est-ce qui est au milieu de la chambre? 12. Y a-t-il un secrétaire dans ce salon? 13. Où est-il? 14. Avez-vous une montre? 15. Quelle heure est-il? 16. Votre montre est-elle remontée? 17. Votre pendule avance-t-elle? 18. La table est-elle plus grande que la chaise? 19. La fenêtre est-elle aussi large que le mur? 20. Écrivez-vous beaucoup de lettres? 21. Lisez-vous beaucoup?

II   Translate into French
1. Do you see my grandfather? 2. He is sitting in the garden. 3. Is she standing

or sitting? 4. Do you play the piano? 5. I don't play, but I often listen, especially to music by Bach. 6. Is your watch made of gold? 7. No, it is made of silver. 8. My alarm clock is smaller than your clock, which is on the mantelpiece. 9. My watch has stopped. 10. Please listen, don't read. 11. What are you writing? 12. A letter to my mother, who is in France.

III

Translate the questions. and say or write down several answers to the questions which can be derived from the following substitution tables. *(Key to I, II and III on pages 151 and 152.)*

1) Est-ce-que	vous êtes je suis mon frère est etc.	plus moins	jeune âgé grand petit fort mince etc.	que	votre frère? mon oncle? notre cousin? sa tante? etc.

2) Est-ce qu'il fait	plus moins	chaud froid	au printemps en été en automne en hiver	qu'	en hiver? en automne? en été? au printemps?

3) Est-ce que les jours les	plus moins	beaux mauvais longs courts	sont	au printemps? en été? en automne? en hiver?

DANS LA BEAUCE

Cette plaine dorée de la Beauce—ce grenier de la France—encore bordée des beaux épis de blé qui l'ont rendue célèbre, est située entre la Seine et la Loire.

Doré	le grenier	épi (m.)	le blé
golden	granary	ear (of corn)	corn

DOUZIÈME LEÇON—*TWELFTH LESSON*

CHARLES SAYS GOODNIGHT

How many objects in the room can you name in French? For key see page 125.

Charles: Je suis très fatigué.
zhe sẅee trai fah-tee-gay.
I am very tired.

Je vais me coucher.
zhe vai me koo-shay.
I am going to bed.

Charles était très fatigué, parce qu'il n'avait pas dormi de toute la nuit.
shahrl ay-tai trai fah-tee-gay, pahrs keel nah-vai pah dor-mee de toot la nẅee.
Charles was very tired because he had not slept the whole night.

La famille Lesage insiste pour que Charles reste chez eux pour la nuit.   **Georges**
lah fah-meey le-sahzh iN-seest poor ke shahrl raist shay-zẅy poor lah nẅee.   zhorzh
The Lesage family insists that Charles stays with them for the night.   *George*

partage sa chambre avec lui.
pahr-tahzh sah shaNbr ah-vaik lẅee.
shares his room with him.

Mme Roberts, avant d'aller à son hôtel, a dit à Charles de ne pas
Mme Robairts ah-vaN dah-lay ah soN-noh-tail ah dee ah shahrl de ne pah-
Mrs. Roberts, before going (lit., to go) to her hotel, has told (lit., said to) Charles not

oublier de se laver.
zoo-blee-ay de se lah-vay.
to forget to wash himself.

PARIS: PORT DE MER (I)

Amarrés dans un bras pittoresque de la Seine, à l'ombre de beaux arbres, ces chalands attendent qu'on les forme en convoi. Pour les mariniers, ce recoin si calme constitue "*leur*" Paris, où, là, ils sont contents.

Amarré (adj.)	**bras** (m.)	**chaland** (m.)	**marinier** (m.)	**recoin** (m.)
Anchored, made fast	arm	barge	bargee	nook, recess

PARIS: PORT DE MER (II)

Ces péniches, poursuivant lentement leur chemin en aval, relient la métropole à la mer, par Rouen et Le Havre. Les péniches sont tantôt formées en convoi que hale un remorqueur, et tantôt mues de leurs propres moyens.

Péniche (f.) à moteur   **en aval**   **remorqueur (m.)**   **mu(e)s de leurs propres moyens**
Motor barge   downstream   tug   moved by their own power

Mme Lesage: **Bonne nuit, Charles, dormez bien.**
bon nῶee shahrl dor-may byiN.
Good night, Charles, sleep well.

Georges: **N'oubliez pas de vous laver.   Vous l'avez promis à votre**
noo-blee-ay pah de voo lah-vay.   voo lah-vay pro-mee ah votr
Don't forget to wash yourself.   You (it) have promised to your

mère, vous savez.   Charles: Sans blague?
mair voo sah-vay.   saN blahg?
mother, you know.   You don't say so! (lit., without a joke)

M. Lesage: **Est-ce que vous voulez être réveillé demain matin de bonne heure?**
ais-ke voo voo-lay-zaitr ray-vai-yay de-miN mah-tiN de bo-nᾶyr?
Do you want to be called in the morning early?[1]

Charles: **Je veux me lever à sept heures.   J'ai beaucoup à faire.**
zhe vᾶy me le-vay ah sai-tᾶyr.   zhay boh-koo-pah fair.
I want to get up at seven o'clock.   I have a lot to do.

M. Lesage: **Vraiment?   Mme L.: Qu'est-ce que vous avez à faire, Charles?**
vrai-maN?   kais-ke voo-zah-vay ah fair shahrl?
Really?   What have you got to do, Charles?

Charles: **Voir Paris; les monuments, les musées, les parcs,**
vwahr pah-ree lay mo-nᾶè-maN lay mᾶè-zay lay pahrk
See Paris; the monuments, the museums, the parks,

enfin tout ce qui est intéressant.
aN-fiN too se kee ay-tiN-tay-rai-saN.
in short everything that is interesting.

M. Lesage: **À la bonne heure.   Charles: Alors bonne nuit tout le monde.**
ah lah bo-nᾶyr.   ah-lor bon nῶee too le moNd.
That's right.[2]   *Good night then everybody (lit., all*
                                          the world).

Charles se lave.
shahrl se lahv.
Charles is washing himself.

---

[1] Lit. "in good time."   [2] **à la bonne heure** is a frequently used expression. meaning "that's good."
"that's right," "all right."

TO WASH, TO GET UP, TO LIE DOWN

laver = *to wash*

se laver = *to wash oneself*

je me lave   (lahv) = *I wash myself*

il se lave   (lahv) = *he washes himself*

elle se lave (lahv) = *she washes herself*

nous nous lavons   (lah-voN) = *we wash ourselves*

vous vous lavez   (lah-vay) = *you wash yourself (-ves)*

ils (elles) se lavent   (lahv) = *they wash themselves*

lavez-vous = *wash yourself!*

lavons-nous = *let us wash ourselves!*

laver by itself means either to wash somebody else or to do some washing. Whereas in English "I wash" is used also in the meaning of "I wash myself," the latter form in French is je me lave; "you wash (yourself)," etc., is as above.

A verb like "to wash oneself" is called a reflexive verb, i.e., one in which the action is done by yourself and to yourself. Many verbs are reflexive in French which are not in English.

se lever = *to get up*

je me ⎫
il se   ⎬ lève   (laiv)   *I am getting up; I get up*
elle se ⎭

nous nous levons   (le-voN)

vous vous levez   (le-vay)

ils   ⎫
elles ⎬ se lèvent   (laiv)

levez-vous = *get up!*

levons-nous = *let us get up!*

se coucher = *to lie down, to go to bed*

je me ⎫
il se   ⎬ couche   (koosh)   *I am lying down, I lie down*
elle se ⎭

nous nous couchons   (koo-shoN)

vous vous couchez   (koo-shay)

ils   ⎫
elles ⎬ se couchent   (koosh)

couchez-vous = *lie down!*

couchons-nous = *let us lie down!*

je ne me lève pas = *I don't get up; I am not getting up*

vous levez-vous? = *are you getting up? do you get up?*

je ne me couche pas = *I don't lie down. I am not lying down*

vous couchez-vous? = *are you lying down? do you lie down?*

I HAD, I WAS, I SPOKE, I PUT, I WASHED

I had, I was having
j'avais   (ah-vai)

il   ⎫
elle ⎬ avait   (ah-vai)

nous avions   (ahv-yoN)
vous aviez   (ahv-yai)

ils   ⎫
elles ⎬ avaient   (ah-vai)

I was, I was being
j'étais   (ay-tai)

il   ⎫
elle ⎬ était   (ay-tai)

nous étions   (ayt-yoN)
vous étiez   (ayt-yay)

ils   ⎫
elles ⎬ étaient   (ay-tai)

I spoke, I was speaking
je parlais   (pahr-lai)

il   ⎫
elle ⎬ parlait   (pahr-lai)

nous parlions   (pahrl-yoN)
vous parliez   (pahrl-yay)

ils   ⎫
elles ⎬ parlaient   (pahr-lai)

I put, I was putting
je mettais   (mai-tai)

il   ⎫
elle ⎬ mettait   (mai-tai)

nous mettions   (mait-yoN)
vous mettiez   (mait-yay)

ils   ⎫
elles ⎬ mettaient   (mai-tai)

I washed, I was washing (myself)
je me lavais   (lah-vai)

il   ⎫
elle ⎬ se lavait   (lah-vai)

nous nous lavions   (lahv-yoN)
vous vous laviez   (lahv-yay)

ils   ⎫
elles ⎬ se lavaient   (lah-vai)

PERFECT AND IMPERFECT

The perfect in French denotes not only what has happened (as the English perfect does), but also what happened. In everyday language it is the tense most frequently used to denote a past event. But when states and conditions in the past are described the Imperfect is used, which is also the tense used to denote habitual or repeated action.

Study the following examples very carefully:

Perfect. (1) What has happened.
J'ai fini ma leçon.
I have finished my lesson.
Où avez-vous mis votre chapeau?
Where have you put your hat?
A-t-il écrit? *Has he written?*
(2) What happened.
Je l'ai vu il y a trois mois.
I saw him three months ago.

À quelle heure avez-vous dîné hier?
At what time did you have dinner yesterday?
Qu'est-ce qu'il a dit? *What did he say?*
Imperfect. (1) What was (description)
Il faisait froid. *It was cold.*
C'était une femme âgée.
It was an old woman.
Le soleil brillait, les oiseaux chantaient.
The sun was shining, the birds were singing.
(2) What used to happen (habitual or repeated action)
Il se couchait tard.
He used to go to bed late.
Nous nous levions toujours à six heures.
We used to get up always at six o'clock.
(3) What was going on when something else happened.
Il écrivait quand je suis arrivé.
He was writing when I arrived.

ARTICLES IN A BEDROOM

le rideau	le store	le divan	le lit	la couverture	l'édredon (m.)
ree-doh	stor	dee-vaN	lee	koo-vair-tẽr	ay-dre-doN
curtain	*window blind*	*couch*	*bed*	*blanket*	*quilt*

le matelas	le drap de lit	l'oreiller (m.)	le traversin
maht-lah	drah de lee	o-rai-yay	trah-vair-siN
mattress	*sheet*	*pillow*	*bolster*

la descente de lit	la pantoufle	la table de nuit	la lampe de chevet
dai-saNt de lee	paN-toofl	tahbl de nw̃ee	laNp de she-vay
(bedside) rug	*slipper*	*bedside table*	*bedside lamp*

la prise de courant	le réveil	une armoire	la glace	le vaporisateur
preez de koo-raN	ray-vaiy	ahr-mwahr	glahs	vah-po-ree-zah-tãyr
plug	*alarm-clock*	*wardrobe*	*mirror*	*scent spray*

le poudrier	la houpette	la brosse	le peigne	le tiroir
pood-ryay	oo-pait	bros	painy	tee-rwahr
powder-box	*powder-puff*	*brush*	*comb*	*drawer*

In the portion of the Lesages' sitting-room shown on p. 123 there is not "a large mirror" over the mantelpiece, but a painting (**peinture**, f.). M. Lesage is not seated at the bureau which is beside the fireplace. The bookcase, as shown in the picture, is really to the left of the fireplace, not on the right as stated, and M. Lesage is not standing in front of it "reading a book." The round table mentioned certainly has an album of photos upon it, but neither vase of flowers nor portrait; and further, since we are only shown a corner of the sitting-room, it cannot be "in the middle of the room," but should correctly be described as "near grandfather Lesage's armchair." The radio is not "on the left of the French windows," but is on the opposite side of the room.

LUCIE LESAGE'S BEDROOM

The list on page 138 has given you the French names of almost all the objects in the room. Cover over the text and see how many of them you know.

Ce tableau nous montre la chambre à coucher de Mademoiselle Lesage.
se tahb-loh noo moNtr lah shaNb-rah koo-shay de mahd-mwah-zail le-sahzh.
This picture shows us the bedroom of Miss Lesage.

Elle a un grand lit confortable, qui est en bois.   À droite on peut
ai-lah uN graN lee koN-for-tahbl kee ay-taN bwah.   ah drwah-toN pay
She has a large comfortable bed, which is of wood.   On the right one can

voir la table de toilette avec une grande glace, devant laquelle
vwahr lah tahbl de twah-lait ah-vaik een graNd glahs de-vaN lah-kail
see the dressing table with a large mirror, in front of which

elle passe beaucoup de temps chaque jour.   La table de toilette a
ail pahs boh-koo de taN shahk zhoor.   lah tahbl de twah-lait ah
she passes a lot of time every day.   The dressing table has

des tiroirs dans lesquels Mademoiselle Lesage met ses bijoux et ses
day tee-rwahr daN lay-kail mahd-mwah-zail le-sahzh mai say bee-zhoo ay say-
some drawers into which Mademoiselle Lesage puts her jewels and her

objets de toilette: ses brosses, ses peignes, ses boîtes à poudres, ses bâtons de rouge
zob-zhay de twah-lait say bros say painy say bwaht-zah poodr say bahtoN de roozh
articles of toilet: her brushes, her combs, her powder boxes, her lipsticks

PARIS QUI DANSE

Tandis qu'en haut un monde cosmopolite se divertit en regardant danser le cancan, en bas, dans un bal-musette du quartier de la Bastille, on danse avec entrain une valse aux sons d'un orchestre composé de violon et d'accordéon.

Se divertir	**bal-musette** (m.)	**entrain** (m.)	**son** (m.)
To amuse oneself	dance hall	liveliness	sound

et ses parfums.   De l'autre côté on voit une armoire
ay say pahr-fuN.   de lohtr koh-tay oN vwah ĕn ahr-mwahr
and her perfumes.   At the other side one sees a cupboard

comprenant deux parties: la garde-robe, qui contient ses robes et une armoire
koN-pre-naN dāy pahr-tee lah gahrd-rob kee koN-tyiN say rob ay ĕn ahr-mwahr
consisting of two parts: the wardrobe, which contains her frocks and a linen

à linge avec beaucoup de rayons.   Près du lit il y a une
ah liNzh ah-vaik boh-koo de ray-oN.   prai dē lee eel-yah ĕn
cupboard with many shelves.   Near the bed is a

petite table de chevet sur laquelle se trouvent[1] un livre, une bonbonnière, une lampe
p'teet tahbl de she-vai sĕr lah-kail se troov uN leevr ĕn boN-bon-yair, ĕn laNp
small bedside table on which there are a book, a box of sweets, a lamp

et un réveil.   Mlle Lesage aime lire dans son lit en mangeant
ay uN ray-vaiy.   mahd-mwah-zail le-sahzh aim leer daN soN lee aN maN-zhaN
and an alarm-clock.   Miss Lesage likes to read in her bed eating

des bonbons ou du chocolat.   Elle dit, que c'est plus agréable et moins
day boN-boN oo dē sho-ko-lah.   ail dee ke say plē-zah-gray-ahbl ay mwiN
sweets or chocolate.   She says that it is more agreeable and less

dangereux que de fumer dans son lit, comme c'est l'habitude de
daN-zhe-rāy ke de fē-may daN soN lee kom say lah-bee-tēd de
dangerous than to smoke in one's bed as it is the habit of

beaucoup de jeunes personnes de nos jours.
boh-koo de zhāyn pair-son de noh zhoor.
lots of young people nowadays (lit. of our days).

Elle lit dans son lit en mangeant des bonbons et du chocolat.
ail lee daN soN lee aN maN-zhaN day boN-boN ay dē sho-ko-lah.
She reads in her bed eating sweets and chocolate.

---

[1] Lit. find themselves.

EXERCISES

I Answer in French

1. Vous couchez-vous de bonne heure? 2. À quelle heure vous levez-vous? 3. Est-ce que Charles se couche à sept heures du soir? 4. Veut-il se lever à neuf heures du matin? 5. Qu'est qu'il veut faire? 6. Est-ce qu'il était très fatigué? 7. Vous lavez-vous dans la salle à manger? 8. Qu'est-ce que vous dites avant de vous coucher? 9. Lisez-vous dans votre lit? 10. Aimez-vous manger du chocolat?

II Translate into French

1. We get up at six o'clock. 2. Don't you go to bed early? 3. They don't wash in the bedroom. 4. You are going to bed at eight o'clock. 5. Are there any chairs in the bedroom? 6. Don't forget to wake me up. 7. He forgot. 8. They went to their hotel. 9. What did he have to do? 10. Everybody was asleep. 11. It was hot. 12. He did not want to wash before breakfast. 13. She was putting her jewels into the third drawer of her dressing table. 14. He liked to read in (his) bed. 15. You are getting up, aren't you?

III Put the following into the Imperfect Tense

1. Je suis malade. 2. Il ne reste pas à l'hôtel. 3. Elle a beaucoup d'argent. 4. Ils sont fatigués. 5. Nous avons faim. 6. Ils n'ont pas de chaises. 7. Est-ce que vous vous couchez? 8. Le train arrive. 9. Il fait beau. 10. Pourquoi mettez-vous les fleurs sur l'armoire? (*Key to I, II and III on page 152.*)

DANS LA CHARENTE

Armées de serpettes, ces braves paysannes de la Charente sont penchées sur les ceps de vigne pour les tailler. La vendange de l'année prochaine s'annonce abondante.

Serpette (f.)	cep (m.)	tailler	vendange (f.)
pruning-bill	vine-stock	to prune	vine-harvest

TREIZIÈME LEÇON

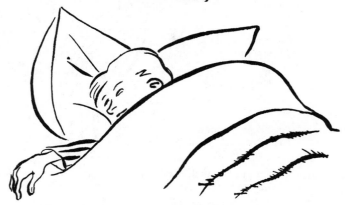

Laissez-moi dormir. Je ne veux pas encore me lever.
lai-say mwah dor-meer. zhe ne vãy pah-zaN-kor me le-vay.
Let me sleep. I don't want yet to get up.

CHARLES GETS UP

Charles: **Entendez-vous, Georges?**
aN-taN-day voo zhorzh?
Do you hear, George?

Georges: **Quoi?**
kwah?
What?

Charles: **On frappe à la porte.**
oN frahp ah lah port.
Someone is knocking at the door.

Georges: **C'est mon père.**
say moN pair.
It is my father.

Charles: **Pourquoi frappe-t-il?**
poor-kwah frahp-teel?
Why does he knock?

Georges: **Pour me réveiller.**
poor me ray-vai-yay.
To wake me.

Charles: **Quelle heure est-il?**
kai-lãyr ay-teel?
What is the time?

Georges: **Il est sept heures.**
ee-lay sai-tãyr.
It is seven o'clock.

Charles: **Est-ce qu'il fait beau ce matin?**
ais-keel fai boh se mah-tiN?
Is the weather fine this morning?

Georges: **Oui, il fait très beau.**
wee eel fai trai boh.
Yes, it is very fine.

Le soleil brille.
le so-laiy breey.
The sun is shining.

Charles: **Avez-vous bien dormi, Georges?**
ah-vay voo byiN dor-mee zhorzh?
Did you sleep well, George?

Georges: **Oui, merci, j'ai bien dormi. Ne voulez-vous pas**
wee mair-see zhay byiN dor-mee. ne voo-lay voo pah
Yes, thank you, I have slept well. Don't you want

vous lever?
voo le-vay?
to get up?

Charles: **Pas encore.   Je**
            pah-zaN-kor.   zhe
            Not yet.   I

            ne suis pas pressé.
            ne sŵee pah prai-say.
            am not in a hurry.

            Je suis en vacances.
            zhe sŵee-zaN vah-kaNs.
            I am on holiday.

            Je n'ai pas besoin de me lever.
            zhe nay pah bezwiN de me le-vay.
            I have no need to get up.

Georges: **Mais hier vous avez dit que vous vouliez être réveillé**
            mai yair voo-zah-vay dee ke voo voo-lyay-zaitr ray-vai-yay
            But yesterday you have said that you wanted to be called

            de bonne heure.   Charles: **J'ai changé d'avis.   Il est si**
            de bo-nŵr.   zhay shaN-zhay dah-vee.   ee-lay see
            early.   *I have changed my mind.   It is so*

            bon de rester au lit.   Georges: **Vous avez dit hier que**
            boN de rais-tay oh lee.   voo-zah-vay dee yair ke
            good to stay in bed.   *You have said yesterday that*

            vous aviez beaucoup à faire.   Charles: **J'ai bien le temps.**
            voo-zah-vyay boh-koo-pah fair.   zhay byiN le taN.
            you had lots of things to do.   *I have plenty of time.*

Georges: **(se levant): Vous êtes heureux.   Je me lève, autrement je serai**
            (se le-vaN) voo-zait-zŵy-rŵy.   zhe me laiv ohtr-maN zhe se-rai
            (getting up): You are lucky.   I am getting up, otherwise I shall be

            en retard.   Je serai habillé avant vous.
            aN re-tahr.   zhe se-ray ah-bee-yay ah-vaN voo.
            late.   I shall be dressed before you.

Charles: **C'est très probable.**   Georges: **C'est curieux.**
            say trai proh-bahbl   say kŵr-yŵy
            That is very likely.   *That's funny.*

Charles: **Qu'avez-vous?**   Georges: **Je ne peux pas**
            kah-vay voo?   zhe ne pŵy pah
            What is the matter with you?   *I can't*

trouver ma chemise.   Charles: La voilà sur le lit.
troo-vay mah she-meez.   lah vwah-lah sễr le lee.
find my shirt.   *There it is on the bed.*

Georges: Merci bien. Pouvez-vous voir mon caleçon?
mair-see byiN. poo-vay voo vwahr moN kahl-soN?
Thank you. Can you see my underdrawers?

Charles: Cherchez-le bien.   Georges: Le voici sous la table.
shair-shay le byiN.   le vwah-see soo lah tahbl.
Look for them well.   *There they are under the table.*

Où sont mes chaussettes?   Charles: Les voilà sur la
oo soN may shoh-sait?   lay vwah-lah sễr lah
Where are my socks?   *There they are on the*

commode.   Georges: Vous êtes un vrai détective.
ko-mod.   voo-zait uN vrai day-taik-teev.
chest of drawers.   *You are a real detective.*

Charles: Peut-être le serai-je un jour.
pễy taitr le se-ray zhe uN zhoor
Perhaps I shall be one, one day.

ARTICLES IN THE BATHROOM

le bain biN *bath*	la baignoire bain-ywahr *bath-tub*	le savon de toilette sah-voN de twah-lait *bath-soap*	le porte-savon port sah-voN *soap-dish*	le gant de toilette gaN de twah-lait *face-flannel*
une éponge ay-poNzh *sponge*		le peignoir de bain pain-ywahr de biN *bath-wrap*	la douche doosh *shower*	le chauffe-bain shohf biN *water heater*
la descente de bain dais-saNt de biN *bath-mat*		le lavabo lah-vah-boh *wash-basin*	le verre à eau vai-rah oh *tumbler*	la brosse à dents bro-sah daN *tooth-brush*
la pâte dentifrice paht daN-tee-frees *tooth-paste*		le flacon d'eau dentifrice flah-koN doh daN-tee-frees *mouth-wash*		le rasoir de sûreté rahz-wahr de sễr-tay *safety-razor*
le savon à barbe sah-voN ah bahrb *shaving soap*		le blaireau blai-roh *shaving-brush*	la serviette de bain sair-vyait de biN *bath-towel*	le porte-serviette port sair-vyait *towel-rail*
le savon sah-voN *soap*	la bascule bahs-kễl *weighing machine*		le bain de siège biN de syaizh *hip-bath*	le W.C. doobl vay say *W.C.*
la chaîne shain *chain*	le couvercle koo-vairkl *lid*	le papier hygiénique pahp-yay eezh-yay-neek *toilet-paper*		le portemanteau port-maN-toh *clothes-rack*

CHARLES IN THE BATHROOM

Try making a list in French of the objects you see before consulting the list on page 145
Then turn back and fill the gaps in your list without making use of the text.

Georges: **Alors aidez-moi à trouver mon rasoir.**
               ah-lor ai-day mwah ah troo-vay moN rahz-wahr.
               Then help me to find my razor.

Charles: **Le voilà sous votre nez.**
               le vwah-lah soo votr nay.
               There it is in front of your eyes (lit., under your nose).

Georges: **Mais ça, c'est extraordinaire.**
               mai sah say-taik-strah-or-dee-nair.
               But that's extraordinary (that is).

Charles: **Peut-être le savon y est-il aussi.**
               pay-taitr le sah-voN ee ay-teel oh-see.
               Perhaps the soap is also there.

Georges: **Vraiment, vous avez raison.   Maintenant j'ai mon pantalon,**
               vrai-maN voo-zah-vay rai-zoN.   miNt-naN zhay moN paN-tah-loN
               Really, you are (lit., have) right.   Now I have my trousers,

               mon gilet, mon col, ma cravate, mes bottines, mon
               moN zhee-lay moN kol mah krah-vaht may bo-teen moN
               my waistcoat, my collar, my tie, my boots, my

veston, et les choses pour me raser. Je vais me raser,
vais-toN ay lay shohz poor me rah-zay.   zhe vai me rah-zay
jacket, and the things for shaving myself.   I am going to shave,

me laver, et m'habiller dans la salle de bain. J'espère que
me lah-vay ay mah-bee-yay daN lah sahl de biN.   zhais-pair ke
to wash, and to dress in the bathroom.   I hope that

vous serez habillé, quand je reviendrai.
voo se-ray zah-bee-yay kaN zhe re-vyiN-dray.
you will be dressed, when I come back.

Charles: **Il n'y a pas de danger.**
eel nyah pah de daN-zhay.
There is no danger of that.

Georges: **Levez-vous, paresseux; je serai prêt avant vous.**
le-vay voo pah-rai-sây; zhe se-rai prai ah-vaN voo.
Get up, lazybones; I shall be ready before you.

Charles: **Cela m'est égal.**
se-lah may-tay-gahl.
I don't care (lit., That to me is equal).

Georges sort.   Charles reste encore quelques minutes
zhorzh sor. shahrl rais-taN-kor kail-ke mee-nêêt
George leaves.   Charles still remains a few minutes

dans son lit.   Puis, après un
daN soN lee.   pŵee ah-prai-zuN
in his bed.   Then, after an

immense effort, il se lève.   Il
nee-maNs ai-for eel se laiv.   eel
immense effort, he gets up.   He

ôte la veste de son pyjama
oht lah vaist de soN pee-zhah-mah
takes off the coat of his pyjamas

et met ses pantoufles.   Il se lave
ay mai say paN-toofl.   eel se lahv
and puts on his slippers.   He washes

les mains, le figure, le cou et les oreilles, après quoi il se sèche
lay miN lah fee-gêêr le koo ay lay-zo-raiy ah-prai kwah eel se saish
his hands, his face, his neck and his ears, after which he dries himself

avec une serviette.   Il se nettoie les dents avec sa brosse à dents et
ah-vai-kêên sair-vyait.   eel se nai-twah lay daN ah-vaik sah bros ah daN ay
with a towel.   He cleans his teeth with his toothbrush and

un peu de dentifrice.   Cela fait, il s'habille.   Il met ses chaussettes, puis
uN p$\widehat{ay}$ de daN-tee-frees.   se-lah fai eel sah-beey.   eel mai say shoh-sait p$\widehat{w}$ee
a little tooth-paste.   That done, he dresses.   He puts on his socks, then

sa chemise, son caleçon, son pantalon et ses bretelles.   Pour mettre sa
sah she-meez soN kahl-soN soN paN-tah-loN ay say bre-tail.   Poor maitr sah
his shirt, his pants, his trousers and his braces.   To put on his

cravate il va devant la glace; il se brosse aussi les
krah-vaht eel vah de-vaN lah glahs eel se bros oh-see lay
tie he goes before the mirror; he also brushes his

cheveux et se peigne.   Après cela il met son gilet, son veston
she-v$\widehat{ay}$ ay se pain$y$.   ah-prai se-lah eel mai soN zhee-lai soN vais-toN
hair and combs it.   After that he puts on his waistcoat, his jacket

et ses souliers.   Il ne se dépêche pas, il prend son temps.   À
ay say sool-yay.   eel ne se day-paish pah eel praN soN taN.   ah
and his shoes.   He does not hurry, he takes his time.   At

neuf heures moins vingt il descend et entre dans la salle à manger, où
n$\widehat{ay}$-v$\widehat{ay}$r mwiN viN eel dais-saN ay aNtr daN lah sahl ah maN-zhay oo
twenty to nine he goes down and enters (in) the dining-room, where

la famille a presque fini le petit déjeuner.   Il dit "bonjour,"
lah fah-meey ah praisk fee-nee le p'tee day-zh$\widehat{ay}$-nay.   eel dee boN-zhoor
the family has almost finished (the) breakfast.   He says "good morning,"

et s'excuse d'être en retard, en disant: "Je vous demande pardon."
ay saik-sk$\widehat{ee}$z daitr aN re-tahr aN dee-zaN zhe voo de-maNd pahr-doN.
and apologises for being late, by saying: "I am sorry."

Mme Lesage répond: "Il n'y a pas de quoi."
mah-dahm le-sahzh ray-poN   eel nyah pah de kwah.
Mme Lesage replies: "Don't mention it."

HOW TO APOLOGISE

Je vous demande pardon, which literally means "I beg your pardon", also stands for "I am sorry", "Excuse me", "I apologise". The usual reply to these is **Il n'y a pas de quoi,** which literally means "There is not of what". "To apologise" is also **s'excuser,** another reflexive verb.

TO KNOCK; TO RING; TO LISTEN

Frapper = to knock, **sonner** = to ring, and **écouter** = to listen to, are regular verbs. On **frappe** means "there is a knock". "someone is knocking"; similarly **on sonne** = "the bell is ringing", "someone is ringing".

VERBS ENDING IN -RE
Entendre = to hear
Present Tense

j'entends   (aN-taN)
il ⎫
elle ⎭ entend   (aN-taN)
nous entendons   (aN-taN-doN)
vous entendez   (aN-taN-day)
ils ⎫
elles ⎭ entendent   'aN-taNd)

Imperfect

j'entendais (aN-taN-dai)

il }
elle } entendait (aN-taN-dai)

nous entendions (aN-taN-dyoN)
vous entendiez (aN-taN-dyay)

ils }
elles } entendaient (aN-taN-dai)

Perfect

j'ai entendu (aN-taN-dœ̄)

il }
elle } a entendu

nous avons entendu

ils }
elles } ont entendu

Répondre=to reply
Present Tense

je réponds (ray-poN)

il }
elle } répond (ray-poN)

nous répondons (ray-poN-doN)
vous répondez (ray-poN-day)

ils }
elles } répondent (ray-poNd)

Imperfect

je répondais (ray-poN-dai)

il }
elle } répondait (ray-poN-dai)

nous répondions (ray-poN-dyoN)
vous répondiez (ray-poN-dyay)

ils }
elles } répondaient (ray-poN-dai)

Perfect

j'ai répondu (ray-poN-dœ̄)

il }
elle } a répondu

nous avons répondu

ils }
elles } ont répondu

Verbs in -re usually have the same forms as given above for **entendre** and **répondre**. Such a regular verb in -re is for instance **vendre**; irregular verbs in -re we have come across so far are **mettre**=to put, **faire**=to make, and **dire**=to say. The Present Tense of these verbs has already

been given in previous pages. Their Imperfects can be derived, as those of every verb whatsoever, from the form of the Present Tense used in connection with **nous**. If you leave out the ending -ons of **mettons, disons** and **faisons** you get **mett-, dis-** and **fais-**. To these stems the Imperfect endings -ais, -ait, -ions, -iez, -aient are added. And this rule holds good for every French verb, except **être**=to be, which, however, is not a proper verb, but a so-called auxiliary verb,

The Perfect of **faire, dire, lire, prendre, écrire** and **mettre** is irregular: **j'ai fait**=I have made, **j'ai dit**=I have said, **j'ai mis**= I have put (on), **j'ai lu**=I have read, **j'ai pris**=I have taken, **j'ai écrit**=I have written.

SOME MORE REFLEXIVE VERBS

se dépêcher=to hurry; **s'habiller**=to get dressed; **se brosser**=to brush (oneself); **se peigner**=to comb (oneself); **se baigner**= to have a bath, to bathe; **se raser**=to shave (oneself) are reflexive verbs, the forms of which are identical with those given in the previous lesson (page 137).

IDIOMATIC EXPRESSIONS

The following have occurred in this lesson:

être pressé=to be in a hurry (lit., to be hurried).

avoir besoin=to need, to require (lit., to have need).

avoir raison=to be right (lit., to have reason).

changer d'avis=to change one's mind (lit., to change of opinion).

j'ai le temps=I have time.

être en retard=to be late (lit., to be in delay).

le voici (voilà)=here (there) it is (if the object referred to is masculine); here (there) he is.

la voici (voilà)=here (there) it is (if the object referred to is feminine); here (there) she is.

les voici (voilà)=here (there) they are.

PARTS OF THE BODY

la tête	tait	*head*
un cheveu	she-vay	*hair*
un œil	ayy	*eye*
le nez	nay	*nose*
la bouche	boosh	*mouth*
la dent	daN	*tooth*
le cou	koo	*neck*
une oreille	oh-raiy	*ear*
le bras	brah	*arm*
la main	miN	*hand*
la jambe	zhaNb	*leg*
le pied	pyay	*foot*

Note.—The plural of **un œil** (ayy) is **les yeux** (lay-zyay); **le cheveu** (she-vay)=*hair* like any other noun ending in **-eu** or **-eau** has the plural ending in **-x** instead of **-s**.

DEFINITE ARTICLE
WITH PARTS OF THE BODY

il se lave les mains=
     he washes his hands.
elle se brosse les cheveux=
     she brushes her hair.
ils se sèchent les mains=
     they dry their hands.
je me nettoie les dents=
     I clean my teeth.
elle a les yeux bleus=
     she has blue eyes.
il a les cheveux courts=
     he has short hair.

When there is no doubt as to the possessor, the definite article is used in French instead of the possessive adjective before parts of the body.

EXERCISES

I Answer in French

1. Où est-ce que Georges avait mis sa chemise? 2. Pourquoi Charles ne voulait-il pas se lever? 3. Avait-il besoin de se lever de bonne heure? 4. Pourquoi pas (=why not)? 5. Qui frappe à la porte de la chambre? 6. Est-ce que Charles se lève à sept heures? 7. Où Georges se lave-t-il? 8. Qu'est-ce qu'on fait avant de s'habiller? 9. Est-ce que vous vous mettez devant une glace pour vous peigner? 10. Qu'est-ce que Charles dit, quand il entre dans la salle à manger? 11. Est-ce que vous vous excusez, quand vous êtes en retard? 12. Qu'est-ce que Mme Lesage répond?

II Translate into English.

1. Pour le déjeuner il y a du café au lait avec du pain et du beurre. 2. Je mets mes chaussettes sur une chaise. 3. Je me lave les mains avec de l'eau chaude et du savon. 4. Il n'y avait pas de savon. 5. Sur la tête il y a les cheveux. 6. Les dents sont dans la bouche. 7. Nous avons deux jambes et deux bras. 8. Les dames ont les cheveux longs. 9. Votre frère a-t-il les cheveux courts? 10. Nous marchons avec les pieds. 11. Avec les yeux nous voyons. 12. Avec les oreilles nous entendons.

III Translate into French

1. Who was knocking? 2. Don't you have to get up? 3. Why did you change your mind? 4. They have plenty of time. 5. I cannot find my collar—here it is. 6. Where are my shoes?—There they are. 7. Won't you brush your hair? 8. Why is she late? 9. She has not heard the alarm-clock. 10. I am sorry for being late, but I was very tired. *(Key to I, II and III on page 152.)*

KEY TO THE EXERCISES

Lesson Nine—I

1. Il est dans le ciel. 2. Il n'est pas visible pendant la nuit. 3. La nuit. 4. Il se lève le matin. 5. Il se couche le soir. 6. À trois heures ou quatre heures. 7. Non, ils sont courts. 8. Oui, elles sont courtes. 9. Non, il fait noir. 10. Nous allumons le gaz ou

l'électricité. 11. Non, il se couche tard. 12. Je ne peux pas voir. 13. Il ne fait plus jour. 14. Ils sont gris. 15. Quelquefois il pleut beaucoup. 16. Non, il ne neige pas en été. 17. Non, ils n'ouvrent pas leurs parapluies. 18. Non, il ne fait pas de soleil. 19. Oui, il fait beau (Non, il ne fait pas beau). 20. Non, il fait froid. 21. Non, il ne neige pas en juillet. 22. J'ai froid (je n'ai pas froid). 23. J'aime les fleurs. 24. L'été. 25. Non, il n'y a pas de violettes en février.

II

1. Quelle heure est-il, s'il vous plaît? 2. Il est onze heures du matin. 3. Le soleil est-il visible maintenant? 4. Fait-il noir? 5. Veuillez allumer le gaz. 6. J'ai toujours froid en hiver. 7. Que fait votre frère? 8. Il fait des bouquets de pensées. 9. Pleut-il (*or* est-ce qu'il pleut)? 10. Il neige quelquefois en hiver.

III

Compare your answers with pages 12, 90 and 112.

Lesson Ten

I

1. Elle est dans un faubourg. 2. Douze. 3. Au rez-de-chaussée. 4. Le salon et le bureau. 5. Au deuxième étage. 6. La mansarde et le grenier. 7. La cave. 8. Un petit jardin. 9. Dans le grand jardin qui est derrière la maison. 10. Au deuxième étage. 11. Dans le cabinet de travail. 12. Dans la cave. 13. Au vestibule. 14. La porte de la maison. 15. Un visiteur et une jeune dame sont dans le vestibule. 16. Il ôte son pardessus. 17. Elle met son chapeau. 18. Une Anglaise, qui donne des leçons. 19. Je prends des leçons de français. 20. Dans le vestibule au fond et à droite.

II

1. -e. 2. -ez. 3. -e. 4. -ons. 5. -ent. 6. -es. 7. -ent. 8. -es. 9. -s. 10. -e.

III

1. Où habitez-vous? 2. Est-ce loin d'ici? 3. Combien de pièces a votre maison? 4. Y a-t-il une salle de bain dans sa maison? 5. À quel étage est la chambre des enfants? 6. Elle est au deuxième étage. 7. Vos malles sont au grenier. 8. Vous avez de beaux parterres de fleurs dans votre jardin, n'est-ce pas? 9. Avez-vous des légumes dans votre jardin? 10. Nous n'avons que quelques fleurs. 11. Est-ce que cet enfant dort? 12. Descendons dans la cave! 13. La cuisine est près de la salle à manger. 14. La salle à manger est à gauche. 15. Le téléphone est à gauche à côté du porte-manteau.

Lesson Eleven

I

1. Le grand-père, la grand'mère, M. et Mme Lesage, etc., sont dans le salon. 2. Il lit. 3. Elle écrit une lettre. 4. Mlle Lesage. 5. Il y a six personnes. 6. Il fume et elle reprise. 7. Une pendule. 8. Dans la niche. 9. Non, il n'est pas debout. 10. M. Lesage. 11. Une table ronde. 12. Oui. 13. Il est à gauche. 14. J'ai une montre (Je n'ai pas de montre). 15. Il est . . . heures. 16. Oui, elle est remontée (Non, elle n'est pas remontée). 17. Il (n') avance (pas.). 18. Oui. 19. Elle n'est pas si large. 20. J'écris (Je n'écris pas) beaucoup de lettres. 21. Je (ne) lis (pas) beaucoup.

II

1. Voyez-vous mon grand-père? 2. Il est assis dans le jardin. 3. Est-elle debout ou assise? 4. Jouez-vous du piano? 5. Je ne joue pas, mais j'écoute souvent, surtout la musique de Bach. 6. Est-ce que votre montre est en or? 7. Non, elle est en argent. 8. Mon réveil est plus petit que votre pendule, qui est sur la cheminée. 9. Ma montre est arrêtée. 10. Écoutez s'il vous plaît, ne lisez pas. 11. Qu'est-ce que vous écrivez? 12. Une lettre à ma mère qui est en France.

III

1. Are you younger (older) than your brother (my uncle), etc.? 2. Is it warmer (less warm; colder) in spring than in winter, etc.? 3. Are the most (least) beautiful (bad, long, short) days in spring, etc.?

Lesson Twelve

I

1. Je (ne) me couche (pas) de bonne heure. 2. Je me lève à ... heures. 3. Non, il ne se couche pas à sept heures. 4. Non, il veut se lever à sept heures. 5. Il veut voir Paris. 6. Oui, il était très fatigué. 7. Non, je ne me lave pas dans la salle à manger. 8. Je dis "bonne nuit". 9. Je (ne) lis (pas) dans mon lit. 10. J'aime (Je n'aime pas) manger du chocolat.

II

1. Nous nous levons à six heures. 2. Ne vous couchez-vous pas de bonne heure? 3. Ils (elles) ne se lavent pas dans la chambre à coucher. 4. Vous allez vous coucher à huit heures. 5. Y a-t-il des chaises dans la chambre à coucher. 6. N'oubliez pas de me réveiller. 7. Il oubliait. 8. Ils allaient à leur hôtel. 9. Qu'est-ce qu'il avait à faire? 10. Tout le monde dormait. 11. Il faisait chaud. 12. Il ne voulait pas se laver avant le petit déjeuner. 13. Elle mettait ses bijoux dans le troisième tiroir de sa table de toilette. 14. Il aimait à lire dans son lit. 15. Vous vous levez, n'est-ce pas?

III

1. J'étais malade. 2. Il ne restait pas à l'hôtel. 3. Elle avait beaucoup d'argent. 4. Ils étaient fatigués. 5. Nous avions faim.

6. Ils n'avaient pas de chaises. 7. Est-ce que vous vous couchiez? 8. Le train arrivait. 9. Il faisait beau. 10. Pourquoi mettiez-vous les fleurs sur l'armoire?

Lesson Thirteen

I

1. Sur son lit. 2. Parce qu'il était paresseux. 3. Non, il n'avait pas besoin de se lever de bonne heure. 4. Parce qu'il était en vacances. 5. Le père de Georges. 6. Non, il ne se lève pas. 7. Il se lave dans la salle de bain. 8. On se lave. 9. Oui, je me mets devant une glace. 10. Il dit "Bonjour". 11. Oui, je m'excuse. 12. Elle répond: "Il n'y a pas de quoi".

II

1. For breakfast there is coffee with milk and bread and butter. 2. I put my socks on a chair. 3. I wash my hands with hot water and soap. 4. There was no soap. 5. On the head is the hair. 6. The teeth are in the mouth. 7. We have two legs and two arms. 8. Ladies have long hair. 9. Has your brother short hair? 10. We walk with our feet. 11. With the eyes we see. 12. With the ears we hear.

III

1. Qui frappait? 2. N'avez-vous pas besoin de vous lever? 3. Pourquoi avez-vous changé d'avis? 4. Ils ont bien le temps. 5. Je ne peux pas trouver mon col —le voici. 6. Où sont mes souliers?—Les voici. 7. Ne voulez-vous pas brosser vos cheveux? 8. Pourquoi est-elle en retard? 9. Elle n'a pas entendu le réveil. 10. Je vous demande pardon d'être en retard, mais j'étais très fatigué(e).

TAKE THE COURSE WITH YOU TO FRANCE!

When next business or pleasure takes you to France, you will be well advised to take the Course with you. It is so designed as to be useful not only to those who wish to learn French at home, but also to those who may wish to take a long motor tour or make an extended stay in France. It may be at the garage when you wish to explain the repairs needed to some part of your car, or at the butcher's when you want to describe some cut of meat, or in the train or on the racecourse, that you will find the Course invaluable.

QUATORZIÈME LEÇON

Could you approach the **grille** (wire partition), pass your sterling through the **guichet** (paying-slot) and change money as Mr. Roberts will do? If not, study the text below, then cover it over and repeat until you are satisfied that you know what you would have to say in French, in order to carry out a similar transaction.

ACHATS DIVERS—VARIOUS PURCHASES

Monsieur Roberts n'a pas d'argent français et pour faire ses achats
m's-yay robairts nah pah dahr-zhaN fraN-sai ay poor fair say-zah-shah
Mr. Roberts has no French money and to do his shopping

il en aura besoin. C'est pourquoi il entre dans un bureau de change.
ee-laN-no-rah bez-wiN. say poor-kwah ee-laNtr daN-zuN bee-roh de shaNzh.
he of it will have need. That is why he enters (in) an exchange office.

M. Roberts: **Monsieur, voulez-vous changer des billets de banque anglais?**
m's-yay voo-lay voo shaN-zhay day bee-yay de baNk aN-glai?
Will you change English banknotes?

Changeur: **Certainement. Combien monsieur veut-il changer?**
sair-tain-maN. koN-byiN m's-yay vay-teel shaN-zhay
Certainly. How much does the gentleman wish to change?

M. Roberts: **Je changerai une livre seulement, s'il vous plaît, monsieur.**
zhe shaNzh-ray een leevr sayl-maN seel-voo plai m's-yay.
I will change one pound only, please.

Changeur: **Comment voulez-vous prendre l'argent[1], en billets ou en monnaie?**
ko-maN voo-lay voo prandr lahr-zhaN aN bee-yay oo aN mo-nai?
How do you wish to take the money, in notes or in silver?

M. Roberts: **Neuf billets de cent francs et de la monnaie[1] pour le reste.**
nãy bee-yai de saN fraN ay de lah mo-nai poor le raist.
Nine notes of 100 *francs and the rest in small change.*

Changeur: **Voici, monsieur, neuf cents francs, cinquante, soixante,**
vwah-see m's-yãy nãy saN fraN, siN-kaNt swah-saNt
Here you are, sir, nine hundred francs, fifty, sixty.

70, 71, 72, 73, 74, 75 francs, cela fait
(see page 112) fraN se-lah fai
70, 71, 72, 73, 74, 75 *francs, that makes*

975 francs.   **M. Roberts (après avoir**
nãy-saN-swah-saNt kiNz fraN.   ah-prai-zahv-wahr
975 *francs*   *(after having*

compté l'argent): Merci, c'est juste.   Bonjour, monsieur.
koN-tay lahr-zhaN.   mair-see, say zhẽẽst.   boN-zhoor m's-yãy.
counted the money): Thanks, that is right.   Good morning, sir.

Ses poches remplies d'argent, M. Roberts entre dans un bistro
say posh raN-plee dahr-zhaN M. ro-bairts aNtr daN-zuN beest-roh
His pockets full of money, Mr. Roberts goes into a public-house

pour acheter des cigarettes.   Il a appris que c'est dans des
poor ahsh-tay day see-gah-rait.   ee-lah ah-pree ke say daN day
to buy some cigarettes.   He has learnt that it is in

bistros qu'on trouve les bureaux de tabac.   Le tabac, les
beest-roh koN troov lay bẽẽ-roh de tah-bah.   le tah-bah lay
public-houses that one finds the tobacco shops.   The tobacco, the

cigarettes, les cigares, les allumettes et les cartes à jouer
see-gah-rait lay see-gahr lay zah-lẽẽ-mait ay lay kahrt ah zhoo-ay
cigarettes, the cigars, the matches and the playing cards

sont des monopoles de l'État, c'est à dire que l'État seul a
soN day mo-no-pol de lay-tah, say-tah deer ke lay-tah sãyl ah
are monopolies of the State, that is to say the State alone has

le droit de les fabriquer et de les vendre.   Dans un bureau de tabac
le drwah de lay fah-bree-kay ay de lay vaNdr.   daN-zuN bẽẽ-roh de tah-bah
the right to manufacture them and to sell them.   In a tobacco shop

---

[1] **l'argent** means both "money" and "silver"; **la monnaie** is "small change" only.

on vend aussi des timbres-poste, des cartes-postales et
oN vaN-toh-see day tiNbr post day kahrt pos-tahl ay
one sells also postage-stamps, postcards and

des cartes-lettres; en outre on y vend des pipes, des blagues, des fume-
day kahrt laitr aN-nootr oN-nee vaN day peep day blahg day fẽẽm
letter-cards; in addition one sells there pipes, pouches, cigar-

cigares, des fume-cigarettes et toutes sortes de choses à l'usage
see-gahr day fẽẽm see-gah-rait ay toot sort de shohz ah lẽẽ-zahzh
holders, cigarette-holders, and all kinds of things for the use

des fumeurs.   M. Roberts s'adresse à la patronne qui vient de
day fẽẽ-mãỹr.   M. ro-bairts sah-drais ah lah pah-tron kee vyiN de
of smokers.   Mr. Roberts addresses himself to the proprietress who has just

vendre[1] quelques timbres-poste à un autre client.
vaNdr kail-ke tiNbr post ah uN-nohtr klee-aN.
been selling some stamps to another customer.

M. Roberts: Bonjour, madame, voulez-vous me donner un paquet de
                boN-zhoor mah-dahm voo-lay voo me do-nay uN pah-kai de
                Good morning, madam, will you give me a packet of

[1] Lit. Comes from selling.

This officer of the French Colonial cavalry dazzles the ladies, but he need not dazzle
you. Our artist has here shown several objects which you know. Consult the list on
page 156 only when your vocabulary breaks down, then turn back. Continue until you
are satisfied that you could cover all your requirements in any French tobacconist's.

cigarettes, s'il vous plaît?
see-gah-rait seel voo plai?
cigarettes, please?

La patronne: Avec plaisir, monsieur, quelles cigarettes désirez-vous?
ah-vaik plai-zeer m's-yâŷ kail see-gah-rait day-zee-ray voo?
With pleasure, sir, what cigarettes do you want?

M. Roberts: Donnez-moi . . . je ne connais pas les marques françaises.
do-nay mwah zhe ne ko-nay pah lay mahrk fraN-saiz.
Give me . . . I don't know the French brands.

Patronne: Désirez-vous des douces ou des fortes?
day-zee-ray voo day doos oo day fort?
Do you want mild or strong ones?

M. Roberts: Vous n'avez pas de cigarettes anglaises, par hasard?
voo nah-vay pah de see-gah-rait-zaN-glaiz pahr-ah-zahr?
You haven't any English cigarettes, by (any) chance?

Patronne: Mais si,[1] monsieur, nous avons toutes les marques connues.
mai see m's-yâŷ noo-zah-voN toot lay mahrk ko-nêê.
But yes, sir, we have all the (well) known brands.

Mr. Roberts: Je préfère les marques anglaises, parce que je ne
zhe pray-fair lay mahrk-zan-glaiz pahrs ke zhe ne
I prefer the English brands, because I don't

AT THE TOBACCONIST'S

le cigare	la cigarette	la pipe	le cigarillo	le fume-cigare
see-gahr	see-gah-rait	peep	see-gah-ril-loh	fêêm see-gahr
cigar	*cigarette*	*pipe*	*small cigar*	*cigar-holder*

le fume-cigarette	la boîte de cigares	le paquet de cigarettes
fêêm see-gah-rait	bwaht de see-gahr	pah-kai de see-gah-rait
cigarette-holder	*box of cigars*	*packet of cigarettes*

un étui à cigares	un étui à cigarettes	une blague	le coupe-cigare
ay-twee ah see-gahr	ay-twee ah see-gah-rait	blahg	koop see-gahr
cigar-case	*cigarette-case*	*tobacco-pouch*	*cigar-cutter*

une boîte d'allumettes	une allumette	le cendrier	la bougie	la tabatière
bwaht dah-lêê-mait	ah-lêê-mait	saN-dryay	boo-zhee	tah-bah-tyair
box of matches	*match*	*ash-tray*	*candle*	*snuff-box*

le paquet de tabac	la pochette d'allumettes	le briquet	le cure-pipe
pah-kai de tah-bah	po-shait dah-lêê-mait	bree-kai	kêêr peep
packet of tobacco	*book matches*	*lighter*	*pipe-cleaner*

---

[1] si is used instead of oui in reply to a negative question.

connais pas les autres. Alors donnez-moi un paquet de
ko-nai pah lay-zohtr ah-lor do-nay mwah uN pah-kay de
know the others. *Then give me a packet of*

vingt Player's.   La patronne: Et Celtique ou Gitane aussi?
viN play-air.   ay sail-teek oo zhee-tahn oh-see?
twenty Player's.   *And Celtic or Gitane also?*

M. Roberts: **Gitane, c'est ça. Donnez-m'en un paquet, s'il vous plaît.**
zhee-tahn say sah. do-nay maN uN pah-kai seel-voo-plai.
Gitane, that's it. Give me (of it) a packet, please.

Et qu'est-ce que ça coûte?
ay kais-ke sah koot?
And how much is that?

La patronne: **Soixante francs le paquet de dix, et cent cinquante francs les Player's.**
swah-saNt fraN le pah-kai de dees ay saN siNkaNt fraN lay play-air
Sixty francs the packet of ten, and 150 francs the Player's.

M. Roberts: **Oh, j'ai presque oublié. Donnez-moi encore une**
oh zhay praisk oo-blee-yay. do-nay mwah aN-kor ẽn
Oh, I have almost forgotten. Give me also a

boîte de cigares de la Havane, c'est pour un parent,
bwaht de see-gahr de lah ah-vahn say poor uN pah-raN
box of Havana cigars, it is for a relation (of mine),

et une boîte d'allumettes.   La patronne: **Ce sera tout?**
ay ẽn bwaht dah-lẽ-mait.   se serah too?
and a box of matches.   *That will be all?*

M. Roberts: **Oui, madame, c'est tout pour aujourd'hui.**
wee mah-dahm say too poor oh-zhoord-ŵee.
Yes, madam, that is all for to-day.

CHEZ LE PAPETIER—AT THE STATIONER'S

M. Roberts a besoin d'écrire beaucoup de lettres et n'a pas
M. ro-bairts a be-zwiN day-kreer boh-koo de laitr ay nah pah
Mr. Roberts has (need) to write lots of letters and has not (got)

ce qu'il faut.   C'est pourquoi il entre chez un papetier
se keel foh.   say poor-kwah ee-laNtr shay-zuN pah-pe-tyay
the necessary things.[1]   That is why he enters (at) a stationer's

pour y faire les achats nécessaires.
poor ee fair lay-zah-shah nay-sai-sair.
to make the necessary purchases.

---

[1] Lit. that which it needs.

Le vendeur: **Qu'y a-t-il pour votre service, monsieur?**
le vaN-dāyr   kyah-teel poor votr sair-vees m's-yāy?
The salesman: *What is there for your service, sir?*

M. Roberts: **Je voudrais du papier à lettres.**
zhe vood-rai dē̃ pahp-yay 'ah laitr.
I want some note-paper.

Vendeur: **De quelle couleur le désirez-vous, monsieur?**
de kail koo-lāyr le day-zee-ray voo m's-yāy?
(Of) what colour do you want it, sir?

M. Roberts: **Montrez-moi du blanc, mais de très belle qualité, s'il vous plaît.**
moN-tray mwah dē̃ blaN mai de trai bail kah-lee-tay seel voo plai.
Show me some white, but of very good quality, please.

Vendeur: **Désirez-vous aussi des enveloppes?**
day-zee-ray voo oh-see day-zaN-ve-lop?
Do you also want envelopes?

M. Roberts: **C'est ça; et puis donnez-moi de l'encre.**
say sah ay pw̃ee do-nay mwah de laNkr.
That's so; and then give me some ink.

This little girl seems to know how to ask for what she wants at the stationer's—can you? Our artist has helped with many objects. Try making your own list in French before you consult the list which is given on the opposite page.

ARTICLES IN THE STATIONER'S

du papier à lettres	**une enveloppe**	**un cahier**	**un carnet**	**un crayon**
pahp-yay ah laitr	aN-ve-lop	kah-yay	kahr-nay	krai-yoN
note-paper	*envelope*	*exercise-book*	*note-book*	*pencil*

de la mine de plomb	**un porte-plume**	**une plume**	**un stylo**	**de l'encre (f.)**	**un encrier**
meen de ploN	port plẽm	plẽm	stee-loh	aNkr	aN-kryay
pencil refill	*pen-holder*	*pen, nib*	*fountain-pen*	*ink*	*inkstand*

une gomme	**un canif**	**une carte**	**un pèse-lettres**	**une carte postale illustrée**
gom	kah-neef	kahrt	paiz laitr	kahrt pos-tahl ee-lẽs-tray
india-rubber	*pen-knife*	*map*	*letter-scale*	*picture postcard*

une carte de visite	**une règle**	**une étiquette**	**de la cire à cacheter**	**un calendrier**
kahrt de vee-zeet	raigl	ay-tee-kait	see-rah kahsh-tay	kah-laN-dryav
visiting card	*ruler*	*label*	*sealing wax*	*calendar*

Vendeur: De l'encre ordinaire ou à stylo?   **M. Roberts:** De l'encre à stylo,
de laNkr or-dee-nair oo ah stee-loh?   de laNkr ah stee-loh
Ordinary ink or for fountain pen?   *Fountain-pen ink,*

noire, s'il vous plaît.   **Avez-vous des cartes postales illustrées?**
nwahr seel voo plai.   avay-voo day kahrt postahl ee-lẽe-stray?
black, please.   *Have you any picture postcards?*

Vendeur: J'en ai même un grand assortiment.   Je vais vous en
zhaN-nay maim uN graN-tah-sor-tee-maN.   zhe vai voo-zaN
I (of them) have (even) a large selection.   *I'll you (of them)*

montrer.   (Il apporte une grande boîte, la met sur le
mon-tray.   ee-lah-por-tẽn graNd bwaht lah mai sẽr le
show.   (He brings a large box, puts it on the

comptoir et l'ouvre.)   Les voici, monsieur.   Il y a des vues
koN-twahr ay loovr.   lay vwah-see m's-yãy.   eel-yah day vẽe
counter and opens it.)   Here they are, sir.   There are views

de la ville, des portraits des vedettes de l'écran, des
de lah veel day por-trai day ve-dait de lay-kraN day
of the town, portraits of the stars of the screen,

reproductions des grandes peintures qui se trouvent[1]
re-pro-dẽeks-yoN day graNd piN-tẽer kee se troov
reproductions of the great paintings which are to be found

au Louvre.[2]   **M. Roberts: Combien celles-ci?**
oh loovr.   koN-byiN sail see?
in the Louvre.   *How much are these?*

---

[1] Lit.   Find themselves   [2] Famous museum.

Vendeur: **25 francs la pièce, monsieur, mais j'en ai encore**
viN-siN fraN lah pyais m's-y@ÿ mai zhaN-nay aNk-or
25 francs each, sir, but I also have

à 150 francs le paquet.   **M. Roberts: Veuillez m'en faire voir,**
a saN-siN-kaNt fraN le pah-kai.   v@ÿ-yay maN fair vwahr
(at) 150 *francs a packet.*   *Will you show me some,*

s'il vous plaît.   **Vendeur: Avec grand plaisir, monsieur.**
seel voo plai.   ah-vaik graN plai-zeer m's-y@ÿ.
please.   *With great pleasure, sir.*

En voici.   **M. Roberts: Je prends ce paquet-ci.**
aN vwah-see.   zhe praN se pah-kai see.
Here are some.   *I'll take this packet.*

Maintenant j'ai tout ce qu'il me faut.   **Voilà un**
miNt-naN zhay toos-keel me foh.   vwah-lah uN
Now I have all that I need.   *There is a*

AU MUSÉE DU LOUVRE

Une foule enthousiaste entoure la statue de la Vénus de Milo, qui possède la réputation de ressembler, comme aucune autre, à l'idéal de la beauté féminine.

Foule (f.)	**enthousiaste** (adj.)	**entourer**	**posséder**	**ressembler**
Crowd	enthusiastic	to surround	to possess	to resemble

billet de mille francs.
bee-yai de meel fraN.
1,000 *francs note.*

monnaie?
mo-nai?
change?

TO BUY AND TO SELL
acheter—*to buy*

j'achète (ah-shait)
il (elle) achète (ah-shait)
nous achetons (ahsh-toN)
vous achetez (ahsh-tay)
ils (elles) achètent (ah-shait)
Imperfect: j'achetais, etc.
Perfect: j'ai acheté, etc.

vendre—*to sell*

je vends (vaN)
il (elle) vend (vaN)
nous vendons (vaN-doN)
vous vendez (vaN-day)
ils (elles) vendent (vaNd)
Imperfect: je vendais, etc.
Perfect: j'ai vendu, etc.

Note that **acheter**, which has e mute in the middle syllable, takes a grave accent when the next syllable has e mute.

DEAR AND CHEAP
Dear—**cher** (m.), **chère** (f.), are both pronounced **shair.**
Cheap—**bon marché** (boN mahr-shay) literally means *good market.*
Cheaper—**meilleur** (mai-yâyr) **marché**, lit., *better market.*
Cheapest—**le meilleur** (mai-yâyr) **marché**, lit., *the best market.*

Note from the above the irregular Comparative and Superlative of **bon, bonne.**

GOOD, BETTER, BEST

Good:	Better:	Best:
bon	meilleur	le meilleur
bonne	meilleure	la meilleure

THE DEFINITE ARTICLE IN PRICE QUOTATIONS
Ces cartes postales coûtent 100 francs la

Vendeur: Monsieur n'a pas de petite
m's-yây nah pah de p'teet
The gentleman has no small

M. Roberts: Je regrette.
zhe re-grait.
I regret (it).

douzaine—*These postcards cost* 100 *francs a dozen.*
150 francs le paquet.—150 *francs a packet.*
Le beurre coûte 200 francs la livre.—(*The*) *butter costs 200 francs a pound.*
J'ai payé 70 francs le mètre.—*I paid* 70 *francs a metre.*

When giving price quotations, measurements, weights, etc., the definite article (**le, la**) is used in French instead of the indefinite article or "per" as used in English.

AGO
Il y a trois mois—*three months ago.*
Il y a quelques jours—*a few days ago.*
Il y a quinze jours—*a fortnight ago.*

WISHES AND REQUESTS
Je voudrais (voo-drai)—*I should like.*
Voudriez-vous (voo-dryai voo)—*would you like?*
Veuillez (vây-yay)—*would you please, will you be so kind as to?*
je désire (day-zeer)—*I wish, I want to.*
je veux (vây)—*I want, I wish to.*
voulez-vous (voo-lay voo)—*do you want, do you wish to?*

THE FUTURE
I shall be

je serai (se-ray)
il (elle) sera (se-ra)
nous serons (se-roN)
vous serez (se-ray)
ils (elles) seront (se-roN)

I shall speak

je parlerai (pahr-le-ray)
il (elle) parlera (pahr-le-rah)
nous parlerons (pahr-le-roN)
vous parlerez (pahr-le-ray)
ils (elles) parleront (pahr-le-roN)

LA BOURSE DE PARIS

En haut, nous voyons une foule rassemblée sur les
marches de la Bourse, occupée à lire la cote affichée par
les courtiers. En bas, ce qui semble une scène de film
arrangée par un régisseur de génie est une véritable
photographie prise un jour de hausse.

The upper photo-
graph shows a crowd
on the steps of the
Stock Exchange,
busily reading the
quotations on the
stockbrokers' lists.
Below, what looks like
a scene from a film
arranged by a clever
director, is an actual
photograph taken on
a day of boom prices.

I shall have
j'aurai (o-ray)
il (elle) aura (o-rah)
nous aurons (o-roN)
vous aurez (o-ray)
ils (elles) auront (o-roN)

I shall reply
je répondrai (ray-poN-dray)
il (elle) répondra (ray-pon-drah)
nous répondrons (ray-poN-droN)
vous répondrez (ray-poN-dray)
ils (elles) répondront (ray-poN-droN)

The Future is usually formed by putting the endings of the present tense of **avoir** on to the Infinitive: **Je parler-ai** is *I have to speak*, i.e., *I shall speak*, etc.

Note that verbs ending in **re** drop the e before the addition of **ai**, etc., e.g., **je répondrai**—*I shall speak*, **je descendrai**—*I shall go down*, **j'entendrai**—*I shall hear*, etc.

EXERCISES

I

Use (*a*) the Present tense, (*b*) the Imperfect, (*c*) the Perfect, (*d*) the Future of the following verbs after the Pronoun **il**:

1. donner. 2. prendre. 3. mettre. 4. acheter. 5. dire.

II   Translate into English

1. Ce livre-ci est un bon livre, mais ce livre-là est meilleur: c'est le meilleur de tous mes livres. 2. Le printemps est la meilleure saison. 3. Georges est le garçon le plus heureux de la ville. 4. Je me laverai dans la salle de bain. 5. Il sera très fatigué. 6. Seront-ils en retard pour le petit déjeuner? 7. Nous passerons les vacances au bord de la mer. 8. Quand serez-vous en vacances? 9. Elle ne changera pas son argent. 10. Pourquoi ne comptez-vous pas la monnaie? 11. Est-ce qu'ils vendront leur maison? 12. Je voudrais me coucher de bonne heure.

III   Translate into French

1. My cigars are better than your cigarettes. 2. The best tobacco is very dear. 3. French cigarettes are cheaper. 4. They are ten francs each. 5. How much is a packet of 10? 6. He will have to write many letters. 7. Will you change your English bank-notes? 8. I shall not forget to buy a box of matches and some ink. 9. Is there a stationer's near here? 10. We shall go into a public-house, where one can buy some stamps. 11. I would like some picture postcards. 12. Would you like to go with me? (*Key on page* 209.)

AVEZ-VOUS ACHETÉ UN DICTIONNAIRE?

Un dictionnaire peut être très utile pour augmenter votre vocabulaire et vous aider à apprendre à mesure que vous avancez. Vous pouvez y chercher les mots que vous rencontrez dans vos lectures ou que vous entendez à la radio et que vous ne connaissez pas. N'importe quel dictionnaire de poche usuel suffira pour le moment. Cependant, assurez-vous que vous connaissez les noms français des objets de tous les jours avant d'essayer d'apprendre des mots difficiles ou rares.

HAVE YOU BOUGHT A DICTIONARY?

A dictionary can be very useful in adding to your vocabulary, and in assisting you to learn as you go along. In it you can look up any word which you read or hear on the radio and do not know. Any ordinary pocket dictionary will serve for the moment. Make certain, however, that you know the French names for everyday things before you attempt to learn any difficult or unusual words.

AUX HALLES CENTRALES

Après minuit, sous de puissantes lampes électriques, les négociants en produits alimentaires viennent s'approvisionner dans ce fameux marché.

Puissant-e (adj.)   **négociant-e** (m.f.)   **produits** (m.pl.) **alimentaires**   **s'approvisionner**
Powerful   (wholesale) merchant   foodstuffs   to lay in stock

QUINZIÈME LEÇON

M. LESAGE AS HOST

Try to describe in French the above picture, in which Mr. and Mrs. Roberts are seen lunching as M. Lesage's guests. For key, see page 401.

DÉJEUNER AU RESTAURANT

M. et Mme Roberts et M. Lesage sont assis autour d'une table dans un
M. ay Mme ro-bairts ay M. le-sahzh soN-tah-see oh-toor dẽn tahbl daN-zuN
Mr. and Mrs. Roberts and Mr. Lesage are sitting around a table in a

restaurant. C'est l'heure du déjeuner.	**M. Lesage: Garçon, donnez-**
rais-toh-raN. say lãyr dẽ day-zhãy-nay.	gahr-soN do-nay
restaurant. It is lunch-time.	*Waiter, give*
moi la carte, s'il vous plaît.	**Garçon: La voici, monsieur.**
mwah lah kahrt seel-voo plai.	lah vwah-see m's-yãy.
me the menu, please.	*Here it is, sir.*

M. Lesage: Merci.   Qu'est-ce que vous prenez comme hors d'œuvre?   Moi, je
mair-see.   kais-ke voo pre-nay kom or-dãyvr?   mwah zhe
Thanks.   What are you taking as hors d'œuvre?   As for me, I

prendrai du filet de hareng. **M. Roberts: La même chose pour moi.**
praN-dray dẽ fee-lay de ah-raN.   lah maim shohz poor mwah.
will take filleted herring.   *The same (thing) for me.*

Mme Roberts: **Je préfère la salade de tomates.**
zhe pray-fair lah sah-lahd de to-maht.
I prefer (the) tomato-salad.

M. Lesage: **Bien. Garçon, apportez-nous deux filets de hareng**
byiN.   gahr-soN ah-por-tay noo dãy fee-lay de ah-raN
Good.   Waiter, bring us two portions of filleted herring

et une salade de tomates et n'oubliez pas le pain.
ay ẽn sah-lad de to-maht ay noo-blyay pah le piN.
and one tomato-salad and don't forget the bread.

Garçon: **Le pain est sur la table, monsieur.**
le piN ay sẽr lah tahbl m's-yãy.
The bread is on the table, sir.

M. Lesage: **Excusez-moi, je ne l'avais pas vu.**
aik-skẽẽ-zay mwah zhe ne lah-vai pah vẽẽ.
Excuse me, I had not seen it.

Garçon: **Qu'est-ce que vous choisissez comme viande, messieurs, dames?**
kais-ke voo shwah-zee-say kom vyaNd mays'yãy dahm?
What do you choose as meat, gentlemen, ladies?

M. Lesage: **Apportez-moi une escalope.   Comme légumes**
ah-por-tay mwah ẽn ais-kah-lop.   kom lay-gẽẽm
Bring me a collop.[1]   As vegetables

je prendrai des pommes de terre et de la salade verte.
zhe praN-dray day pom de tair ay de lah sah-lahd vairt.
I'll take potatoes and green salad.

Garçon: **C'est entendu.**   **Mme Roberts: Pour moi**
say-taN-taN-dẽẽ.   poor mwah
Very good, sir (lit., this is understood).   *For me*

une tranche de bœuf avec des champignons, s'il vous plaît.
ẽn traNsh de bãyf ah-vaik day shaN-peen-yoN seel voo plait.
(a portion of) roast beef with mushrooms, please.

M. Roberts: **Pouvez-vous recommander votre lapin rôti?**
poo-vay voo re-ko-maN-day votr lah-piN roh-tee?
Can you recommend your roast rabbit?

Garçon: **Je vous le recommande beaucoup, nous le servons**
zhe voo le re-ko-maNd boh-koo noo le sair-voN
I (to you) recommend it very much, we serve it

---

[1] The French word **escalope** is more often used for this thin slice of meat.

PARIS QUI MANGE

En haut, on déguste dans un fameux restaurant des mets de choix et des vins de marque. En bas, des employés de la Halle aux Vins savourent un bon "gueuleton."

Déguster	**mets** (m.)	**vins de marque**	**savourer**	**gueuleton** (m.) (slang)
To taste	viand; (prepared) food	vintage wines	to relish	"blow-out"

CARTE DU JOUR—MENU

HORS D'ŒUVRE[1]

Filet de hareng	**Anchois**	**Maquereaux au vin blanc**	**Beurre**
fee-lai de ah-raN	aN-shwah	mak-roh oh viN blaN	bᾶyr
Filleted herring	*Anchovies*	*Mackerel in white wine*	*Butter*
Huitres	**Paté de lapin**	**Hors d'œuvre variés**	**Saucissons**
ῆeetr	pah-tay de lah-piN	or dᾶyvr vah-ryay	soh-see-soN
Oysters	*Rabbit pie*	*Assorted hors d'œuvre*	*Sausage*

SOUPES

Soupe à l'oignon	**Consommé Julienne**
soop ah lon-yoN	koN-so-may zhᾶel-yain
Onion soup	*Clear vegetable soup*

ENTRÉES

Salade de bœuf	**Veau sauté petits pois**	**Homard mayonnaise**
sah-lahd de bᾶyf	voh soh-tay p'tee pwah	o-mahr mah-yo-naiz
Beef salad	*Stewed veal with peas*	*Lobster with mayonnaise*

Omelette paysanne	**Œufs brouillés aux pointes d'asperge**
om-lait pai-ee-zahn	ᾶy broo-yay oh pwiNt dahs-pairzh
Omelette with chopped vegetables	*Scrambled eggs with asparagus tips*

LÉGUMES—VEGETABLES

Pommes nouvelles au beurre	**Haricots verts à l'huile**	**Asperges**
pom noo-vail oh bᾶyr	ah-ree-koh vair ah lῆeel	ah-spairzh
New potatoes in butter	*French beans in oil*	*Asparagus*
Petits pois au lard	**Chou-fleur au gratin**	**Céleri braisé**
p'tee pwah oh lahr	shoo-flᾶyr oh grah-tiN	sayl-ree brai-zay
Peas in bacon fat	*Cauliflower au gratin*	*Braised celery*

RÔTIS—JOINTS

Noix de veau rôtie	**Faisan rôti**	**Côte de porc sauce piquante**
nwah de voh roh-tee	fai-saN roh-tee	koht de por sohs pee-kaNt
Roast knuckle of veal	*Roast pheasant*	*Rib of pork, piquant sauce*

Aloyau, pommes nouvelles	**Côtelette de mouton aux pommes soufflées**
ah-lwah-yoh pom noo-vail	koht-lait de moo-toN oh pom soof-lay
Sirloin of beef, new potatoes	*Mutton chop, puffed potatoes*

FROMAGES—CHEESE

Crème d'Isigny	**Camembert**	**Roquefort**	**Gruyère**	**Brie**
kraim dee-zeen-yee	kah-maN-bair	rok-for	grᾶe-yair	bree
Creme d'Isigny	*Camembert*	*Roquefort*	*Gruyère*	*Brie*
(Cream cheese)		*(Kind of strong cheese)*		

DESSERTS

Compote de pêches	**Glaces**	**Confitures**	**Fraises**	**Gâteaux**	**Cerises**
koN-pot de paish	glahs	koN-fee-tᾶer	fraiz	gah-toh	se-reez
Stewed peaches	*Ices*	*Jams*	*Strawberries*	*Cakes*	*Cherries*

[1] Usually, but incorrectly, spelt in English **hors d'œuvres**. The French words **hors d'œuvre** (without final **s**) mean "outside the (finished) work," in other words, a side-dish.

Here our artist has done half the work for you, since you can scarcely miss which are lobsters, oysters, salmon, mussels, etc. But there are still others for which you must consult the list below. Use this list as in other lessons, until you feel satisfied that you could order anything you wanted at the fishmonger's.

LE POISSON—FISH

le hareng	le maquereau	la carpe	l'anguille (f.)	l'anchois (m.)	la sardine
ah-raN	mahk-roh	kahrp	aN-geey	aN-shwah	sahr-deen
herring	*mackerel*	*carp*	*eel*	*anchovy*	*sardine*

la truite	l'éperlan	le saumon	la perche	la raie	la barbue
trw̃eet	ay-pair-laN	soh-moN	pairsh	rai	bahr-bw̃
trout	*smelt*	*salmon*	*perch*	*skate*	*brill*

le thon	l'aigrefin (m.)	la morue	la sole	le homard	la langouste	l'huître (f.)
toN	aygr-fiN	mo-rw̃	sohl	o-mahr	laN-goost	w̃eetr
tunny	*haddock*	*cod*	*sole*	*lobster*	*sea crayfish*	*oyster*

la crevette	l'escargot (m.)	la moule	la tortue	le carrelet	les crustacés
kre-vait	ais-kahr-goh	mool	tor-tw̃	kahr-lay	krw̃-stah-say
shrimp	*snail*	*mussel*	*turtle*	*plaice*	*shell fish*

le poisson d'eau douce	le poisson de marée	mariné	étuvé	frit
pwah-soN doh doos	pwah-soN de mah-ray	mah-ree-nay	ay-tw̃-vay	free
fresh-water fish	*salt-water fish*	*pickled, soused*	*stewed*	*fried*

au four	à la brochette	grillé	au bleu	en coquille	aux câpres
oh foor	ah lah bro-shait	gree-yay	oh blw̃	aN ko-keey	oh kahpr
baked	*broiled*	*grilled*	*cooked in wine*	*served in shell*	*with caper sauce*

bonne femme	Colbert	maître d'hôtel	friture (f.)
bon fahm	kol-bair	maitr doh-tail	free-tw̃r
with bitter sauce	*with white sauce*	*done in butter*	*dish of small fried fish*

FRC—F*

au vin blanc, c'est délicieux, monsieur.
oh viN blaN say day-lees-yây m's-yây.
with white wine, it is delicious, sir.

M. Roberts: Bon, j'ai confiance en vous.   **Garçon:** Qu'est-ce que vous
boN zhay koN-fyaNs aN voo.   kais-ke voo
Good, I have confidence in you.   *What do you*

prenez comme légumes, monsieur?
pre-nay kom lay-gêm m's-yây?
take as vegetables, sir?

M. Roberts: Des petits pois, s'il vous plaît.   **Garçon:** Comme vin je
day p'tee pwah seel voo plai.   kom viN zhe
Peas, if you please.   *As (a) wine I*

vous recommande surtout notre Bordeaux rouge.
voo re-ko-maNd sêr-too notr bor-doh roozh.
recommend you especially our red Bordeaux.

Il est exquis.   **M. Lesage:** Non, apportez-nous plutôt
ee-lay-taik-skee.   noN ah-por-tay noo plêê-toh
It is exquisite.   *No, bring us rather*

une demi-bouteille de Montrachet avec les
êen de-mee-boo-taiy de moN- rah-shay ah-vaik lay
a half-bottle of Montrachet with the

hors-d'œuvre et une bonne bouteille de Bourgogne rouge
or-dâyvr ay êen bon boo-taiy de boor-gony roozh
hors-d'œuvres and a good bottle of red Burgundy

avec le rôti.   **Garçon:** Bien, monsieur, et qu'est-ce que
ah-vaik le roh-tee.   byiN m's-yây ay kais-ke
with the (roast) meat.   *All right, sir, and what*

vous prenez comme dessert?   **M. Lesage:** Du fromage et des
voo pre-nay kom dai-sair?   dêê fro-mahzh ay day
will you take as dessert?   *Cheese and*

fruits pour moi.   **Mme Roberts:** La même chose pour nous.
frŵee pour mwah.   lah maim shohz poor noo.
fruit for me.   *The same (thing) for us.*

Garçon: Je vais vous servir tout de suite, messieurs, dames.
zhe vai voo sair-veer tood-sŵeet mays-yây dahm.
I am going to serve you at once, gentlemen, ladies.

Mme Roberts: C'est un coquet petit restaurant.
say-tuN ko-kai p'tee rais-toh-raN.
It is a charming little restaurant.

M. Lesage: Un de mes amis me l'a recommandé; il semble qu'on y
uN de may-zah-mee me lah re-ko-maN-day eel saNbl koN-nee
One of my friends has recommended it to me; it seems that one (here)

mange bien et pas cher.
maNzh byiN ay pah shair.
eats well and not expensively.

LÉGUMES (m.pl.)—VEGETABLES

les petits pois	les haricots	haricots verts	la tomate	le concombre	l'asperge (f.)
p'tee pwah	ah-ree-koh	ah-ree-koh vair	to-maht	koN-koNbr	ahs-pairzh
green peas	*beans*	*French beans*	*tomato*	*cucumber*	*asparagus*

le radis	la carotte	le raifort	le poireau	l'oignon	le céleri	l'épinard
rah-dee	kah-rot	rai-for	pwah-roh	on-yoN	sayl-ree	ay-pee-nahr
radish	*carrot*	*horse-radish*	*leek*	*onion*	*celery*	*spinach*

le chou	le chou de Bruxelles	le chou-fleur	la laitue	la pomme de terre	la betterave
shoo	shoo de br@k-sail	shoo-fl@yr	lai-t@	pom de tair	bait-rahv
cabbage	*Brussels sprouts*	*cauliflower*	*lettuce*	*potato*	*beetroot*

le cresson	le navet	la courge	la chicorée	l'artichaut (m.)	la citrouille, le potiron
krai-soN	nah-vai	koorzh	shee-koh-ray	ahr-tee-shoh	see-trooy po-tee-roN
watercress	*turnip*	*marrow*	*endive*	*artichoke*	*pumpkin*

Certain popular vegetables are here clearly shown—but supposing you wanted a lettuce, cress, beetroot and radishes for a salad? Consult the list above, then cover it over and practise making in French your own lists of the things shown on these greengrocers' stalls.

M. Roberts: **Est-ce que l'avenue des Champs-Élysées est loin d'ici?**
ais-ke lah-ve-nê͡e day shaN-zay-lee-zay ay lwiN dee-see?
Is the avenue des Champs Elysees far from here?

M. Lesage: **Non, nous sommes tout près des Champs-Élysées.   Avez-vous**
noN noo som too prai day shaN-zay-lee-zay.   ah-vay voo
No, we are quite near the Champs Elysees.   Have you

l'intention d'y aller après le repas?
liN-taNs-yoN dee ah-lay ah-prai le re-pah?
the intention to go there after the meal?

Mme Roberts: Je voudrais tant prendre une tasse de café à
zhe voo-drai taN praNdr ê͡en tahs de kah-fay ah
I should like so much to have a cup of coffee at

la Hungaria après le déjeuner.   On
lah uN-gahr-yah ah-prai le day-zhâ͡y-nay.   oN
the Hungaria after (the) lunch.   One

m'a dit qu'il y a là un bon orchestre hongrois avec
mah dee kee-lyah lah uN boN-nor-kaistr oN-grwah ah-vaik
has told me that there is a good Hungarian band with

des chanteurs tziganes.   **M. Lesage: J'ai une course à**
day shaN-tâ͡yr tsee-gahn.   zhay ê͡en koors ah
gipsy singers.   *I have an errand to*

faire, mais je veux bien vous accompagner jusqu'à la
fair mai zhe vâ͡y byiN voo-zah-koN-pahn-yay zhê͡es-kah lah
do, but I should like very much to accompany you to the

Hungaria.   Si vous pouvez m'attendre, je vous y
uN-gahr-yah.   see voo poo-vay mah-taNdr zhe voo-zee
Hungaria.   If you can wait for me, I shall

rejoindrai vers quatre heures et demie.
re-zhwiN-dray vair kaht-râ͡yr ay de-mee.
rejoin you there towards half-past four.

Mme Roberts: Bien sûr, nous vous attendrons.   Nous n'avons
byiN sê͡er noo voo-zah-taN-droN.   noo nah-voN
Certainly, we shall wait for you.   We have

rien à faire de tout l'après-midi.   Voilà le
ryiN-nah fair de too lahp-rai mee-dee.   vwah-lah le
nothing to do the whole afternoon.   Here comes the

garçon qui arrive.   **Garçon: Veuillez m'excuser,**
gahr-soN kee ah-reev.   vâ͡y-yay maik-skê͡e-zay
waiter.   *Will you excuse me,*

LE JOUEUR D'ACCORDÉON

Par cette belle après-midi d'automne les passants sont rares, mais c'est peut-être l'art pour l'art qui retient ce musicien à son poste sur le quai.

Accordéon (m.)	**passant-e** (m.f.)	**l'art pour l'art**	**quai** (m.)
Melodeon, concertina	passer-by	art for art's sake	embankment

madame, il n'y a plus de tomates.   **Mon collègue vient**
mah-dahm eel nyah plẽ de to-maht.   moN ko-laig vyiN
madam, there are no more tomatoes.   *My colleague has*

de servir¹ les dernières.
de sair-veer lay dairn-yair.
just served the last.

Mme Roberts: **C'est dommage.** **Alors apportez-moi des sardines.** **Il y en a**
say do-mahzh.   ah-lor ah-por-tay mwah day sahr-deen. eel yaN nah
That's a pity.   *Then bring me some sardines.*   *There are some*

encore, j'espère?
aN-kor zhais-pair?
left, I hope?

Garçon: **Sans aucun doute, madame.** **Je vous les servirai tout de suite.**
saN-zoh-kuN doot mah-dahm.   zhe voo lay sair-vee-ray tood-swẽet.
Without any doubt, madam.   *I shall serve them to you at once.*

M. Lesage: **Ne nous faites pas trop attendre, je vous prie.**
ne noo fait pah troh pah-taNdr zhe voo pree
Don't let us wait too much, I beg you.

Garçon: **Il y a tant de monde aujourd'hui, mais je ferai mon**
ell-yah taN de moNd oh-zhoor-dŵee mai zhe fe-ray moN
There are so many people today, but I shall do all

possible, monsieur. **(Il s'éloigne.)**
po-seebl m's-yãy.   eel say-lwahny.
I can, sir. *(He goes off.)*

M. Lesage: **Pas de tomates!** **Enfin, c'est vrai, il y a beaucoup de**
pah de to-maht!   aN-fiN say vrai eel-yah boh-koo de
No tomatoes!   *After all, it's true there are lots of*

monde, soyons indulgents. **Garçon: Voilà les filets de**
moNd swah-yoN-ziN-dẽel-zhaN.   vwahl-ah lay fee-lai de
people, let's be tolerant. *Here are the fillets of*

hareng et les sardines. **Je vous apporte en même temps**
ah-raN ay lay sahr-deen.   zhe voo-zah-port aN maim taN
herring and the sardines. *I bring you at the same time*

votre Montrachet. **La viande et les légumes vont suivre dans**
votr moN- rah-shay.   lah vyaNd ay lay lay-gẽm voN sŵeevr daN
your Montrachet.   *The meat and the vegetables will follow in*

¹ Lit. comes from serving.

un instant.   **M. Lesage: Bien. (Il lève son verre.)   À votre**
zuN-niN-staN.   byiN.   eel laiv soN vair.   ah votɪ
a moment.   *Good.   (He raises his glass.)   You*

santé. (Tout le monde boit.)   Je voulais vous faire
saN-tay.   too le moNd bwah.   zhe voo-lai voo fair
health.   (They all drink.)   I wanted to let you

goûter de ce Montrachet, l'un de nos vins blancs bien
goo-tay de ce moN- rah-shay luN de noh viN blaN byiN
taste this Montrachet, one of our white wines far

trop peu connu à l'étranger.
troh pö kon-nö ah lay-traN-zhay.
too little known abroad.

M. Roberts: **Il est délicieux.   Je vous en suis vraiment**
eel ay day-lees-yö.   zhe voo-zaN sẅee vrai-maN
It is delicious.   I am really grateful to you

reconnaissant.   **M. Lesage (un peu plus tard): La cuisine**
rek-on-nai-saN.   uN pö plö tahr: lah kẅee-zeen
for (introducing me to) it.   *(a little later): The cooking*

DANS UN VIGNOBLE DE BEAUNE

Les grappes de raisins tombent dans les paniers. Les vignerons auront tôt fait d'achever
la vendange. Votre verre de Bourgogne est assuré!

Vignoble (m.)	**grappe (f.)**	**vigneron (m.)**	**avoir tôt fait de**	**vendange (f.)**
Vineyard	bunch	vine-grower	not to be long in (doing)	wine-harvest

n'est pas mauvaise, pas mauvaise du tout, n'est-ce pas?
nay pah mo-vaiz pah mo-vaiz dẽ too nais pah?
is not bad, not bad at all, isn't it so?

M. Roberts: **Quant à moi, je suis très content.**
kaN-tah mwah zhe sŵee trai koN-taN.
As for me, I am very pleased.

Garçon: **Voilà le fromage et le dessert.**
vwah-lah le fro-mahzh ay le dai-sair.
Here is the cheese and the dessert.

M. Lesage: **Je vous remercie.   Vous nous servez vraiment vite.**
zhe voo re-mair-see.   voo noo sair-vay vrai-maN veet.
I thank you.   You serve us really quickly.

Maintenant apportez l'addition, s'il vous plaît.
miNt-naN ah-por-tay lah-dees-yoN seel voo plai.
Now, bring the bill, please.

Garçon: **Bien, monsieur.**
byiN m's-yãy.
Good, sir.

M. Lesage (s'adressant à un vendeur de
sah-drai-saN ah uN vaN-dãyr de
(addressing himself to a

journaux qui passe): Donnez-moi Paris-Midi!
zhoor-noh kee pahs do-nay mwah pah-ree mee-dee!
newspaper seller who passes) Give me Paris-Midi!

M. Roberts: **Il y a du nouveau?**
eel yah dẽ noo-voh?
Is there any news?

M. Lesage: **Rien d'extraordinaire.**
ryiN daik-strah-or-dee-nair.
Nothing extraordinary.

Tiens!   On a arrêté le
tyiN!   oN-nah ah-rai-tay le
I say! One has (they have) arrested the

meurtrier de la rue de Clichy.
mãyr-tryay de lah rẽ de klee-shee.
rue de Clichy murderer.

Mme Roberts: **Vous lisez les histoires de meurtres?**
voo lee-zay lay-zees-twahr de mãyrtr?
You read (the) stories of murders?

M. Lesage: C'est un cas extraordinaire, vous n'en avez pas
say-tuN kah aik-strah-or-dee-nair voo naN-nah-vay pah-
It is an extraordinary case, you haven't heard

entendu parler? Mais tout Paris en parle. C'était
zaN-taN-dæ pahr-lay? mai too pah-ree aN pahrl. say-tai
speak of it? But all Paris is speaking of it. It was

il y a deux ou trois jours . . .
eel yah dæy-zoo trwah zhoor
two or three days ago . . .

Garçon: Voilà l'addition, messieurs.
vwah-lah lah-dees-yoN mays-yæy.
Here is the bill, gentlemen.

M. Lesage: Je vais régler ça. Voilà, gardez le reste!
zhe vai rayg-lay sah vwah-lah gahr-day le raist!
I am going to settle this. Here you are, keep the rest!

DANS UNE RÔTISSERIE PARISIENNE
Devant soi, en plein restaurant, on voit tourner à la broche le poulet qu'on a choisi
pour déjeuner. C'est avec difficulté qu'on réprime son impatience.

En plein restaurant	tourner à la broche	rôtisserie (f.)	réprimer
Right in the restaurant	to turn on the spit	grill-room	to repress

Mme Roberts: **Alors nous pouvons partir.**
ah-lor noo poo-voN pahr-teer.
Now we can go.

M. Lesage: **Je vous raconterai l'histoire du meurtre en route.**
zhe voo rah-koN-tray lees-twahr d@@ m@yrtr aN root.
I will tell you the story of the murder on the way.

C'est vraiment sensationnel.   Quelle chance qu'on ait
say vrai-maN saN-sah-syon-ail.   kail shaNs koN-nai
It is really sensational.   What luck that one has

pu arrêter le meurtrier si vite.   Elle travaille
p@@ ah-rai-tay le m@yr-tryay see veet.   ail trah-vah*y*
been able to arrest the murderer so quickly.   It works

bien, la police, il faut l'avouer.   Mais je veux
byiN lah po-lees eel foh lah-voo-ay.   mai zhe v@y
well, the police, one has to admit it.   But I want

commencer par le commencement.   Alors c'était . . .
ko-maN-say pahr le ko-maNs-maN.   ah-lor say-tai
to start with the beginning.   Well, there was . . .

(Ils quittent le restaurant.   Dans la rue M. Lesage continue
eel keet le rais-toh-raN.   daN lah r@@ m's-y@y le-sahzh koN-tee-n@@
(They leave the restaurant.   In the street Mr. Lesage continues

à raconter l'histoire étrange du meurtre de la rue de Clichy.)
ah rah-koN-tay lees-twahr ay-traNzh d@@ m@yrtr de lah r@@ de klee-shee.
to tell the strange story of the murder in the rue de Clichy.)

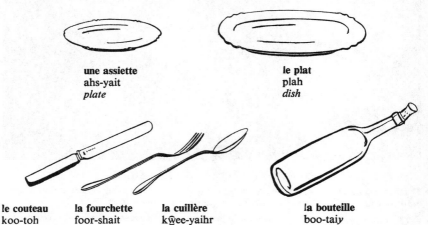

une assiette   le plat
ahs-yait   plah
plate   *dish*

le couteau   la fourchette   la cuillère   la bouteille
koo-toh   foor-shait   k@ee-yaihr   boo-tai*y*
knife   *fork*   *spoon*   *bottle*

LA VIANDE—MEAT
LE GIBIER—GAME
LA VOLAILLE—POULTRY

le bœuf	le veau	le porc	le mouton	l'agneau (m.)	le lapin	le lièvre	la bécasse
bäyf	voh	por	moo-toN	ahn-yoh	lah-piN	lyaivr	bay-kahs
ox	*calf*	*pig*	*mutton*	*lamb*	*rabbit*	*hare*	*woodcock*

la caille	la perdrix	le faisan	le coq de bruyère	le pluvier
kahy	pair-dree	fai-zaN	kok de brêê-yair	plêêv-yay
quail	*partridge*	*pheasant*	*grouse*	*plover*

le poulet	le canard	l'oie	la dinde	le dindon	la pintade	le chevreuil
poo-lai	kah-nahr	wah	diNd	diN-doN	piN-tahd	shev-rãy-y
chicken	*duck*	*goose*	*turkey (hen)*	*turkey (cock)*	*guinea-fowl*	*roe-buck*

du bœuf—*beef*
du veau—*veal*
du porc—*pork*
de la viande de bœuf—*beef*
de la viande de veau—*veal*
de la viande de porc—*pork*
du rôti de bœuf—*roast beef*
du rôti de veau—*roast veal*
du rôti de porc—*roast pork*
l'aile (f.)—*wing (of poultry)*
le bifteck (beef-taik)—*beefsteak*
au pot (oh poh)—*boiled*
en ragoût—*stewed*
en daube—*braised*
bouilli (boo-yee)—*boiled*
grillade (gree-yahd)—*grilled*
sur le gril—*grilled*
à la casserole—*stewed in stewpan*
au four—*baked*
hachis—*minced*
le rognon (ron-yoN)—*kidney*
le foie—*liver*
la langue (laNg)—*tongue*
le pied (pyay)—*foot*
la cervelle—*brain*
le collet (co-lai)—*neck*
la côte—*rib*
la côtelette—*chop, cutlet*
le dos (doh)—*saddle*
la tête—*head*

la poitrine (pwaht-reen)—*breast*
le gigot—*leg of mutton*
la cuisse—*leg of game or poultry*
le cuissot—*leg of venison*
le ris (ree)—*sweetbread*
farci—*stuffed*
le jambon (zhaN-boN)—*ham*
la saucisse (soh-sees)—*sausage*
le saucisson—*large sausage eaten cold*
le lard (lahr)—*bacon*
andouille (aN-dooy)—*sausage of tripe*
blanquette—*stew in thick white sauce*
bouchée (boo-shay)—*pie or patty*
le boudin—*black pudding*
bourguignon—*with carrots and onions*
châteaubriant—*fillet of steak with fried potatoes*
cocotte—*cooked with bacon in casserole*
cœur de filet—*tender loin steak*
escalope (f.)—*thin slice of meat*
financière—*with mushrooms and truffles in Madeira wine*
jardinière—*with mixed vegetables*
maître d'hôtel—*done in butter*
velouté de—*creamed or pulped*
pot-au-feu—*boiled beef and broth*
civet de—*jugged*
fricandeau—*stew of larded meat*
vol-au-vent—*raised pie filled with goose liver, kidneys, mushrooms, &c.*

FOR STUDENTS TO REMEMBER!

Le commencement est la moitié de tout.
Well begun is half done.

L'oisiveté est la mère de tous les vices.
Idleness is the root of all evil.

MANGER=TO EAT; BOIRE=TO DRINK

Present Tense

(See Lesson 8, page 100)

Imperfect

je mangeais (maN-zhai)

il
elle } mangeait (maN-zhai)

nous mangions (maN-zhyoN)
vous mangiez (maN-zhyay)

ils
elles } mangeaient (maN-zhai)

je buvais (bẽ-vai)

il
elle } buvait (bẽ-vai)

nous buvions (bẽv-yoN)
vous buviez (bẽv-yay)

ils
elles } buvaient (bẽ-vai)

Future

je mangerai (maNzh-ray), etc.
je boirai (bwah-ray), etc.

Perfect

j'ai mangé (maN-zhay)
j'ai bu (bẽ), etc.

Nous mangeons (maN-zhoN) la soupe avec une cuillère. Nous mangeons la viande avec une fourchette. Nous coupons la viande avec un couteau.

Nous buvons le vin dans un verre. Nous buvons le thé dans une tasse. On apporte la viande sur un plat, mais nous la mangeons dans une assiette.

Note.—The g in **manger** is soft (pronounced like the s in "pleasure"). g is always soft before **e** and **i**, otherwise it is hard (as in "go").

Now, in order to indicate that the g remains soft when used in connection with **nous** an e is inserted before the ending **ons**. The same is done in the Imperfect. Notice that this extra e is not pronounced.

HIM, HER, THEM

Connaissez-vous M. Lesage? Je le connais.
Do you know Mr. Lesage?   I know him.

Je ne le connais pas.
I don't know him.
Prenez-vous ce billet? Je le prends.
Do you take this ticket?   I take it.
Je ne le prends pas.
I don't take it.
Connaissez-vous Mme Lesage?   Je la connais.
Do you know Mrs. Lesage?   I know her.
Je ne la connais pas.
I don't know her.
Prenez-vous cette boîte?   Je la prends.
Do you take that box?   I take it.
Je ne les prends pas.
I don't take them.
Connaissez-vous les Lesage? Je les connais.
Do you know the Lesages?   I know them.
Je ne les connais pas.
I don't know them.
Prenez-vous ces billets (boîtes)?
Do you take these tickets (boxes)?
Je les prends.
I take them.
Je ne les prends pas.
I don't take them.
Voici le garçon. Appelez-le.
Here is the waiter. Call him.
Voici le billet. Prenez-le.
Here is the ticket. Take it.
Ne le prenez pas.
Don't take it.
Voici la serveuse. Appelez-la.
Here is the waitress. Call her.
Ne l'appelez pas. Voici la boîte.
Don't call her. Here is the box.
Prenez-la. Ne la prenez pas.
Take it. Don't take it.
Voici les billets (boîtes).
Here are the tickets (boxes).
Prenez-les. Ne les prenez pas.
Take them. Don't take them.

When we are constantly referring to a certain person we do not consider it necessary to repeat his (or her) name over and over again: we refer to him as "he", to her as "she", to a thing as "it", to several persons or things as "they". Words like "he", "she", "it", "they", "them", etc., which are used instead of nouns are called Pronouns. "I", "he", "she", and "they", are used as subjects of sentences;

"me", "him", "her", and "them", are used as objects. "It", "you", can be used either as subjects or objects, e.g. "it is beautiful" ("it" is the subject of the sentence); "can you see it?" (here "it" is the object, "you" the subject); "I like you" ("I" is the subject, "you" the object). Careful study of the above examples will show you that in French: 1. Le is used both for "him" and for "it" (when the object is masculine). 2. La is used both for "her" and for "it" (when the object is feminine). 3. Les is used for "them".

With regard to the order of words in the sentence note that:

1. Pronouns, when objects, are placed before the verb instead of after it as in English.

2. When the verb expresses a command, i.e., when it is in the Imperative Affirmative, the Pronoun Object is placed after the verb and joined on to it by a hyphen.

3. If the Imperative is negative (i.e., begins with Don't) pronoun objects are placed before the verb.

Prenez-le but **ne le prenez pas.**
Voyons-les but **ne les voyons pas.**
Écoutez-nous but **ne nous écoutez pas.**

Note from the last example that there is no difference in French between "we" and "us", both forms rendered by **nous**.

ME

Est-ce qu'il vous connaît? Does he know you?
Il me connaît. He knows me.
Il ne me connaît pas. He does not know me.
Écoutez-moi. Listen to me.
Attendez-moi. Wait for me.
Ne m'attendez pas. Don't wait for me.

Note.—1. When me is to be placed after the verb in the Imperative it becomes **moi** (mwah). 2. me, le, la, become **m', l', l',** before a vowel or mute h.

IT

1. **Voici le vin. Il est bon.**
   Here is the wine. It is good.
2. **Je le prends.** I take it.
3. **Voici la bière. Elle est bonne.**
   Here is the beer. It is good.
4. **Je la prends.** I take it.

In these four lines we have the four equivalents for English "it".

1. In the first line the "it" in "it is good" must be translated by **il**, because "it" is the subject and replaces a masculine noun.

2. In the second line "it" must be translated by **le**, because it is the object, replacing a masculine noun.

3. In the third line "it" is the subject, replacing a feminine noun.

4. In the fourth line "it" is the object, replacing a feminine noun.

IL ("he" or "it") replaces any masculine noun, if the subject.

ELLE ("she" or "it") replaces any feminine noun, if the subject.

LE ("him" or "it") replaces any masculine noun, if the object.

LA ("her" or "it") replaces any feminine noun, if the object.

SUMMARY
(Sentence building)

je (ne)	le la les	regarde donne prends connais mange	(pas)
il elle (ne)	le la les	regarde donne prend connaît mange	(pas)
vous (ne)	le la les	regardez donnez prenez connaissez mangez	(pas)
ils elles (ne)	le la les	regardent donnent prennent connaissent mangent	(pas)

EXERCISES

I Replace the words in bold type by Pronouns

1. **Charles** n'écoute pas le **professeur**.
2. Les enfants regardent **les belles fleurs**.

3. Nous allons voir **nos parents.** 4. Elle met **la main** sur sa bouche. 5. Il ne mange pas **les légumes.** 6. Aimez-vous **la bière?** 7. Il ne trouve pas **ses livres.** 8. Elle attend **son oncle.** 9. **Les enfants** ne ferment pas **la porte.** 10. **Le professeur** prend-t-il **la boîte?**

II Translate into French

1. Are you taking (the) salad? Yes, I am taking it. 2. Is she taking herring? She is not taking it. 3. Does the teacher open the window? No, he does not open it. 4. They eat meat, vegetables and fruit. 5. I don't eat fish. 6. I like to eat strawberries. 7. Do you like to eat cherries? 8. Do you put sugar in your (the) coffee? 9. I put three lumps in my coffee. 10. The waiter has not brought us the wine. 11. The cheese is very good; I recommend it.

12. I cannot accompany them. 13. Wait for me. 14. Don't wait for me. 15. Wait for her. 16. Don't wait for her.

III Answer in French

1. Y a-t-il quelque chose sur la table de votre salle à manger? 2. Mangez-vous beaucoup de pain? 3. Buvez-vous du vin? 4. Mangez-vous des fruits? 5. Mettez-vous du lait dans le café? 6. Buvez-vous du café noir? 7. Avec quoi mangez-vous la soupe? 8. Avec quoi coupons-nous la viande? 9. Aimez-vous manger du fromage? 10. Aimez-vous boire de la bière? 11. Aimez-vous lire les histoires de meurtre? 12. M. Lesage, qu'est-ce qu'il prend comme dessert? 13. M. et Mme Roberts, où vont-ils après le déjeuner? 14. Qui les accompagne? 15. Quand M. Lesage les rejoindra-t-il? (*Key on pp.* 209 *and* 210).

SOUS LES PONTS DE PARIS

Même le voisinage menaçant de la Sûreté qu'on entrevoit à travers le crépuscule ne suffit plus à émouvoir ces pauvres loques humaines.

Voisinage (m.) Neighbourhood   **Sûreté** (f.) French C.I.D.   **crépuscule** (m.) twilight   **loques** (f.) **humaines** human wreckage

SEIZIÈME LEÇON

From the text below and the list on the next page, you can learn how to buy all you want at the fruiterer's. Try afterwards to make specimen lists in French on your own.

AT THE FRUITERER'S, THE BUTCHER'S AND THE BAKER'S

Mme Lesage a invité ses parents pour un grand dîner de famille
mah-dahm le-sahzh ah iN-vee-tay say pah-raN poo-ruN graN dee-nay de fah-meey
Mrs. Lesage has invited her relations to a great family dinner

et est en train de faire les achats nécessaires chez quelques
ay ay-taN triN de fair lay-zah-shah nay-sai-sair shay kail-ke
and is about to make the necessary purchases at some

marchands de son quartier.   Elle entre d'abord dans une
mahr-shaN de soN kahr-tyay.   ail aNtr dah-bor daN-zeen
shopkeepers of her district.   She enters first into a

boutique de fruits et de primeurs.
boo-teek de frwee ay de pree-meer.
shop of fruit and early vegetables.

Le fruitier: Bonjour, madame; vous désirez, madame?
bon-zhoor mah-dahm voo day-zee-ray mah-dahm?
Good morning, madam; what would you like, madam?

Mme L.:   **Donnez-moi une douzaine de bananes, s'il vous plaît,**
do-nay mwah ên doo-zain de bah-nahn seel voo plai
Give me a dozen bananas, please,

mais de la meilleure qualité.   Ensuite vous pouvez me donner
mai de lah mai-yâyr kah-lee-tay.   aN-swêet voo poo-vay me do-nay
but of the best quality.   Then you can give me

une livre de cerises anglaises.   Je ne
ên leevr de se-reez aN-glaiz.   zhe ne
a pound of English cherries.   I don't

les aime pas personnellement, seulement j'ai des
lay-zaim pah pair-so-nail-maN sâyl-maN zhay day-
like them personally, only I have

invités anglais à dîner.
ziN-vee-tai-zaN-glai ah dee-nay.
English guests for dinner.

Fruitier: **Goûtez-les, madame, elles sont excellentes.**
goo-tay lay mah-dahm ail soN-taik-sai-laNt.
Taste them, madam, they are excellent.

Mme L.:   **Non, merci, pour moi je préfère les cerises sucrées.**
noN mair-see poor mwah zhe pray-fair lay se-reez sêk-ray.
No, thank you, as for me, I prefer the sweet cherries.

Fruitier: **C'est tout ce que vous désirez, madame?**
say toos ke voo day-zee-ray mah-dahm?
That is all that you want, madam?

Regardez les belles pêches.   Ne voulez-vous pas
re-gahr-day lay bail paish.   ne voo-lay voo pah-
Have a look at the beautiful peaches.   Wouldn't you like

FRUIT

la banane	l'abricot	la pêche	la prune	la figue	la datte	le melon
bah-nahn	ahb-ree-koh	paish	prên	feeg	daht	me-loN
banana	*apricot*	*peach*	*plum*	*fig*	*date*	*melon*

l'orange (f.)	le citron	la mandarine	la groseille	la groseille à maquereau
oh-raNzh	see-troN	maN-dah-reen	gro-zaiy	gro-zaiy ah mah-kroh
orange	*lemon*	*tangerine*	*red currant*	*gooseberry*

le cassis	l'amande (f.)	la noix	la noisette	la noix d'Amérique
kah-sees	ah-maNd	nwah	nwah-zait	nwah dah-may-reek
black currant	*almond*	*walnut*	*hazel-nut*	*Brazil nut*

la châtaigne	le coing	la framboise	le raisin	la pomme	la poire
shah-tainy	kwiN	fraN-bwahz	rai-ziN	pom	pwahr
chestnut	*quince*	*raspberry*	*grape*	*apple*	*pear*

en prendre une livre?
zaN praNdr ẽn leevr?
to have a pound of them?

Mme Lesage: **Donnez-moi plutôt**
do-nay mwah plẽe-toh
Give me rather

un kilo d'abricots.
uN kee-loh dahb-ree-koh.
a kilo of apricots.

Fruitier: **Voilà, madame.**
vwah-lah mah-dahm.
Here you are, madam.

Mme Lesage: **Combien vous dois-je?**
koN-byiN voo dwah zhe?
How much do I owe you?

Fruitier: **Ça vous fait 360 francs, madame.**
sah voo fai trwah saN swah-saNt fraN mah-dahm.
That makes 360 francs, madam.

Mme Lesage: **Voilà quatre cents francs, donnez-moi une livre de reines-Claude**
vwah-lah kahtr saN fraN do-nay mwah ẽn leevr de rain klohd
Here is four hundred francs, give me a pound of greengages

pour faire un compte juste.
poor fair uN koNt zhẽest.
to make up the difference.

Mme Lesage quitte la boutique et se rend chez le boucher.   Elle regarde
mah-dahm le-sahzh keet la boo-teek ay se raN shay le boo-shay.   ail re-gahrd
Mrs. Lesage leaves the shop and goes to the butcher's.   She looks at

l'étalage et examine le prix.   Puis elle entre dans la boucherie
lay-tah-lahzh ay eg-zah-meen lay pree.   pw̃ee ail aNtr daN lah boo-shree
the shop-window and considers the prices.   Then she enters into the butcher's

et s'adresse à un garçon boucher.
ay sah-drais ah uN gahr-soN boo-shay
and addresses an assistant.

Mme L.:   **Bonjour, monsieur!   Je ne suis pas contente de vous.**
boN-zhoor m's-ỹaỹ zhe ne sw̃ee pah koN-taNt de voo.
Good morning.   I am not satisfied with you.

Les biftecks que vous m'avez vendus l'autre jour étaient
lay beef-taik ke voo mah-vay vaN-dẽe lohtr zhoor ay-tai
The beefsteaks which you sold me the other day were

tellement durs qu'il était impossible de les manger.
tail-maN dẽer kee-lay-tai-tiN-po-seebl de lay maN-zhay.
so tough that it was impossible to eat them.

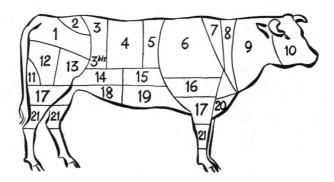

LE BŒUF

1. **la culotte** kẽẽ-lot
2. **le romsteck** rom-staik
3. **l'aloyau** (m.) ah-lwah-yoh
3 *bis.* **le filet** fee-lay
4. **le faux filet** foh fee-lay
5. **côtes** (f.pl.) koht
6. **les entrecôtes** aNtr-koht
7. **la surlonge** sẽẽr-loNzh
8. **le talon de collier** tah-loN de kol-yay
9. **le collier** kol-yay
10. **la tête** tait
11. **le quasi** kah-zee

12. **le gîte à la noix** zhee-tah lah nwah
13. **la tranche grasse** traNsh grahs
14. **la bavette d'aloyau** bah-vait dah-lwah-yoh
15. **les plates côtes** (f.) plaht koht
16. **la boîte à moelle** bwaht ah mwail
17. **le gîte** zheet
18. **le flanchet** flaN-shai
19. ⎱
20. ⎰ **la poitrine** pwaht-reen
21. **la crosse** kros

LE VEAU

1. **le quasi** kah-zee
2. **le filet** fee-lai
2 *bis.* **la panse** paNs
3. **le carré** kah-ray
4. **le collet** ko-lai
5. **la tête** tait

6. **le cuisseau** kw̃ee-soh
7. **le tendron** taN-droN
8. **l'épaule** (f.) ay-pol
9. **la poitrine** pwaht-reen
10. **le jarret** zhah-rai

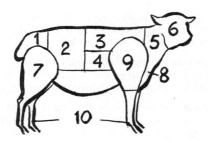

LE MOUTON

1. **la selle**   sail
2. **le filet**   fee-lai
3. **le carré**   kah-ray
4. **le haut de côtelettes**   oh de koht-lait
5. **le collet**   ko-lai

6. **la tête**   tait
7. **le gigot**   zhee-goh
8. **la poitrine**   pwaht-reen
9. **l'épaule** (f.)   ay-pol
10. **les pieds** (m. pl.)   pyay

LE PORC

1. **le jambon**   zhaN-boN
2. **le lard gras**   lahr grah
2 *bis*. **le filet**   fee-lai
3. **les côtes** (f. pl.)   koht
4. **la tête**   tait

5. **le ventre (la poitrine)** vaNtr (pwaht-reen)
6. **l'épaule** (f.)   ay-pol
7. **le jambonneau**   zhaN-bo-noh
8. **les pieds** (m. pl.)   pyay

ENGLISH EXPLANATION OF DIAGRAMS
(In certain cases there are no equivalent cuts)

Beef: 1. Buttock. 2. Rump-steak. 3. Sirloin. 3a. Fillet (undercut). 4. Fore-rib. 5. Ribs. 6. Roasting ribs. 7. No equivalent. 8. Clod. 9. Neck. 10. Head. 11. Chump-end. 12. Silverside. 13. Round (top-rump). 14. Top of sirloin. 15. Top ribs. 16. Stewing steak. 17. Leg of beef. 18. Flank. 19/20. Brisket. 21. Knuckle.

Veal: 1. Chump-end. 2. Fillet. 2a. Belly. 3. Loin. 4. Neck. 5. Head. 6. Leg fillet. 7. Gristle. 8. Shoulder. 9. Breast. 10. Knuckle.

Mutton: 1. Saddle. 2. Fillet. 3. Loin. 4. Best ribs. 5. Neck. 6. Head. 7. Leg. 8. Breast. 9. Shoulder. 10. Feet.

Pork: 1. Leg of pork. 2. Fat bacon. 2a. Loin. 3. Ribs. 4. "Pig's Cheek". 5. Belly. 6 and 7 correspond to "Hand and spring" and "Half-leg". 8. Feet.

Le boucher: Je m'excuse, madame, je ne comprends pas . . .
zhe maik-skẽz mah-dahm zhe ne koN-praN pah
I apologize, madam, I don't understand . . .

Mme Lesage: N'en parlons plus, mais servez-moi bien cette
naN pahr-loN plẽ mai sair-vay mwah byiN sait
Don't let us speak about it any more, but serve me well this

fois; j'ai des invités et je ne veux pas qu'ils se
fwah zhay day-ziN-vee-tay ay zhe ne vãy pah keel se
time; I have guests and I don't want them to

cassent les dents en mangeant vos biftecks.
kahs lay daN aN maN-zhaN voh beef-taik.
break their teeth by eating your beefsteaks.

Boucher: Comptez sur moi, madame!   Que désirez-vous aujourd'hui?
koN-tay sẽr mwah mah-dam! ke day-zee-ray voo oh-zhoord-w̃ee?
Count on me, madam!   What do you want today?

Mme L.:   Donnez-moi un beau morceau de noix de veau—disons un
do-nay mwah uN boh mor-soh de nwah de voh dee-zoN uN
Give me a good piece of knuckle of veal—let us say one

kilo; et deux petites tranches de foie.
kee-loh ay dãy p'teet traNsh de fwah.
kilo; and two small slices of liver.

Boucher: Du foie de veau, madame, ou de bœuf?
dẽ fwah de voh mah-dahm oo de bãyf?
Calves' liver, madam, or ox's?

Mme L.:   Du veau.   C'est pour mes petits-enfants, je leur achète
dẽ voh. say poor may p'tee-zaN-faN zhe lãyr ah-shait
Calves'.   It's for my grandchildren, I buy them

toujours le meilleur.
too-zhoor le mai-yãyr.
always the best.

Après avoir fait ses achats, Mme Lesage paye sa note à la
ah-prai-zah-vwahr fai say-zah-shah mah-dahm le-sahzh pay sah not ah lah
After having made her purchases, Mme Lesage pays her bill at the

caisse et se rend chez le boulanger.
kais ay se raN shay le boo-laN-zhay.
cash-desk and betakes herself to the baker.

Le boulanger: Bonjour, Madame Lesage, comment allez-vous?
boN-zhoor, mah-dahm le-sahzh, ko-man-tah-lay voo?
Good morning, Mme Lesage, how are you?

Without looking at the text, you should now be able to make a list in French of everything you can recognise in this butcher's and poulterer's. If you cannot do so, study the last Lessons again.

Mme Lesage: **Ça va, je vous remercie, et vous, ça va toujours**
sah vah zhe voo re-mair-see ay voo sah vah too-zhoor
Very well, thank you, and you are keeping

bien?[1] **Quelle chaleur!** **Donnez-moi une livre de pain de**
byiN? kail shah-lāyr! do-nay mwah ēēn leevr de piN de
well? *What heat!* *Give me one pound of household*

ménage et un kilo de pain bis . . . oh, comme j'ai chaud!
may-nahzh ay uN kee-loh de piN bee . . . oh kom zhay shoh!
bread and one kilo of brown bread . . . oh, how hot I am!

Le boulanger: **Voilà, Madame Lesage.** **Mme L.:** **Donnez-moi encore une**
vwah-lah mah-dahm le-sahzh.   do-nay mwah aN-kor ēēn
Here it is, Mme Lesage.   *Give me also a*

douzaine de croissants et deux morceaux de gâteau.
doo-zain de krwah-saN ay dāy mor-soh de gah-toh.
dozen crescent rolls and two pieces of cake.

Le boulanger: **Ah, je vois, c'est pour les petits-enfants.**
ah zhe vwah say poor lay p'tee-zaN-faN.
Ah, I see, this is for the grand-children.

[1] Lit. "It goes, I thank you, and you, it goes always well?"

L'AVENUE DES CHAMPS-ÉLYSÉES

Paris est redevable de cette noble avenue au génie du Baron Haussman (1809–91).
Devenu préfet de la Seine, il entreprit la reconstruction de la ville entière. L'Arc de

| Être redevable de q'ch à q'qn | génie (m.) | devenir | entreprendre |
| To be indebted to s'one for s'thing | genius | to become | to undertake |

ET L'ARC DE TRIOMPHE

Triomphe fut érigé pour célébrer les victoires de Napoléon 1er. Consacrée autrefois aux hôtels particuliers, l'Avenue est aujourd'hui devenue quartier commerçant.

Ériger	**consacrer à**	**hôtel** (m.) **particulier**	**quartier** (m.) **commerçant**
To erect	dedicated to	private house	business quarter

Je vous ai vue dans la rue avec les gosses.
zhe voo-zai vẽ daN lah rẽ ah-vaik lay gos.
I saw you in the street with the youngsters.

Ils sont gentils, très gentils.
eel soN zhaN-tee trai zhaN-tee.
They are nice, very nice.

Mme L.: **Je crois bien**[1]
zhe krwah byiN
I think (indeed)

qu'ils sont gentils, mes petits-enfants.
keel soN zhaN-tee may p'tee-zaN-faN.
that they are nice, my grandchildren.

Quelle heure est-il?
kai-lẽr ay-teel?
What time is it?

Onze heures? **Il faut que je me sauve**[2] **... au revoir.**
oN-zẽr? eel foh ke zhe me sohv oh re-vwahr.
Eleven o'clock? *I must hurry . . . goodbye.*

THE USE OF "EN"

1. **Avez-vous du pain? Oui, j'en ai.** Have you any bread? Yes, I have some.
   Avez-vous de la viande? J'en ai. Have you any meat? I have some.
   Avez-vous des sardines? J'en ai. Have you any sardines? I have some.
   Je n'en ai pas. I haven't any.

   The French for "some" or "any" used instead of the noun is **en**, which is placed directly before the verb.

2. **Avez-vous des cigarettes? Oui, monsieur, j'en ai.** Yes, I have.
   Combien de cigarettes avez-vous? J'en ai trois. I have three.
   Avez-vous de l'argent? Oui, j'en ai. Yes, I have.
   Je n'en ai pas. I haven't.
   J'en ai beaucoup. I have much.

   Note that **en** must be inserted when standing for a noun used with the partitive article, even in cases where the English word may be omitted.

3. Meaning "of it," "of them", "with it", "with them", "for it", "for them", etc.
   J'en ai assez. I have enough of it.
   N'en parlons plus. Don't let us speak about it any more.
   Il a volé l'argent; j'en suis sûr. He has stolen the money; I am sure of it.
   J'ai vu la maison et j'en suis charmé. I have seen the house and I am delighted with it.
   Combien a-t-il d'enfants? Il en a quatre. How many children has he? He has four (of them).
   J'ai payé la note; en voici le reçu. I paid the bill; here is the receipt for it.
   Est-ce qu'il y a des cigares? Are there any cigars?
   Il y en a plusieurs. There are several (of them).

4. **en** may also be a preposition:
   en été In summer
   en hiver In winter
   en automne In autumn
   en France. In France
   en Angleterre In England
   en Allemagne In Germany.

POSITION OF ADJECTIVES

Le grand garçon est intelligent. The big boy is intelligent.
Le grand garçon intelligent est le fils de mon ami. The big intelligent boy is the son of my friend.
C'est une jolie petite fille. She is a pretty little girl.
Ces jeunes filles françaises. These French girls.
Elle est assise sur la vieille chaise. She is sitting on the old chair.

---

[1] **Je crois bien** here means something like "I should jolly well think."
[2] Lit. "save myself."

Quel mauvais temps!
What bad weather!
Ils mangent de bons raisins.
They eat good grapes.
Elle regarde de jolis tableaux.
She is looking at pretty pictures.
Ils ont de gros melons.
They have big melons.
Il aime de vieux vin rouge.
He likes old red wine.

Most adjectives in French usually follow the noun. But a number of short and frequently used adjectives precede it. Among the latter are: **grand, petit, bon, mauvais, jeune, vieux, beau, joli, cher, gros.**

Note that when the noun is preceded by an adjective, **de** only is used instead of **du, de la, de l'**, or **des:**

du gâteau cake
de bon gâteau good cake
de la viande meat
de bonne viande good meat
des enfants children
de petits enfants little children
de l'argent money
de mauvais argent bad money
des chiens dogs
de jolis chiens pretty dogs
but: **des chiens intelligents,**
de l'argent anglais, etc.

SENTENCE BUILDING

Question		Answer
Avez-vous	du pain? du poisson? du vin rouge? de la viande? de l'argent?	J'en ai. I have some.
Voulez-vous	des légumes? des fruits? des oranges? beaucoup de pain? de jolis crayons? de l'argent français? de l'encre noire?	Merci, j'en ai déjà. Thank you, I have some already. Je n'en ai pas. I haven't any.
Voulez-vous } Pouvez-vous } me donner	de bonnes oranges? un peu de fromage? de beaux tableaux? de bon vin blanc? de vieux vin rouge?	Je regrette infiniment, mais je n'en ai pas. I greatly regret, but I have not any.

EXERCISES

I Answer in French

1. Est-ce que vous avez beaucoup d'argent? 2. Mangez-vous des fruits? 3. Avez-vous beaucoup de livres français? 4. Où achetez-vous des légumes? 5. Où est-ce qu'on achète de la viande? 6. Qui vend des fruits? 7. Avez-vous assez de pain? 8. Est-ce que Mme Lesage achète des poires? 9. Qu'est-ce qu'elle achète? 10. Est-ce qu'elle était contente de son boucher? 11. Pourquoi pas? 12. Combien prend-elle de gâteaux? 13. Est-ce que M. Robert est chez le boulanger? 14. Où a-t-il acheté ses cigarettes? 15. Qu'est-ce qu'il a fait dans le bureau de change?

II Replace with pronouns the words in bold type

1. **La grand'mère** achète **du pain.** 2. On mange **de la viande.** 3. Elle a **des crayons** dans sa valise. 4. **Mon père** boit **le vin blanc.** 5. **Mon père** boit **du vin blanc.** 6. **Ma sœur** a acheté **la viande.** 7. **Sa cousine** achète **de la viande.** 8. **Le garçon** apporte

les légumes. 9. Mes parents mangent beaucoup de légumes. 10. Ils regardent les livres. 11. Elle n'a pas de livres français. 12. Il veut de l'encre rouge.

III Translate into French

1. I have some bread, but I have no butter. 2. Have you got any? 3. I have a little. 4. I haven't any. 5. There are no cherries at the fruiterer's. 6. Are there none? 7. Don't you drink red wine? 8. Do you never drink any? 9. I want some good oranges. 10. Have you got any? 11. I have apples, but I haven't any pears. 12. Does your father drink white wine? 13. Your aunt asks if there is any meat. 14. The maid says that there is not any. 15. She is going to buy cheese, vegetables and meat. (*Key on page* 210).

PARIS: LA CONCIERGERIE

Cette ancienne prison, dont la construction remonte au XVᵉ siècle, fut la dernière demeure de Marie Antoinette avant sa mort sur l'échafaud. Aujourd'hui elle fait partie du Palais de Justice.

Remonter à	**demeure (f.)**	**échafaud (m.)**	**Palais (m.) de Justice**
To date back to	dwelling	scaffold	Law Courts

DIX-SEPTIÈME LEÇON

LE DÎNER CHEZ LES LESAGE

L'appartement de grand-père et grand'mère Lesage.   Dans la
la-pahr-te-maN de graN-pair ay graN-mair le-sahzh.   daN lah
The flat of grandfather and grandmother Lesage.   In the

salle à manger la table est mise pour six personnes.
sah-lah maN-zhay lah tahbl ay meez poor see pair-son.
dining room the table is laid for six persons.

Grand-père	**(regardant sa montre): Je ne comprends pas. Il est sept heures** re-gahr-daN sah moNtr zhe ne koN-praN pah. ee-lay sai-tâyr *(looking at his watch): I don't understand. It is past seven* **passées, et ils n'arrivent toujours pas.** pah-say ay eel nah-reev too-zhoor pah. *o'clock, and they still don't arrive.*
Grand'mère:	**Il ne faut pas oublier qu'ils ne sont pas Parisiens.** eel ne foh pah-zoo-blee-yay keel ne soN pah pah-reez-yiN. *One must not forget that they are not Parisians.*
Grand-père:	**Tout de même, j'ai une faim de loup.** too de maim zhay ên fiN de loo. *Nevertheless, I have a wolf's hunger ("I'm as hungry as a hunter").*
	(On sonne.) oN son. *(The bell is ringing.)*
Grand-père:	**Les voilà, enfin. (M. et Mme Roberts entrent.)** lay vwah-lah aN-fiN. *There they are at last.*
Mme Roberts:	**Bon soir tout le monde! Veuillez nous excuser,** bon-swahr too le moNd! vây-yay noo-zaik-skêe-zay *Good evening, everybody! Will you excuse us,* **mais ce n'est vraiment pas notre faute si nous sommes en retard.** mai se nay vrai-maN pah notr foht see noo som-zaN re-tahr. *but it is really not our fault if we are late.*
M. Roberts:	**C'est vrai. Le métro était** say vrai. le mayt-roh ay-tai *It is true. The tube was* **bloqué pendant un bon quart d'heure. Je ne sais pas pour** blo-kay paN-daN uN boN kahr dâyr. zhe ne sai pah poor *blocked during a good quarter of an hour. I don't know for*

DINNER AT GRANDMOTHER LESAGE'S

Here you have a typically French interior on an evening when a cosy repast is being prepared for a few intimate friends.

Before consulting the list on the next page, it should now be easy for you to name in French twenty objects on the table or in the room. For key see page 198.

quelle raison. J'espère qu'il n'y a pas eu
kail rai-zoN. zhais-pair keel nyah pah-zę̃
what reason. I hope that there has not been
d'accident. Donc, excusez notre retard.
dahk-see-daN. doNk aik-skę̃-zay notr re-tahr.
an accident. Therefore excuse our being late.

La bonne: **Le dîner est servi, madame.**
le dee-nay ay sair-vee mah-dahm.
Dinner is served, madam.

Grand-père: **Vous êtes tous excusés.**
voo-zait toos aik-skę̃-zay.
You are all excused.

Mais maintenant vite à table. **Vous prenez l'apéritif?**
mai miNt-naN vee-tah tahbl. voo pre-nay lah-pay-ree-teef?
But now quick to (the) table. *You take an appetiser?*

M. Roberts: **Non, merci, nous n'aimons pas ça.**
noN mair-see noo nai-moN pah sah.
No, thanks, we don't like that.

Grand-père: **Tant pis pour vous.** **Mais vous ne déclinerez pas notre**
taN pee poor voo. mai voo ne day-kleen-ray pah notr
So much the worse for you. *But you will not refuse our*

LA SALLE À MANGER—THE DINING-ROOM

La table mise pour le dîner tahbl meez poor le dee-nay *table laid for dinner*	**le buffet** bę̃-fai *sideboard*	**la nappe** nahp *table-cloth*	**la desserte** dai-sairt *side-table*
la lampe à suspension laNp ah sę̃s-paN-syoN *hanging lamp*	**la soupière** soo-pyair *soup-tureen*	**la gravure** la gravure *picture*	**une assiette plate** ah-syait plaht *flat plate*
une assiette creuse ah-syait krą̃yz *deep plate*	**le couteau** koo-toh *knife*	**la fourchette** foor-shait *fork*	**la cuillère à potage** kw̃ee-yair ah po-tahzh *soup spoon*
la serviette sair-vyait *serviette, dinner-napkin*	**le moutardier** moo-tahr-dyay *mustard-pot*	**la saucière** sohs-yair *sauce-dish*	**la salière** sahl-yair *salt-cellar*	**la cloche à fromage** klosh ah fro-mahzh *cheese dish*
la bouteille de vin boo-taiy de viN *bottle of wine*	**la cuillère à dessert** kw̃ee-yair ah dai-sair *dessert-spoon*	**la carafe** kah-rahf *decanter*	**le couvert à poisson** koo-vair ah pwah-soN *fish knife and fork*
la corbeille à pain kor-baiy ah piN *bread basket*	**le légumier** lay-gę̃m-yay *vegetable-dish*	**une assiette à dessert** ahs-yait ah dai-sair *dessert-plate*	**le plat à rôti** plah ah roh-tee *meat dish*
l'huilier w̃eel-yay *oil cruet*	**le verre à vin** vair ah viN *wine glass*	**la ménagère** may-nah-zhair *cruet-stand*	**le vinaigrier** vee-naig-ree-ay *vinegar cruet*

bon vin de France, j'espère.   M. Roberts: **Tout au**
boN viN de fraNs zhais-pair.   too-toh
good wine of France, I hope.   *Quite on the*

contraire. Votre vin, je le préfère à tout autre.
koN-trair. votr viN zhe le pray-fair ah too-tohtr.
contrary. Your wine I prefer to any other.

Grand'mère: **Voulez-vous du potage, mon gendre?**
voo-lay voo dê po-tahzh moN zhaNdr?
Do you want some soup, my son-in-law?

M. Roberts: **J'en prendrai un tout petit peu.**
zhaN praN-dray uN too p'tee pây.
I'll (of it) have only very little.

Georges: **Voulez-vous me passer le pain, s'il vous plaît? Merci.**
voo-lay voo me pah-say le piN seel voo plai?   mair-see.
Will you pass me the bread, please?   Thank you.

Grand-père: **Avez-vous déjà visité la ville?**
ah-vay voo day-zhah vee-zee-tay lah veel?
Have you already visited the town?

M. Roberts: **Nous avons visité des musées, surtout le Louvre.   Hier**
noo-zah-voN vee-zee-tay day mê-zay sêr-too le loovr.   yair
We have visited some museums, especially the Louvre.   Last

soir nous étions au théâtre du Châtelet.   C'était
swahr noo zayt-yoN-zoh tay-ahtr dê shaht-lai.   say-tai
night we were in the Châtelet theatre.   It was

vraiment très amusant.   Vous avez de bons
vrai-maN trai-zah-mê-zaN.   voo-zah-vay de boN-
really very amusing.   You have good

acteurs à Paris.   Mme Roberts: Demain soir nous
zahk-tâyr ah pah-ree.   de-miN swahr noo-
actors in Paris.   Tomorrow night we

irons à l'Opéra.   Paul nous a invités.
zee-roN-zah lo-pay-rah.   pol noo-zah iN-vee-tay.
shall go to the Opera.   Paul has invited us.

Grand'mère: **Et les enfants, vont-ils bien?   N'oubliez pas de**
ay lay-zaN-faN voN-teel byiN?   noo-blyay pah de
And the children, are they all right?   Don't forget

Twenty objects (p. 196) are: **la table, la chaise, la fenêtre, la lampe, la portière, la tasse, la soucoupe, le pain, le fromage, l'assiette, le vin, le verre à vin, le couteau, la fourchette, la cuillère, du sel, de la moutarde, de l'huile, la gravure, la corbeille à fleurs.**

les amener avec vous demain pour le déjeuner.
lay-zah-me-nay ah-vaik voo de-miN poor le day-zhãy-nay.
to bring them along with you tomorrow for lunch.

Comment la ville leur plaît-elle?
ko-maN lah veel lãyr plai-tail?
How do they like the town?

M. Roberts: Oh, ils trouvent
oh eel troov
Oh, they find

Paris très intéressant.
pah-ree trai-ziN-tay-rai-saN.
Paris very interesting.

Georges: Avez-vous déjà
ah-vay voo day-zhah
Have you already

été à Versailles?
ay-tay ah vair-sahy?
been to Versailles?

M. Roberts: Non, pas encore. Mais je
noN pah-zaN-kor. mai zhe
No, not yet. But I

ne partirai pas sans l'avoir vu. Est-ce loin d'ici?
ne pahr-tee-ray pah saN lah-vwahr vẽ. ais lwiN dee-see?
won't leave without having seen it. Is it far from here?

Georges: **Pas du tout! Vous n'avez qu'à prendre le métro**
pah dẽ too! voo nah-vay kah praNdr le may-troh
Not at all! You only have to take the underground

jusqu'au pont de Sèvres. Là vous prendrez l'autobus.
zhẽs-koh poN de saivr. lah voo praN-dray loh-toh-bẽs.
up to Sèvres bridge. There you'll have to take the bus.

C'est très simple. Vous y serez dans une heure
say trai siNpl. voo-zee se-ray daN-zẽen-ãyr
It's very simple. You will be there in one hour

environ. D'ailleurs je peux vous accompagner, si vous le
aN-vee-roN. dah-yãyr zhe pãy voo-zah-koN-pahn-yay see voo le
approximately. Besides I can accompany you, if you

voulez. Qu'en dites-vous?
voo-lay. kaN deet voo?
want to. What do you say to that?

Mme Roberts: **Nous acceptons avec le plus grand plaisir.**
noo-zahk-saip-toN ah-vaik le plẽ graN plai-zeer.
We accept with the greatest pleasure.

Vous nous accompagnerez aussi, chère cousine?
voo noo-zah-koN-pahn-ye-ray oh-see shair koo-zeen?
You will also accompany us, dear cousin?

Mlle Lesage: **Très volontiers. Quand voulez-vous faire l'excursion?**
trai vo-loN-tyay. kaN voo-lay voo fair laik-skẽer-syoN?
Very gladly. When do you want to make the excursion?

VERSAILLES: LA VILLE ROYALE

En haut, le Palais, aujourd'hui un musée, où Louis XIV, le Roi Soleil, tenait jadis sa cour, qui servait de modèle à toute l'Europe. En bas, les jardins où, les jours des "Grandes Eaux", les citoyens viennent admirer les fontaines.

"Le Roi Soleil"
"The Sun King," flatterers' title for Louis XIV

"Les Grandes Eaux"
Special fountain displays at Versailles

Je suis libre presque tous les jours.
zhe sŵee leebr praisk too lay zhoor.
I am free almost every day.

M. Roberts: **Disons après-demain, pour ne pas remettre trop**
dee-zoN ah-prai de-miN poor ne pah re-maitr troh
Let us say the day after tomorrow, in order not to put it off too

longtemps. **Mlle Lesage:** **C'est entendu pour après-demain.**
loN-taN   say-taN-taN-dē̃e poor ah-prai de-miN.
long.   *That's arranged for the day after tomorrow.*

Grand'mère: **Eh bien, je crois que nous pouvons passer à la viande.**
eh byiN zhe krwah ke noo poo-voN pah-say ah lah vyaNd.
Well, I think that we can pass on to the meat.

(Elle sonne la bonne.) **La bonne:** **Madame a sonné?**
ail son lah bon.   mah-dahm ah so-nay?
(She rings for the servant.)   *Did you ring, Madam?*

Grand'mère: **Vous pouvez changer les assiettes et servir la viande.**
voo poo-vay shaN-zhay lay-zahs-yait ay sair-veer lah vyaNd.
You can change the plates and serve the meat.

(On sert la viande et ils mangent tous avec beaucoup
oN sair lah vyaNd ay eel maNzh toos ah-vaik boh-koo
(The meat is served and they all eat with much

d'appétit.) **Grand-père:** **Voulez-vous du vin rouge ou**
dah-pay-tee.   voo-lay voo dē̃e viN roozh oo
appetite.)   *Will you have red wine or*

du blanc? **M. Roberts:** **Du rouge, s'il vous plaît.** **Ah, quelle**
dē̃e blaN?   dē̃e roozh seel voo plai.   ah kail
white?   *Some red, please.*   *Ah, how*

merveille! **On dirait du Bordeaux de marque.**
mair-vaiy!   oN dee-rai dē̃e bor-doh de mahrk.
marvellous!   *One would say choice (or vintage) claret.*

Grand-père: **C'est bien cela.** **Il sort de ma propre cave.** **On dirait**
say byiN se-lah.   eel sor de mah propr kahv.   oN dee-rai
That's what it is.   *It comes from my own cellar.*   *One would*

du soleil en bouteille. **Un peu plus tard vous allez**
dē̃e so-laiy aN boo-taiy.   uN pŵy plē̃e tahr voo-zah-lay
say sunshine in a bottle.   *A little later you are going to*

déguster un autre vin rouge.
day-gē̃es-tay uN-nohtr viN roozh.
taste another red wine.

Grand'mère: Encore un peu de ce rôti?
aN-kor uN pây de se roh-tee?
Some more of this joint?

M. Roberts: Rien qu'un petit morceau, s'il vous plaît.   Ça c'est
ryiN kuN p'tee mor-soh seel voo plai.   sah say
Only a tiny piece, please.   That is

beaucoup trop. Mme Roberts: Merci, j'en ai eu suffisamment.
boh-koo troh.   mair-see zhaN-nay ê sê-fee-zah-maN.
far too much.   Thank you, I have had plenty.

Grand'mère: Voilà le gâteau et les fruits. Après vous aurez
vwah-lah le gah-toh ay lay frŵee.   ah-prai voo-zoh-ray
Here is the cake and the fruit.   Afterwards you'll have

de bon café. J'espère que vous êtes tous contents.
de boN kah-fay.   zhes-pair ke voo-zait toos koN-taN.
some good coffee.   I hope you are all pleased.

M. Roberts: C'était excellent.   C'est vraiment très agréable
say-tai-taik-sai-laN.   say vrai-maN trai-zah-gray-ahbl
It was excellent.   It really is very nice (to be)

chez vous.   Mlle Lesage: Comme il est bon ce gâteau!
shay voo.   ko-mee-lay boN se gah-toh!
with you.   How good this cake is!

Grand'mère: Je l'ai fait moi-même.   C'en était du travail.   Il y a de
zhe lay fai mwah maim.   saN-nay-tai dê trah-vay.   eel yah de
I made it myself.   It was some work.   There are some

bonne choses là-dedans.   Mme Lesage: On le note tout de suite.
bon shohz lah de-daN.   oN le not tood sŵeet.
good things inside.   You realise it at once.

Grand-père: Vous fumez le cigare?
voo fê-may le see-gahr?
You smoke a cigar?

M. Roberts: Merci, je préfère une cigarette.
mair-see zhe pray-fair ên see-gah-rait.
No thank you, I prefer a cigarette.

Grand'mère: Georges, pourquoi ne mangez-vous pas votre dessert?
zhorzh poor-kwah ne maN-zhay voo pah votre dai-sair?
George, why don't you eat your dessert?

Georges: Oh, vous savez, je n'aime pas les choses sucrées.
oh voo sah-vay zhe naim pah lay shohz sê-kray.
Oh, you know, I don't like sweet things.

Grand'mère: **Mais il y a des fruits. Puis-je vous peler une orange?**
mai eel yah day frŵee. pŵee zhe voo pe-lay ẽ-no-raNzh?
But there is fruit. May I peel an orange for you?

Grand-père: **Où donc est mon briquet?** **(Il cherche dans ses poches.)**
oo doNk ay moN bree-kay? eel shairsh daN say posh.
Where on earth is my lighter? *(He looks in his pockets.)*

M. Roberts: **J'ai des allumettes sur moi. Voilà.** **(Il lui**
zhay day-zah-lẽ-mait sẽr mwah. vwah-lah. eel lwee
I have matches with me. There you are. (He

offre du feu.) **Grand-père: Merci. Vous jouez aux cartes?**
ofr dẽ fŵy. mair-see. voo zhoo-ay oh kahrt?
offers him a light.) *Thanks. Do you play cards?*

M. Roberts: **Assez rarement. Mais si je me rappelle bien, vous**
ah-say rahr-maN. mai see zhe me rah-pail byiN voo
Very rarely. But if I remember right, you

jouiez aux échecs. Grand-père: C'est exact. Alors
zhoo-yay oh-zay-shaik. say-taig-zahkt. ah-lor
used to play chess. That's right. So let

faisons une partie! **M. Roberts: Avec plaisir.**
fe -zoN-zẽn pahr-tee! ah-vaik plai-zeer.
us have a game! *With pleasure.*

D'ailleurs, un ami va me téléphoner.
dah-yŵyr uN-nah-mee vah me tay-lay-fo-nay.
By the way, a friend (of mine) is going to ring me up.

Je me suis permis de donner votre numéro de
zhe me sŵee pair-mee de do-nay votr nẽ-may-roh de
I took the liberty of giving your telephone

téléphone. J'espère que cela ne vous gênera pas.
tay-lay-fon. zhais-pair ke se-lah ne voo zhain'rah pah.
number. I hope that this will not inconvenience you.

Grand-père: **Mais non, pas du tout. Allez faire votre partie**
mai noN pah dẽ too. ah-lay fair votr pahr-tee
But no, not at all. Go and have your game

d'échecs. Je vous appellerai quand votre ami vous
day-shaik. zhe voo-zah-pail-ray kaN vot-rah-mee voo
of chess. I'll call you when your friend will

demandera. **Grand'mère: Je me sens un peu fatiguée,**
de-maNd-rah zhe me saNz-uN pŵy fah-tee-gay
ask for you. *I feel a bit tired,*

et je vais m'étendre pour une demi-heure. Amusez-
ay zhe vai may-taN-dr poor ẽn de-mee-ãyr. ah-mẽẽ-zay
and I am going to lie down for half an hour. Have a good

vous bien. À tout à l'heure!
voo byiN. ah too-tah-lãyr!
time. Until later!

Les autres:	**À tout à l'heure! Reposez-vous bien!**
lay-zohtr:	ah too-tah-lãyr! re-poh-zay voo byiN!
The others:	*Until later ! Have a good rest !*

Mlle Lesage: Avez-vous envie de faire une petite promenade?
ah-vay voo aN-vee de fair ẽn p'teet prom-nahd?
Would you like to go for a little walk?

Georges: Pour moi, j'accepte. Et vous‿ma chère tante?
Poor mwah zhahk-saipt. ay voo mah shair taNt?
As for me, I accept. And you, my dear aunt?

Mme Roberts: Je veux bien, si vous n'allez pas trop loin.
zhe vãy byiN see voo nah-lay pah troh lwiN.
I should love to, if you don't go too far.

Georges: Oh, non, nous n'allons faire qu'un petit tour.
oh noN, noo nah-loN fair kuN p'tee toor.
Oh no, we are only going for a little stroll.

(riant) C'est bon pour la digestion, vous savez.
ryaN   say boN poor lah dee-zhaist-yoN voo sah-vay.
(laughing) That is good for the digestion, you know.

Mme Roberts: Dans ce cas, je vous accompagne. Je vais seulement
daN se kah zhe voo-zah-koN-pahny. zhe vai sãyl-maN
In that case, I'll come with you. I am only going

chercher mon chapeau et mon sac.
shair-shay moN shah-poh ay moN sahk.
to get my hat and my handbag.

Georges: Prenez votre temps. Nous vous attendons. (Quelques minutes
pre-nay votr taN. noo voo-zah-taN-doN. kail-ke mee-nẽẽt-
Take your time. We'll wait for you. (A few minutes

après, Mme Roberts revient, et ils s'en vont.)
zah-prai mah-dahm ro-bairts re-vyiN ay eel saN voN.
later Mrs. Roberts comes back, and they go away.)

S'EN ALLER—TO GO (AWAY)
Present Affirmative

je m'en vais I am going
il (elle) s'en va he (she) is going
nous nous en allons we are going
vous vous en allez you are going
ils (elles) s'en vont they are going

Present Negative
je ne m'en vais pas, etc.

Present Interrogative
s'en va-t-il? is he going?
vous en allez-vous? are you going?

Imperative Affirmative
allons-nous-en! let us go!
allez-vous-en! go away!

Imperative Negative
ne nous en allons pas! don't let us go!
ne vous en allez pas! don't go!

COMPRENDRE—TO UNDERSTAND
Present
je comprends
il (elle) comprend
nous comprenons
vous comprenez
ils (elles) comprennent

Imperfect
je comprenais, etc.

Future
je comprendrai, etc.

Perfect
j'ai compris, etc.

SOME VERBS ENDING IN -IR
partir = to leave; **dormir** = to sleep;
servir = to serve; **sentir** = to feel, to smell;
sortir = to go out; **venir** = to come.

Present

je pars	**je dors**
il (elle) part	**il (elle) dort**
nous partons	**nous dormons**
vous partez	**vous dormez**
ils (elles) partent	**ils (elles) dorment**

je sers	**je sens**
il (elle) sert	**il (elle) sent**
nous servons	**nous sentons**
vous servez	**vous sentez**
ils (elles) servent	**ils (elles) sentent**

je sors	**je viens**
il (elle) sort	**il (elle) vient**
nous sortons	**nous venons**
vous sortez	**vous venez**
ils (elles) sortent	**ils (elles) viennent**

Imperfect

je partais	**je dormais**	**je servais**
je sentais	**je sortais**	**je venais**

Future

je partirai	**je dormirai**	**je servirai**
je sentirai	**je sortirai**	**je viendrai**

Perfect

je suis parti	**j'ai dormi**	**j'ai servi**
j'ai senti	**je suis sorti**	**je suis venu**

THE PAST PARTICIPLE

je dîne I am having dinner; I dine — **j'ai dîné** I have had dinner; I dined

il dort he is asleep; he sleeps — **il a dormi** he has been sleeping; he slept

elle vend des bas she sells (is selling) stockings — **elle les a vendus** she has sold them: she sold them

Forms of the verb like "dined," "slept," "sold," "arrived," "left," etc., are called Past Participles. In English the usual ending of the Past Participle is **-ed** (the same as for the past tense). In French the usual ending of the Past Participle is **-é**: it is the ending of all verbs of which the Infinitive ends in **-er**.

Infinitive	Past Participle
dîner = to dine	**dîné** = dined
aller = to go	**allé** = gone
donner = to give	**donné** = given
dormir = to sleep	**dormi** = slept
vendre = to sell	**vendu** = sold
prendre = to take	**pris** = taken

The endings of the past participle are:
-é with all verbs in -er.
-i with most verbs in -ir.
-u with most verbs in -re.

je sors	je suis sorti(e)
(I am going out)	(I have gone out)
le train part	le train est parti
(the train is leaving)	(the train has left)
ils arrivent	ils sont arrivé(e)s
(they arrive)	(they have arrived)

The Perfect Tense of the vast majority of French verbs is formed (as in English) by the Present Tense of avoir (j'ai, il a, etc.) and the Past Participle.

A few verbs (they are mostly verbs denoting motion from one place to another) form their Perfect with être (je suis, il est, etc.). Instead of saying, for example: "he has gone," the French say il est allé ("is gone").

The following verbs form their Perfect with être, unless they are used transitively, that is, with an object:

aller = to go; venir = to come; entrer = to enter; sortir = to go out; arriver = to arrive; partir = to leave; monter = to go (come) up; descendre = to go (come) down; tomber = to fall; rester = to stay; naître = to be born;

mourir = to die; retourner = to come back; and all verbs formed from them, such as rentrer, devenir, etc.

1. Mon oncle est venu.
   My uncle has come.
   Il est arrivé à six heures.
   He arrived at six o'clock.
2. Ma tante est venue.
   My aunt has come.
   Elle est arrivée à onze heures.
   She arrived at eleven o'clock.
3. Mes cousins sont venus.
   My cousins have come.
   Ils sont arrivés à une heure.
   They arrived at one o'clock.
4. Mes cousines sont venues.
   My cousins (women) have come.
   Elles sont arrivées à midi et demi.
   They arrived at half past twelve.

Note from the above: 1. The Perfect Tense in French denotes not only what has just been happening, but also what happened in the past.

2. The Past Participle used in connection with être agrees with the subject. (In sentence 2, the subject is feminine, therefore -e is added to venu and arrivé; in sentence 3, the subject is masculine plural, therefore -s is added; in 4, the subject is feminine plural, so -es is added.)

SENTENCE BUILDING

j'ai	I have, etc.
vous avez	
nous avons	
il (elle) a	
ils (elles) ont	
je n'ai pas	I haven't, etc.
vous n'avez pas	
nous n'avons pas	
il n'a pas	
elle n'a pas	
ils n'ont pas	
elles n'ont pas	
(n') { ai-je / avez-vous / avons-nous / a-t-il (elle) / ont-ils (elles) }	Have I (Haven't I), etc. (pas)

mangé	eaten
déjeuné	lunched
dîné	dined
fermé la porte	shut the door
ouvert la fenêtre	opened the window
été en France	been in France
regardé les fleurs	looked at the flower
parlé français	spoken French
dit au revoir	said goodbye
pris un bain	taken a bath
eu des lettres	had letters
fait les malles	packed the trunks
bien dormi	slept well
mis des gants	put on gloves
vu Paris	seen Paris
lu ce roman	read this novel
écrit des lettres	written letters
demandé pardon	apologized

I have, etc.
je suis
vous êtes
nous sommes
il ⎫
elle ⎬ est
ils ⎭
elles ⎫ sont

I haven't, etc.
je ne suis pas
vous n'êtes pas
il n'est pas
elle n'est pas
nous ne sommes pas
ils ne sont pas
elles ne sont pas

Have I (haven't I), etc.
(ne) suis-je
(n') êtes-vous
(n') est-il
(n') est-elle ⎬ (pas)
(ne) sommes-nous
(ne) sont-ils
(ne) sont-elles

allé(es) à Paris	gone to Paris
arrivé(es) en auto	arrived in a car
venu(es) hier	come yesterday
sorti(es) de la maison	left the house (gone out of)
entré(es) tard	come in late
parti(es) pour l'Amérique	left for America
monté(es) l'escalier	gone up the stairs
descendu(es) pour le dîner	come down for dinner
tombé(es) dans l'eau	fallen into the wate
resté(es) à la maison	stayed indoors

Note.—Add -e to the Past Participle if the subject of the sentence is feminine; -s if it is masculine plural; -es if feminine plural. These endings do not affect the pronunciation.

SOME FRENCH PROVERBS

Quand le chat n'y est pas, les souris dansent. When the cat is away the mice play.

Quand les fous vont au marché, les marchands se réjouissent. When fools go buying there is joy in the market place.

Quand on sème le vent, on récolte la tempête. Sow the wind and reap the whirlwind.

Qui dort, dîne. Sleeping is as good as eating.

Qui ne risque rien, n'a rien. Nothing venture, nothing win.

Qui s'excuse, s'accuse. He who excuses himself accuses himself.

Rira bien qui rira le dernier. He who laughs last, laughs longest.

Tel père tel fils. Like father like son.

Tout est bien qui finit bien. All's well that ends well.

Vouloir c'est pouvoir. Where there's a will there's a way.

EXERCISES

I Put into the Perfect

1. Je ne comprends pas. 2. Il est malade. 3. J'ai une faim de loup. 4. Est-ce que Madame sonne? 5. Elle n'aime pas la bière. 6. Nous ne fermons pas les yeux. 7. Il prend le métro. 8. La domestique apporte la viande. 9. Personne ne veut de potage. 10. Elle fait une robe.

II Answer in French

1. Avez-vous lu beaucoup de livres? 2. À quelle heure avez-vous dîné hier? 3. Avez-vous bu du vin hier? 4. Avez-vous mangé quelque chose ce matin? 5. Avez-vous fait une promenade hier soir? 6. M. Roberts a-t-il pris du potage? 7. M. et Mme Roberts ont-ils déjà visité la ville?

GENS DE LOISIR

Des "trimardeurs" et des gens quasi respectables font la sieste sur les bords du fleuve.

Loisir (m.)	**trimardeur** (m.)	**quasi** (adv.)	**sieste** (f.)	**fleuve** (m.)
Leisure	tramp (slang)	almost	siesta, after-lunch sleep	river

8. Ont-ils déjà été à Versailles? 9. Qui a fait le gâteau? 10. Qui est allé faire une promenade? 11. Êtes-vous allé au théâtre hier soir? 12. Êtes-vous resté à la maison dimanche dernier (dairn-yay=last)? 13. Êtes-vous sorti mardi dernier? 14. Êtes-vous allé à Paris l'année dernière? 15. M. et Mme Roberts sont-ils arrivés en retard?

III Translate into French

1. At what time do you have dinner? 2. At what time did you have dinner yesterday? 3. Did you drink wine last night? 4. Have you been to Paris? 5. Not yet, but I shall go in summer. 6. I have been to Boulogne. 7. Last year we went to Nice. 8. They have not arrived yet. 9. They left for America last month. 10. We stayed in the theatre (for) four hours. 11. I did not go out last night. 12. My parents have arrived. We went to the station.

(*Key on page* 210)

KEY TO THE EXERCISES

Lesson Fourteen

I

1. il donne, donnait, a donné, donnera. 2. il prend, prenait, a pris, prendra. 3. il met, mettait, a mis, mettra. 4. il achète, achetait, a acheté, achètera. 5. il dit, disait, a dit, dira.

II

1. This book is a good one, but that book is a better one; it is the best of all my books. 2. Spring is the best season. 3. George is the happiest boy of the town. 4. I shall wash in the bathroom. 5. He will be very tired. 6. Will they be late for breakfast? 7. We shall spend the holidays at the seaside. 8. When will you have your holidays? 9. She will not change her money. 10. Why don't you count your change? 11. Will they sell their house? 12. I should like to go to bed early.

III

1. Mes cigares sont meilleurs que vos cigarettes. 2. Le meilleur tabac est très cher. 3. Des cigarettes françaises sont meilleur marché. 4. Elles sont dix francs la pièce. 5. Combien coûte le paquet de dix? 6. Il aura à écrire beaucoup de lettres. 7. Changerez-vous vos billets de banque anglais? 8. Je n'oublierai pas d'acheter une boîte d'allumettes et de l'encre. 9. Y a-t-il une papeterie près d'ici? 10. Nous entrerons dans un bistro, où l'on peut acheter des timbres-poste. 11. Je voudrais des cartes postales illustrées. 12. Voudriez-vous aller avec moi?

Lesson Fifteen

I

1. Il ne l'écoute pas. 2. Ils les regardent. 3. Nous allons les voir. 4. Elle la met sur la bouche. 5. Il ne les mange pas. 6. L'aimez-vous? 7. Il ne les trouve pas. 8. Elle l'attend. 9. Ils ne la ferment pas. 10. La prend-il?

II

1. Prenez-vous la salade? Oui, je la prends. 2. Est-ce qu'elle prend du hareng? Elle ne le prend pas. 3. Est-ce que le professeur ouvre la fenêtre? Non, il ne l'ouvre pas. 4. Ils mangent de la viande, des légumes et des fruits. 5. Je ne mange pas de poisson. 6. J'aime manger des fraises. 7. Aimez-vous manger des cerises? 8. Mettez-vous du sucre dans le café? 9. Je mets trois morceaux dans mon café. 10. Le garçon ne nous a pas apporté le vin. 11. Le fromage est très bon; je le recommande. 12. Je ne peux pas les accompagner. 13. Attendez-moi. 14. Ne m'attendez pas. 15. Attendez-la. 16. Ne l'attendez pas.

III

1. Il y a quelque chose (il n'y a rien). 2. Je mange beaucoup de pain (je ne mange pas beaucoup de pain). 3. Je bois du vin (je ne bois pas de vin). 4. Je mange des

fruits. 5. Je (ne) mets (pas de) du lait dans le café. 6. Je (ne) bois (pas de) du café noir. 7. Je la mange avec une cuillère. 8. Nous la coupons avec un couteau. 9 and 10. Je l'aime (Je ne l'aime pas). 11. J' (je n') aime (pas) les lire. 12. Du fromage et des fruits. 13. Ils vont à un café. 14. M. Lesage les accompagne. 15. Il les rejoindra à quatre heures et demie.

Lesson Sixteen

I

1. J'en ai beaucoup (je n'en ai pas beaucoup). 2. J'en mange (je n'en mange pas). 3. Same as 1. 4. J'en achète chez le fruitier. 5. Chez le boucher. 6. Le fruitier en vend. 7. J'en ai assez. 8. Elle n'en achète pas. 9. Elle achète des cerises et des abricots. 10. Non, elle n'était pas contente de son boucher. 11. Il avait vendu de la viande dure. 12. Elle en prend deux. 13. Non, il n'est pas chez le boulanger. 14. Dans un bureau de tabac. 15. Il a changé de l'argent anglais.

II

1. Elle en achète. 2. On en mange. 3. Elle en a. 4. Il le boit. 5. Il en boit. 6. Elle l'a achetée. 7. Elle en achète. 8. Il les apporte. 9. Ils en mangent beaucoup. 10. Ils les regardent. 11. Elle n'en a pas. 12. Il en veut.

III

1. J'ai du pain, mais je n'ai pas de beurre. 2. En avez-vous? 3. J'en ai un peu. 4. Je n'en ai pas. 5. Il n'y a pas de cerises chez le fruitier. 6. N'y en a-t-il pas? 7. Ne buvez-vous pas de vin rouge? 8. N'en buvez-vous jamais? 9. Je veux de bonnes oranges. 10. En avez-vous? 11. J'ai des pommes, mais je n'ai pas de poires. 12. Est-ce que votre père boit du vin blanc? 13. Votre tante demande s'il y a de la viande. 14. La bonne dit qu'il n'y en a pas.

15. Elle va acheter du fromage. des légumes et de la viande.

Lesson Seventeen

I

1. Je n'ai pas compris. 2. Il a été malade. 3. J'ai eu une faim de loup. 4. Est-ce que Mme a sonné? 5. Elle n'a pas aimé la bière. 6. Nous n'avons pas fermé les yeux. 7. Il a pris le métro. 8. La domestique a apporté la viande. 9. Personne n'a voulu de potage. 10. Elle a fait une robe.

II

1. J'en ai lu beaucoup (je n'en ai pas lu beaucoup). 2. Hier j'ai dîné à sept heures. 3. Je n'en ai pas bu hier. J'en ai bu hier. 4. Oui, j'ai mangé quelque chose ce matin. 5. Je n'ai pas fait de promenade. J'ai fait une promenade hier soir. 6. Il en a pris. 7. Ils l'ont déjà visité. 8. Ils n'ont pas encore été à Versailles. 9. Mme Lesage l'a fait. 10. Mme Roberts, Mlle Lesage et Georges sont allés faire une promenade. 11. Je (ne) suis (pas) allé au théâtre hier soir. 12. Je (ne) suis (pas) resté à la maison. 13. Je (ne) suis (pas) sorti mardi dernier. 14. Je (ne) suis (pas) allé à Paris l'année dernière. 15. Oui, ils sont arrivés en retard.

III

1. À quelle heure dînez-vous? 2. À quelle heure avez-vous dîné hier? 3. Avez-vous bu du vin hier soir? 4. Avez-vous été à Paris? 5. Pas encore, mais j'irai cet été. 6. J'ai été à Boulogne. 7. L'année dernière nous sommes allés à Nice. 8. Ils ne sont pas encore arrivés. 9. Ils sont partis pour l'Amérique le mois dernier. 10. Nous sommes restés au théâtre quatre heures. 11. Je ne suis pas sorti hier soir. 12. Mes parents sont arrivés. Nous sommes allés à la gare.

ANOTHER FRENCH PROVERB
Le menteur n'est plus écouté, quand même il dit la vérité.
A liar is no longer listened to, even when he speaks the truth.

PRONUNCIATION AT SIGHT

WE have now reached a stage in this Course where we no longer consider it necessary to provide students with phonetic transcriptions. We feel sure that by now every one of our readers will be able to pronounce at sight frequent words as **monsieur, madame, mademoiselle, je suis, un peu, tu, du** and **s'il vous plaît.** The phonetic transcriptions have been given so often, that it would really amount to a complete waste of space to continue giving them.

As we explained in the beginning, our system of imitated pronunciation did not claim to do more than to offer a nearest English equivalent, not an exact reproduction of French sounds. For that reason we advised students to listen in to French being spoken by Frenchmen, and to check their own pronunciation as they listened. Many students will have done this, and the material which follows should aid them in the task of perfecting what they have learned.

While in English the same letter or combination of letters is quite often sounded differently in different words, in French every letter and every combination of letters can—with very few exceptions—be pronounced in one way only. Whereas *ou* is pronounced differently in *soup, soul, house, enough,* etc., French **ou** is always pronounced the same, namely as in English *soup*; whereas English *au* is pronounced differently in *daughter, laughter, automatic,* etc., French **au** is almost always pronounced **oh**; whereas English "u" is differently sounded in *but, sure, supply, survey,* etc., French **u** is always pronounced "œ" when not forming part of a nasal sound. It is clearly impossible to give, to a foreign student of English, rules of pronunciation that will enable him to pronounce correctly words that he has never heard before. But it is the object of this section to show how every letter and every combination of letters should be pronounced in French.

I. THE VOWELS

Vowels are generally either long or short (*see* page 214).   *Examples*

a } as in "far," when long, and like the "a" in "rat"
à } when short.   *page, dame, par, la, a, ma, papa.*

â as in "bah!", always long.   *âme* (soul), *âge, tâche* (task).

é like "ay" in "gay," but shorter.   *été, donné, thé.*

è like "ai" in "pair."   *père, mère, je lève.*

e as in "her," at the end of a word or syllable.   *le, me, retenir* (to retain).

   like **é** when followed by a mute consonant.   *les, mes, ses.*

   like **è** when followed by a sounded consonant. *elle, lettre, terre* (earth).

i like "ee" in "seen."   *qui, il, ici, ami.*

î like **i**, but always long.   *île* (island).

o long as in "home."   *rose, poser.*

   short like "aw" in "lawyer."   *comme, poste, robe.*

ô as in "home," always long.   *trône* (throne), *tôt, rôti.*

u } "œ" with closely rounded lips.   *lu, vu, mûr* (ripe), *sûr.*
û }

y like **i**, but always long.   *style, y, cylindre.*

ai usually like **è**.   *vrai, jamais, palais.*

   like **é** in *gai, j'ai* (but **è** in *ai-je*) and the termination of the first person singular Future.   *je donnerai.*

   like **e** in "her" in *faisons*, and in Imperfect of *faire.*   *je faisais*, etc.

   like **a** if followed by *l* or *ll*. *travailler, le travail, volaille.*

ay like **è**.   *crayon, payer.*

au ⎱ like "oh."   *auto, au, autre.*
eau ⎰   *beau, couteau, eau.*

ei like **è**, always long.   *reine* (queen), *peine.*

eu like "i" in "fir" when followed by a hard consonant;   *neuf, beurre.*
like **é** pronounced with rounded lips when followed   *deux, feu, heureuse.*
by a soft consonant or by a silent consonant, or
at the end of a word.

like **ę**, when meaning "had" (past participle of   *J'ai eu peur.*
avoir) or in *eut*, the Preterite of *avoir*.

oi like "wah."   *trois, moi, froid.*

œu like "i" in "fir" (in the plural of œuf—"egg," the *œu*   *cœur, sœur, œuf.*
is sounded like "ay" pronounced with rounded lips).

ou like "oo" in "tool."   *poule, fou, jour, pour.*

oy like **oi**.   *nettoyer, royal, loyer* (lwah-yay).

ui like **u+i** making the u very short, the i following   *lui, huit, nuit, puis.*
immediately.

II. CONSONANTS

(unless mentioned below, they are the same as in English)

c pronounced "k" before *a, o, u* or a consonant.   *cage, cacao, crédit.*
pronounced "s" before *e, i, y*.   *ce, cigare, bicyclette.*

cc pronounced "k" before *a, o, u* or a consonant,   *occuper* (o-kę-pay),
"ks" before *e* or *i*.   *accepter* (ahk-saip-tay),
     accident (ahk-see-daN).

ç always like "s."   *Français, garçon.*

ch like English "sh."   *chien, cheval, chef.*
"k" in some words.   *écho, Christ, chrétien* (kray-tyiN
=Christian), *chœur* (kāyr
=choir), *choléra, technique
orchestre.*

g hard as in "go" before *a, o, u* or a consonant other   *gare, goût, guide* (geed), *grand.*
than *n*.
soft, like "s" in "measure," before *e, i, y*.   *gentil, gilet, gymnastique.*

ge like soft "g" before *a, o, u* (the "e" is mute here, it   *je mangeais, nous mangeons.*
is merely an indication that the "g" is soft).

gn like "ni" in English "onion."   *oignon, Bretagne, signe.*

gu like hard "*g*" (the "*u*" is mute here, it only shows   *langue, guerre, guitare.*
that the "*g*" retains its hard sound).

h is always silent. Most words beginning with "h"   *l'heure, l'homme, l'hôtel, les*
are treated exactly as if they began with a vowel   *heures* (lay-zāyr), *les hommes*
(mute "*h*").   (lay-zom).
in some words, however, the "h" is treated as a con-   *le hareng* (herring); *le hasard*
sonant (*h aspiré*), i.e. there is neither liaison nor   (chance, risk); *la hâte*
elision. Some of the most frequent ones are given   (haste); *haut* (oh=high);
opposite: *la Hollande* (Holland); *la
Hongrie* (Hungary), *le Havre*.

(This difference is made because *h aspiré* was sounded in former times. In modern French both are equally silent.)

j like soft g (zh). — *je, jamais, journal.*

l as in "lamp" (never as in "all"). — *la, lampe, boule* (ball).

ll preceded by *i* pronounced double "l" when a word begins with "ill." — *illégal, illustration.*

pronounced like "y" in English *yes* in the middle or at the end of a word. — *fille, bouteille, famille.*

like single "l" in — *mille, million, ville, village, tranquille* and in a few others.

q } like "k." — *coq, cinq, que, quand, question.*
qu

r resembles the sound of gargling (see p. 12). — *rose, Charles, rouge.*

s at the beginning of a word as in "see." — *sont, sac, sucre.*

between vowels like "z" also in the following words (although preceded by a consonant): — *Alsace, alsacien, transaction, transition, transatlantique.*

ss always like "s" in "see." — *poisson, assassinat* (murder).

sc like "sk" before *a, o, u* or a consonant. — *scandale, sculpteur.*

like "s" (in "see") before *e, i,* or *y.* — *descendre, science.*

t usually as in English. — *tenir, question, vingtième.*

like "s" (in "see") in words ending in *-tial, -tiel, -tience, -tieux, -tie, -tion* (when not *-stion*) — *nation, essentiel, patience, partial, ambitieux, aristocratie.*

th like t. — *thé, théâtre.*

w like English "v." — *wagon.*

x—"gz" when at the beginning followed by a vowel or *h.* — *exact, exagérer, exhibition.*

like "z" in — *deuxième, sixième, dixième.*

like "ks" in all other cases. — *luxe, excuse, excellent.*

III. FINAL LETTERS

Final e without any accent is not sounded, unless it is the only vowel of the word, as in *je, le, me,* etc.

Final consonants are usually not pronounced, except final **c, f, k, l, q** and **r**; e.g. *parc, sac, avec,* etc. (c pronounced as k.)

f is pronounced in *bref* (short); *sauf* (except); *soif* (thirst); *neuf,* etc.

k final only in foreign words: *Danemark; bifteck, bock,* etc.

is pronounced in *il; fil; mil; avril; exil;* and others.

q final is pronounced as **k**: *coq* (cock).

r final is usually pronounced (*mer; cher; hiver; hier; car; par; sortir; or; noir; cour;* etc.) but it is mute in the ending of the infinitive *-er,* which is pronounced like *é,* and the ending *-ier,* which is pronounced "yay."

ent, the ending of the 3rd person plural is silent: *ils donnent.* But the t is pronounced in *donnent-ils.*

Exceptions to the rules given above:—

b final is pronounced in proper names and in foreign words: Jacob, club.

c final is mute in *tabac, estomac* (stomach), *porc, caoutchouc* (rubber).

d final is pronounced in *sud* (south) and in proper names like *David.*

f final is mute in *clef* (key), also written *clé.*

l final is mute in *fusil* (rifle), *gentil* (nice), *outil* (tool), *sourcil* (eyebrow). **il** is pronounced "y" in *travail* (work), *soleil* (sun), *fauteuil* (armchair) and a few others. For the pronunciation of *ille* see Section II above.

m final: see section IV (below).
n final: see section IV (below).
r final: the "r" is pronounced in *hier* (yesterday) and *fier* (proud); it is mute in *monsieur* and *messieurs*.
s final is pronounced in *omnibus*; *tennis*; *gratis*; *as*; *atlas*; *hélas*; *bis* (twice); *ours* (bear), and in certain proper names.
t final is pronounced in *mat, net, sept, est* (east), *ouest* (west), *déficit, tact, strict,*

huit, except when followed by a word it multiplies which begins with a consonant or an aspirated "h": *huit cents*; *huit livres*, etc.
x final is pronounced "s" in *six* and *dix*, but silent when followed by a plural beginning with a consonant (*six livres*). etc.
z final is sounded in *gaz* and in foreign words.

IV. NASALS

Nasals occur whenever a vowel comes before *m* or *n* at the end of a word, or when these letters are followed by one or several consonants. They are purely vowel sounds, and there is no difference whether *n* or *m* follows. How to nasalize vowels has been explained in the Introduction to French Pronunciation in the first part of this Course.

an, am, en, em nasalized "ah"
anglais, lampe, patient, temps;

on, om nasalized "o"
on, concert, bon, nom, compliment;

un, um nasalized "a̅y̅"
un, commun, parfum, humble;
in, im, ain, aim, ein, eim, yn, ym nasalized "ai"
vin; *quinze, impossible, bain, faim, plein, Reims, sympathique, syncope* (fainting fit).
en is pronounced like "iN" in *vient, tient, mien, bien, combien, examen, européen. égyptien, parisien* and *moyen* (=means).
Note.—If the **m** or **n** is followed by a vowel (or "*h*") or doubled, it loses its nasal sound: *une, bonne, immense, bonheur, brune,* etc.

V. SIGNS AND ACCENTS

(1) **l'accent aigu** (´) to show that e is pronounced *ay*: *été, donné, thé.*
(2) **l'accent grave** (`) to show that e is pronounced *ai*: *père, mère, il lève*; to distinguish meanings, without changing pronunciation, e.g., *a*=has; *à*= to; *ou*=or, *où*=where; *la*=the; *là*=there.
(3) **l'accent circonflexe** (^) to show that e is open and long: *tête, fenêtre*; to

lengthen other vowels: *âme* (soul) *île* (island), *côte* (coast).
(4) **le tréma** (¨) to show that the vowel bearing it is not blended with the preceding vowel: *Noël* (Christmas), *naïf* (nah-eef).
(5) **la cédille** (say-deey) to give the ç the sound of "s" before "a, o, u": *ça, leçon, reçu.*
(6) **l'apostrophe** to indicate the omission of a vowel: *l'hôtel, j'ai, s'il.*

VI. LENGTH OF VOWELS

Vowels are long:

(1) Before a single soft consonant (*vr, ch,* and *ll* when sounded "y" count as one consonant):
page, dame, rouge, rose, livre. fille, gauche.
(2) When having a circumflex accent: *tête, côte, sûr.*

Vowels are short:

(1) When followed by a hard consonant or by two consonants:
os, force, juste, carte, lourd.
(2) When a final syllable ends in a vowel sound:
ma, la, si, est, vous, tu, bleu, couteau.
(3) When é or e:
je, me, été, fermé, donner, cheval, revenir.

Vowels are of medium length:
In all other cases.
Nasals are long:
When followed by a consonant which is sounded:

France, oncle, tante, ronde, grande.
Nasals are of medium length:
In all other cases.
Nasals are short:Never.

VII. LIAISON

When a word ending in a consonant stands before a word beginning with a vowel or **h** mute, the consonant is frequently pronounced and the two words joined in pronunciation. They are spoken as if the final consonant were detached from its own word and became the initial sound of the following one, e.g., *mes amis* is pronounced *may-zah-mee*, etc.

It is impossible to give definite and infallible rules as to where liaison should or should not take place. It is less frequent in conversation than in reading aloud.

Liaison is obligatory, if the two words are closely connected in sense, namely:

(1) after *les, des, ces, aux, nous, vous, ils, elles: les amis, des enfants, ces hommes, des hôtels, aux États-Unis, nous avons, ils ont, elles aiment.*

(2) Between adjectives and the following nouns: *le petit enfant, un grand amour, plusieurs hôtels, quelques amis, trois hommes.*

(3) Between prepositions and the following words: *en été, dans un jardin, sous une table, pendant une heure, chez elle,* etc.

(4) Between *bien, très, plus, moins,* and a following adjective: *très actif, plus intéressant, moins intelligent.*

(5) After auxiliary verbs (but not after *tu es* or *tu as*): *il est occupé, elles ont entendu, ils sont arrivés, il avait eu, ils ont acheté,* etc.

(6) In expressions and compounds: *tout à coup* (=suddenly), *de temps en temps* (=from time to time), *vis à vis* (face to face, opposite), *de plus en plus* (=more and more), etc.

Liaison must never be used:

(1) Between a noun used as a subject and *est*: *la maison est belle.*

(2) With a mute consonant following "r": *il sort à midi, cela ne sert à rien.*

(3) after infinitives in *-er*: *il faut aller immédiatement, elle va retourner à Paris.*

(4) Before aspirated "h," before *huit* or *onze*: *la Hollande, les huit jours, les onze harengs.*

(5) after *et*=*and*: *une fourchette et un couteau.*

NOTE:

(1) In liaison, **d** is sounded like "t," **f** like "v," **s** and **x** like "z": *un grand hôtel, neuf heures, deux enfants, trois images,* etc.

(2) When the n of a nasal sound is sounded in liaison, the preceding vowel may lose some of its nasal quality, particularly in rapid speech.

PUNCTUATION MARKS

. *point*
, *virgule*
: *deux points*
; *point-virgule*
! *point d'exclamation*
? *point d'interrogation*
- *trait d'union*
— *tiret*
" " *guillemets*
( ) *parenthèses*

THREE MORE PROVERBS

Il ne faut pas mettre le doigt entre l'arbre et l'écorce. Do not interfere between a man and his wife. (Literally: One must not put one's finger between the tree and the bark.)

Pierre qui roule n'amasse pas mousse. A rolling stone gathers no moss.

Loin des yeux, loin du cœur. Out of sight. out of mind.

AU VIEUX MONTMARTRE

On mange en plein air sur la fameuse Place du Tertre, au sommet de la Butte Montmartre. À l'arrière-plan, la flèche de la Basilique du Sacré-Cœur.

Manger en plein air	**tertre** (m.)	**butte** (f.)	**à l'arrière-plan**	**flèche** (f.)
To eat in the open	hillock	knoll	in the background	spire (of church)

DIX-HUITIÈME LEÇON

EN VILLE—IN TOWN

M. et Mme Roberts désireux de connaître Paris se promènent dans les rues
Mr. and Mrs. Roberts desirous to know Paris are walking in the streets

en regardant les vieux quartiers et les vieilles maisons qui ont déjà vu
looking at the old parts and the old houses which have already seen

tant de siècles.   Ils visitent le vieux Montmartre avec ses petites rues montantes
so many centuries.   They visit old Montmartre with its small steep streets

et ses innombrables escaliers.   Ils visitent le "Père-Lachaise" et
and its countless stairs.   They visit the "Père-Lachaise" and

regardent les tombeaux des célébrités qui y reposent.   Ils ont déjà vu
look at the tombs of the famous who rest there.   They have already seen

tant de choses que finalement Mme Roberts dit à son mari:
so many things that finally Mrs. Roberts says to her husband:

LE PEINTRE MONTMARTROIS
Nullement gêné par la présence des laïques, le peintre poursuit sa tâche.

Nullement (adv.)	**gêner**	**laïque** (m.f.)	**poursuivre**	**tâche** (f.)
Not at all, in no way	to embarrass	layman	to continue with	task

Ne trouves-tu pas que nous en avons assez vu aujourd'hui?
Don't you find that we have seen enough today?

M. Roberts: **Plus je regarde Paris, plus je l'aime.** **Je ne veux pas**
The more I look at Paris, the more I like it. I don't want

quitter cette ville sans en avoir vu le plus possible.
to leave this town without having seen as much as possible.

Mme Roberts: **Pour vraiment connaître Paris il faudrait des années . . .**
In order really to know Paris one would need years . . .

M. Roberts: **Je sais, mais je veux tout de même voir ce que tout étranger**
I know, but I want, nevertheless, to see what every foreigner

visite à Paris. **Mme Roberts: Je te comprends parfaitement;**
visits in Paris. I understand you perfectly;

néanmoins, je suis trop fatiguée aujourd'hui. **Je te ferai une**
nevertheless, I am too tired today. I'll make you a

LE CIMETIÈRE DU PÈRE-LACHAISE

Le "Monument des Morts" au Père-Lachaise. Dans ce cimetière sont ensevelis Héloïse et Abélard, amants tragiques dont le roman a attristé le monde entier, et Oscar Wilde, exilé volontaire après avoir été relâché de la prison de Reading.

Cimetière (m.)	**ensevelir**	**attrister**	**relâcher**
Cemetery	to bury	to sadden	to release

proposition. Tu verras l'Arc de Triomphe sans moi, et moi,
suggestion.   You will see the Arc de Triomphe without me, and

j'attendrai dans ce petit café, où je prendrai
I shall wait in this little café, where I shall have

une glace. M. Roberts: Bien, tu es très gentille ma chère;
an ice-cream.   All right, you are very kind, my dear;

à tout à l'heure. (S'adressant à un passant): Monsieur,
bye-bye, until later.   (Addressing himself to a passer-by): Sir.

pouvez-vous m'indiquer le chemin pour aller à l'Arc de Triomphe?
can you indicate to me the way (to go) to the Arc de Triomphe?

Passant: Je regrette, monsieur, je ne suis pas du quartier.
I regret, sir, I am a stranger myself (lit., I am not of the district).

Voilà un facteur qui pourra certainement
There is a postman who will certainly be able

vous renseigner.   M. Roberts: Merci beaucoup, monsieur.   (Il
to direct you.   Thank you very much, sir.   (He

s'approche du facteur.)   Pardon,
goes up to the postman.)   Excuse me,

monsieur, pouvez-vous me dire quel
sir, could you tell me which

chemin je dois prendre pour aller
way I have to take to go

à l'Arc de Triomphe?   Facteur: Avec
to the Arc de Triomphe?   With

plaisir, monsieur.   Suivez cette rue
pleasure, sir.   Follow that street

jusqu'au bout, puis tournez à droite et continuez tout
up to the end, then turn to the right and continue straight

droit.   Vous arriverez à un carrefour, d'où vous verrez
ahead.   You will arrive at a cross-roads, where you will see

l'Arc de Triomphe au bout de la deuxième rue à gauche.
the Arc de Triomphe at the end of the second street on the left.

M. Roberts: Vous êtes très aimable.   Est-ce loin?
That is very kind of you.   Is it far?

Facteur: Pas du tout, c'est tout près, à peine dix minutes d'ici.
Not at all, it's quite near, hardly ten minutes from here.

M. Roberts: Merci bien, monsieur. (Il suit
Thanks very much, sir. (He follows

le chemin indiqué pendant dix minutes,
the way indicated for ten minutes,

à peu près, sans arriver à son
approximately, without arriving at his

but. Alors il s'adresse à un agent de police.)
goal. Then he speaks to a policeman.)

Pardon, monsieur l'agent, est-ce bien par
Excuse me, officer, is it (right) by

ici que je peux arriver a l'Arc de Triomphe?
this way that I can get to the Arc de Triomphe?

Agent: Pas du tout, monsieur, c'est juste dans le sens opposé.
Not at all, sir, it's just in the opposite direction.

Retournez jusqu'à la première à gauche,
Go back as far as the first street on the left,

prenez la grande avenue que vous trouverez devant vous,
take the broad thoroughfare which you will find in front of you,

et vous verrez l'Arc de Triomphe au bout de cette avenue.
and you will see the Arc de Triomphe at the end of this avenue.

Je t'aime
I love you

"THOU" IN FRENCH

The Familiar Form.—While in English the familiar form—THOU, THY, THEE—is almost extinct, it is used in French when speaking to small children and intimate friends.

Present Tense

Ordinary Form	Familiar Form	
vous avez	tu as	you have
vous êtes	tu es	you are
vous parlez	tu parles	you speak
vous donnez	tu donnes	you give
vous aimez	tu aimes	you love
vous allez	tu vas	you go
vous faites	tu fais	you make
vous prenez	tu prends	you take
vous mettez	tu mets	you put
vous venez	tu viens	you come

vous dormez	tu dors	you sleep
vous partez	tu pars	you leave
vous sortez	tu sors	you go out
vous attendez	tu attends	you wait
vous pouvez	tu peux	you can
vous voulez	tu veux	you want, wish, will

Note that the forms of the verb used in connection with **tu**, as far as pronunciation is concerned, are identical with the forms used in connection with **il** or **elle**. With regard to spelling, however, note that they all, with the exception of the last two examples given, end in -s.

Other Tenses

vous aviez	tu avais	you had
vouz étiez	tu étais	you were
vous parliez	tu parlais	you spoke
vous donniez	tu donnais	you gave
vouz aimiez	tu aimais	you loved
vous alliez	tu allais	you went
vous faisiez	tu faisais	you made
vous disiez	tu disais	you said
vous veniez	tu venais	you came
vous dormiez	tu dormais	you slept
vous partiez	tu partais	you left
vous attendiez	tu attendais	you waited
vous pouviez	tu pouvais	you could
vous vouliez	tu voulais	you wanted
vous aurez	tu auras	you will have
vous serez	tu seras	you will be
vous parlerez	tu parleras	you will speak
vous donnerez	tu donneras	you will give
vous irez	tu iras	you will go
vous viendrez	tu viendras	you will come
vous ferez	tu feras	you will make
vous direz	tu diras	you will say
vous prendrez	tu prendras	you will take
vous mettrez	tu mettras	you will put
vous dormirez	tu dormiras	you will sleep
vous partirez	tu partiras	you will leave
vous pourrez	tu pourras	you will be able
vous voudrez	tu voudras	you will want
vous avez eu	tu as eu	you have had
vous avez été	tu as été	you have been
vous avez parlé	tu as parlé	you have spoken

vous avez donné	tu as donné	you have given
vous avez fait	tu as fait	you have made
vous avez dit	tu as dit	you have said
vous avez pris	tu as pris	you have taken
vous avez attendu	tu as attendu	you have waited
vous avez dormi	tu as dormi	you have slept
vous êtes venu(e/s/es)	tu es venu(e)	you have come
vous êtes parti(e/s/es)	tu es parti(e)	you have left
vous êtes sorti(e/s/es)	tu es sorti(e)	you have gone out

Note that all these forms, as far as pronunciation is concerned, are identical with the forms used in connection with **il** or **elle,** and that with regard to spelling they all end in -s, which, however, is not sounded.

Imperative

donnez!	donne!	give!
parlez!	parle!	speak!
mangez!	mange!	eat!
attendez!	attends!	wait!
prenez!	prends!	take!
dormez!	dors!	sleep!
allez!	va!	go!
ayez!	aie!	have . . .!
soyez!	sois!	be . . .!

Note that the Imperative singular is the same as the first person (i.e. the form of the present tense used in connection with **je**), with the exception of the last three examples given above.

The Possessive Adjective

votre livre	ton livre	your book
votre chaise	ta chaise	your chair
votre père	ton père	your father
votre mère	ta mère	your mother
vos parents	tes parents	your parents
vos livres	tes livres	your books
vos chaises	tes chaises	your chairs

Ton (toN), ta (tah), tes (tay) are the French equivalents for "thy."

Ton is used with masculine nouns, singular, and before a feminine singular noun beginning with a vowel or mute h; ta with feminines (singular) and tes with plurals (masculine and feminine). Compare mon, ma, mes with ton, ta, tes:

mon chapeau...............	my hat
ton chapeau................	thy hat
ma robe.....................	my dress
ta robe.....................	thy dress
mes chapeaux...............	my hats
tes chapeaux...............	thy hats
mes robes..................	my dresses
tes robes..................	thy dresses

The Object Pronoun

je vous vois	je te vois	I see you
je vous aime	je t'aime	I love you
vous vous lavez	tu te laves	you wash yourself
vous habillez-vous?	t'habilles-tu?	are you getting dressed?
levez-vous!	lève-toi!	get up!
ne vous levez pas!	ne te lève pas!	don't get up!
vous vous en allez	tu t'en vas	you are going away
allez-vous-en!	va-t'en!	go away!
ne vous en allez paz!	ne t'en va pas!	don't go away!

The familiar form of the object pronoun is te or t' in front of a vowel or mute h.

va-t-en!
go away!

ne t'en va pas!
don't go away!

Compare te (t') with me (m'):

il me vois.................	he sees me
il te vois.................	he sees thee
elle m'aime...............	she loves me
elle t'aime...............	she loves thee

POUVOIR—TO BE ABLE

I can	*Can I?*
je peux	puis-je?
tu peux	peux-tu?
il (elle) peut	peut-il (elle)?
nous pouvons	etc.
vous pouvez	
ils (elles) peuvent	

I cannot	*I could*
je ne peux pas	je pouvais
or: je ne puis pas	tu pouvais
tu ne peux pas	il pouvait
etc.	etc.

I shall be able	*I have been able*
je pourrai	j'ai pu
tu pourras	tu as pu
il pourra	il a pu
etc.	etc.

The English "I can" is a defective verb. i.e., it has only a Present and a Past Tense; for the other tenses "to be able" has to be used. In French, however, "I can" is a full verb, capable of forming all tenses, except the Imperative.

Note that the first person of the Present Interrogative is irregular, and also that there is an alternative form for the first person of the Present Negative, which is frequently used.

EXERCISES

I Answer in French

1. Est-ce que tu es plus grand que ton père? 2. Est-ce que tu écris beaucoup de lettres? 3. Est-ce que tu as parlé français hier? 4. Est-ce que tu manges des pommes? 5. Qu'est-ce que tu as mangé pour le petit déjeuner? 6. Est-ce que tu prends du sucre dans ton café? 7. M'as-tu vu hier soir? 8. Bois-tu de bon vin blanc? 9. As-tu bu du vin à midi? 10. Quel livre lis-tu maintenant? 11. As-tu lu "Les Misérables" par Victor Hugo? 12. T'es-tu levé de bonne heure aujourd'hui?

II Replace vous, votre, vos by the more intimate form—tu, te, ton, ta, tes, etc.

1. Vous mettez les fruits sur la table. 2. Ne prenez-vous pas de légumes? 3. N'écrivez-vous pas? 4. Vous êtes bien aimable. 5. Avez-vous vos cartes? 6. Regardez-vous votre tableau? 7. Vous pouvez venir avec votre frère. 8. Vous vous couchez tard. 9. Il vous voit. 10. Ne vous lavez-vous pas? 11. Partez-vous avec votre fille? 12. Vous vous en allez.

III Translate

1. Do you want to go for a walk? 2. I shall not be able to go out today. 3. Don't you want to see your sister? 4. Will you not be able to see her? 5. Have you seen your friends? 6. Can you tell me please which way I have to go to get to Rue Montmartre? 7. I am sorry, I cannot tell you. 8. There is a policeman who will be able to tell you. 9. I saw you last night. 10. Did you see me too? 11. I have seen your brother and your parents, but I haven't seen your sister. 12. Don't do that. 13. Don't speak so fast! 14. Don't go. 15. Wait, please.

(Key on page 252.)

L'AVENUE DES CHAMPS-ÉLYSÉES VUE DE L'ARC DE TRIOMPHE

En descendant l'Avenue, bordée tout le long de beaux platanes, l'on traverse le Rond-Point des Champs-Élysées pour aboutir à la Place de la Concorde.

platane (m.)
plane tree

rond-point (m.)
circus (meeting of several roads)

aboutir
to end in, at

DIX-NEUVIÈME LEÇON

LA FAMILLE ROBERTS AU VIEUX MONTMARTRE

Madame et Monsieur Roberts visitant le Vieux Montmartre ont monté la colline. Ils remarquent quelques maisons délabrées, ils longent quelques ruelles écartées et ils grimpent d'anciens escaliers de tout genre.

colline (f.)	**délabré-e** (adj.)	**écarté-e** (adj.)	**grimper**
hill	dilapidated	secluded	to climb

M. et Mme Roberts se promènent dans les rues de Paris et visitent plusieurs
Mr. and Mrs. Roberts are walking in the streets of Paris and visit several

magasins, pour y faire des achats. Leurs enfants, Charles et Madeleine,
shops to make some purchases there. Their children, Charles and Madeleine,

les accompagnent. En ce moment ils entrent dans un magasin à prix unique.
accompany them. At this moment they are entering a one-price store.

M. Roberts (s'adressant à une vendeuse): Pardon, mademoiselle, où
(addressing himself to a saleswoman): Pardon, miss, where

    est le rayon des articles de toilette, s'il vous plaît?
    is the department for toilet articles, please?

La vendeuse: **Par là, monsieur, vous le trouverez au bout de ce passage.**
        That way, sir, you will find it at the end of this passage.

M. Roberts: **Merci, mademoiselle.**   **Vendeuse: À votre service, monsieur.**
       Thank you, miss.   At your service, sir.

Charles: **Maman, tu ne vas pas oublier ce que tu m'as promis?**
Mummy, you won't forget what you have promised me?

Mme Roberts: **Tu auras ta glace tout à l'heure.**   **Ne peux-tu pas**
You will have your ice-cream in a moment.   Can't you

          patienter un peu?   **Charles: Oui, maman, mais tu m'as promis**
          be patient a little?   Yes, mummy, but you have promised me

          encore autre chose . . .   **Mme Roberts: Ah, le ping-pong?**
          still something else . . .   Ah, the ping-pong?

          Petit polisson, n'as-tu pas confiance en ta mère?   **D'ailleurs,**
          Little rascal, have you no trust in your mother?   Besides,

          avec qui veux-tu jouer?   **Tu n'as pas de copain à Paris.**
          with whom will you play?   You have no friend in Paris.

Charles: **Ça ne fait rien.**   **Je peux jouer avec Madeleine, et puis**
That doesn't matter   I can play with Madeleine, and then

          Georges voudra sûrement jouer au ping-pong avec moi.
George would surely (like to) play ping-pong with me.

M. Roberts: **Nous y voilà.**   **Vous me servez, mademoiselle?**
Here we are.   Are you serving me, miss?

Une vendeuse: **Certainement, monsieur, que désirez-vous?**
Certainly, sir, what would you like?

M. Roberts: **Donnez-moi un morceau de ce savon!**
Give me a cake of this soap!

Vendeuse: **Le voilà, monsieur!**   **C'est tout ce qu'il vous faut?**
There you are, sir!   Is that all (that) you require?

M. Roberts: **Non, mademoiselle, donnez-moi encore ce paquet**
No, miss, give me also this packet

          de lames de rasoir; elles sont bonnes, j'espère?
          of razor blades; they are good, I hope?

Vendeuse: **Ah oui, monsieur, ce sont les meilleures.**   **C'est une marque**
Oh, yes, sir, these are the best.   It's a well-known

          très connue.   **M. Roberts: Ça sera tout pour aujourd'hui.**   **Combien**
          brand.   That will be all for to-day.   How much

          est-ce que je vous dois?   **Vendeuse: Ça fait cent francs, monsieur.**
          do I owe you?   A hundred francs, sir.

A FRENCH TOWN

With the text below covered, how many objects in the picture can you name in French? If you have to consult the text, cover it over again, and fill in any gaps in your list.

La mairie Town hall	**le stationnement des véhicules** taxi-rank		**le marché** market	**la grand'rue** main street
les (sapeurs) pompiers Fire brigade		**la mouette** seagull	**la place** square	**l'aiguille** (f.) spire
e faubourg Suburb	**l'usine** (f.) factory		**le clocher** belfry, steeple	**la caserne** barracks

M. Roberts: **Les voilà. Au revoir, mademoiselle.**
Here it is. Good bye, miss.

Mme Roberts: **J'aimerais mieux aller dans un magasin de nouveautés.**
I would prefer to go to a draper's stores.

Je ne crois pas que je trouve ici ce qu'il me faut.
I don't think that I shall find here what I want.

M. Roberts: **Ça m'est égal, allons-y!**
It's all the same to me, let's go there!

Charles: **Mais, maman, comme ça je n'aurai pas ce que tu m'as promis.**
But, mummy, like this I won't get what you have promised me.

Mme Roberts: **Charles, vraiment, tu m'énerves.**
Charles, really, you are unnerving (worrying) me.

(Ils quittent le magasin à prix unique et entrent dans une maison de nouveautés.)
(They leave the one-price shop and enter (in) a draper's stores.)

Un vendeur: **Bonjour, monsieur, dame! Vous désirez?**
Good day, sir, madam! You want something?

Mme Roberts: **Je cherche un sac-à-main; où est-ce que je peux trouver ça?**
I am looking for a handbag; where can I find that?

Le vendeur: **Le rayon de maroquinerie se trouve au premier étage,**
The leather goods department is on the first floor,

madame. Si vous voulez prendre l'ascenseur . . .
madam. If you will take the lift . . .

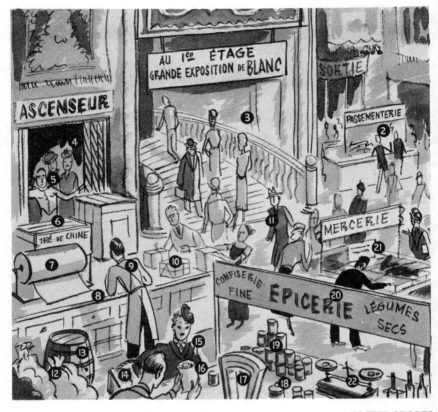

English

1. Jewellery; 2. Trimmings; 3. Grand staircase; 4. Lift; 5. Liftman; 6. Tea chest; 7. Wrapping paper; 8. Packing counter; 9. Shop assistant; 10. Package; 11. Male customer; 12. Sack; 13. Barrel; 14. Shopping basket; 15. Female customer; 16. Paper bag; 17. Scales (Spring balance); 18. Jar; 19. Tins; 20. Show-board; 21. Haberdashery; 22. Scales; 23. Shopwalker; 24. Price-ticket; 25. Knitted goods; 26. Notice; 27. Paying-in window; 28. Cashier (f.); 29. Cash-desk; 30. Clock Dept.; 31. Commissionaire; 32. Shopfront; 33. Shop-window; 34. Goods in window; 35. Tailor's dummy; 36. Revolving door; 37. Showcase for watches.

French

1. Bijouterie (f.); 2. Passementerie (f.); 3. Grand escalier (m.); 4. Ascenseur (m.); 5. Garçon d'ascenseur, liftier (m.); 6.

Further Useful Expressions	**Le dernier cri** The latest fashion	le dernier chic the last word (in smartness)	**marchander** to bargain

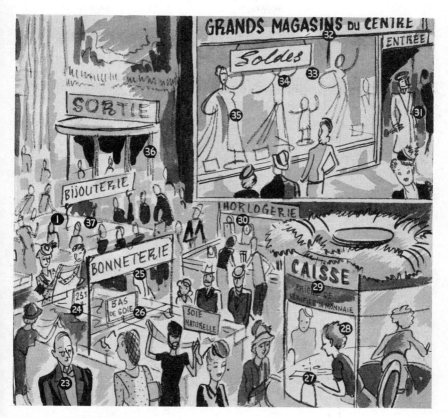

DANS UN GRAND MAGASIN

Caisse (f.) à thé ; 7. Papier (m.) d'emballage ; 8. Comptoir (m.) d'emballage ; 9. Employé-e (m.f.) de magasin ; vendeur-se (m.f.) ; 10. Paquet, colis (m.) ; 11. Chaland, client (m.) ; 12. Sac (m.) ; 13. Tonneau, baril, fût (m.) ; barrique (f.), etc. (according to nature of contents) ; 14. Panier, cabas (m.) ; 15. Chalande, cliente (f.) ; 16. Sac en (or de) papier ; 17. Peson (m.) ; balance (f.) à ressort ; 18. Pot, bocal (m.) ; jarre (f.), etc. (according to the contents) ; 19. Boîte (f.) à, de, conserves ; 20. Planche (f.) à affiche ; écriteau (m.) d'annonces ; 21. Mercerie (f.) ; 22. Balance (f.) ; 23. Chef (m.) de rayon ; 24. Étiquette (f.) ; 25. Bonneterie (f.) ; 26. Pancarte (f.) ; 27. Guichet (m.) ; 28. Caissière (f.) ; 29. Caisse (f.) ; 30. Horlogerie (f.) ; 31. Portier, commissionnaire (m.) ; 32. Devanture (f.) ; 33. Vitrine (f.) ; 34. Étalage (m.) ; 35. Figure (f.) de cire ; 36. Porte (f.) revolver ; 37. Vitrine (f.), porte-montres.

faire son marché to do one's shopping	**les bas indémaillables** run-proof stockings	**un fromage bien à point** a cheese nicely ripe

Mme Roberts: Ça ne vaut pas la peine.   Nous prendrons l'escalier.
That's not worth while.   We shall go by the staircase.

Je vous remercie, monsieur.
I thank you, sir.

(Ils montent au premier étage où ils s'adressent à
(They go up to the first floor, where they address themselves to

une vendeuse du rayon de maroquinerie.   Mme Roberts, après avoir
a saleswoman of the leather goods department.   Mme Roberts, after having

longtemps hésité s'est enfin décidée à acheter un très beau et
hesitated for a long time, has at last decided to buy a very beautiful and

très solide sac-à-main.   Après avoir payé, les Roberts visitent encore
strong handbag.   After having paid, the Robertses also visit

d'autres rayons.   Ils achètent des bas, des chaussettes, du linge, et même une
other departments.   They buy stockings, socks, linen, and even a

jolie robe pour Madeleine.   Mme Roberts a tenu parole en achetant quelques
pretty frock for Madeleine.   Mrs. Roberts has kept her word by buying some

jouets pour les enfants, et Charles, tout fier et heureux, est enfin devenu
toys for the children, and Charles, all proud and happy, has at last become

le propriétaire d'un ping-pong.)
the owner of a ping-pong set.)

M. Roberts: Tu dois être très fatiguée?   Je te propose d'aller prendre un
You must be very tired.   I suggest that you have a (some)

rafraîchissement au salon de thé.   Moi, j'irai acheter
refreshment in the tea-room   I shall go and buy

des cigarettes dans un bureau de tabac, et je vous rejoindrai
cigarettes in the tobacconist's, and I will rejoin you

dans un quart d'heure.
in a quarter of an hour.

SHOPPING EXPRESSIONS

The word used for the designation of the shop usually also applies to the designation of the trade or business and often also to the goods handled. **La mercerie** means not only the haberdasher's shop, but also his trade and his goods. **L'épicerie** means (1) the grocer's shop, (2) groceries, (3) the grocery business.

At the grocer's is.................... **chez l'épicier,** or **dans l'épicerie.**
At the butcher's.................... **chez le boucher,** or **dans la boucherie,** etc.
At a stationer's.................... **chez un libraire** or **dans une librairie,** etc.

La boutique is only "the small shop." The usual word for "shop" is **le magasin;** a department store is **un grand magasin.**

to go shopping   **faire des courses**
a bargain   **une occasion**
reduced in price   **à prix réduit**
to pay cash   **payer comptant**
a deposit   **des arrhes** (ahr) f.pl.
to leave a deposit of 1,000 francs   **laisser mille francs d'arrhes**
by instalments   **par acomptes**
the invoice   **la facture**
the bill   **la note**
a receipt   **un reçu**
to pack   **emballer**
the size   **le numéro; la pointure** (of shoes, gloves and stockings)
the colour   **la couleur**
the quality   **la qualité**
something in blue   **quelque chose de bleu**
dark blue   **bleu foncé**⎫ invariable
light blue   **bleu clair**⎭ compound adj.
How much is it?   **Combien est-ce?**
It is too dear   **C'est trop cher**
I'll have it   **Je le (la) prendrai**
I'll have them   **Je les prendrai**
I'll take it (them) with me   **Je (les) l'emporterai avec moi**
Please have it sent to this address   **Veuillez me le livrer à cette adresse**
I have not enough money with me   **Je n'ai pas assez d'argent sur moi**
I shall pay on delivery   **Je paierai à la livraison**
cash on delivery   **Contre remboursement**

Idiomatic Expressions

tout à l'heure   a moment ago; in a moment; just now
par ici   this way
par là   that way
ça ne fait rien   that does not matter
le voilà!   there he is! *or* there it is!
me voici!   here I am!
nous voilà!   there we are!
nous y voilà   we are there

j'aimerais mieux   I would rather, I should prefer (lit. I would like better)
tout ce qu'il faut   all that is needed
tout ce qu'il me faut   all that I need
je n'en peux plus   I can't go on any longer
je vous en prie   I beg you

THERE

Où est la lettre? Elle est là sur la table.   Where is the letter? It is there on the table.

Est-il à Paris? Oui, il y est.   Is he in Paris? Yes, he is (there).

Où est la gare? Elle est là au bout de la rue.   Where is the station? It is there at the end of the street.

Je vais à la gare. J'y vais aussi.   I am going to the station. I am going there too.

Ce magasin est très grand. On y trouve tout ce qu'on peut désirer.   This shop is very big. One finds there all that one can want.

If the word "there" is being used to point to a certain place it is translated by **là.**

If "there" indicates a place already mentioned, it is translated by **y.**

Note that **y** is placed before the verb.

When **en** and **y** are together, the order is always **y en.**

THERE IS, THERE ARE

voilà votre journal   there is your newspaper
voilà vos journaux   there are your newspapers
il y a un article intéressant dans le journal   there is an interesting article in the newspaper.
il y a des nouvelles importantes   there is important news.
qu'est-ce qu'il y a de nouveau?   what news is there?
il n'y a rien   there is nothing
il n'y a pas de nouvelles   there is no news.
y a-t-il des lettres?   are there any letters?
il y en a trois   there are three
il y en a une   there is one

THE SHOPPING STREET

Here our artist has in many cases made it clear what types of goods these various shops are handling. With the help of the drawing make a list of the types of businesses

La librairie; le libraire
Bookshop; bookseller

la crémerie; le/la crémier-ère
dairy; dairyman/woman

la pharmacie; le pharmacien
chemist's; chemist

La pâtisserie; le/la pâtissier-ère
Pastrycook's; pastrycook

la chapellerie; le/la chapelier-ère
hatter's; hatter

You should also know the following, not shown on the drawing.

La boucherie; le boucher
Butcher's; butcher

la mercerie; le/la mercier-ère
haberdasher's; haberdasher

La bijouterie; le bijoutier
Jeweller's; jeweller

le tailleur
tailor

la couturière
dressmaker

LA RUE COMMERÇANTE

and the titles of those who run them. Fill in any blanks by reference to the key below which gives masculine and feminine. Such businesses are frequently run by women.

l'épicerie; l'épicier-ère grocer's; grocer	le coiffeur; la coiffeuse male and female hairdresser	la quincaillerie; le quincaillier ironmonger's; ironmonger
	la plomberie; le plombier plumber's; plumber	la serrurrie; le serrurier locksmith's; locksmith

---

la charcuterie; le/la charcutier-ère
cooked meats shop; pork butcher

la boulangerie; le/la boulanger-ère
bakery; baker

le magasin d'étoffes; le marchand d'étoffes
cloth-merchant's; cloth-merchant

le magasin (le marchand) de chaussures
bootshop; proprietor

Use **voilà** when pointing to persons or things, and use **il y a** when not pointing. The English sentence "There is bread" can either mean a general statement that there is bread available, or that bread is actually there and being pointed out. In French, the general statement is: **Il y a du pain.** The pointing to it is expressed by: **"Voilà du pain."**

REFLEXIVE VERBS
Se promener = to go for a walk

Present
I am going for a walk, I go for a walk
Je me promène
tu te promènes
il se promène
elle se promène
nous nous promenons
vous vous promenez
ils se promènent
elles se promènent

Imperfect
I was going for a walk
Je me promenais
etc.

Future
I shall go for a walk
Je me promènerai
tu te promèneras
il se promènera
elle se promènera
nous nous promènerons
vous vous promènerez
ils se promèneront
elles se promèneront

Perfect
I went for a walk, I have been for a walk
je me suis promené(e)
tu t'es promené(e)
il s'est promené
elle s'est promenée
nous nous sommes promené(e)s
vous vous êtes promené(e-s)
ils se sont promenés
elles se sont promenées

Se décider = to make up one's mind

Present
je me décide
tu te décides etc.

Imperfect
je me décidais
tu te décidais etc.

Future
je me déciderai
tu te décideras etc.

Perfect
je me suis décidé(e)
tu t'es décidé(e)
il s'est décidé
elle s'est décidée
nous nous sommes décidé(e)s
vous vous êtes décidé(e-s)
ils se sont décidés
elles se sont décidées

Note.—The perfect of reflexive verbs is conjugated with être, e.g., **je me suis lavé** I have washed myself; **s'est-il habillé?** has he got dressed? **elle s'est couchée** she has lain down.

DEVENIR = to become
All the forms of the verb **devenir** are like **venir** (see page 205).
Note that "I have become" is **je suis devenu,** "he has become" is **il est devenu** etc.

PROMETTRE = to promise
This verb is conjugated like **mettre** (see pages 122, 137); "I have promised" is **j'ai promis;** "I will promise" is **je promettrai.**

EXERCISES
I   Replace the words in italic type by le, la, les, en or y

1. Le petit garçon achète *des pommes.* 2. Je mets *les jouets sur la table.* 3. Charles regarde *le sac-à-main.* 4. Elle a vendu *les robes.* 5. Nous irons voir *notre grand'-mère.* 6. Il achète *le gâteau chez le boulanger.* 7. Il achète *du gâteau chez le boulanger.* 8. Elle achète *les sardines chez l'épicier.* 9. Il a acheté *ses cigarettes dans*

un bistro. 10. Il a acheté *des cigarettes dans un bureau de tabac.*

II   Answer in French

1. Mme Roberts était-elle fatiguée? 2. M. et Mme Roberts, où sont-ils allés? 3. Sont-ils restés longtemps dans le premier magasin? 4. Quel est le rayon qui intéresse Mme Roberts? 5. Qu'est-ce que Charles veut avoir? 6. De quoi parle-t-il toujours? 7. Avec qui veut-il jouer? 8. Le magasin à prix unique vend-il des automobiles? 9. À qui parle Mme Roberts dans le magasin de nouveautés? 10. Que font-ils après avoir fait leurs achats? 11. M. Roberts accompagne-t-il sa famille dans le salon de thé? 12. Où va-t-il?

III   Translate into French

1. There is a pencil. Where is it? There it is. 2. There are the books. Where are they? There they are. 3. Have you got any paper? 4. Have you got any? 5. I have some. 6. There is some in the bookcase. 7. There is some. 8. Haven't you got any envelopes? 9. There are some in the drawer. 10. There are not any. 11. There isn't any ice-cream. 12. There isn't any bread. 13. There isn't any. 14. Isn't there any? 15. Are you going there? 16. Did he go there? 17. I am not going there. 18. He did not go there. 19. They are not going there any more. 20. There is your ticket. Where is it? There on the table, and there is one at the cash-desk. (*Key on page* 252.)

Another reminder:
Are you listening in daily to broadcasts in French?

PRÈS D'ÉPERNAY (CHAMPAGNE): LA VENDANGE

Le champagne n'est ni un vin ancien ni le vin favori des Français mais c'est lui qui tient la première place dans le commerce extérieur. Des affaires importantes dont le chiffre s'élève à des milliards de francs s'exécutent journellement entre la France et presque tous les pays du monde.

Affaires (f.pl.)	**chiffre** (m.)	**journellement**	**pays** (m.)	**monde** (m.)
Business	amount	daily	country	world

VINGTIÈME LEÇON

A PARIS BUS

Here is a typical Paris bus, and below are a few phrases connected with it. Learn these, then read carefully the account of the Roberts' bus journey. Then close the book and make a list of the terms needed on any ordinary Paris bus journey.

Un arrêt d'autobus	**le chauffeur**	**la plate-forme**	**le marchepied**
Bus-stop	driver	platform	step
Les voyageurs	**la banquette**	**le conducteur**	**le contrôle**
Passengers	seat	conductor	ticket-inspection

DANS L'AUTOBUS—IN THE BUS

Château de Vincennes, terminus d'une ligne de métro, point de départ de
Castle of Vincennes, terminus of a line of the metro, starting point of

nombreux autobus partant pour des centres d'excursion dans la banlieue de
numerous buses leaving for excursion centres in the outskirts of

Paris. M. et Mme Roberts avec leurs enfants Charles et Madeleine et
Paris. Mr. and Mrs. Roberts with their children Charles and Madeleine and

leur oncle, Monsieur Paul Lesage, à l'arrêt d'un autobus.
their uncle, Mr. Paul Lesage, at the stopping place of a bus.

M. Lesage (au conducteur): Pardon, monsieur, est-ce qu'on peut aller au bord
         (to the conductor): Excuse me, conductor, can one go to the banks

         de la Marne par cette ligne?
         of the Marne by this line?

Conducteur:	**Ça dépend! À quel endroit voulez-vous aller?** It depends! To what place do you want to go?
Charles:	**Là naturellement où nous pourrons nous baigner.** There, of course, where we shall be able to bathe.
Conducteur:	**Vous pouvez aller à Noisy-le-Grand, par exemple.** You can go to Noisy-le-Grand, for instance.
	Prenez le 120, ici à côté. Take the 120, here close by.
M. Lesage:	**Merci beaucoup, monsieur. (Toute la famille se rend à l'arrêt** Thank you very much, sir. (The whole family goes to the sto
	du 120, mais le conducteur ne les admet¹ pas.) of the 120 bus, but the conductor does not admit them.)
Conducteur:	**Complet! Prenez le prochain, qui partira dans dix minutes.** Full up! Take the next (one), which will leave in ten minutes

(Le conducteur sonne, l'autobus part, le suivant arrive.   Comme il y a
(The conductor rings, the bus leaves, the following arrives.   As there are

beaucoup de gens qui attendent, ils montent vite et prennent place en
many people who wait, they get in quickly and take (their) seats in the

première classe.   En deuxième il n'y a plus de place libre.   Même la plate-form(
first class.   In the second there is no seat left.   Even the platform

est pleine de monde.   Déjà le conducteur s'écrie "Complet!"   Une vieille
is full of people.   Already the conductor is calling out "Full up!" An old

dame, qui n'a pas trouvé de place, reste debout à l'intérieur.)
lady, who has not found a seat, remains standing in the inside.)

Conducteur:	**Vous ne pouvez pas rester dans le passage, madame; voulez-vous** You cannot stand in the gangway, madam; will you
	aller sur la plate-forme, s'il vous plaît? go on to the platform, please?
Mme Roberts (s'adressant à son fils):	**Lève-toi, Charles, et offre ta** (addressing herself to her son): Stand up, Charles, and offer your
	place à cette dame. seat to this lady.

---

¹ From **admettre**—to admit, conjugated like **mettre**.

Charles: Oui, maman, je veux bien. (Il se lève et s'adresse à la vieille
Yes, mummy, I should like to. (He stands up and addresses the old

dame.) Pardon, madame, puis-je vous offrir ma place?
lady.) Excuse me, madam, may I offer you my seat?

La dame: Merci, beaucoup, mon petit ami, c'est très gentil de votre part.
Thank you very much, my little friend, it's very nice of you.

Charles: Il n'y a pas de quoi,[1] madame.
Don't mention it, madam.

M. Lesage: (à M. Roberts): Il est bien élevé,[2] ton fils.
He is well mannered, your son.

M. Roberts: C'est tout naturel d'offrir sa place à une vieille dame.
It is quite natural to offer one's seat to an old lady.

Conducteur: Vous avez vos billets?
You have (got) your tickets?

M. Lesage: Non. Combien de billets[3] faut-il pour Noisy-le-Grand?
No. How many tickets does one need for Noisy-le-Grand?

Conducteur: Cinq par personne, monsieur.
Five each (lit., per person), sir.

M. Lesage: Eh, bien, nous sommes cinq personnes, donnez-moi 25 billets.[3]
Well, then, we are five persons, give me 25 tickets.

Conducteur: Ne voulez-vous pas prendre deux carnets?
Won't you take two booklets?

Cela vous coûtera moins cher.
That will cost you less (dear).

M. Roberts: Combien de billets y a-t-il dans un carnet?
How many tickets are there in one booklet?

Conducteur: Vingt, monsieur. Si vous prenez deux carnets, vous pourrez utiliser
Twenty, sir. If you take two booklets, you will be able to use

le reste au retour.
the rest on the return (journey).

---

[1] Lit. there isn't of what. [2] Lit. well brought up. [3] Bus-fares in Paris are cheaper if you buy **un carnet,** a booklet of 20 tickets. **Un billet** is good for one section only. For a longer journey, several **billets,** according to the number of fare stages, are required.

M. Lesage: **C'est entendu, monsieur, donnez-moi deux carnets, s'il vous plaît.**
All right, conductor, give me two booklets, please.

Conducteur: **Voilà! Ça fait 200 francs, monsieur.**
There you are. That makes 200 francs, sir.

M. Lesage (à M. Roberts): **As-tu de la monnaie? Je n'ai qu'un**
Have you any change? I have only a

> **billet de 1,000 francs.** M. Roberts: **Je crois que oui. (Il cherche**
> 1,000 franc note. I think so. (He searches
>
> **dans ses poches.) Voilà 200 francs. Dites, monsieur, quand est-ce**
> in his pockets.) Here is 200 francs. Tell me, conductor, when shall
>
> **que nous serons à Noisy-le-Grand?**
> we be at Noisy-le-Grand?

Conducteur: **Dans une demi-heure à peu près.**
In half an hour, approximately.

M. Roberts: **Est-ce qu'il y a un arrêt fixe à Noisy-le-Grand?**
Is there a compulsory stop at Noisy-le-Grand?

Conducteur: **Bien sûr, monsieur, puisque c'est le terminus.**
Certainly, sir, since it is the terminus.

EN ROUTE—ON THE ROAD

un autobus bus	**un autocar** coach	**une limousine** limousine	**une conduite intérieure** saloon car
une torpédo open tourer	**un cabriolet** convertible coupé	**une auto de course** racing car	**une bicyclette** bicycle
une motocyclette motorcycle	**un camion** truck	**le chauffeur** driver	**un dépôt d'essence** gas station
la route road	**un chemin de traverse** side-road, short cut	**un passage à niveau** level crossing	
un poteau indicateur road sign	**un virage** bend	**vidange gratuite** "sump drained free"	
gonflage gratuit "free air" (gonfler—to pump up)		**l'huile (f.)** lubrication-oil	**la bougie** spark plug

THREE MORE PROVERBS

Il faut prendre les hommes comme ils sont, et les choses comme elles viennent.
One must take men as they are and things as they come.

Le bon marché coûte toujours cher.
Cheap things are always dear

Chien qui aboie ne mord pas.
Barking dogs don't bite.

All the vehicles and objects shown in this drawing of a typical section of road near Paris are in the list on the preceding page. Study this, until you can make your own list in French without having to consult the text.

TERMES CONTRAIRES—OPPOSITE TERMS

gras(se) fat	**maigre** lean	**grand(e)** tall	**petit(e)** short, small	**long(ue)** long	**court(e)** short
corpulent(e) stout	**mince** slim	**large** wide	**étroit(e)** narrow	**vide** empty	**plein(e)** full
épais(se) thick	**mince** thin	**haut(e)** high; tall	**bas(se)** low	**premier** **première** first	**dernier** **dernière** last
léger(ère) light	**lourd(e)** heavy	**droit(e)** straight	**courbé(e)** curved	**heureux** **heureuse** happy	**malheureux** **malheureuse** unhappy
droit(e) upright	**incliné(e)** slanting	**ouvert(e)** open	**fermé(e)** closed		
tranchant(e) sharp	**émoussé(e)** blunt	**vertical(e)** perpendicular	**horizontal(e)** horizontal	**clair(e)** light	**obscur(e)** dark; dim
chaud(e) hot	**froid(e)** cold	**riche** rich	**pauvre** poor	**généreux(se)** generous	**avare** miserly
vrai(e) true	**faux(sse)** false	**gauche** left	**droit(e)** right	**lent(e)** slow	**rapide** fast

ENDINGS OF ADJECTIVES

Ce monsieur est furieux, parce
This man is furious, because

que le beau chapeau neuf de sa
the beautiful new hat of his

femme est trop cher.
wife is too dear.

Cette femme est furieuse, parce
This woman is furious, because

que la belle robe neuve de sa
the beautiful new dress of her

fille est trop chère.
daughter is too dear.

Note.—(1) Adjectives ending in **-eux** form their feminine by changing **-eux** into **-euse.**

Masculine	Feminine	
furieux	furieuse	furious
heureux	heureuse	happy
malheureux	malheureuse	unhappy
nombreux	nombreuse	numerous
dangereux	dangereuse	dangerous

(2) Adjectives ending in **-er** take a grave accent beside adding **-e:**

cher	chère	dear
premier	première	first
dernier	dernière	last

(3) Adjectives ending in **-f**, change the **f** into **ve** (compare with English "leaf," "leaves," etc.)

neuf	neuve	new
actif	active	active
vif	vive	lively

(4) The following adjectives double their last consonants before adding **-e:**

Masculine	Feminine	
naturel	naturelle	natural
bon	bonne	good
européen	européenne	European
indien	indienne	Indian
gentil	gentille	nice
gros	grosse	big
gras	grasse	fat
sot	sotte	stupid
bas	basse	low

(5) Irregular feminines are:

blanc	blanche	white
doux	douce	sweet
faux	fausse	false
frais	fraîche	fresh
long	longue	long
sec	sèche	dry
complet	complète	complete

Ces vieux messieurs sont heureux

(6) The following adjectives have two masculine as well as the feminine forms:

Masculine		Feminine	
Before a consonant	Before a vowel or mute h		
beau	bel	belle	beautiful
fou	fol	folle	foolish, mad
nouveau	nouvel	nouvelle	new
mou	mol	molle	soft
vieux	vieil	vieille	old
ce	cet	cette	this, that

(7) Adjectives ending in -x do not add -s in the plural, e.g., **Ces vieux messieurs sont heureux.**

NEW

la nouvelle mode   the new fashion.

un nouveau roman   a new novel.

un vêtement neuf   a new garment.

habillé de neuf   dressed in new clothes.

neuf, neuve   new, i.e., never before used.

nouveau, nouvel (see above), **nouvelle** (f.), new, i.e., not previously seen or heard, fresh, another.

In the meaning of "never before seen or heard" it follows the noun.

In the meaning of "fresh" or "another" it precedes the noun, e.g.,

un nouveau livre   another book.

un livre nouveau   a new book (which has just been published).

un livre neuf   a new book (not a second-hand book).

TO SIT DOWN

Infinitive: s'asseoir

Present Tense:

je m'assieds	nous nous asseyons
tu t'assieds	vous vous asseyez
il (elle) s'assied	ils (elles) s'asseyent

Imperfect: **Future:**

je m'asseyais, etc.   je m'assiérai, etc

Perfect: **Imperative:**

je me suis assis, etc.   assieds-toi
                               asseyez-vous
                               asseyons-nous

Note.—The non-reflexive form **asseoir** has the meaning of *to seat, to place, to set.*

Alternative forms are also used, for the present tense: **assois, assoit, assoyons, assoyez, assoient.** For the Future **assoirai.** etc.

EXERCISES

I   Translate into English

1. A-t-il un chapeau neuf? 2. Ces jeunes filles étaient heureuses parce qu'elles avaient des robes neuves. 3. Il n'est pas heureux, parce que sa femme a acheté une robe qui coûte très cher. 4. Cette dame avait une

corbeille (basket) pleine de pommes. 5. N'avait-il pas un pardessus noir, des gants bruns et un chapeau gris? 6. Ma vieille grand'mère est très vive pour son âge. 7. Je n'aime pas le porc gras. 8. Grand-père est assis dans son fauteuil qui est devant la fenêtre ouverte. 9. Il fume une grosse pipe. 10. Le petit poulet que tu as acheté est maigre. 11. L'Écossais est malheureux parce que son verre est vide. 12. Notre rue est étroite et courte.

II Replace the dashes by suitable adjectives

1. Le poulet est —. 2. Le crayon est —. 3. La fenêtre est —. 4. Les verres sont —. 5. Est-ce que les couteaux sont —? 6. Le pied de la table est —. 7. Le — chien est —. 8. Cette — plume est —. 9. Ces — jeunes filles sont —. 10. Mes souliers — sont —.

III Translate into French

1. The bus is full up. 2. There are numerous buses. 3. The next one will be empty. 4. Let us get in quickly. 5. The bottle is full. 6. Is there no seat for that old lady? 7. That is a good system. 8. Your new sideboard is very expensive. 9. Have you seen the new maid? 10. Isn't she pretty? 11. Are you happy, (my) boys? 12. This is our new house. (*Key on pages 252 and 253.*)

UN CHÂTEAU DE L'ALLIER

Ce château du Département de l'Allier au Centre de la France, juché sur une hauteur boisée et entouré par des chaumières, nous porte à l'esprit une communauté moyenâgeuse —la demeure seigneuriale dominant les taudis des vilains, pour donner protection contre l'ennemi. Est-ce moins banal que la vérité? L'on aime bien les effets de l'imagination quelquefois!

Juché-e (p.p.) Perched	**hauteur** (f.) height	**boisé-e** (adj.) wooded	**entourer** to surround	**communauté** (f.) community
demeure (f.) **seigneuriale** baronial hall		**taudis** (m.) hovel	**vilain-e** (m.f.) villein, serf	**vérité** (f.) truth

VINGT ET UNIÈME LEÇON

THE ROBERTSES GO VISITING

In this drawing of the Roberts family calling on French friends, there are shown the objects listed on page 245. But below we give some other terms connected with the illustration.

Un chat pie	un tapis d'escalier	des tringles d'escalier	la maîtresse de maison
black and white cat	stair carpet	stair-rods	mistress of the house

UNE VISITE—A VISIT

M. et Mme Roberts, avec leurs enfants Charles et Madeleine, sont
Mr. and Mrs. Roberts, with their children Charles and Madeleine, have been

invités chez des amis.   À quatre heures précises ils
invited to the house of some friends.   Exactly at four o'clock they

s'arrêtent devant une porte et sonnent.   Une charmante jeune
stop before a door and ring the bell.   A charming young

femme ouvre.
woman opens (the door).

La jeune femme: Bonjour, M. Roberts, bonjour, chère Madame,
Good afternoon, Mr. Roberts, good afternoon, Madam,

bonjour, les enfants.   Comment allez-vous?
good afternoon, children.   How are you?

SUR L'ESCALIER—ON THE STAIRCASE

l'escalier (m.)	la rampe	le palier	la porte d'entrée	la clef
stairs	banisters	landing	hall-door	key

le trou de la serrure	la serrure	la clef de sûreté	l'éclairage
key-hole	lock	latch-key	light

la poignée	la sonnette	le guichet de la boîte aux lettres
door-handle	bell	letter-box slit

le commutateur	le visiteur	la visiteuse
switch	visitor (man)	visitor (woman)

Mme Roberts: **Comment allez-vous vous-même?   Je suis très heureuse de vous**
How are you yourself?   I am very happy to see you

retrouver à Paris.   Et votre mari, comment va-t-il?
again in Paris.   And your husband, how is he?

La jeune femme: **Je vous remercie, madame, nous allons tous bien.   Mon mari**
I thank you, madame, we are all well.   My husband

vous attend déjà.   Voulez-vous avoir l'amabilité de me suivre?
is expecting you already.   Will you have the kindness to follow me?

Le mari: **Ah, voilà nos invités.   Je suis heureux, monsieur, de faire**
Ah, here are our guests.   I am delighted, sir, to make

votre connaissance.   Enchanté, madame.   Ma femme m'a beaucoup
your acquaintance.   Delighted, madam.   My wife has spoken to me

parlé de vous.
a lot about you.

La jeune femme: **Mais asseyez-vous donc, je vous en prie.   Vous êtes sans doute**
But do sit down, please (lit., I beg you).   You are no doubt

très fatigués.   Veuillez m'excuser quelques instants.
very tired.   Will you please excuse me a few moments.

Je vais vous préparer un petit rafraîchissement.
I will get ready a little refreshment for you.

Mme Roberts: **Vous êtes trop aimable, mais il ne faut pas vous déranger, madame.**
You are too kind, but please do not trouble, madam.

Le mari: **Vous ne refuserez pourtant pas une tasse de thé et**
You won't, however, refuse a cup of tea and

quelques petits gâteaux, n'est-ce pas?
some little cakes, will you?

M. Roberts: Comment pourrions-nous refuser, puisque vous insistez avec
How could we refuse, since you insist with

tant de bonne grâce?
so much charm?

Le mari: Vous nous faites plaisir en acceptant.
You make us happy by accepting.

M. Roberts: Comme vous êtes charmants, vous autres Français.
How charming you are, you French people.

Le mari: Je suis très flatté, M. Roberts.   Je trouve d'ailleurs que nous
I am very flattered, Mr. Roberts.   Besides, I find that we

sommes comme les autres; seulement nous nous exprimons d'une
are like others; only we express ourselves in a

façon différente.   Aimez-vous la pêche, M. Roberts?
different way.   Are you fond of fishing, Mr. Roberts?

M. Roberts: J'aime tous les sports, mais je ne suis jamais allé à la pêche.
I like all (the) sports, but I have never gone fishing.

Je préfère le golf; je trouve qu'il est plus intéressant
Personally I prefer golf; I find that it is more interesting

que la pêche, qui m'ennuierait.
than fishing, which would bore me.

Le mari: (riant) Quel dommage!   Nos goûts sont donc tout à fait
(laughing) What a pity!   Our tastes are therefore entirely

différents.   Moi, j'aime tant la tranquillité.   Je peux passer
different.   Personally I like so much peacefulness.   I can spend

des heures et des heures au bord d'une rivière ou d'un lac,
hours and hours on the bank of a river or of a lake,

sans bouger, dans l'attente patiente de . . .
without moving, in the patient expectation of . . .

La jeune femme (rentrant): Voilà, le thé est servi.
There we are, tea is ready.

---

[1] Although the use of such expressions may seem somewhat profuse to us, among French people similar terms are part of the usual conversation on such occasions.

MÊME DANS PARIS, L'ON PÊCHE

L'ami français de M. Roberts n'est pas le seul amateur de pêche en France. Ici, même en plein centre de Paris, les fervents s'adonnent à leur sport favori. Les uns, de la berge, les autres, de bateaux amarrés dans le fleuve, jettent leurs lignes et attendent que la plongée du flotteur indique la présence d'un poisson trop téméraire attiré par l'appât.

Fervent-e (m.f.)	**s'adonner**	**flotteur** (m.)	**téméraire** (adj. inv.)	**appât** (m.)
Enthusiast	to devote oneself	float	rash	bait

Note.—Fishing is a passion among Frenchmen to a degree unknown elsewhere. During the coarse-fishing season, which commences on June 15, visitors can observe for themselves how every stretch of water is utilised.

Mme Roberts: Je me suis permis de vous apporter un petit souvenir de
I permitted myself to bring you a little souvenir from

Londres.   Faites-moi le plaisir d'accepter ce petit cadeau,
London.   Make me the pleasure to accept this little present,

chère Madame.
dear madam.

La jeune femme: Oh, comme vous êtes gentille, chère Madame Roberts.   En le
Oh, how charming of you, dear Mrs. Roberts.   When

regardant, je penserai toujours à vous.   Oh, comme c'est mignon!
looking at it I shall always think of you.   Oh, how dainty it is!

Charles: Maman, veux-tu me passer le sucre, s'il te plaît.
Mummy, will you pass me the sugar, please.

Mme Roberts: Le voilà, mon chéri.   Charles: Merci, maman.
There you are, my darling.   Thank you, mother

La jeune femme: Quel beau temps après tant de jours de pluie!
What beautiful weather after so many rainy days!

Mme Roberts: Oui, il fait beau aujourd'hui.   Quand nous étions à Versailles
Yes, it is fine today.   When we were at Versailles

il pleuvait tout le temps.
it was raining all the time.

Le mari: C'est vraiment dommage.   Mais Versailles n'est pas loin;
That's really a pity.   But Versailles is not far;

ne voudriez-vous pas y retourner?
wouldn't you like to go back there?

M. Roberts: Pourquoi pas?   Nous restons encore plusieurs semaines à Paris.
Why not?   We still remain several weeks in Paris.

Le mari: Il est plus intéressant d'y aller par beau temps.   Il y a de
It is more interesting to go there in fine weather.   There are

belles forêts tout près.   N'oubliez surtout pas de visiter
beautiful woods quite near.   Above all, don't forget to visit

Fontainebleau.   C'est un peu plus loin, mais là vous serez au
Fontainebleau.   It is a bit farther, but there you will be in the

grand air.   Mme Roberts: Nous pensons y aller avec
open air.   We are thinking of going there with

nos parents français qui connaissent bien le pays, et qui
our French relations who know well the country, and who will

ne manqueront pas de nous montrer toutes les beautés aux environs
not fail to show us all the beauties in the surroundings.

de Paris.   M. Roberts: Chers amis, veuillez bien nous excuser,
of Paris.   Dear friends, will you please excuse us,

mais nous sommes obligés de vous quitter pour aujourd'hui.
but we have to leave you for today.

Nous avons encore un tas de choses à faire.
We still have a lot of things to do.

Mme Roberts: Mille fois merci pour votre aimable accueil.   N'oubliez pas de
Thanks a thousand times for your charming welcome.   Don't forget

nous rendre visite un de ces jours.   Quand viendrez-vous
to pay us a visit one of these days.   When will you

LE PALAIS DE FONTAINEBLEAU

L'étang qui entoure cette maison royale de campagne fourmille de carpes séculaires tellement apprivoisées qu'elles mangent sans peur de la main du visiteur.

| Étang (m.) | fourmiller | séculaire (adj. inv.) | apprivoiser |
| Pond | to swarm | century-old | to tame |

nous voir?   Samedi vous conviendrait-il?
come to see us?   Would Saturday suit you?

La jeune femme: Oui, mes amis, nous aurons le plaisir de vous voir samedi.
Yes, my friends, we shall have the pleasure to see you on Saturday

Mme Roberts: À quelle heure pourrions-nous vous attendre?
At what time could we expect you?

La jeune femme: Disons, à quatre heures de l'après-midi, si cela vous convient.
Let us say at four o'clock in the afternoon, if that suits you.

Mme Roberts: C'est entendu.   Au revoir!   **Tous: Au revoir!**
That's all right.   Good-bye!   Good-bye!

THE TEA TABLE

You should now be able to name practically everything on this table without looking at the list below. Glance at it only to check that you are word-perfect before continuing with the Course. If necessary, look back to earlier lessons, which give most of the words.

LA TABLE MISE POUR LE THÉ—THE TABLE LAID FOR TEA

la table à thé tea table	**du pain grillé** toast	**des gâteaux** assorted pastries	**de la confiture** jam
du beurre butter	**des tartines de beurre** slices of bread and butter	**un gâteau** cake	**la théière** tea-pot
la tasse cup	**le sucrier** sugar basin	**des petits-fours** fancy biscuits	**la soucoupe** saucer
une assiette plate	**le couteau** **la cuillère** knife spoon	**le plateau** tray	**un vase de fleurs** vase with flowers

APPELER = to call

Present:

J'appelle   I call, I am calling
tu appelles
il appelle
nous appelons
vous appelez
ils appellent

Imperfect: j'appelais, etc.

Future: j'appellerai, etc.

S'APPELER = to be called

Je m'appelle   I am called, my name is, I
   call myself
tu t'appelles
il s'appelle
nous nous appelons
vous vous appelez
ils s'appellent

Imperfect: je m'appelais, etc.

Future: je m'appellerai, etc

CONDITIONAL TENSE

Je donnerais   I should (would) give
tu donnerais
il donnerait
nous donnerions
vous donneriez
ils donneraient

Similarly:

je prendrais	I should (would) take	
je serais	,,	,, be
j'aurais	,,	,, have
j'irais	,,	,, go
je ferais	,,	,, do
je viendrais	,,	,, come
je m'appellerais,,	,, call myself	

The Conditional Tense is formed by adding -ais, -ait, -ions, -iez, -aient, to the Infinitive. Note that the Conditional has exactly the same endings as the Imperfect.

If the Future of the verb shows some irregularity, the same irregularity appears in the Conditional, e.g.,

Future:

j'irai   I shall (will) go
je pourrai   I shall (will) be able
j'aurai   I shall (will) have

Conditional:

j'irais   I should (would) go
je pourrais   I should (would) be able; I
   could
j'aurais   I should (would) have

Note.—In English "I could" may be either Imperfect as in "I could not come last night," or Conditional as in "Couldn't you lend me this book?" In French the two "could's" must be translated differently; "I could not come last night"—Je ne pouvais pas venir hier soir; "Couldn't you lend me this book?"—Ne pourriez-vous pas me prêter ce livre?

EXERCISES

I   Translate into English

1. Charles ne se couche pas tard. 2. Il se lève de bonne heure. 3. Il se lave et met vite ses vêtements (= clothes). 4. Après le petit déjeuner il va se promener avec sa sœur. 5. Dans la rue ils rencontrent une dame anglaise avec son petit chien. 6. Quel beau chien! s'écrie-t-il. 7. Comment s'appelle-t-il? 8. Quel âge a-t-il? 9. Les enfants s'en vont. 10. Ils vont se promener. 11. Ils se promènent dans les grandes rues. 12. Le temps est si beau; sinon nous rentrerions plus tôt.

II   Answer in French

1. Comment s'appelle le père de Charles? 2. Comment vous appelez-vous? 3. Comment s'appelle votre tante? 4. Vous promenez-vous à cinq heures du matin? 5. Te lèves-tu de bonne heure? 6. Te couches-tu après le dîner? 7. Auriez-vous beaucoup de voitures si vous aviez beaucoup d'argent? 8. Feriez-vous beaucoup de voyages si vous aviez un million? 9. Vous coucheriez-vous si vous étiez fatigué? 10. Êtes-vous plus âgé que Charles? 11. Quel âge a-t-il? 12. Allez-vous vous promener avant le petit déjeuner?

III Give the French opposite of
1. noir. 2. large. 3. gras. 4. long. 5. ouvert.
6. plein. 7. le premier jour. 8. un paquet
lourd. 9. un couteau tranchant. 10. la
poule grasse. 11. la rue étroite. 12. la tour
haute. 13. le vieux chapeau. 14. l'année
prochaine. 15. la petite fille heureuse.

(Key on page 253.)

KEY TO THE EXERCISES

Lesson Eighteen

I

1. Je (ne) suis (pas) plus grand que mon père. 2. J'en écris beaucoup (je n'en écris pas . . .) 3. Oui, j'ai (non, je n'ai pas) parlé français hier. 4. Oui, j'en mange. 5. J'ai mangé du pain bis et du beurre. 6. Oui, j'en prends. 7. Je (ne) t'ai (pas) vu. 8. J'en bois (je n'en bois pas). 9. J'en ai bu (je n'en ai pas bu). 10. Je lis un roman de Galsworthy. 11. Je (ne) l'ai (pas) lu. 12. Je (ne) me suis (pas) levé de bonne heure aujourd'hui.

II

1. Tu mets les fruits sur la table. 2. Ne prends-tu pas . . . 3. N'écris-tu pas . . .? 4. Tu es . . . 5. As-tu tes . . .? 6. Regardes-tu ton . . .? 7. Tu peux venir avec ton . . . 8. Tu te couches tard. 9. Il te voit. 10. Ne te laves-tu pas? 11. Pars-tu avec ta . . .? 12. Tu t'en vas.

III

1. Voulez-vous aller vous promener? 2. Je ne pourrai pas sortir aujourd'hui. 3. Ne voulez-vous pas voir votre sœur? 4. Ne pourrez-vous pas la voir? 5. Avez-vous vu vos amis? 6. Pouvez-vous me dire quel chemin je dois prendre pour aller à la Rue Montmartre, s'il vous plaît? 7. Je regrette, je ne peux pas vous le dire. 8. Voilà un agent qui pourra vous le dire. 9. Je vous ai vu hier soir. 10. M'avez-vous vu aussi? 11. J'ai vu votre frère et vos parents, mais je n'ai pas vu votre sœur. 12. Ne faites pas cela. 13. Ne parlez pas si vite! 14. Ne vous en allez pas (ne t'en va pas). 15. Attendez, s'il vous plaît (attends, s'il te plaît).

Lesson Nineteen

I

1. Il en achète. 2. Je les y mets. 3. Il le regarde. 4. Elle les a vendues. 5. Nous irons la voir. 6. Il l'y achète. 7. Il y en achète. 8. Elle les y achète. 9. Il les y a achetés. 10. Il y en a acheté.

II

1. Oui, elle était fatiguée. 2. Ils sont allés dans des magasins pour faire des achats. 3. Non, ils n'y sont pas restés longtemps. 4. Le rayon de maroquinerie l'intéresse. 5. Il veut avoir un jeu de ping-pong. 6. Il en parle toujours. 7. Il veut jouer avec son cousin. 8. Il n'en vend pas. 9. Elle parle à une vendeuse. 10. Ils vont prendre un rafraîchissement. 11. Il ne l'y accompagne pas. 12. Il va acheter des cigarettes.

III

1. Voilà un crayon. Où est-il? Le voilà. 2. Voilà les livres. Où sont-ils? Les voilà. 3. Avez-vous du papier? 4. En avez-vous? 5. J'en ai. 6. Il y en a dans la bibliothèque. 7. En voilà. 8. N'avez-vous pas d'enveloppes? 9. Il y en a dans le tiroir. 10. Il n'y en a pas. 11. Il n'y a pas de glace. 12. Il n'y a pas de pain. 13. Il n'y en a pas. 14. N'y en a-t-il pas? 15. Y allez-vous? 16. Y est-il allé? 17. Je n'y vais pas. 18. Il n'y est pas allé. 19. Ils n'y vont plus. 20. Voilà votre billet. Où est-il? Là sur la table et en voilà un à la caisse.

Lesson Twenty

I

1. Has he got a new hat? 2. These girls were happy because they had new dresses.

3. He is not happy, because his wife has bought a dress which is very dear. 4. That woman had a basket full of apples. 5. Didn't he have a black overcoat, brown shoes and a grey hat? 6. My old grandmother is very lively for her age. 7. I don't like fat pork. 8. Grandfather is sitting in his easy chair, which is in front of the open window. 9. He smokes a big pipe. 10. The small chicken you bought is lean. 11. The Scotsman is unhappy, because his glass is empty. 12. Our street is narrow and short.

II

1. gras. 2. long. 3. fermée. 4. vides. 5. tranchants. 6. courbe. 7. petit — gris. 8. nouvelle — jaune. 9. petites — anglaises. 10. neufs — étroits.

III

1. L'autobus est complet. 2. Il y a de nombreux autobus. 3. Le prochain sera vide. 4. Montons vite! 5. La bouteille est pleine. 6. N'y a-t-il pas de place pour cette vieille dame? 7. C'est un bon système. 8. Votre nouveau buffet est très cher. 9. Avez-vous vu la nouvelle bonne? 10. N'est-elle pas jolie? 11. Êtes-vous heureux, mes garçons? 12. Ceci est notre nouvelle maison.

Lesson Twenty-one
I

1. Charles does not go to bed late. 2. He gets up early. 3. He washes and puts on his clothes quickly. 4. After breakfast he goes for a walk with his sister. 5. In the street they meet an English lady with her little dog. 6. What a beautiful dog! he exclaims. 7. What's his name? 8. How old is he? 9. The children are going away. 10. They are going for a walk. 11. They are walking in the streets. 12. The weather is so beautiful; otherwise we would go back earlier.

II

1. Il s'appelle M. Roberts. 2. Je m'appelle . . . 3. Elle s'appelle . . . 4. Je ne me promène pas si tôt. 5. Je (ne) me lève (pas) de bonne heure. 6. Je (ne) me couche (pas) après le dîner. 7. Je (ne) les aurais (pas). 8. J'en ferais beaucoup. 9. Je me coucherais. 10. Je (ne) suis (pas) plus âgé que lui. 11. Il a douze ans. 12. Je (ne) vais (pas) me promener avant le petit déjeuner.

III

1. blanc. 2. étroit. 3. maigre. 4. court. 5. fermé. 6. vide. 7. le dernier jour. 8. un paquet léger. 9. un couteau émoussé. 10. la poule maigre. 11. la rue large. 12. la tour basse. 13. le chapeau neuf. 14. l'année dernière. 15. La grande fille malheureuse.

ROUND THE TOWN

Quand on Voyage en France

N'oubliez pas, quand vous voyagez en France, que tous les bagages doivent être enregistrés, et que par conséquent vous devez arriver à la gare assez à l'avance du départ du train, pour accomplir cette tâche.

Si vous voyagez en auto, il vaut la peine de vous fournir avant votre départ de la liste d'hôtels et de restaurants approuvés par l'Auto Club. Comme ça, vous pouvez bien manger dans n'importe quelle ville en France. Et surtout, n'oubliez jamais de demander la spécialité locale, en viande ou en vin, dans chaque ville.

When Travelling in France

Don't forget, when travelling in France, that all luggage must be registered, and that in consequence you should arrive at the station in sufficient time before the departure of the train, in order to accomplish this task.

If you are travelling by car, it's worth while to obtain a copy of the (French) Automobile Club's list of approved hotels and restaurants before you start. In that way, you can have a good meal anywhere in France. And, above all, never forget to ask for the local speciality, in meat or in wine, in each town.

VINGT-DEUXIÈME LEÇON

MR. ROBERTS AT THE POST-OFFICE

Your exercise here is to translate the notices and describe in French the actions of the persons in the post-office, before reading the text in the pages which follow. Use these later to fill in any gaps in the lists which you have made in English and French.

AU BUREAU DE POSTE—AT THE POST-OFFICE

M. Roberts avec plusieurs lettres dans la poche et un petit paqet sous
Mr. Roberts with several letters in his pocket and a small parcel under

le bras se rend dans un bureau de poste.   Il entre et s'adresse à
his arm is on his way to a post-office.   He goes in and addresses himself to

un employé qui est assis derrière le guichet.
an employee who is sitting behind the counter.

M. Roberts: **Un timbre de 30 francs, s'il vous plaît.**
               A 30 francs stamp, please.

L'employé: **Veuillez vous adresser au guichet No. 5.**
               Please address yourself to counter No. 5.

M. Roberts: **(à l'employé du guichet 5) Voici trois lettres.   Voulez-vous**
               Here are three letters.   Will you

avoir l'amabilité de les affranchir? Ce sont des lettres pour
have the kindness to put stamps on them.   They are letters for

l'étranger; celle-ci je voudrais bien l'envoyer comme
abroad; this one I should like to send (it) as (a)

lettre recommandée, celle-là comme lettre ordinaire, et celle-là
registered letter, that one as an ordinary letter, and that one

comme imprimé ou échantillon sans valeur.
as printed matter or sample without value.

L'employé: **Je veux bien mettre des timbres sur ces lettres, mais pour**
I will put stamps on these letters, but for

la lettre recommandée il faut d'abord remplir cette
the registered letter one has first to fill in this

petite feuille jaune—ah, je vois que vous êtes étranger . . . alors
little yellow form—oh, I see that you are a foreigner . . . well

mettez là le nom et l'adresse du destinataire, et ici
put there the name and the address of the addressee and here

le vôtre.   C'est bien, comme ça . . . voilà le reçu.
yours.   That's right, like this . . . here is the receipt.

M. Roberts: **C'est bien amiable à vous, monsieur; permettez-moi encore une**
That is very kind of you, sir; allow me another

question.   Où se trouve le guichet pour les colis?
question.   Where is (to be found) the counter for parcels?

L'employé: **Là-bas, au guichet trois.   Il faudra[1] faire la queue . . .**
Down there, on counter three.   You will have to queue up . . .

il y a beaucoup de monde . . . attendez . . . donnez-moi
there are lots of people . . . wait (a minute) . . . give me

votre colis, je ferai une exception pour vous.
your parcel, I'll make an exception for you.

M. Roberts: **Mais j'ai vraiment de la chance . . . le voici . . .   Dites, monsieur,**
But I am really lucky . . . here it is . . .   Tell me, sir,

les lettres qu'on met dans la boîte aux lettres
the letters which one puts into the letter-box

---

[1] Lit. it will be necessary.

aujourd'hui, seront-elles en Angleterre demain?
today, will they be in England tomorrow?

L'employé: Certainement, monsieur, elles seront distribuées demain.
Certainly, sir, they will be delivered tomorrow.

VOCABULAIRE

la cabine téléphonique
telephone box

le pèse-lettres
letter-scales

le guichet des timbres-poste
stamp-counter

l'employé du guichet
official at counter

le guichet des versements
payment counter

la boîte de la poste aérienne
air-mail box

le tarif postal
postage rate

l'entrée
entrance

le guichet des colis postaux
parcels counter

la bascule
scales

le colis postal
parcel

le pupitre
desk

un monsieur écrivant une lettre
gentleman writing a letter

une petite fille achetant des timbres
little girl buying stamps

une dame envoyant un télégramme
lady sending a telegram

la boîte aux lettres
letter-box

CABINE TÉLÉPHONIQUE
Sign over telephone box

TIMBRES-POSTE
Sign over stamp counter

VERSEMENTS
Sign over payment counter

TELEGRAMMES
Sign over telegram counter

LETTRES RECOMMANDÉES
Sign over registered letters counter

POSTE RESTANTE
"To be called for" counter

COLIS POSTAUX
Sign over parcels counter

TARIF POSTAL
Headline of poster

TELEPHONE EXPRESSIONS

Un coup de téléphone	a telephone call
Demander interurbain	to ask for "long distance"
Poste 123	extension 123
On nous a coupés	We've been cut off

PARIS QUI JOUE

En haut, les Courses de Nuit à Longchamp attirent un monde chic. En bas, c'est
également le hasard qui tente ces habitués d'un café louche.

Attirer	**également** (adv.)	**hasard** (m.)	**tenter**	**louche** (adj.)
To attract	likewise	chance, luck	to tempt	disreputable

LA LETTRE—LETTER	**la signature** signature
le papier à lettre notepaper	**une enveloppe** envelope
la date date	**le timbre-poste** postage stamp
la suscription opening greeting	**l'adresse** address
le texte de la lettre text of the letter	**une carte postale** postcard
la salutation finale final greeting	**un télégramme (une dépêche)** telegram

THIS ONE, THAT ONE, THESE, THOSE

Quel gâteau prenez-vous?   Which cake are you taking?
Celui-ci est meilleur marché que celui-là.   This one is cheaper than that one.

Quelle chaise voulez-vouz?   Which chair do you want?
Celle-ci ou celle-là?   This one or that?

Quels gâteaux prenez-vous?   Which cakes are you taking?
Ceux-ci ou ceux-là?   These or those?

Quelles chaises voulez-vous?   Which chairs do you want?
Celles-ci ou celles-là?   These or those?

"This one" when replacing a masculine noun	=	**Celui-ci**
"That one" when replacing a masculine noun	=	**Celui-là**
"This one" when replacing a feminine noun	=	**Celle-ci**
"That one" when replacing a feminine noun	=	**Celle-là**
"These" when replacing masculine nouns	=	**Ceux-ci**
"Those" when replacing masculine nouns	=	**Ceux-là**
"These" when replacing feminine nouns	=	**Celles-ci**
"Those" when replacing feminine nouns	=	**Celles-là**

Note that the above expressions are used only when replacing nouns.

(1) Followed by a noun **ce (cet)** and **cette** are used for "this" and "that," **ces** for "these" and "those."

(2) "This," "that," "these," "those" are translated by **ce (c')** if employed with a tense of "to be": **C'est mon journal**= This (that) is my newspaper. **Ce sont mes livres**= These (those) are my books. **N'est-ce pas votre chaise?**= Is this not your chair?

(3) "This" when not replacing a noun is **ceci**. "That" when not replacing a noun is **cela**, or **ça. Voulez-vous ceci ou cela?**= Do you want this or that? **Ceci est pour vous**= This is for you. **Ne faites pas ça**= Don't do that. **C'est ça**= That's it.

IL FAUT—IT IS NECESSARY, IT MUST

il faut travailler= one must work.
il me faut y aller= I must go there (lit., it is necessary for me to go there).

il vous faut y aller= you must go there (lit., it is necessary for you to go there).

il faut le faire= it must be done.
il fallait le faire= it had to be done.
il faudra le faire= it will have to be done.
il ne faut pas fumer trop= one must not smoke too much.
il faut lire ce livre= you must read this book.

The verb **falloir** means "to be necessary"; it is also translated by "must" and "to have to". While the English "must" can be used with any person, the French **falloir** can only be used in connection with the prefix **il**:

il faut= it is necessary
    (I, you, he, she, it, we, they must).
il fallait= it was necessary
    (I, you, he, she, it, we, they had to).
il faudra= it will be necessary
    (I, you, etc., will have to).
il faudrait= it would be necessary
    (I, you, etc., would have to).

SUMMARY

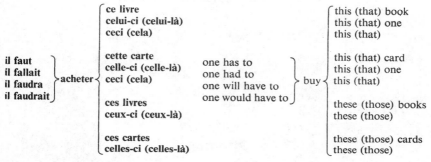

	ce livre			this (that) book
	celui-ci (celui-là)			this (that) one
	ceci (cela)			this (that)
il faut	cette carte	one has to		this (that) card
il fallait	celle-ci (celle-là)	one had to		this (that) one
il faudra } acheter	ceci (cela)	one will have to } buy		this (that)
il faudrait		one would have to		
	ces livres			these (those) books
	ceux-ci (ceux-là)			these (those)
	ces cartes			these (those) cards
	celles-ci (celles-là)			these (those)

EXERCISES

I Translate into English

1. Je vais à la poste. 2. Il me faut des timbres. 3. Où est le bureau de poste? 4. Y a-t-il des lettres pour moi? 5. En voilà une. 6. De qui est-elle? 7. Elle est de mon ami. 8. Qu'est-ce qu'il écrit? 9. Pas grand'chose. 10. Donnez-moi trois timbres de quatre-vingt-dix centimes. 11. Veuillez recommander cette lettre. 12. Voulez-vous envoyer ce télégramme? 13. Avez-vous mis votre lettre à la boîte? 14. Quand pensez-vous que cette lettre arrivera? 15. Il faut l'envoyer poste-restante.

II Replace the nouns by pronouns

1. Voilà deux lettres; cette lettre-ci est pour moi, cette lettre-là est pour vous. 2. Ce colis est pour vous. 3. Je n'aime pas ces cigarettes. 4. Prenez-vous ce vin blanc ou ce vin rouge? 5. Sa maison est dans cette rue. 6. J'ai acheté cette cravate dans ce magasin-là. 7. Voulez-vous ce melon? 8. Merci, je préfère ce melon-ci. 9. Ces fleurs sont très belles. 10. Cette chaise n'est pas confortable, prenez ce fauteuil. 11. Prenez-vous ces gants-là? 12. Donnez-moi ce pain, s'il vous plaît.

III Translate into French

1. Do you know these ladies? 2. Are you reading this book? 3. Did they buy this house? 4. Which wine do you want, this one or that one? 5. Do you want these cigarettes? No, thanks, I prefer those. 6. In which store did you buy your gloves, in this one or in that one? 7. You must read this book; it is very interesting. 8. We must speak French now. 9. Where is the post-office? 10. I want some stamps. 11. Two twenty-franc stamps and five postcards, please. 12. Have you got a ten-franc stamp?

(*Key on pages* 288 *and* 289.)

THE TWENTY-FOUR-HOUR CLOCK

All over France you will find the twenty-four-hour clock in use, both on the radio and in railway time-tables. For English people there is a very simple way of calculating it in terms of pence. Thus, 19 pence is 1/7 and 19 hours is 7 o'clock (p.m.).

L'HORLOGE DES VINGT-QUATRE HEURES

Partout en France le système horaire de vingt-quatre heures est d'usage, soit à la radio, soit dans les indicateurs des chemins de fer. Les Anglais, habitués à leur système monétaire duodécimal, n'ont qu'à se dire que 19 "pence" équivalent à 1 shilling et 7 pence, ce dernier chiffre donnant là traduction de "19 heures."

VINGT-TROISIÈME LEÇON

LAUNDRY FOR GRANDMOTHER LESAGE

You ought now to be able to name in French practically every object shown in this drawing. Make a list, and to correct yourself consult the text below—and look back to previous lessons. The washerwoman's basket is called **un panier à linge.**

LA BLANCHISSEUSE—THE LAUNDRY-WOMAN

La blanchisseuse rapporte le linge chez grand'mère Lesage.   Elle lui remet
The laundry woman brings back the washing to grandmother Lesage. She hands her

la note et Mme Lesage commence à compter.
the bill and Mrs. Lesage begins to count.

Mme Lesage: 3 chemises d'hommes, 3 chemises de femme, 5 chemises de nuit.
          3 men's shirts, 3 women's chemises, 5 nightdresses.

   7 cols mous et 4 cols durs, 12 mouchoirs, 2 caleçons.
   7 soft collars and 4 stiff collars, 12 handkerchiefs, 2 pairs of underdrawers.

   8 paires de bas et 10 paires de chaussettes, un soutien-gorge,
   8 pairs of stockings and 10 pairs of socks, one brassière,

   5 culottes, 3 pyjamas, 2 jupons, un tablier, 14 serviettes.   En
   5 knickers, 3 pyjamas, 2 petticoats, 1 apron, 14 napkins.   Here

   voici une qui n'est pas à moi; tout le reste est en ordre.
   is one which is not mine; everything else is correct.

Voici la liste de mon linge sale; il me le faut
Here is the list of my soiled linen; I must have it

mardi au plus tard.　　**La blanchisseuse: Bien, madame.**
on Tuesday at the latest.　　All right, madam

LES SOUS-VÊTEMENTS—UNDERWEAR

le cache-corset	**la chemise**	**la chemise de nuit**	**le pyjama**	**la veste**
camisole	chemise	nightdress	pyjama	jacket

le pantalon	**le peignoir**	**le soutien-gorge**	**la combinaison**	**la culotte**
trousers	dressing gown	brassière	combinations	knickers

le jupon	**la ceinture sport**	**la jarretelle**	**le bas**	**le mouchoir**
petticoat	sports-corset	sock suspender	stocking	handkerchief

le tablier	**le calecon**	**le tricot**	**le col**	**le bouton de col**
apron	underdrawers	vest; pullover	collar	collar-stud

la manchette	**le fixe-manche**	**les bretelles**	**la ceinture**	**la cravate**
cuff	armband	braces	belt	tie

le fixe-cravate	**le nœud papillon**	**la chaussette**	**la blanchisserie**
tie-clip	bow-tie	sock	laundry

le linge	**la lingerie**	**faire blanchir**	**nettoyer**
linen	underwear	to have washed	to clean

raccommoder	**repriser**	**coudre**	**recoudre**	**le bouton**	**repasser**
to mend	to darn	to sew	to sew on	button	to iron

THE INDIRECT OBJECT (TO HIM, TO HER, TO THEM, ETC.)

Il m'écrit = He writes to me.
Il lui écrit = He writes to him (*or* to her).
Je leur écris = I write to them.
Ils nous écrivent = They write to us.
Nous vous écrivons = We write to you.
Je vous donne le livre = I give you the book.

Vous me donnez trop = You give me too much.
Il lui donne de l'argent = He gives him (*or* her) money.
Elle leur donne des leçons = She gives them lessons.

Ils ne nous donnent pas de viande=They don't give us meat.

Je lui donne le livre=I give him the book.

Je donne le livre à mon père=I give my father the book.

Let us look at the last example. Here we have two objects, "father" and "book." But clearly "book" is more directly an object than "father": we do not really give the father, we give to the father. "Book" is accordingly the Direct Object, "father" the Indirect Object. In English the Indirect Object is shown by the word *to*, which, however, can frequently be omitted. In French the Indirect Object is indicated by the use of **à**, which may be contracted with **le** to **au** and with **les** to **aux**.

The following are the Indirect Object Pronouns:—

me=to me, **te**=to thee, **lui**=to him or to her, **nous**=to us, **vous**=to you, **leur**=to them, **se**=to himself, herself, itself, oneself, themselves.

Note that with the exception of **lui** and **leur** the Indirect Object pronouns are the same as the Direct Object pronouns.

With regard to word order, the following rules apply:—

(1) Both Direct and Indirect Object pronouns are placed before the verb, except in the Imperative Affirmative (**je lui donne**, but **donnez-lui**).

(2) In negative sentences these pronouns must come between **ne** and the verb (**je ne lui écris pas**=I don't write to him; **ne lui écrivez pas!**=don't write to him!)

Further examples:—

Je lui donne un cadeau=I give him (*or* her) a present.

Nous leur achetons des bonbons=We buy them sweets.

Ils me vendent leur maison=They sell me their house.

Parlez-lui=Speak to him (*or* her).

Ne lui parlez pas=Don't speak to him (*or* her).

Écrivez-nous=Write to us.

Ne leur écrivez pas=Don't write to them.

Écrivez-moi=Write to me.

Ne m'écrivez pas=Don't write to me.

Apportez-nous du café=Bring us some coffee.

Ne leur apportez pas de thé=Don't bring them tea.

Je lui ai téléphoné=I telephoned to him (*or* her).

Leur avez-vous téléphoné?=Did you ring them up?

Ils ne nous ont pas écrit=They did not write to us.

Je l'ai vu hier=I saw him yesterday.

Réveillez-les=Wake them up.

Ne les réveillez pas=Don't wake them up.

Lève-toi
Levez-vous }=Get up.

Ne te lève pas
Ne vous levez pas }=Don't get up.

Note from the above examples that **me** and **te** become **moi** and **toi** when used with the Imperative Affirmative.

Le professeur donne un livre à l'élève=The teacher gives a book to the pupil.

Il lui donne un livre=He gives him a book.

Il le lui donne=He gives it to him.

ROUND THE TOWN
En France

La circulation prend toujours le côté droit de la rue.

Un monsieur accompagnant une dame marche toujours à sa gauche.

Le fromage se mange avant le fruit.

On boit souvent le porto comme apéritif.

Le champagne se boit seulement à la fin du repas.

On serre la main, même si on se voit tous les jours.

In France

Traffic always keeps to the right of the road.

A gentleman accompanying a lady walks always on her left.

Cheese is eaten before fruit.

Port is often drunk as an appetiser.

Champagne is drunk only at the end of a meal.

People shake hands, although they see each other every day.

La petite fille montre sa langue au médecin.
The little girl shows her tongue to the doctor.

Elle lui montre sa langue.
She shows him her tongue.

Elle la lui montre.
She shows it to him.

Je montre mes tableaux à mes amis.
I show my pictures to my friends.
Je leur montre mes tableaux.
I show them my pictures.

Avez-vous le paquet?
Have you got the parcel?
Donnez-le-lui.
Give it to him (or her).
Ne le lui donnez pas.
Don't give it to him (or her).

Avez-vous la valise?
Have you got the suitcase?
Montrez-la-lui.
Show it to him (or her).
Ne la lui montrez pas.
Don't show it to him (or her).

Avez-vous les allumettes?
Have you got the matches?
Donnez-les-lui.
Give them to him (or her).
Donnez-les-leur.
Give them to them.

Voici le jardin.
Here is the garden.
Montrez-le-leur.
Show it to them.
Ne le leur montrez pas.
Don't show it to them.

Voilà la maison.
There is the house.
Montrez-la-leur.
Show it to them.
Ne la leur montrez pas.
Don't show it to them.

Voilà les bouteilles.
There are the bottles.
Apportez-les-leur.
Bring them to them.
Ne les leur apportez pas.
Don't bring them to them.

Note that le, la and
les precede lui and leur

**Je vous donne la
pomme.**
I give you the apple
Je vous la donne.
I give it to you.

YOU SHOULD BE ABLE TO TRANSLATE THIS

Le cidre est une
boisson populaire en
Normandie, et la
liqueur normande
Calvados est également extraite de la
pomme.

LA CONCIERGE EST BIEN LOGÉE!

C'est un gîte confortable, encadré d'arbustes, qu'a trouvé cette concierge! Même Mimi et Minou semblent approuver ce domicile si coquet et si parisien.

Gîte (m.)	encadré-e (p.p.)	arbuste (m.)	Mimi, Minou	coquet (adj.)
Lodging	framed	shrub	names for cats	trim, neat

Je vous donne le journal.
I give (*or* am giving) you the newspaper.

Je vous le donne.
I give it to you.

Je vous donne les livres.
I give you the books.

Je vous les donne.
I give them to you.

Il me montre son tableau.
He shows me his picture.

Il me le montre.
He shows it to me.

Il me vend sa maison.
He sells me his house.

Il me la vend.
He sells it to me.

Il m'apporte les journaux.
He brings me the newspapers.

Il me les apporte.
He brings them to me.

Nous vous donnons ces livres.
We give you these books.

Nous vous les donnons.
We give them to you.

Il nous envoie l'argent.
He sends us the money.

Il nous l'envoie.
He sends it to us.

Ils te donnent leurs tableaux.
They give you their pictures.

Ils te les donnent.
They give them to you.

Note that **me, te, nous** and **vous** precede **le, la** and **les**.

SUMMARY

Present tense:

$$
\text{je} \left\{ \text{(ne)} \left\{ \begin{array}{l} \text{le} \\ \text{la} \\ \text{les} \end{array} \right. \left\{ \begin{array}{l} \text{lui} \\ \text{leur} \end{array} \right. \left\{ \begin{array}{l} \text{donne} \\ \text{montre} \\ \text{envoie} \\ \text{apporte} \\ \text{écris} \\ \text{dis} \\ \text{fais} \end{array} \right\} \text{(pas)} \right.
$$

$$
\text{vous} \left\{ \text{(ne)} \left\{ \begin{array}{l} \text{le} \\ \text{la} \\ \text{les} \end{array} \right. \left\{ \begin{array}{l} \text{lui} \\ \text{leur} \end{array} \right. \left\{ \begin{array}{l} \text{donnez} \\ \text{montrez} \\ \text{envoyez} \\ \text{apportez} \\ \text{écrivez} \\ \text{dites} \\ \text{faites} \end{array} \right\} \text{(pas)} \right.
$$

Present Tense:

il / elle { (ne) { le / la / les { lui / leur { donne, montre, envoie, apporte, écrit, dit, fait } (pas)

je { (ne) { te / vous { le / la / l' / les { donne, montre, envoie, etc. } (pas)

nous { (ne) { le / la / les { leur { donnons, montrons, envoyons, apportons, écrivons, disons, faisons } (pas)

il / elle { (ne) { me / te / nous / vous { le / la / l' / les { donne, montre, envoie, etc. } (pas)

ils { (ne) { me / te / nous / vous { le / la / l' / les { donnent, montrent, envoient, etc. } (pas)

ils / elles { (ne) { le / la / les { lui / leur { donnent, montrent, envoient, apportent, écrivent, disent, font } (pas)

elles { (ne) { me / te / nous / vous { le / la / l' / les { donnent, montrent, envoient, etc. } (pas)

nous { (ne) { te / vous { le / la / l' / les { donnons, montrons, envoyons, etc. } (pas)

vous { (ne) { me / nous { le / la / l' / les { donnez, montrez, envoyez, etc. } (pas)

Imperative:

donnez, montrez, envoyez, apportez, écrivez, dites, faites { -le / -la / -les { -moi / -lui / -leur / -nous

Perfect:

je (ne) { te / vous { l' / les { ai (pas) { donné (e, s, es), montré (e, s, es), envoyé (e, s, es), etc.

ne { le / la / les { lui / leur { donnez, montrez, envoyez, apportez, écrivez, dites, faites } pas

Perfect:

je { (ne) { le / la / les { lui / leur { ai (pas) { donné (e,s,es), montré (e,s,es), envoyé (e,s,es), apporté (e, s, es), écrit (e, s, es), dit (e, s, es), fait (e, s, es)

EXERCISES

I Replace the words in italic type by pronouns

1. Je ne lui donne pas *le couteau.* 2. *Charles* envoie *les livres* à *ses amis.* 3. *Le garçon* apporte *le café.* 4. Nous envoyons *le linge sale* à *la blanchisseuse.* 5. Écrivez à *ma tante!* 6. Ne parlez pas à *mes parents.* 7. Elles donnent *les fleurs au professeur.* 8. Je donnerai *ces fleurs à mon amie.* 9. Il y a *trois tasses.* 10. On voit *ces dames* chaque jour. 11. *Mon amie* me

montre *ses livres*. 12. *Le professeur* montre *les timbres-poste* à ses élèves.

II Answer the following questions, using pronouns instead of the nouns

1. Que donnez-vous à votre frère? 2. Que donne le professeur à ses élèves? 3. Madame Roberts parle-t-elle à Mademoiselle Lesage? 4. À qui envoyez-vous cette lettre? 5. Qu'est-ce que vous envoyez à vos amis? 6. Qu'est-ce que le boulanger vend à ses clients? 7. À qui apportez-vous ces fleurs? 8. Me donnez-vous votre argent? 9. Envoyez-vous la lettre à Mme Roberts? 10. Le professeur donne-t-il les livres aux élèves?

III Translate into French

1. Write to me. 2. Do not write to him. 3. Did you write to them? 4. The laundress brings her the clean linen. 5. You did not send him the newspapers. 6. You did not send them to him. 7. Wake them up. 8. He sends us three shirts, twelve handkerchiefs and six pairs of socks. 9. She has not given us our laundry-list. 10. I don't want to give them her address. 11. Do it tomorrow. 12. Don't do it. 13. Don't give them to him. 14. Show her your picture. 15. Don't show it to them.

(*Key on page* 289.)

PARIS CAMPAGNARD
Le vieux moulin à vent donne un air de campagne à la rue Lepic à Montmartre.

Campagnard-e (adj.)	**moulin à vent** (m.)	**air** (m.)	**campagne** (f.)
Rustic	windmill	appearance	country

VINGT-QUATRIÈME LEÇON

CHEZ LA COUTURIÈRE—AT THE DRESSMAKER'S

Mme Roberts est allée voir une couturière qui lui a été recommandée par
Mrs. Roberts has gone to see a dressmaker who has been recommended to her by

Madame Lesage.   C'est aujourd'hui qu'a lieu le premier essayage
Mrs. Lesage.   It's today that is taking place the first fitting

d'une robe d'après-midi, et le deuxième essayage d'un tailleur et
of an afternoon frock, and the second fitting of a tailor-made costume and

d'un manteau d'été.
of a summer coat.

Mme Roberts: Pas trop mal pour le premier essayage.   Seulement un peu
Not too bad for the first fitting.   Only a little

       trop étroit des hanches.
       too tight over the hips.

Couturière: En effet, madame.   Je vais l'élargir un peu.   Et comme
Yes, indeed, madam.   I will let that out a bit.   And how

       longueur?
       is it for length?

Mme Roberts: Un tout petit peu trop long, ne trouvez-vous pas?
Just a little bit too long, don't you think?

Couturière: Peut-être bien, madame.   Je la raccourcirai d'un centimètre.
Perhaps it is, madam.   I'll shorten it by one centimetre.

       Autrement il n'y a rien à changer.   Voulez-vous avoir la
       Otherwise there is nothing to alter.   Will you have the

       bonté d'essayer le tailleur maintenant?
       kindness to try on the tailor-made costume now?

Mme Roberts: Avec plaisir, mademoiselle.   En tout je suis très contente,
With pleasure, miss.   In general I am very pleased,

       seulement la jupe ne tombe pas encore assez bien.
       only the skirt still does not fall quite well.

       Par contre, les poches et le col peuvent rester comme
       On the other hand, the pockets, and the collar can remain as

ils sont maintenant.
they are at present.

Couturière: Il faudra un nouvel
Another fitting will be

essayage pour le tailleur, madame. **Je vais rectifier**
necessary for the tailor-made costume, madam. I will put the

la jupe. **Est-ce qu'il vous conviendrait de revenir demain**
skirt right. Would it suit you to come back tomorrow

dans l'après-midi? **Mme Roberts: C'est entendu.**
in the afternoon? That's all right.

Couturière: **Voilà l'échantillon du drap que vous avez voulu voir**
Here is the sample of the cloth which you wanted to see

l'autre jour, madame.
the other day, madam.

Mme Roberts: J'ai changé d'idée. **Je crois que je choisirai une robe de**
I've changed my mind. I think that I'll choose a frock of

velours de soie, mais nous en parlerons plus tard.
chiffon velvet, but we shall discuss that later.

Couturière: **Est-ce que vous verrez Mademoiselle Lesage ces jours-ci, madame?**
Will you see Miss Lesage one of these days, madam?

Mme Roberts: Oui, je la verrai demain ou après-demain; avez-vous
Yes, I shall see her tomorrow or the day after tomorrow; have you

quelque chose à lui faire dire?
any message to give to her?

Couturière: **Oui, madame, si cela ne vous dérange pas trop, voulez-vous**
Yes, madam, if it is not too much trouble for you, will you

avoir la gentillesse de dire à mademoiselle que je l'attends
have the kindness to tell mademoiselle that I expect her

pour l'essayage de la robe qu'elle a commandée
for the fitting of the dress which she ordered

il y a une quinzaine de jours?
a fortnight ago?

Mme Roberts: Bien, je le lui dirai. **Couturière: Je vous remercie, madame.**
Good, I'll tell her. Thank you, madam.

THE TAILOR—LE TAILLEUR

English.—1. Dinner jacket; 2. Lounge suit; 3. Raincoat; 4. Riding breeches; 5. Roll of cloth; 6. Suit length; 7. Overcoat; 8, 9 and 10. Coat, white waistcoat and trousers of evening dress; 11. Measuring tape; 12. Morning coat; 13. Striped trousers; 14. Patent leather shoes; 15, 16 and 17. Lapels, sleeve and jacket of lounge suit; 18. Norfolk jacket.

French.—1. Smoking (m.); 2. Complet veston (m.); 3. Imperméable; 4. Culotte (f.) de cheval; 5. Pièce (f.) d'étoffe; 6. Coupon (m.) de complet; 7. Pardessus (m.); 8, 9, 10, Jaquette (f.) *or* frac (m.), gilet blanc et pantalon d'habit (*or* de tenue de soirée); 11. Centimètre (m.); 12. Jaquette (f.); 13. Pantalon (m.) rayé; 14. Souliers (m.pl.) vernis; 15, 16, 17, Revers (m.), manche (f.) et veston (m.); 18. Veston Norfolk.

Further Useful Expressions	**Un tailleur en vogue** A fashionable tailor	**un pardessus de facture soignée** a well-tailored overcoat
	Un vêtement confectionné A ready-made garment	**un vêtement sur commande** a bespoke garment

THE DRESSMAKER—LA COUTURIÈRE

English.—1. Evening dress; 2. Raincoat; 3. Sports coat; 4. Mirror wardrobe; 5. Sleeve; 6. Collar; 7. Dress (frock); 8. Pullover; 9. Belt; 10. Fur collar; 11. Winter coat; 12. Muff; 13. Pin-cushion; 14. Skirt; 15. Blouse; 16. Tailor-made jacket; 17. Sweater; 18. Tailor-made skirt.

French.—1. Tenue (f.) de soirée; 2. Manteau (m.) de pluie; 3. Manteau de sport; 4. Armoire (f.) à glace; 5. Manche (f.); 6. Col (m.); 7. Robe (f.); 8. Pullover (m.); 9. Ceinture (f.); 10. Col de fourrure; 11. Manteau d'hiver; 12. Manchon (m.); 13. Pelote (f.) à épingles; 14. Jupe (f.); 15. Blouse (f.); 16. Jaquette (f.) tailleur; 17. Tricot (m.); 18. Jupe tailleur.

Être élégante sans recherche	**une coiffure bien seyante** (from seoir)
To be faultlessly but simply dressed	a very becoming hat or hair style
Être affreusement affublée	**à la mode** **démodé (e)**
To be got up like a scarecrow	in the fashion out of fashion

VÊTEMENTS (ACCESSOIRES)—CLOTHING (ACCESSORIES)

le mouchoir handkerchief
le monogramme initials
le foulard scarf
le ceinture belt
une aiguille needle
le bouton button
le fil cotton (thread)
la ruche frill
le bouton pression press button
une agrafe et un œillet hook and eye

une épingle pin
une épingle de sûreté safety-pin
les ciseaux scissors
la fermeture éclair zip-fastener
le gant glove
le sac à main handbag
une agrafe clasp
le manchon muff
la manchette gauntlet cuff
la dentelle lace

IDIOMATIC EXPRESSIONS

avoir lieu=to take place
en effet=indeed
par contre=on the other hand
un tout petit peu=a tiny little bit
changer d'idée=to change one's mind
ces jours-ci=one of these days
pas du tout=not at all

il y a une quinzaine=a fortnight ago
il y a quelques semaines (mois)=a few weeks (months) ago
dans un jour=in one day
dans une quinzaine=in a fortnight
dans quelques jours (semaines)=in a few days (weeks)

POSITION OF Y AND EN

Il laisse sa femme à la maison.
  He leaves his wife at home.
Il l'y laisse.
  He leaves her there.

Vous avez des cigarettes.
  You have got cigarettes.
Donnez-m'en.
  Give me some.
Ne lui en donnez pas.
  Don't give him any.

Je vous quitte à la gare.
  I leave you at the station.
Je vous y quitte.
  I leave you there.

Elle met les fourchettes sur la table.
  She puts the forks on the table.
Elle les y met.
  She puts them there.

Nous leur parlons de notre jardin.
  We speak to them about our garden.
Nous leur en parlons.
  We speak to them about it.

Ils nous donnent des pommes.
  They give us apples.
Ils nous en donnent.
  They give us some.

Il n'y a pas de vin.
There isn't any wine.

Il n'y en a pas.
There isn't any.

Il n'y a pas d'allumettes.
There aren't any matches.

Il n'y en a pas.
There aren't any.

Note.—(1) When **y** or **en** is used with any other object pronoun the **y** or **en** is always put last; (2) **y** precedes **en**.

SUMMARY

The order of pronoun objects preceding a verb is this:—

me				
te	le	lui		
se	la	leur	y	en
nous	les			
vous				

EXERCISES

I Replace the words in italic type by pronouns

1. Charles n'écrit pas *ses lettres* dans la cuisine. 2. Elle vous donnera *du pain*. 3. Elles m'ont donné *de la viande*. 4. Ne nous donnez-vous pas *de pommes?* 5. Nous mangeons souvent *du chocolat dans la chambre à coucher.* 6. Nous donnons *des fleurs à Madame X.* 7. Il apporte *des roses à Mesdames X. et Y.* 8. On trouve de jolies *fleurs dans son jardin.* 9. La tante a envoyé *des bonbons aux enfants.* 10. J'enverrai *mes enfants à la campagne.*

II Answer the following questions using pronouns instead of nouns

1. Avez-vous beaucoup de travail à faire aujourd'hui? 2. Donnez-vous du pain aux chiens? 3. Est-ce que vous donnez du vin à un chat? 4. Est-ce que votre père est en Amérique? 5. Est-ce que vous allez souvent au cinéma? 6. Me donnez-vous des pommes? 7. Est-ce que je vous donne de l'argent? 8. Pouvez-vous envoyer des lettres à M. Roberts? 9. Est-ce que la couturière vous fait beaucoup de robes? 10. Voulez-vous m'envoyer des bonbons? 11. Écrivez-vous beaucoup de lettres à vos amis? 12. À qui envoyez-vous des colis?

III Translate into French

1. What will you give us? 2. I will give you a French lesson. 3. What do you send us? 4. I send you shirts, handkerchiefs and socks. 5. To whom do you send this parcel? 6. I send it to my sister, who is at present in France. 7. I can send you some underwear. 8. Did you write to him about it? 9. I shall give you some chocolate; but don't give any to my brother; I gave him enough. 10. Where are my handkerchiefs? There are some in that box.

(Key on page 289)

AROUND THE TOWN

Les Midinettes de Paris

Derrière la façade fastueuse des grands établissements de mode, où des dames élégantes viennent choisir les toilettes du dernier chic parisien qui font l'envie de leurs amies, se trouve une personne de grande importance dans l'organisation. C'est la petite "arpète" (apprentie) qui coud dans les ateliers du sous-sol et qui met dans son travail la vraie délicatesse parisienne. Paris la connaît sous le sobriquet de "midinette," parce qu'elle rentre d'habitude dîner chez elle à midi. Elle est facile à reconnaître dans la rue par le chic qu'elle parvient à atteindre malgré son budget restreint.

Paris "Midinettes'"

Behind the sumptuous façade of the great houses of fashion, to which elegant ladies come to choose clothes—the last word in Paris smartness—which arouse the envy of their friends, is a person of the first importance in the organization. This is the little "arpète" (apprentice) who sews in the basement work-rooms and puts the true Parisian touch into her work. Paris knows her under the nickname of "midinette," because she usually goes home to lunch at midday, easy to recognize in the street by the elegance which she succeeds in achieving, despite her restricted budget.

LE PALAIS BOURBON

Construit en 1722 sur l'ordre de la duchesse douairière de Bourbon, le Palais Bourbon fait partie aujourd'hui de L'Assemblée Nationale. Ici nous voyons l'entrée de derrière.

Douairière (f.)	**faire partie**	**L'Assemblée Nationale (f.)**
Dowager	form part	The National Assembly (French Parliament)

VINGT-CINQUIÈME LEÇON

LE TAILLEUR—THE TAILOR

M. Roberts attend le tailleur avec lequel il a fixé un
Mr. Roberts waits for the tailor with whom he has made an

rendez-vous pour cet après-midi. On sonne. M. Roberts va
appointment for this afternoon. The bell is ringing. Mr. Roberts goes

lui-même ouvrir la porte, et le tailleur entre.
himself to open the door, and the tailor comes in.

M. Roberts: **Je suis très pressé. Prenez vite mes mesures,**
I am in a great hurry. Take my measurements quickly,

s'il vous plaît, monsieur. Je vous ai déjà dit qu'il me
please. I have already told you that I

faut un complet-veston. Voilà l'échantillon de l'étoffe
need a lounge suit. This is the sample of the material

que j'ai choisie.
which I have chosen.

Le tailleur (en prenant les mesures): Quelle sorte de doublure désirez-vous,
(taking the measurements): What sort of lining do you want,

monsieur?
sir?

M. Roberts: **Je la desire en soie. Quand pourrons-nous essayer?**
I want it in silk. When shall we be able to have a fitting?

Le tailleur: **Après-demain, monsieur. Je pourrai venir chez vous, si cela**
The day after tomorrow, sir. I could call on you, if it

vous convient. M. Roberts: Non, je passerai chez vous.
suits you.   No, I shall come along to your place.

L'ESSAYAGE—THE FITTING

Le tailleur: **Bonjour, M. Roberts, quel beau temps nous avons aujourd'hui!**
Good day, Mr. Roberts, what fine weather we have today!

Votre complet est prêt. Si vous voulez bien l'essayer,
Your suit is ready. If you will be good enough to try it on,

nous allons voir comment il va.
we shall see how it fits.

M. Roberts a mis le complet, et le tailleur voit son client
Mr. Roberts has put on the suit, and the tailor sees his customer

froncer les sourcils.
frowning.

Le tailleur: Est-ce que vous êtes content, M. Roberts?
Are you satisfied, Mr. Roberts?

M. Roberts: Comme-ci comme-ça. Le veston me gêne sous les bras.
So so. The coat is too tight under the arms.

Le tailleur: Ce n'est rien; au premier essayage il y a toujours
That's nothing; at the first fitting there are always

quelques retouches à faire. Je vais faire le nécessaire.
a few alterations to be made. I will see to it.

Que pensez-vous de la coupe, monsieur?
What do you think of the cut, sir?

M. Roberts: La coupe est très bonne, mais le pantalon est trop long.
The cut is very good, but the trousers are too long.

J'aime les pantalons un peu courts, car ils ne ramassent pas
I like trousers rather short, because they do not pick up

la boue quand il pleut, ni la poussière quand il fait sec. J'ai
mud when it rains, nor dust when it is dry. I have

aussi remarqué qu'ils ne s'usent pas si vite aux bords.
also noticed that they do not wear out so quickly at the edges.

Le tailleur: Vous avez raison, monsieur.
You are right, sir.

M. Roberts: Je pense que ce beau temps ne va pas durer, et que
I think that the fine weather is not going to last, and that

bientôt nous aurons le grand froid. Prenez mes
soon we shall have severe cold. Take my

mesures pour un pardessus.
measurements for an overcoat.

Le tailleur: Certainement, monsieur, et quel genre d'étoffe désirez-vous?
Certainly, sir, and what kind of cloth do you want?

LA PLACE DE LA BASTILLE

Le monument actuel s'élève sur l'emplacement où jadis se trouvait la forteresse de la Bastille. La destruction de celle-ci par les émeutiers de 1789 fut le premier pas vers la Révolution, qui entraîna plus tard l'exécution de Louis XVI et de Marie Antoinette.

Emplacement (m.)	**jadis** (adv.)	**émeutier-ère** (m.f.)	**entraîner**
Site	formerly	rioter	to entail, involve

M. Roberts: **Je voudrais un tissu doux, assez épais et d'une**
I should like a soft cloth, rather thick and of a
couleur sombre.   C'est un pardessus d'hiver dont j'ai besoin.
dark colour.   It is a winter overcoat of which I have need.

LES CHAPEAUX—HATS

le chapeau haut-de-forme   top hat
le chapeau melon   bowler hat
le chapeau mou   soft hat
le bord   brim
le ruban   ribbon
le panama   panama
la casquette   cap
le capuchon   hood

la coiffe   bonnet
le béret   beret
la voilette   veil
le chapeau tyrolien sports hat (Tyrol shape)
le chapeau cloche   sports hat (with turned-down brim)
le chapeau de paille   straw hat (wide brim)
le chapeau relevé   hat with turned-up brim

CHAUSSURES—FOOTWEAR

le magasin de chaussures   shoe-shop
la pantoufle   slipper
la sandale   sandal
le soulier à bride   shoe with strap
le soulier à lacets   tie shoe
l'escarpin   court shoe
la guêtre   (men's) spats
le soulier   shoe

la bottine   boot
la botte   high boot
le soulier verni   patent leather shoe
le talon   heel
la semelle   sole
le bout   cap
la languette   tongue
les lacets (m.)   laces

AROUND THE TOWN

La Mode Masculine à Paris

Pour l'Anglais moyen il peut sembler drôle que M. Roberts, notre "héros," qui doit rentrer en Angleterre dans quelques mois, se soit avisé de se faire faire des vêtements par un tailleur français. Mais de nos jours, la mode masculine européenne tend à se rationaliser, et c'est ainsi que des vêtements faits sur mesure par un bon tailleur parisien, ne sembleraient plus extraordinaires aux amis londoniens de M. Roberts. Il existe à Paris beaucoup de firmes spécialisées dans la coupe anglaise, et plusieurs tailleurs français qui ont fait leur apprentissage à Londres.

Paris Men's Fashions

It may seem strange to the average Briton that Mr. Roberts, our "hero," who has to return to England in a few months, should have got the idea of having clothes made by a French tailor. But in these days European men's fashions tend to become rationalized, so that clothes made to measure by a good Paris tailor would no longer seem strange to Mr. Roberts's London friends. There exist in Paris many tailors specializing in English cut, and several French tailors have served their apprenticeship in London.

ON DÉMÉNAGE

Quoique prise près de Paris, cette photographie d'un déménagement villageois offre toute l'ambiance de la vie champêtre loin de la métropole et de sa vie turbulente.

Déménager	**villageois-e** (adj.)	**ambiance** (f.)	**métropole** (f.)
To move (house)	village	atmosphere, environment	metropolis

PERSONAL PRONOUNS USED APART FROM VERBS

Qui vient? = Who is coming?
Moi = I (am)
Lui = He (is)
Elle = She (is)
Nous = We (are)
Vous = You (are)
Eux = They (are) (m.)
Elles = They (are) (f.)
Toi = You (are) (familiar form)
Qui veut aller à la gare? = Who wants to go to the station?
Moi, monsieur = I, sir
Qui a pris mon stylo? = Who has taken my fountain-pen?
Lui, madame = He (has), madam
Je viendrai avec vous / toi = I shall come with you
Qui fait tant de bruit? = Who is making so much noise?
Ce sont eux = They are
Viendras-tu avec moi? = Will you come with me?
N'allez pas sans lui = Don't go without him
Ne sortez pas sans eux = Don't go out without them (men or boys)
Ne sortez pas sans elles = Don't go out without them (women or girls)
C'est moi qui ai fait cela = It is I, who have done it
C'est lui qui a acheté le couteau = It is he who has bought the knife
C'est elle qui a fait la cuisine = It is she who has done the cooking
Ce sont eux qui n'ont pas encore mangé = It is they who have not eaten yet

All the personal pronouns which have occurred so far have been used with verbs only.

e.g. **Vous parlez très bien. Il me donne de l'argent. Elle lui écrit souvent. Il me l'a dit. Il n'y en a pas.**

They are called weak pronouns, because they cannot stand alone and are used in connection with verbs only. In this lesson we met various strong pronouns, i.e., those used apart from verbs.

You must distinguish between:

WEAK PRONOUNS *used in connection with verbs*	STRONG PRONOUNS *used apart from verbs*	
je	moi	I
tu	toi	thou
vous	vous	you
il	lui	he
elle	elle	she
nous	nous	we
ils	eux	they (m.)
elles	elles	they (f.)

Four of the pronouns are the same in both lists above; there are special words only for I, thou, he and they (masc.).

The strong pronouns are more emphatic than the weak ones. The following constructions are therefore used to throw more emphasis on to the pronoun. In English this emphasis is usually shown by the voice only.

e.g., **Moi, je l'ai trouvé** = *I* have found it
    Ce n'est pas moi qui l'ai fait, c'est lui = *I* did not do it, *he* did
    Lui et moi l'avons apporté = *He* and *I* have brought it
    Charles et moi le ferons = *Charles* and *I* will do it
    Lui et moi, nous allons = (He and I) *we* are going
    Vous et lui, vous jouez = (You and he) *you* play
    Vous, allez-vous-en! = *You* (emphatic) go away from here!

Note that strong pronouns are used when the subject consists of two pronouns, or a noun and a pronoun.

AT HOME

Je suis chez moi = I am at home
Il est chez lui = He is at home
Elle est chez elle = She is at home

Nous sommes chez nous = We are at home
Ils sont chez eux
Elles sont chez elles } They are at home
Êtes-vous chez vous?
Es-tu chez toi? } Are you at home?

MINE, THINE, YOURS, HIS, HERS, ETC.

C'est à moi = That is mine
C'est à lui = That is his
C'est à elle = That is hers
C'est à nous = That is ours
C'est à vous ⎱
C'est à toi ⎰ = That is yours
C'est à eux ⎱
C'est à elles ⎰ = That is theirs
Ce chapeau est à Charles = This hat is Charles's (belongs to Charles)
Il est à lui = It is his (it belongs to him)

MYSELF, YOURSELF, HIMSELF, HERSELF, ETC.

Je le ferai moi-même = I shall do it myself.
L'a-t-il fait lui-même? = Did he do it himself?
Elle me l'a dit elle-même = She told me herself.
Vous n'avez que vous-même à blâmer = You have only yourself to blame.

Ils le font eux-mêmes ⎱ They are doing
Elles le font elles-mêmes ⎰ it themselves.
Nous ne le savons pas nous-mêmes = We don't know it ourselves.

Note.—moi-même = myself; toi-même = yourself; lui-même = himself; elle-même = herself; nous-mêmes = ourselves; eux-mêmes = themselves (m.); elles-mêmes = themselves (f.); vous-même = yourself; vous-mêmes = yourselves.

RIRE—TO LAUGH

Present:

Je ris	nous rions
tu ris	vous riez
il rit	ils rient

Imperfect: je riais, etc.
Future: je rirai, etc.
Conditional: je rirais, etc.
Perfect: j'ai ri, etc.

EXERCISES

II Translate into English

1. Je pense à lui. 2. Ne pensez pas à elle. 3. Ce crayon est à moi. 4. Ce journal est-il à vous? 5. Non, il n'est pas à moi. 6. Cette maison est-elle à lui? 7. Ce parapluie est-il à elle? 8. Je n'ai pas discuté (= discussed) la question avec eux. 9. Vous pouvez compter (= count) sur lui. 10. Avez-vous des lettres pour moi? 11. Elle n'est pas chez elle. 12. Il l'a acheté chez Woolworth. 13. Il l'a fait lui-même. 14. Vous me l'avez dit vous-même. 15. Ils ne le savent pas eux-mêmes.

III Translate into French

1. Can you recommend her to me? 2. Are you thinking of her? 3. Does this umbrella belong to him? 4. Does this belong to her? 5. Is he satisfied with them? 6. Did he speak of me? 7. Are you dissatisfied with him? 8. What does she think of them. 9. Is he at home? 10. Is Miss Smith at home? 11. No, she went to her dressmaker. 12. Did you come from home? 13. I did it myself. 14. Did you do it yourself? 15. Tell him to do it himself. 16. Have you anything for them? 17. My friend and I. 18. Who is hungry? I am. 19. Whom have you seen? Him. 20. Those pencils are not yours; they are Madeleine's.

(Key on pages 289 and 290.)

LA CHOSE SE PASSE AU CAFÉ

Premier consommateur: Monsieur, je crois que nous nous sommes déjà rencontrés, l'année dernière, à ce café.

Deuxième consommateur: Vous croyez me reconnaître?

Premier: Pas vous, mais votre parapluie.

Deuxième: Mon parapluie? Mais je ne l'avais pas à cette époque.

Premier: En effet, mais moi, je l'avais.

La chose, thing; **se passer,** to happen; **consommateur,** customer; **croire,** to believe; **se rencontrer,** to meet; **reconnaître,** to recognize; **le parapluie,** umbrella; **à cette époque,** at that time; **en effet,** that's right.

VINGT-SIXIÈME LEÇON

AU THÉÂTRE—AT THE THEATRE

Pour célébrer l'anniversaire de sa fille Mme Roberts amena ses
To celebrate her daughter's birthday Mrs. Roberts took her

enfants au théâtre. Après avoir consulté les affiches dans les
children to the theatre. After having studied the posters in the

rues et les colonnes des spectacles dans les journaux Mme Roberts
streets and the theatre-columns in the newspapers Mrs. Roberts

avait décidé de les amener à la Comédie Française où
decided to take them to the Comédie Française where

l'on jouait "Le Malade Imaginaire" de Molière. Quand elle était en
Molière's "Le Malade Imaginaire" was being played. When she was in

ville pour faire des achats elle avait retenu trois places au
town to do some shopping she had booked three seats in the

parterre. Le soir de la représentation, quand ils arrivèrent
orchestra. On the evening of the performance, when they arrived

au théâtre Mme Roberts alla d'abord au vestiaire pour y
at the theatre Mrs. Roberts went first to the cloakroom to

laisser son manteau et son chapeau. Puis ils donnèrent leurs
leave her coat and her hat there. Then they gave their

billets à l'ouvreuse, qui les conduisit à leurs places. Charles
tickets to the usherette, who led them to their seats. Charles

acheta un programme et donna un pourboire à l'ouvreuse.[1]
bought a programme and gave a tip to the usherette.[1]

Charles (à l'ouvreuse): Pouvez-vous nous louer des jumelles?
(to the usherette): Can you hire us a pair of opera-glasses?

L'ouvreuse: Certainement, monsieur, c'est cinquante francs.
Certainly, sir, it's fifty francs.

Charles: Voici cent francs; avez-vous de la monnaie? (Il est très
Here is a hundred francs; have you any change? (He is very

---

[1] It is customary in France to tip the **ouvreuse**, and she expects it.

> fier, parce que c'est la première fois qu'on
> proud, because it is the first time that he has been

> l'a appelé "monsieur").
> called "sir").

L'ouvreuse: **Non, monsieur, mais je vais aller vous en chercher.**
No, sir, but I'll go to get you some.

(Charles ajuste ses jumelles et regarde autour de lui.)
(Charles adjusts his opera-glasses and looks round.)

LE THÉÂTRE FRANÇAIS (COMÉDIE FRANÇAISE)

L'eau étincelante forme une espèce de rideau devant le foyer des "Sociétaires".

Étincelant-e (adj.)   **rideau** (m.)   **"Sociétaires"**
Sparkling   curtain   designation of Comédie Française players

Charles: Le théâtre est bondé.
                    The theatre is crowded.

Madeleine: Il n'y a pas une place de libre.
                    There is not one seat free.

L'ouvreuse (à Charles): Voici votre monnaie, monsieur.
(to Charles): Here is your change, sir.

Mme Roberts: Attention, on frappe les trois coups. C'est comme cela
Listen, there are the three knocks. That is how the

qu'on annonce en France le commencement du spectacle.
beginning of the play is announced in France.

Charles: Quel drôle de coutume.
                    What a funny custom.

Mme Roberts: Chut! On commence.
Quiet! It's starting.

(Le rideau se lève et on joue la première scène du "Malade Imaginaire",
(The curtain rises and they play the first scene of "Le Malade Imaginaire",

comédie brillante d'un fou qui n'est point malade et qui
a brilliant comedy of a hypochondriac who is not ill and who

s'entoure de médecins.)
surrounds himself with doctors.)

PAST TENSES

(1) **Il a visité le cinéma deux fois cette semaine** = He has visited the cinema twice this week.

(2) (a) **Le cinéma était bondé** = the cinema was crowded.

(b) **Il visitait le cinéma deux fois par semaine** = He visited (used to visit) the cinema twice a week.

(c) **Nous demeurions à Paris pendant six mois** = We lived in Paris for six months.

(3) **Il entra, acheta un billet et le donna à l'ouvreuse** = He entered, bought a ticket and gave it to the usherette.

AROUND THE TOWN

Les "Girls" de Paris

La plupart des touristes anglais font au moins une visite dans un des grands music-halls où le genre de spectacle n'exige pas une grande connaissance de la langue française. Là ils voient parmi les troupes de danseuses beaucoup de leurs compatriotes. Les "Girls" de Paris sont renommées, et il y avait longtemps à Paris un pasteur anglais, le Révérend Basil Cardew, qui se dévouait à leurs besoins.

The "Girls" of Paris

Most English tourists make at least one visit to one of the big music-halls where the type of entertainment does not require any great knowledge of French. There they see among the troupes of dancing girls many of their fellow-countrywomen. The "Girls" of Paris are famous, and for a long time in Paris there was an English parson, the Rev. Basil Cardew, who ministered to their needs.

(4) **Quand il entra la représentation avait déjà commencé**=When he entered the performance had already begun.

In the last two foregoing sentences a new tense makes its appearance, which is called the Preterite. It is used in narratives of a historic or literary nature, in telling of past actions that happened once, as distinct from habitual or continuous actions (compare the last two sentences with sentence 1). For descriptions (see sentence 2a), and habitual (2b) or continuous action (2c), the Imperfect is used. In French conversation, however, past incidents are given in the Perfect (sentence 1).

The imperfect may be translated in three different ways.

je donnais $\begin{cases} \text{I gave} \\ \text{I was giving} \\ \text{I used to give} \end{cases}$

Students who are learning French for conversational purposes only may ignore the Preterite, since it is never used in conversation.

THE PRETERITE

donner=to give	finir=to finish
je donnai	je finis
tu donnas	tu finis
il donna	il finis
nous donnâmes	nous finîmes
vous donnâtes	vous finîtes
ils donnèrent	ils finirent

perdre=to lose	recevoir=to receive
je perdis	je reçus
tu perdis	tu reçus
il perdit	il reçut
nous perdîmes	nous reçûmes
vous perdîtes	vous reçûtes
ils perdirent	ils reçurent

Note that the regular endings of the Preterite are:

-er verbs	-ir and -re verbs	-oir verbs
-ai	-is	-us
-as	-is	-us
-a	-it	-ut
-âmes	-îmes	-ûmes
-âtes	-îtes	-ûtes
-èrent	-irent	-urent

avoir=to have	être=to be
j'eus=I had	je fus=I was
tu eus	tu fus
il eut	il fut
nous eûmes	nous fûmes
vous eûtes	vous fûtes
ils eurent	ils furent

venir=to come

je vins=I came	nous vînmes
tu vins	vous vîntes
il vint	ils vinrent

aller=to go, same as **donner** (j'allai, etc.)
tenir=to hold, same as **venir** (je tins, etc.)
faire=to make—je fis, etc.
prendre=to take—je pris, etc.
mettre=to put—je mis, etc.
dire=to say—je dis, etc.
boire=to drink—je bus, etc.
lire=to read—je lus, etc.
écrire=to write—j'écrivis, etc.
connaître=to know—je connus, etc.
courir=to run—je courus, etc.
mourir=to die—je mourus, etc.
voir=to see—je vis, etc.
pouvoir=to be able—je pus, etc.
croire=to believe—je crus, etc.
savoir=to know—je sus, etc.
s'asseoir=to sit down—je m'assis, tu t'assis, il s'assit, etc.
pleuvoir=to rain—il plut

The Preterite is used in the literary language only. It expresses a particular fact or event which took place (once) at some definite past time (there must be an interval of at least one day).

English

1. Stage door; 2. Dress circle; 3. Upper circle; 4. Box; 5. Spotlight; 6. Curtain; 7. Limelights; 8. Proscenium; 9. Safety-curtain; 10. Scenery; 11. Stage-hands; 12. Stage-manager; 13. Star (man); 14. Star (woman); 15. Supporting cast; 16. Foot-lights; 17, 18. Prompter and prompter's box; 19, 20. Orchestra and orchestra pit; 21. Conductor; 22. Emergency exit; 23. Opera-glasses; 24. Sweets-seller; 25. Seating attendant; 26. Orchestra stalls; 27. Programme-girl; 28. Box office; 29. Foyer; 30. Bar.

French

1. Entrée (f.) des artistes; 2. Premier

Further Useful Expressions			
	Faire fureur To be a "riot"	**faire four** to be a "flop"	**costumière** (f.) wardrobe-mistress
	Effets sonores (m.pl.) Sound effects	**coulisses** (f.pl.) wings	**metteur** (m.) **en scène** producer

LE THÈÂTRE

balcon (m.); 3. Seconde galerie (f.); 4. Loge (f.); 5. Projecteur (m.); 6. Rideau (m.); 7. Lumière (f.) oxhydrique; 8. Avant-scène; 9. Rideau métallique; 10. Décors (m.pl.); mise (f.) en scène; 11. Machinistes (m.pl.); 12. Régisseur (m.); 13. Acteur de premier rôle; vedette (f.); 14. Actrice de premier rôle; vedette; 15. Troupe (f.); 16. Rampe (f.); 17, 18. Souffleur-euse (m.f.); trou du souffleur; 19, 20. Orchestre (m.); fosse (f.) d'orchestre; 21. Chef (m.) d'orchestre; 22. Sortie (f.) de secours; 23. Jumelles (f.pl.) (when hired from theatre) en location; 24. Vendeuse de bonbons; 25. Ouvreuse (f.); 26. Fauteuils (m.pl.) d'orchestre; 27. Vendeuse de programmes; 28. Location (f.); 29. Foyer (m.); 30. Buffet (m.).

Nom (m.) **de théâtre**	**spectateur-trice** (m.f.)	**habilleuse** (f.)	**effets scéniques** (m.pl.)
Stage-name	theatre-goer	dresser	effects

Se faire acteur (actrice)	**droits** (m.pl) **de production**	**trac** (m.)	**aparté** (m.)
To go on the stage	stage-rights	stage-fright	stage-whisper, aside

	He had an
Il eut une entrevue	interview
hier	yesterday
la semaine dernière	last week
le mois passé	last month
l'année dernière	last year

but: **il a eu une entrevue aujourd'hui** = he had an interview today (lit., he has had)

Learn this tongue-twister by heart:

Didon dîna, dit-on, du dos d'un dodu dindon
Queen Dido dined, they say, off the back of a fat turkey.

conduire = to lead, to drive
je conduis, tu conduis, il conduit
nous conduisons, vous conduisez
ils conduisent
Imperfect: **je conduisais,** etc.
Preterite: **je conduisis,** etc.
Future: **je conduirai,** etc.
Perfect: **j'ai conduit,** etc.

paraître = to appear
je parais, tu parais, il paraît
nous paraissons, vous paraissez
ils paraissent
Imperfect: **je paraissais,** etc.
Preterite: **je parus,** etc.
Future: **je paraîtrai,** etc.
Perfect: **j'ai paru,** etc.

EXERCISES

I Write these sentences using the Preterite Tense

1. Je (recevoir) la lettre hier soir. 2. Il (venir) à Paris. 3. Ils ne nous (répondre) pas. 4. Ils (visiter) le musée. 5. Nous (aller) chez lui. 6. Quand on (ouvrir) la porte je (entrer). 7. Elle (faire) venir le médecin. 8. Ils (écrire) des lettres. 9. Elle (répondre) à sa question. 10. Il (finir) sa leçon.

II Translate into English

1. Ils ne nous répondirent pas. 2. Il arriva le soir. 3. Elle me donna son billet. 4. Elles choisirent des robes élégantes. 5. Il coupa le pain. 6. Elle chantait pendant que je jouais. 7. Elle chantait quand il entra. 8. Quand je fus à Paris je visitai l'Opéra. 9. Elles donnèrent de l'argent à la pauvre femme. 10. La porte de la chambre fut ouverte.

III

Re-write the sentences from Exercise II in conversational language (using the perfect instead of the preterite)

1. Ils ne nous ont pas répondu, etc.

IV Answer these Questions in French

1. Y a-t-il beaucoup de théâtres à Paris? 2. Avez-vous déjà été dans un théâtre français? 3. Quelle comédie Charles et Madeleine vont-ils voir? 4. Dans quel théâtre la joue-t-on? 5. Quelles places ont-ils? 6. Leur mère laisse-t-elle son chapeau au vestiaire? 7. Qui les conduit à leurs places? 8. Pourquoi Charles est-il fier? 9. Qu'est-ce qu'ils pensaient de la représentation? 10. Qu'est-ce qu'ils ont fait pendant l'entr'acte?

(Key on page 290)

KEY TO THE EXERCISES

Lesson Twenty-two

I

1. I am going to the post-office. 2. I must have some stamps. 3. Where is the post-office? 4. Are there any letters for me? 5. There is one. 6. Whom is it from? 7. It is from my friend. 8. What is he writing? 9. Nothing important. 10. Give me three 90-centime stamps. 11. Will you register this letter. 12. Do you want to send this telegram? 13. Did you post your letter? 14. When do you think this letter will arrive? 15. You will have to send it poste restante (or "I'll have," "We'll have," etc., according to the context).

II

1. Les voilà; celle-ci est pour moi; celle-là est pour vous. 2. Ceci est pour vous. 3. Je n'aime pas celles-ci. 4. Prenez-vous celui-ci ou celui-là? 5. Elle y

est. 6. Je l'y ai achetée. 7. Le voulez-vous? 8. Je préfère celui-ci. 9. Elles (celles-ci) sont très belles. 10. Celle-ci n'est pas confortable, prenez celui-là. 11. Prenez-vous ceux-là? 12. Donnez-moi celui-ci (celui-là), s'il vous plaît.

III

1. Connaissez-vous ces dames? 2. Lisez-vous ce livre? 3. Ont-ils acheté cette maison? 4. Quel vin voulez-vous, celui-ci ou celui-là? 5. Voulez-vous ces cigarettes? Non, merci, je préfère celles-là. 6. Dans quel magasin avez-vous acheté vos gants, dans celui-ci ou dans celui-là? 7. Il faut lire ce livre; il est très intéressant. 8. Il faut parler français maintenant. 9. Où est la poste? 10. Il me faut des timbres. 11. Deux timbres de vingt francs et cinq cartes postales, s'il vous plaît. 12. Avez-vous un timbre dix francs?

Lesson Twenty-three
I

1. Je ne le lui donne pas. 2. Il les leur envoie. 3. Il l'apporte. 4. Nous le lui envoyons. 5. Écrivez-lui! 6. Ne leur parlez pas. 7. Elles les lui donnent. 8. Je les lui donnerai. 9. Il y en a trois. 10. On les voit chaque jour. 11. Elle me les montre. 12. Il les leur montre.

II

1. Je lui donne une cravate. 2. Il leur donne une leçon. 3. Elle lui parle. 4. Je l'envoie à mon ami. 5. Je leur envoie des lettres. 6. Il leur vend du pain. 7. Je les apporte à ma mère. 8. Je ne vous le donne pas. 9. Je la lui envoie. 10. Il les leur donne.

III

1. Écrivez-moi. 2. Ne lui écrivez pas. 3. Leur avez-vous écrit? 4. La blanchisseuse lui apporte le linge propre. 5. Vous ne lui avez pas envoyé les journaux. 6. Vous ne les lui avez pas envoyés. 7. Réveillez-les. 8. Il nous envoie trois chemises, douze mouchoirs, et six paires de chaussettes. 9. Elle ne nous a pas donné notre liste de blanchissage. 10. Je ne veux

pas leur donner son adresse. 11. Faites-le demain. 12. Ne le faites pas. 13. Ne les lui donnez pas. 14. Montrez-lui votre tableau. 15. Ne le leur montrez pas.

Lesson Twenty-four
I

1. Charles ne les écrit pas dans la cuisine. 2. Elle vous en donnera. 3. Elles m'en ont donné. 4. Ne nous en donnez-vous pas? 5. Nous y en mangeons souvent. 6. Nous lui en donnons. 7. Il leur en apporte. 8. On y en trouve de jolies. 9. Elle leur en a envoyé. 10. Je les y enverrai.

II

1. Je n'en ai pas beaucoup à faire aujourd'hui. 2. Je leur en donne. 3. Je ne lui en donne pas. 4. Non, il n'y est pas. 5. Non, je n'y vais pas souvent. 6. Je vous en donne. 7. Vous ne m'en donnez pas. 8. Je peux lui en envoyer. 9. Elle m'en fait beaucoup. 10. Je vous en enverrai demain. 11. Je leur en écris tous les jours. 12. J'en envoie à ma cousine.

III

1. Que nous donnerez-vous? 2. Je vous donnerai une leçon de français. 3. Que nous envoyez-vous? 4. Je vous envoie des chemises, des mouchoirs et des chaussettes. 5. À qui envoyez-vous ce colis? 6. Je l'envoie à ma sœur qui est maintenant en France. 7. Je peux vous envoyer des sous-vêtements. 8. Lui avez-vous écrit à ce sujet? 9. Je vous donnerai du chocolat; mais n'en donnez pas à mon frère; je lui en ai assez donné. 10. Où sont mes mouchoirs? Il y en a dans cette boîte.

Lesson Twenty-five
I

1. I am thinking of him. 2. Don't think of her. 3. This pencil is mine. 4. Is this paper yours? 5. No, it is not mine. 6. Does this house belong to him? 7. Does this umbrella belong to her? 8. I haven't discussed the question with them. 9. You can count on him. 10. Have you any letters

for me? 11. She is not at home. 12. He bought it at Woolworth's. 13. He did it himself. 14. You told me yourself. 15. They don't know themselves.

II

1. Pouvez-vous me la recommander? 2. Pensez-vous à elle? 3. Est-ce que ce parapluie est à lui? 4. Est-ce que ceci est à elle? 5. Est-il content d'eux (or d'elles). 6. A-t-il parlé de moi? 7. Êtes-vous mécontent de lui? 8. Qu'est-ce qu'elle pense d'eux? 9. Est-il chez lui? 10. Miss Smith est-elle chez elle? 11. Non, elle est allée chez sa couturière. 12. Est-ce que vous êtes venu de chez vous? 13. Je l'ai fait moi-même. 14. L'avez-vous fait vous-même? 15. Dites-lui de le faire lui-même. 16. Avez-vous quelque chose pour eux (or elles)? 17. Mon ami et moi. 18. Qui a faim? Moi. 19. Qui avez-vous vu? Lui. 20. Ces crayons ne sont pas à vous; ils sont à Madeleine.

Lesson Twenty-six
I

1. reçus. 2. vint. 3. répondirent. 4. visitèrent. 5. allâmes. 6. ouvrit, j'entrai. 7. fit. 8. écrivirent. 9. répondit. 10. finit.

II

1. They did not answer us. 2. He arrived in the evening. 3. She gave me her ticket. 4. They selected some elegant frocks. 5. He cut the bread. 6. She sang while I played. 7. She was singing when he entered. 8. When I was in Paris I visited the Opera. 9. They gave the poor woman money. 10. The door of the room was opened.

III

1. Ils ne nous ont pas répondu. 2. Il est arrivé le soir. 3. Elle m'a donné son billet. 4. Elles ont choisi des robes élégantes. 5. Il a coupé le pain. 6. Elle a chanté pendant que j'ai joué. 7. Elle chantait quand je suis entré. 8. Quand j'étais à Paris j'ai visité l'Opéra. 9. Elles ont donné de l'argent à la pauvre femme. 10. La porte de la chambre a été ouverte.

IV

1. Il y en a beaucoup. 2. Je n'y ai pas encore été, or je n'y suis pas encore allé. 3. Ils vont voir "Le Malade Imaginaire." 4. On la joue à la Comédie Française. 5. Ils ont des places au parterre. 6. Elle l'y laisse. 7. Une ouvreuse les y conduit. 8. Parce qu'on l'appelle "Monsieur." 9. Ils en étaient très contents. 10. Ils se sont promenés au foyer.

AROUND THE TOWN
Les Halles Centrales

Les Halles Centrales de Paris, où l'on vend en gros (wholesale) presque tout ce qui est mangeable, offrent du crépuscule jusqu'à l'aube, un spectacle des plus pittoresques. Ce qui attire surtout les curieux, ce sont les restaurants du marché qui restent ouverts toute la nuit. On ne peut pas s'appeler un vrai Parisien, si l'on n'a pas mangé une soupe à l'oignon chez le Père Tranquille, à quatre heures du matin.

Paris Central Markets

The Halles Centrales or Central Markets of Paris, which deal in pretty nearly everything eatable, offer a lively picture from dusk till dawn. The attraction for many visitors is the market restaurants, which remain open all night. You cannot call yourself a real Parisian unless you have eaten a soupe à l'oignon at the Père Tranquille, at four o'clock in the morning.

JEU DE MOTS

Réflexion mélancolique d'un mari:— Avant mon mariage, ma femme m'était chère et j'étais son trésor. . . . Mais, maintenant, elle m'est plus chère encore, et je suis son trésorier.

Jeu de mots, play with words, pun; **un mari,** husband; **un trésor,** treasure; **un trésorier,** treasurer.

VINGT-SEPTIÈME LEÇON

READY FOR THE JOURNEY

When you know that Grandpa Lesage can be called **un vieillard** (old man), what you have learned in previous lessons should enable you to describe everything and everybody in this picture. If not, you should regard it as a "Stop!" notice, and go back for further study to earlier lessons where these words are encountered.

PROJETS DE VOYAGE—TRAVELLING PLANS

Monsieur et Madame Lesage ont décidé d'aller passer les vacances au bord de la mer,
M. and Mme Lesage have decided to spend the holidays at the seaside,

et pour que tout marche bien ils arrangent tous les
and in order that everything may go well, they arrange all the

détails à l'avance.
details beforehand.

Mme Lesage: **Puisque grand-père et grand'mère Lesage veulent bien nous**
As grandfather and grandmother Lesage wish to come with us,

accompagner, nous serons six.
we shall be six.

M. Lesage: **Ce qui nous permettra d'obtenir un billet de famille, et de**
This will enable us to obtain a family ticket, and to

voyager à prix réduit et aussi plus confortablement, puisque nous
travel at a reduced price, and also more comfortably, as we

ROUEN: RUE DE LA GROSSE HORLOGE

Cette ancienne horloge, chef-d'œuvre de l'art horlogier, surmonte l'arche de la rue à laquelle elle donne son nom. Jeanne d'Arc fut brûlée près de là.

Chef-d'œuvre (m.) (pron. shai-dā̃yvr)	surmonter	arche (f.)	brûler
Masterpiece; outstanding achievement	to surmount	arch	to burn

aurons un compartiment pour nous seuls.
shall have a compartment entirely to ourselves.

Georges: **Et notre oncle, notre tante et nos deux cousins, que vont-**
And uncle, aunt and our two cousins—what are they

ils faire?   Je crois qu'ils aimeraient aussi aller au bord
going to do?   I think they would also like to go to the seaside

de la mer durant leur séjour en France.   Cela me ferait
during their stay in France.   It would give me great

plaisir de les conduire en auto à Dieppe.   J'aurais pu emmener
pleasure to drive them by car to Dieppe.   I could take at

au moins cinq personnes.   Je pensais que nous pourrions passer
least five persons.   I thought we could go

par Rouen afin de visiter la magnifique
via Rouen so that we could visit the beautiful

cathédrale gothique.
Gothic cathedral.

Mme Lesage: **En voilà une bonne idée.   Et quand ils reviendront avec Lucie**
That's a very good idea.   And when they return with Lucie

de leur visite au Jardin Zoologique nous discuterons
from their visit to the Zoological Gardens we will discuss

le projet avec eux.
the plan with them.

Grand'mère: **Je crois les entendre maintenant.**
I think I hear them now.

(La porte s'ouvre, et Mme Roberts, Madeleine, Charles, et Lucie Lesage entrent.)
(The door opens, and Mrs. Roberts, Madeleine, Charles, and Lucie Lesage enter.)

Charles: **Nous voilà, grand'maman.   Nous nous sommes amusés follement.**
Here we are, grandmama.   We have had such a marvellous time.

Ma sœur et moi, nous sommes montés sur un éléphant.
My sister and I, we mounted an elephant.

Madeleine avait très peur comme toutes les petites filles,
Madeleine was very frightened like all little girls,

mais pas moi!
but not me!

PARIS: LE JARDIN D'ACCLIMATATION

En haut, la cacahuète qu'offre le petit garçon ne constitue guère une ripaille pour le grand éléphant. En bas, les lions ont l'air d'écouter comme des écoliers sages le discours du dompteur. Les spectateurs peuvent bien sourire car un fossé les sépare des lions.

Cacahuète (f.)	**ripaille** (f.)	**écolier** (m.)	**dompteur-euse** (m.f.)
Peanut; monkey-nut	feast	pupil	tamer

Mme Roberts: **Si tu te vantes comme ça, je ne te sortirai plus.**
If you boast like that, I shall not take you out any more.

Georges: **Écoutez bien, ma tante. Cela vous ferait-il plaisir**
Listen, auntie. Would you like

d'aller tous en auto à Dieppe en passant par
to go to Dieppe by car by way of

Rouen où nous pourrions visiter la cathédrale? La voiture peut
Rouen where we could visit the Cathedral? The car can

contenir cinq personnes, y compris moi, si cela ne vous fait rien
take five people, including myself, if you don't mind

d'être un peu serrée à l'arrière. Les autres pourront prendre
being rather squashed at the back. The rest can go by

le train, et comme vous êtes si nombreux, vous pouvez
train, and as there are so many of you, you will be able to

voyager à prix réduit.
travel at a reduced rate.

M. Roberts: **Très bonne idée, et je propose que les grand-parents, vos**
That is a very good idea, and I suggest that your grandparents,

parents et moi voyagions par chemin de fer et que les autres
your father and mother and I, travel by rail, and the rest

partent en auto avec Georges demain. (Tous sont d'accord.)
go with George by car tomorrow. (All agree.)

PETITES HISTOIRES

These little stories in French are intended to test your knowledge. Words which you cannot be expected to know are translated. Other examples are given elsewhere.

IL CHERCHAIT UN GRATTE-CIEL!

Quel est le prix de vos chambres, monsieur le gérant?

Cinq cents francs au premier étage, quatre cents au second, trois cents au troisième et deux cents au quatrième.

Merci, et excusez-moi de vous avoir dérangé inutilement, mais votre hôtel n'est pas assez haut pour moi.

AUX TROPIQUES

Et qu'est-ce que vous faites contre les microbes?

Eh bien, d'abord je fais bouillir l'eau.

Ah! et puis?

Et puis je la stérilise.

Très bien, et puis?

Et puis je bois de la bière!

IL ENTRAIT EN FRAPPANT

Comment avez-vous connu votre second mari?

Il a écrasé mon premier dans un accident d'auto.

Aux Tropiques means "In the Tropics"; **écraser** (in this sense) means "to run over," and **stériliser** you can guess from the English word, which is spelt like it.

English

1. Two-seater open tourer with rumble-seat; 2. Studded pedestrian crossing; 3. Box-tricycle; 4. Truck; 5. Cyclist; 6. "No Parking"; 7. Limousine with sliding roof; 8. Driver's mirror; 9. Windshield wiper; 10. Headlights; 11. Bumpers; 12. Number; 13. Motor-cyclist; 14. Convertible coupé; 15. Spare wheel; 16. Mudguard; 17. Running board; 18. Back wheel; 19. Window; 20. Hood; 21. Gas pump; 22. "Have Your Air Tested"; 23. Garage hand; 24. Front wheel; 25. Tyre; 26. Radiator; 27. Radiator fan; 28. Distributor; 29. Cylinder head; 30. Carburettor; 31. Air filter; 32. Jack; 33. Valves; 34. Steering column; 35. Gear box; 36. Gear lever; 37. Steering wheel; 38. Front seat; 39. Door; 40. Back seat.

French

1. Torpédo (f.) à deux places avec spider; 2. Passage (m.) clouté; 3. Bicyclette (f.) de livreur; 4. Camion (m.); 5. Cycliste (m. or

LA RUE ET L'AUTO

f.); 6. "Stationnement (m.) Défendu"[1];
7. Limousine (f.) à toit découvrable; 8.
Miroir (m.) rétroviseur; 9. Essuie-glaces
(m.); 10. Phares (m.); projecteurs (m.);
11. Pare-chocs (m.); 12. Numéro (m.) de
police; 13. Motocycliste (m. or f.); 14.
Coupé (m.) à capote rabattable; 15. Roue
(f.) de secours; 16. Pare-boue (m.); 17.
Marchepied (m.); 18. Roue arrière (or
d'arrière); 19. Glace (f.); 20. Capot (m.);

21. Pompe (f.) à essence; 22. "Vérifiez la
pression de vos pneus"; 23. Garagiste (m.);
employé (m.) de garage; 24. Roue d'avant;
25. Pneumatique (m.); 26. Radiateur (m.);
27. Ventilateur (m.); 28. Distributeur (m.)
d'allumage; 29. Culasse (f.); 30. Carburateur (m.); 31. Épurateur (m.) d'air; 32.
Lève-auto (m.); 33. Soupapes (f.pl.); 34.
Colonne (f.) de direction; 35. Boîte (f.) de
vitesses; 36. Levier (m.) des vitesses; 37.
Volant (m.); 38. Siège (m.) d'avant;
39. Portière (f.); 40. Siège d'arrière.

---

[1] Indicated by letter "P" with stroke through it.

MOTORING TERMS

la corne horn
corner to sound one's horn
allumer to switch on *(lights)*
éteindre to switch off
doubler to overtake
croiser to pass *(in opposite direction)*
parquer to park
glisser, déraper to skid

un parc à autos parking-place
le garage garage
remiser to garage
la panne breakdown
la réparation repair
la carrosserie body
le châssis chassis
le moteur engine

ADVERBS

Il fait terriblement froid
    It is terribly cold
C'est certainement une erreur
    That is certainly an error
Il travaille énormément
    He works very hard
Elle joue rarement
    She rarely plays
Je l'ai totalement oublié
    I completely forgot it
Ils viendront immédiatement
    They will come immediately
Je l'ai trouvé, heureusement
    I found it, fortunately
Je l'ai perdu, malheureusement
    I lost it, unfortunately
Il me l'a dit distinctement
    He clearly said it to me
Elle marche gracieusement
    She walks gracefully
Il parle sérieusement
    He speaks seriously

The ending **-ment** corresponds to the English adverbial ending "-*ly*"; it is added to the feminine of the adjective. If the masculine adjective ends with a vowel **-ment** is added to the masculine.

Le professeur est distrait
    The professor is absent-minded

Il traverse la rue distraitement
    He crosses the road absent-mindedly

LES ENFANTS! ...

Un dîner de cérémonie. La petite Sophie, huit ans, interpelle son grand-père:

Grand-papa . . .

Mais le grand-papa interrompt:
Les petites filles doivent se taire et écouter.

À la fin du repas le grand-père, devenu bienveillant, interroge l'enfant:

Que me voulais-tu, mon enfant? Parle maintenant.

Trop tard: il y avait une mouche dans votre salade et vous l'avez mangée.

Interpeller means "to address," **interrompre** "to interrupt," **se taire** "to be silent," **bienveillant** "kind, benign," and **interroger** "to question."

Masculine	Feminine		Adverb	
heureux	heureuse	happy, fortunate	heureusement	happily, fortunately
malheureux	malheureuse	unhappy, unfortunate	malheureusement	unfortunately
poli	polie	polite	poliment	politely
fier	fière	proud	fièrement	proudly
distrait	distraite	absent-minded	distraitement	absent-mindedly
sage	sage	wise	sagement	wisely
franc	franche	frank	franchement	frankly
lent	lente	slow	lentement	slowly
doux	douce	sweet	doucement	sweetly
triste	triste	sad	tristement	sadly
énorme	énorme	enormous	énormément	enormously
patient	patiente	patient	patiemment	patiently
constant	constante	constant	constamment	constantly
évident	évidente	evident	évidemment	evidently

Note that the last four of these adverbs are formed slightly irregularly.

Comparison of Adverbs:

Poliment	plus poliment
Politely	more politely

le plus poliment
most politely

For the comparative, prefix **plus,** for the superlative, **le plus** (same as the comparison of Adjectives; see page 130).

Irregular Comparison:

bien = well	mieux = better
peu = little	moins = less
beaucoup = much	plus = more
mal = ill, badly	pis or plus mal = worse

le mieux = best
le moins = least
le plus = most
le pis or le plus mal = worst

Distinguish carefully between these irregular adverbs and the irregular adjectives:

Adverb:

il parle bien = he speaks well
il parle mieux = he speaks better
il parle le mieux = he speaks best

Adjective:

un bon vin = a good wine
un meilleur vin = a better wine
le meilleur vin = the best wine

Adverb:

il parle mal = he speaks badly
il parle plus mal = he speaks worse
il parle le plus mal = he speaks worst

Adjective:

une mauvaise organisation
        a bad organisation
une plus mauvaise organisation
        a worse organisation
la plus mauvaise organisation
        the worst organisation

Position of Adverbs:

il neige souvent = it often snows
il a souvent neigé = it has often snowed

Adverbs are usually placed just after the verb, or in compound tenses after the auxiliary.

For emphasis, however, the adverb frequently stands at the beginning or end of the sentence, e.g. **fièrement il me l'a montré** or **il me l'a montré fièrement** = proudly he showed it to me.

EXERCISES

I Form adverbs from the following adjectives:

1. joli. 2. premier. 3. long. 4. bon.
5. mauvais. 6. curieux. 7. général
8. complet. 9. meilleur. 10. absolu.

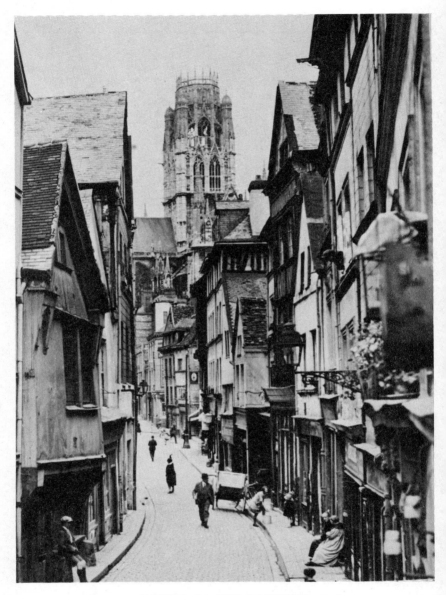

ROUEN: LA RUE DAMIETTE

Les façades, les toitures, les pignons—tout évoque le passé dans cette rue ancienne.

Façade (f.)	**toiture** (f.)	**pignon** (m.)	**évoquer**
Front	roof, roofing	gable, gable-end	to evoke, to recall

II Translate into English

1. C'est un bon homme. 2. C'est le meilleur homme du monde. 3. Ce dîner est bien fait. 4. Il est mieux que celui d'hier. 5. Votre hôtel est meilleur que le mien. 6. Vous le faites mieux que lui. 7. C'est mon meilleur ami. 8. Il parle mieux le français que moi. 9. Elle parle très mal. 10. Il va plus mal ce matin. 11. Il est moins intelligent que son père. 12. J'ai extrêmement faim. 13. Il fait terriblement chaud. 14. Malheureusement je ne pouvais pas le trouver. 15. Évidemment il est gravement malade. 16. J'aime beaucoup le tennis, mais j'aime mieux le golf. 17. Hier elle se portait bien, mais aujourd'hui elle se porte plus mal. 18. Il parle peu, mais sa femme parle beaucoup moins. 19. J'ai fini mon travail. Tant mieux (so much the better) pour vous. 20. Il faut partir immédiatement.

III Translate into French

1. I like this picture very much. 2. They are enormously rich. 3. She speaks better than her sister. 4. She is a very good girl; she always works well. 5. Unfortunately he has lost the book. So much the worse (tant pis) for him. 6. This is not his best book. 7. Do you like him better than her? 8. Did you sleep well? 9. You have written this letter badly. 10. Worse than ever. 11. Is your father better? 12. No, he is much worse than yesterday. 13. I am terribly thirsty. 14. Can you do it immediately? 15. Fortunately I am free at present. 16. He is generally at home from five to six. 17. Please speak more distinctly. 18. Unfortunately I did not find her at home. 19. He naturally thinks that you will come. 20. That is exactly my opinion. (*Key on pages* 334 *and* 335.)

CHAMONIX EN HIVER

À une allure vertigineuse, leurs bâtons de ski en l'air, les skieurs descendent la piste.

Allure (f.)   **vertigineux-euse** (adj.)   **bâton** (m.) **de ski**   **piste** (f.)
Speed, gait, bearing   giddy, dizzy   skiing-stick   track

VINGT-HUITIÈME LEÇON

OFF TO THE SEASIDE

In this picture you see the Lesage children leaving by car. You should now be able to describe in French other features shown in the illustration.

Encaisseur (m.)	**bouche** (f.) **d'égout**	**bouche** (f.) **d'incendie**	**voiture** (f.) **d'enfant**
Bank messenger	drain cover	hydrant	perambulator

A JOURNEY BY CAR

(Les portières claquent; les autres Lesage et M. Roberts agitent des mouchoirs,
(The doors slam; the other Lesages and Mr. Roberts wave their handkerchiefs,

et voilà les enfants partis. Charles est très intrigué par la voiture.
and away the children go. Charles is very much interested in the car.

Il ne connaît jusqu'à présent que les automobiles anglaises.)
Up to now he only knows British cars.)

Charles: **Quelle est la marque de cette voiture?**
                What make is this car?

Georges: **C'est une Renage. Elle tient très bien la route, et les freins sont**
                It is a Renage. It holds the road well, and the brakes are

                très bons. Regardez cette reprise.
                very good. Look how she responds.

(Le compteur de vitesse commence à grimper d'une façon impressionnante:
(The speedometer begins to mount in an impressive manner:

90——100——110——115 kilomètres par heure.)
approximately 56—63—69—72 miles an hour.)

Mme Roberts: Georges, pas si vite; vous savez que votre mère vous a demandé
Not so fast, George.   You know your mother asked you not

de ne pas dépasser le 100.
to exceed 100 (63 m.p.h.).

(Georges, jetant un coup d'œil dans le rétroviseur et s'apercevant
(George, giving a glance in the mirror and noticing that the three

que les trois passagers n'avaient pas l'air à l'aise, ralentit.
passengers did not look very happy, slows down.

Il faisait très beau; on avait glissé le toit ouvrant vers l'arrière, et toutes
The weather was very fine; they had pushed back the sunshine roof, and all

les glaces étaient baissées.   Mais voilà qu'en montant une côte un peu
the windows were down.   But just as they are climbing a rather

raide le moteur a une panne.   Georges descend et ouvre le capot.)
steep hill, the engine gives out.   Georges gets out and opens the bonnet.)

Georges: Il doit y avoir une saleté dans le carburateur;
                There must be some dirt in the carburettor;

                je vais le démonter.
                I shall take it to pieces.

(Georges sort un tournevis de la boîte à outils, et se met au travail.   Les deux
(George takes out a screwdriver from the tool-box, and sets to work.   The two

garçons, appuyés côte à côte sur le garde-boue, nettoient bien vite les
boys, leaning side by side on the mudguard, quickly clean the

différents gicleurs.   Georges vérifie le niveau de l'eau et essaie de mettre en marche;
different jets.   George tests the water in the radiator and tries to start up;

enfin le moteur démarre.   Arrivant dans une petite ville, Georges
in the end the engine starts.   Arriving at a small town, George

hésite; la route n'est pas bien indiquée.   Il hèle une vieille dame.)
hesitates; the route is not very clearly indicated.   He hails an old lady.)

Georges: Pour Rouen, s'il vous plaît, madame?
                Which is the way to Rouen, please?

La vieille dame: C'est tout droit, mon bon ami; et puis vous prendrez
                Straight on, my boy; and then you take

la deuxième à droite.
the second on the right.

Georges: Merci bien, madame.
Thanks so much.

(Le voyage se poursuit sans
(The journey continues without

autre encombre jusqu'à la tombée
further hindrance until

de la nuit. Ils arrivent à Rouen sans avoir
nightfall. They arrive at Rouen without having

besoin d'allumer les phares. C'est assez heureux,
to use their headlights. This is rather lucky,

car Georges s'aperçoit le lendemain que le feu rouge
as George notices next day that the red light

ne marche pas. Ils se dirigent vers un très bon hôtel que leur avaient
is not working. They make their way to a very good hotel which their friends

recommandé des amis. C'est là qu'ils passent la nuit.)
had recommended to them. There they pass the night.)

MORE MOTORING TERMS

conduire *(je conduis, il conduit, nous* | **mettre en marche** to start up
  conduisons, j'ai conduit) to drive | **mettre en première (deuxième) vitesse** to
tenir le volant to take the wheel | put in first *(second)* gear
le conducteur the driver | **la vitesse** speed
le permis de conduire driving licence | **accélérer** to accelerate
le permis de circulation car licence | **ralentir** to slow down
l'essence gasoline | **freiner** to brake

TO, AT, IN (A PLACE, ETC.)

La France	=France	**en France**	=to *or* in France
La Grande-Bretagne	=Great Britain	**en Grande-Bretagne**	=to *or* in Great Britain
l'Angleterre	=England (Britain)	**en Angleterre**	=to *or* in England (Britain)
La Belgique	=Belgium	**en Belgique**	=to *or* in Belgium
La Suisse	=Switzerland	**en Suisse**	=to *or* in Switzerland
La Russie	=Russia	**en Russie**	=to *or* in Russia
La Bretagne	=Britanny	**en Bretagne**	=to *or* in Britanny
La Normandie	=Normandy	**en Normandie**	=to *or* in Normandy
L'Écosse	=Scotland	**en Écosse**	=to *or* in Scotland
L'Irlande	=Ireland	**en Irlande**	=to *or* in Ireland
L'Allemagne	=Germany	**en Allemagne**	=to *or* in Germany
L'Italie	=Italy	**en Italie**	=to *or* in Italy
L'Europe	=Europe	**en Europe**	=to *or* in Europe

L'Amérique	=America	en Amérique	=to *or* in America
L'Asie	=Asia	en Asie	=to *or* in Asia
Le Japon	=Japan	au Japon	=to *or* in Japan
Le Danemark	=Denmark	au Danemark	=to *or* in Denmark
Le Portugal	=Portugal	au Portugal	=to *or* in Portugal
Le Brésil	=Brazil	au Brésil	=to *or* in Brazil
Les États-Unis	=United States	aux États-Unis	=to *or* in the U.S.A.
Les Indes	=India	aux Indes	=to *or* in India

The names of all the continents and of most countries are feminine. . . . With the names of countries and continents, **en** is used for "*in*" or "*to*"; but if the name is Masculine, **au** (or **aux**) is used.

à Paris   =   in, to *or* at Paris
à Londres =   in, to *or* at London
à Douvres =   in, to *or* at Dover
au Havre =   in, to *or* at Le Havre
à La Haye=   in, to *or* at The Hague

With the names of towns, **à**="*in*," "*to*," or "*at*." In some cases (e.g. **Le Havre, La Haye**) the definite article forms part of the name of the town.

à la campagne=
in the country *or* to the country

à l'Hôtel de Ville=
at the Town Hall *or* to the Town Hall

dans le nord de l'Angleterre=
in the north of England

dans tous les pays=
in all countries

dans la pharmacie=
in the chemist's shop (compare **chez le pharmacien**=at the chemist's)

je partirai dans trois minutes=
I shall leave in three minutes

Ils vont au théâtre

Ils sont au théâtre

Note that **à** is equivalent to "*on*" in the following expressions:—

aller à pied = to go on foot
aller à cheval = to go on horseback
aller à bicyclette = to ride on a bicycle, etc.

Note also:—

aller en auto	= to go by car
aller en chemin de fer	= to go by rail
aller en bateau	= to go by boat
aller en autocar	= to go by coach

Elles vont à l'église

Elles sont à l'église

Il est à la poste

Il est dans (or à) la poste

EXERCISES

I Translate into English

Versailles est près de Paris. De Paris à Versailles il y a dix-huit kilomètres. Quelle est la distance de Paris au Havre? Le Havre est à 288 kilometres de Paris. Du Havre on peut aller en bateau à New York. Combien de jours faut-il pour aller d'Europe en Amérique? Environ (=about) cinq ou six jours. Combien d'heures faut-il pour aller de Paris au Havre? De trois à quatre heures. Voici un indicateur. Il y a un express qui part à midi trente. Un rapide part de Paris à sept heures. A cinq heures de l'après-midi il y a un train omnibus (slow train). Mais il est très lent (slow); il s'arrête à toutes les gares.

II Translate into French

1. Is Versailles far from Paris? 2. Do you live far from here? 3. Our house is five minutes from here; we live near the church. 4. How far is it from here to the station? 5. About three kilometres; half an hour on foot. 6. Will you go by boat or by train? 7. How many hours does it take to go from here to the seaside? 8. Is there an express train in the morning? 9. There is only a slow train. It stops at all stations. 10. Are there no fast trains? 11. The best train is a fast train which leaves at noon and arrives at 8.35 p.m. 12. It stops only twice. (*Key on page* 335.)

DIEPPE: ANCIENNE ET MODERNE

Tout change dans ce monde-ci, et la forteresse sur la colline fut érigée en 1435 comme défense contre les Anglais, qui luttaient à cette époque sous le commandement du duc de Bedford pour établir les droits de succession de leur roi Henri VI au trône de France.

De nos jours les ennemis d'autrefois sont devenus de bons amis et c'est une invasion d'une autre sorte qui menace Dieppe, puisque des milliers d'Anglais vont chaque année en pélerinage à Dieppe. Les hôtels qui longent la plage sont pour la plupart occupés par des touristes anglais, venant chercher la santé et le repos.

Derrière les hôtels modernes, on entrevoit la vieille ville avec sa cathédrale.

Colline (f.)	ériger	lutter	pélerinage (m.)	longer	santé (f.)	repos (m.)
Hillock	to erect	to struggle	pilgrimage	to lie along	health	rest

VINGT-NEUVIÈME LEÇON

AT THE SWIMMING POOL

A swimming pool vocabulary is on page 314. Study this in conjunction with the other vocabularies contained in this lesson, until you are able to make out your own list in French of the things shown and what everyone in this picture is wearing or doing.

AU BORD DE LA MER—AT THE SEASIDE

Les Lesage avaient décidé avec les Roberts de prendre un appartement
The Lesages had decided with the Robertses to take furnished rooms

meublé à Dieppe.   Cela revient bien meilleur marché que d'aller à l'hôtel.
at Dieppe.   This comes much cheaper than going to a hotel.

Le premier jour, tandis que Mme Roberts est occupée à déballer les vêtements et
On the first day, while Mrs. Roberts is busy unpacking their clothes and

à les ranger, la jeunesse va faire un tour du côté de
putting them away, the youngsters go off to take a turn in the direction of

la plage.
the beach.

Madeleine: **Quel dommage!   Nous n'avons pas encore nos maillots de bain.**
What a pity!   We have not got our bathing costumes yet.

                 Nous aurions pu aller jouer sur la plage et nous baigner.
We should have been able to play on the beach and to bathe.

Lucie: **Nous irons tout a l'heure.   Il y aura plus de place, car la**
We will go later on.   There will be more room, as the

marée sera basse.
tide will be low.

Charles: **Regardez le grand bateau tout là-bas à l'horizon.   Je me**
Look at the big boat right over there on the horizon.   I

demande où il va.
wonder where she is going.

Georges: **Ce doit être le bateau qui vient d'Angleterre.   Il y a un**
It must be the boat coming from England.   There is a

service de jour et un service de nuit.
day and night service.

Charles: **Moi, j'aime mieux aller de jour.   On peut au moins se promener**
I prefer to go by day.   One can at least walk about

sur le pont et voir ce qui se passe.
on the deck and see what is going on.

Madeleine: **Oh, regardez le petit chalutier qui sort du port.**
Oh, look at the little trawler going out of the harbour.

Lucie: **Il est d'une jolie couleur brune.   Je pense qu'il part à la pêche.**
It is a very pretty brown colour.   I think it is going fishing.

Georges: **Demandons à ce vieux pêcheur quels poissons on prend ici.**
Let us ask this old fisherman what fish they catch here.

AT THE BATHING BEACH

By carefully memorising the French names of everything shown in this picture, as set out on page 313, in conjunction with the Swimming Pool vocabulary on page 314, you can equip yourself for your next seaside holiday in France. Now that you are at an advanced stage of the Course, and should be in possession of a sound knowledge of colloquial French, this seems an objective well worth while. Therefore, we leave it to you to study the vocabularies until you feel that you could name anything here in French, and become a happy (and vocal) member of the cheerful crowd on the sea front of this typical holiday resort.

(**Le vieil homme était assis sur le rebord de pierre de la promenade et**
(The old man was seated on the stone edge of the esplanade and

reparait des filets.)
was mending some nets.)

Georges: **Pardon, monsieur. Quels sont les poissons que l'on pêche par ici?**
Excuse me. What fish are caught in this neighbourhood?

Le vieux pecheur (souriant): Vous voulez donc devenir pêcheurs.
(smiling): So you want to become fishermen.

C'est un rude métier. Eh bien, il y a des bateaux
It is a hard calling. Well, some boats are

qui vont pêcher le hareng dans la mer du Nord, et
going to fish for herring in the North Sea, and

d'autres la morue du côté de Terre-Neuve.
others to catch cod near Newfoundland.

Madeleine: **C'est loin cela!**
That is a long way!

Le pêcheur: **Mais oui, c'est loin, ma petite fille. Je vois que tu**
Yes, it is a long way, my little lass. I see that you

sais déjà bien ta géographie.
know your geography well already.

Georges: **Nous, nous nous contenterons de pêcher la crevette et**
As for us, we will content ourselves with catching shrimps and

la moule, si toutefois il y en a.
mussels, if there happen to be any.

Le pêcheur: **Oui, vous en trouverez facilement.**
Yes, you'll find some easily.

Lucie: **Il y en a même à déjeuner aujourd'hui.**
There are even some for lunch today.

Georges: **Et comme les autres seront probablement déjà arrivés,**
And as the other people will have probably arrived by now,

rentrons vite.
let's go back quickly.

Charles: **Ça c'est une bonne ideé, car j'ai une faim de loup.**
That is a good idea, for I am famished.

(Ils sont revenus à l'hôtel pour déjeuner.)
(They returned to the hotel to have lunch.)

Ils sont restés deux semaines au bord de la mer.   Deux fois par jour,
They stayed for two weeks at the seaside.   Twice a day

ils se baignaient.   Après le deuxième bain ils jouaient au tennis ou
they bathed.   After the second bathe they played tennis or

allaient sur la jetée pour voir le départ des pêcheurs.   Charles s'amusait
went on the pier to see the departure of the fishermen.   Charles amused himself

à construire des châteaux de sable.   Le soir on admirait le coucher du soleil,
by building sand-castles.   In the evening they admired the sunset,

ou dansait tandis que leurs parents risquaient quelques francs
or danced while their parents risked some francs

dans les salles de jeu du casino.
in the gaming room of the casino.

AU CASINO

En plein ou à cheval, pair ou impair? Madame semble trouver le choix difficile.

En plein	**à cheval**	**pair-e, impair-e** (adj.)
All out on one number	stake divided between two numbers	even, odd

CÔTÉ

le côté side, direction, way, part
d'un côté, de l'autre côté on the one hand, on the other hand
à côté close by, beside
de ce côté-ci on this side
de ce côté-là on that side
de quel côté est la gare? whereabout is the station?
du côté de Paris towards *(in the direction of)* Paris

venez de ce côté come this way; come on this side
la maison est tout à côté the house is quite near
à côté de by the side of, next to
il habite à côté de nous he lives next door to us
de mon côté on my side; for my part

N.B.—**la côte** (koht)=the coast, or the rib, or the hill.

AU BORD DE LA MER—AT THE SEASIDE

la mer sea
la plage beach
le brise-lames breakwater
la jetée pier
la tente tent
la cabine de plage bathing cabin
la cabine roulante bathing machine
le poste de sauvetage life-saving station
la bouée de sauvetage life-buoy
la ceinture de natation cork-jacket
le canot rowing-boat
l'ombrelle (f.) sunshade
le peignoir de bain bathing wrap

le maillot de bain bathing suit
la serviette de bain bathing towel
le soulier de bain bathing shoe
le bonnet de bain bathing cap
le caleçon de bain bathing slip
la vague wave
le banc de sable sandbank
la mouette sea-gull
la promenade (le quai) promenade (front)
le kiosque à musique bandstand
un hôtel hotel
le casino casino

LA NAGE—SWIMMING

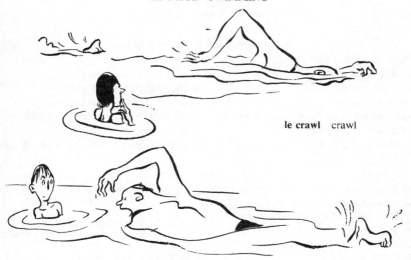

le crawl crawl

la nage indienne overarm stroke

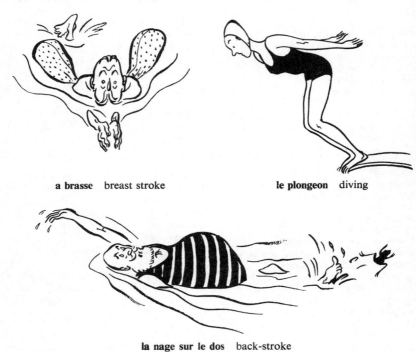

a **brasse** breast stroke   **le plongeon** diving

la nage sur le dos back-stroke

LA PISCINE—SWIMMING BATH

le **bain de soleil** sun-bathing
la **cabine de bain** dressing cubicle
la **douche** shower-bath
le **bassin de natation** swimming pool
le **professeur de natation** swimming instructor
le **tremplin** diving board
la **glissoire** water-chute

la **bête en caoutchouc** rubber animal
le **nageur** swimmer (man)
la **nageuse** swimmer (woman)
le **caleçon de bain** bathing-slip
le **costume de bain** bathing costume
le **bonnet de bain** bathing cap
le **peignoir de bain** bathing wrap

ON

On dit qu'il est riche=They say he is rich.
On vous demande au téléphone=
    You are wanted on the phone.
On frappe=Someone is knocking.
On sonne=The bell is ringing.
On voit la mer d'ici=
    The sea can be seen from here.

Où peut-on trouver cela?=
    Where can one find that?

On cultive beaucoup de vignes en France=
    Vines are much grown in France.

Que dit-on dans le journal?
    What do they say in the paper?

DIEPPE: ARRIVÉE DU PAQUEBOT

Dans ce tohu-bohu, les stewards arrivent quand même à dénicher les bagages de leurs patrons de passage.

Tohu-bohu (m.)	**arriver à quand même**	**dénicher**	**de passage**
Hurly-burly, muddle	to succeed in nevertheless	to ferret out	temporary

On is much more widely used than its English equivalent "*one*." It is employed as a general term meaning "*people*," "*some one*," "*you and I*"; it is also used instead of the English passive voice. The sentence "*French is spoken here*" is in the so-called Passive Voice. In French this is rendered in the Active Voice, by using **on: Ici on parle français.** There is also a Passive form of French verbs, but it is used less frequently than the English Passive, so that we can deal with it at a later stage of this course. In the meantime use **on** and the Active Voice.

WORDS DENOTING A QUANTITY

Un peu d'eau=a little water

beaucoup de viande=much meat

peu de chiens=few dogs

beaucoup de Français=many Frenchmen

combien d'argent=how much money

combien de chevaux=how many horses

trop de sucre=too much sugar

trop de gens=too many people

. . . **plus de café**=more coffee

moins de chocolat=less chocolate

moins de cigarettes=fewer cigarettes

Je n'ai pas autant d'argent que lui=I have not so much money as he.

J'ai autant de cartes que lui=I have as many cards as he.

Vous avez eu assez de vin=You have had enough wine.

C'est quelque chose de nouveau=That is something new.

Il a bu plus de six verres=He has drunk more than six glasses.

Vous avez travaillé moins de trois heures=You worked less than three hours.

Note that words denoting a quantity, like "*much*," "*little*," "*more*," "*less*," etc., are followed by **de** before the noun.

ADVERBS OF QUANTITY

beaucoup de=much, many, a great deal of;   **peu de**=little, few;

trop de=too much, too many;   **beaucoup trop de**=far too much (many);

plus de=more;   **beaucoup plus de**=much more;   **moins de**=less;

beaucoup moins de=much less, far less;   **assez de**=enough;   **tant** or **autant de**=so much, so many.

ADVERBS IN COMPARISON

aussi . . . que=as . . . as . . . **(si . . . que,** often used in negative sentences instead of **aussi . . . que);** **autant que**=as much as, so much as; **plus que**=more than; **moins que**=less than.

When there is no Comparison:

J'ai lu plus de vingt pages=I read more than twenty pages.

Il a écrit moins de deux pages=He wrote less than two pages.

ADVERBS OF MANNER

bien=well

très bien, fort bien=very well

assez bien=fairly well

mieux=better

bien mieux=rather better

beaucoup mieux=much better

mal=badly

assez mal=rather badly

beaucoup plus mal=much worse

vite=fast, quickly

presque=almost

davantage=more

LA GLACE À LA FRAISE (VANILLE)—STRAWBERRY (VANILLA) ICE-CREAM

1. Paul a beaucoup de glace.
2. Gustave a moins de glace que Paul, mais il en a assez.
3. Richard a assez de glace.
4. Gaston n'a pas autant de glace que Richard.

5. Robert a peu de glace.
6. André n'a pas de glace du tout *(at all)*.
7. Charles a trop de glace.
8. Georges a autant de glace que Paul.

SI

1. Il n'est pas venu?=He has not come?
Si, monsieur=Yes, sir, he has.
N'est-il pas venu?=Has he not come?
Si! il est venu=Yes, he has come.
si="Yes" in answer to a negative or interrogative negative.

2. Je suis si heureux de vous voir=I am so glad to see you.
Il n'est pas si intelligent que son frère= He is not so intelligent as his brother
si=so.

3. Si vous le cherchez, vous le trouverez=If you look for it you will find it.
Si je l'avais su, je vous l'aurais dit=If I had known it, I would have told it to you.
Je le ferai, si j'ai le temps=I shall do it, if I have time.
S'il fait beau demain, nous irons au bord de la mer=If it's fine tomorrow we shall go to the seaside.

S'il vient, vous lui direz de m'attendre= If he comes, tell him to wait for me.

Si vous étiez à ma place, le feriez-vous?= If you were in my place, would you do it?

Si vous me donniez le livre, je serais très heureux=If you gave me the book, I should be very glad.

EXERCISES

I Answer the following questions in French (referring to the top of this page)

1. Paul a-t-il de la glace? 2. Gustave a-t-il autant de glace que Paul? 3. Richard a-t-il beaucoup de glace? 4. Robert en a-t-il assez? 5. André a-t-il de la glace? 6. Charles a-t-il autant de glace que Paul? 7. Qui en a le plus? 8. Qui en a le moins? 9. Qui n'en a pas? 10. Qui a trop de glace?

II Translate into English

1. Combien de personnes y aura-t-il chez vous? 2. Avez-vous autant d'argent que Rockefeller? 3. Je n'ai pas assez d'argent. 4. Voulez-vous donner un peu d'argent à ce pauvre garçon? 5. Il y avait trop de personnes chez lui. 6. J'ai bu autant que lui. 7. J'ai tant travaillé que je suis fatigué. 8. Vous ne travaillez pas assez. 9. Il ne parle pas autant qu'elle. 10. Ne fumez pas tant. 11. Il ne fume pas beaucoup. Si, il fume beaucoup. 12. Est-ce qu'ils boivent beaucoup? 13. Non, pas beaucoup. 14. Ces moules (=mussels) sont-elles fraîches? Je pense bien (=I should say so).

III Translate into French

1. You are not eating enough vegetables. 2. There will be too many people. 3. You are drinking too much beer. 4. You have given too much meat to my son. 5. Will there be enough wine? 6. He is not reading enough. 7. I read more than three hours. 8. How many letters have you written? 9. You had not so much appetite as your brother. 10. You did not work? Why, yes, I did. 11. She does not smoke very much. 12. You are not writing enough exercises. 13. If you will go to bed now I shall leave. 14. If he pays me, I shall pay you. 15. If he comes, tell him that I am waiting for him. (*Key on pages 335 and 336.*)

LYON: HÔTEL DE VILLE ET FONTAINE

Lyon, deuxième cité de France et chef-lieu du Département du Rhône, est le centre d'une région industrielle. La ville, renommée pour ses soieries et notoire par son climat pluvieux, est située au confluent du Rhône avec la Saône.

Chef-lieu (m.)	renommé -e (adj.)	soieries (f.)	notoire (adj.)
County town	famous, celebrated	silk goods	notorious

Note that Lyon is spelt in French without a final "s."

TRENTIÈME LEÇON

CHARLES HAS AN ACCIDENT

When you have studied the lesson, you will find out the whys and the wherefores of the accident. Charles has ignored an important French traffic rule. In case you think of taking your bike to France, you must regard this picture as a warning.

CHEZ LE PHARMACIEN—AT THE CHEMIST'S

Monsieur Roberts n'a pas pu passer toutes les vacances avec sa famille.   Il
Mr. Roberts was not able to spend all the holidays with his family.   He

a dû rentrer pour affaires à Londres.   Bonne aubaine pour Charles,
was obliged to return to London on business.   A stroke of luck for Charles,

qui n'ose pas faire trop de bêtises en présence de son père.
who does not dare to do so many stupid things in his father's presence.

Charles a en effet très envie d'emprunter la bicyclette de Jean,
Charles is in fact very keen on borrowing the bicycle of Jean,

fils du concierge, pour aller faire un petit tour.   Dès le départ de son père,
the porter's son, to go for a little ride.   As soon as his father has gone,

il va trouver Jean, qui consent à lui prêter son vélo moyennant
he goes to find Jean, who consents to lend him his bike in exchange for

quelques billes.   Charles, au comble de la joie, grimpe sur la
some marbles.   Charles, very thrilled, jumps on the

machine et se met à pédaler de toutes ses forces.   Malheureusement, au détour
machine, and goes pedalling off at a great rate.   Unfortunately, at a turn

du chemin, il voit une automobile se diriger droit sur lui.   Les freins ne sont
of the road, he sees a car coming straight for him.   The brakes are not

pas assez bons, et sa machine s'écrase contre le pare-chocs de la voiture;
good enough, and his machine crashes against the bumper of the car;

il fait un vol-plané par-dessus le capot de l'automobile, atterrissant
he flies over the bonnet of the car; landing

fort brutalement sur le gravier de la route.   Voilà ce que c'est d'oublier que
heavily on the gravel of the road.   This is what happens if one forgets

l'on conduit à droite en France.
to ride on the right in France.

L'automobiliste (accourant vers Charles): T'es-tu fait mal, petit bandit?
        (running towards Charles): Are you hurt, you little scamp?

Charles (les genoux et les mains en sang, et s'efforçant de ne pas
        (his knees and hands covered with blood, and trying not

        pleurer): Oui, un peu, monsieur.
        to cry): Yes, a little.

L'automobiliste: Tu as de la chance; il y a une pharmacie tout près.
        You are lucky; there happens to be a chemist's shop quite close.

        (À un passant).   Pourriez-vous m'aider à porter ce chenapan
        (To a passer-by).   Would you mind helping me to carry this rascal

        jusqu'à cette pharmacie, s'il vous plaît, monsieur?
        to that chemist's, please?

(Quelques instants après, le pharmacien tâte Charles pour voir s'il n'a rien
(A few minutes later, the chemist feels Charles to see if he has broken

de cassé, tandis que son aide lui nettoie ses plaies.   Charles a bien
anything, while his assistant cleans his wounds.   Charles is very much

envie de crier quand on lui touche le genou avec un tampon d'alcool.)
inclined to cry out when they touch his knee with a spirit dressing.)

Le pharmacien: Tiens, tu t'es cogné la tête aussi.   Tu as un peu de sang
        Well, you've bumped your head, too.   You have a little blood

        dans les cheveux.   Il va falloir t'en couper quelques-uns et
        in your hair.   We shall have to cut some off and

te nettoyer la tempe avec de l'eau oxygénée.
clean your temple with peroxide.

(Le lendemain Charles est dans sa chambre, allongé sur un divan; sa mère est
(The next day Charles is in his room, lying on a sofa; his mother is

auprès de lui et coud.   La sonnette retentit.)
beside him, sewing.   The bell rings.)

Mme Roberts: Le médecin!
         The doctor!

Charles: J'espère qu'il ne me fera pas mal.
         I hope he won't hurt me.

Le Médecin (entrant): Alors voilà notre cycliste.   Il paraît qu'il a
         (entering): Well, and how's our cyclist?   It seems that he has

une côte cassée, un œil au beurre noir, une épaule démise, une
a broken rib, a black eye, a dislocated shoulder, a

cheville foulée, etc., etc. . . .!
sprained ankle, etc., etc. . . .!

Mme Roberts (riant): Non, Docteur, heureusement, ce n'est pas si grave
         (laughing): No, Doctor, it is fortunately not so bad

que cela—quelques petites écorchures seulement.
as that—only a few slight grazes.

Le Médecin (défaisant le bandage du genou de Charles): Voyons cette
         (undoing the bandage on Charles's knee): Let's see how this

plaie, si elle se referme bien.   Ah, très bien, mon petit.   Mais
wound is healing.   Well, very good, my boy.   But

plus de vélo pour quelques semaines, n'est-ce pas!
no more bikes for some weeks!

(Quelques jours après, Charles était tout-à-fait guéri.)
(A few days later, Charles had entirely recovered.)

LE CORPS HUMAIN—THE HUMAN BODY

la tête head
les cheveux hair
le front forehead
un œil (pl. **les yeux**) eye
une oreille ear
la joue cheek
la bouche mouth
la gorge throat
le cou neck
le tronc trunk
une épaule shoulder
la poitrine chest

le ventre stomach
le nombril navel
le bras arm
le coude elbow
la main hand
la jambe leg
la cuisse thigh
le genou knee
le mollet calf
le pied foot
l'orteil (m.) toe
le talon heel

LA MAIN—THE HAND

les doigts (m.pl.) fingers
le pouce thumb
l'index (m.) index finger, forefinger
le majeur middle finger
l'annulaire (m.) ring finger
l'auriculaire (m.) little finger
le poignet wrist
la paume palm of the hand
le pouls pulse

MEDICAL VOCABULARY

le médecin doctor
le chirurgien surgeon
un hôpital hospital
malade ill
la maladie illness
le mal complaint; pain
le mal de tête headache
le mal de cœur sickness
le mal de gorge sore throat
le malaise indisposition
un rhume cold
la fièvre temperature
la douleur pain

la grippe influenza
la blessure wound
blessé wounded
une ambulance ambulance
écrasé run over
renversé knocked down
faire venir un médecin to send for a doctor
une ordonnance prescription
une opération operation
opérer to operate
aller mieux to be getting better
aller plus mal to be getting worse
être guéri to be healed; to be well again

mourir to die
mort dead
le pharmacien chemist
la pharmacie chemist's
le remède (contre) remedy (for)
préparer une ordonnance to make up a
    prescription
le poison poison
le bandage bandage
le coton cotton wool
une lotion lotion
une pastille lozenge
une potion draught
un onguent ointment
une pilule pill
un emplâtre plaster
une poudre powder

Une cuillerée à bouche
A tablespoonful

**de trois heures en trois
heures**
every three hours

Agiter avant de s'en servir
Shake before use

CHEZ LE MÉDECIN—AT THE DOCTOR'S

Monsieur a mal à la tête
        The man has a headache
Madame a mal aux yeux
        The lady has eye trouble
Le vieux monsieur a mal au dos
        The old man has the back-ache
Le petit garçon a mal au nez
        The little boy has nose trouble

La petite a mal au bras gauche
        The little girl has a bad left arm
Mademoiselle a mal au pied droit
        The young lady has a bad right foot
Monsieur a mal à la gorge
        The man has throat trouble
Madame a mal aux oreilles
        The lady has ear trouble

MINE, THINE, HIS, ETC.

Singular

	masculine	*feminine*
mine	le mien	la mienne
thine	le tien	la tienne
his, hers	le sien	la sienne
ours	le nôtre	la nôtre
yours	le vôtre	la vôtre
theirs	le leur	la leur

Plural

	masculine	*feminine*
mine	les miens	les miennes
thine	les tiens	les tiennes
his, hers	les siens	les siennes
ours	les nôtres	les nôtres
yours	les vôtres	les vôtres
theirs	les leurs	les leurs

mon jardin et le sien
   my garden and his (or hers)
ma maison et la sienne
   my house and his (or hers)
mes chiens et les siens
   my dogs and his (or hers)
mes pommes et les siennes
   my apples and his (or hers)

Note.—The above words stand for nouns and show possession; they are therefore possessive pronouns and in French agree in number and gender with the nouns to which they refer.

Further examples:

Ma mère et la sienne = My mother and his (or hers)

Sa chambre est plus petite que la vôtre = His room is smaller than yours.

Son appartement est plus luxueux que le mien = His flat is more luxurious than mine.

Il a reçu des cadeaux de ma mère et de la tienne = He has received presents from my mother and yours.

Son auto est plus chère que la mienne = His (her) car is dearer than mine.

Le pardessus de votre frère ressemble au mien = Your brother's overcoat is similar to mine.

Je ne parle pas de votre gramophone, je parle du sien = I am not speaking of your gramophone, I am speaking of his.

À qui est cette chaise? Elle est à moi = Whose chair is this? It is mine.

N.B.—Mine, yours, his, etc., when used in connection with *is* or *are* are generally translated by **à moi, à vous, à lui,** etc. (see page 281).

DANS—OUT OF

Note the following expressions:

Je bois dans une tasse =
   I drink out of a cup.
Je lis dans un livre =
   I read out of a book.
Je mange dans une assiette =
   I eat out of a plate.
Je prends la clef dans ma poche =
   I take the key out of my pocket.

FRACTIONS

1/2 = **un** (or **une**) **demi(e)** or **la moitié**
1/4 = **un quart**
3/4 = **trois quarts**
1/3 = **un tiers**
2/3 = **deux tiers**
1/5 = **un cinquième**
2/5 = **deux cinquièmes**
1/6 = **un sixième**
5/6 = **cinq sixièmes**, etc.

Une livre et demie de beurre =
   A pound and a half of butter
Une demi-heure de récréation =
   Half an hour's recreation
Une heure et demie =
   An hour and a half
Un demi-siècle =
   Half a century
La moitié de six est trois =
   Half of six is three.
Il m'a donné la moitié de sa poire =
   He gave me half his pear.
Je vous en donnerai la moitié =
   I shall give you half *(of it)*

Note on the word "half"—

From the above examples it should be noted that

(1) When **demi** is used after **et** it takes the gender of the noun to which it refers.

(2) When used before a noun **demi** forms a compound word and is invariable.

(3) When *half* is a noun it must be translated by **la moitié**.

COLLECTIVE NUMBERS

Une dizaine de verres =
About ten glasses
Une douzaine d'oranges =
A dozen oranges
Une quinzaine =
A fortnight *(first and last days being included)*
Une quinzaine d'enfants =
About fifteen children
Une vingtaine d'huîtres =
About twenty oysters
Une trentaine de personnes =
About thirty persons
Une centaine d'hommes =
About a hundred men
Des centaines d'hommes =
Hundreds of men
Un millier de bouteilles =
About a thousand bottles
Des milliers de bouteilles =
Thousands of bottles
Cela m'a coûté une centaine =
That has cost me about a hundred francs.

ONCE, TWICE, ETC.

Une fois = Once
Deux fois = Twice
Trois fois = Three times
Quatre fois = Four times
Cinq fois = Five times, etc.

Deux fois six font douze = $2 \times 6 = 12$
Sept fois trois font vingt et un = $7 \times 3 = 21$
La première fois = The first time
La dernière fois = The last time
Une fois pour toutes = Once and for all

Je ne peux pas vous comprendre, si vous parlez tous à la fois = I can't understand you if you all speak at the same time.

SANS—WITHOUT

Ne sortez pas sans parapluie = Don't go out without an umbrella.
Prenez-vous le café avec ou sans lait? = Do you drink coffee with or without milk?
Avec du lait, mais sans sucre = With milk, but with no sugar.
On ne peut pas y entrer sans billet = You can't go in there without a ticket.

On peut y aller sans passeport = You can go there without a passport.

Note that a noun after **sans** does not have an article.

EXERCISES

I   Translate into English

1. Deux et trois font cinq. 2. Combien font seize et onze? 3. Je le lui ai dit cent fois. 4. Ce monsieur va à l'église tous les jours à dix heures et demie. 5. Il part pour Paris dans une demi-heure. 6. Combien de fois leur a-t-il écrit? 7. Ils partent pour l'Amérique dans un quart d'heure. 8. Il dort la moitié du temps. 9. Donnez-lui la moitié de cette pomme. 10. Donnez-lui le tiers de cela. 11. Combien d'oranges désirez-vous? 12. Donnez m'en une douzaine, s'il vous plaît. 13. Charles a perdu son crayon. En voici un; est-ce le sien? 14. Vos parents sont avec les miens. 15. À qui est ce gâteau? C'est le leur.

II   Translate into French

1. This chair is his, but this armchair is yours. 2. What a beautiful picture! Is it yours? 3. Our garden is smaller than yours. 4. Whose are those flowers? These are mine; yours are in the other room. 5. Would you like some of this cake? I can give you half of it. 6. How many pages of this book have you read? I have read about twenty. 7. I paid about a thousand francs for it. 8. What time is it? 9. It is a quarter past five. 10. It is half past nine p.m. 11. Seven and six are thirteen. 12. How much are five times eight? 13. I have no pencils. 14. Here are about ten. 15. I forgot my pen. Here is mine. 16. Do not take his (hat). 17. You are taking hers (hat). 18. Have you found his (box)? 19. I haven't got hers (box). 20. How many oranges do you want? Give me half a dozen.

III   Give the following times in French

1. 6.30 a.m. 2. 9.00 a.m. 3. 10.45 a.m. 4. 12.15 p.m. 5. 1.30 p.m. 6. 6.50 p.m. 7. 8.05 p.m. 8. 0.03 a.m.

(Key on page 336.)

TRENTE-ET-UNIÈME LEÇON

CHEZ LE COIFFEUR—AT THE HAIRDRESSER'S

Mme Roberts et Madeleine sont allées chez un coiffeur.   **Il y a un salon**
Mrs. Roberts and Madeleine have gone to a hairdresser's.   There is a saloon

pour dames et un salon pour messieurs.   **En passant Madeleine aperçoit un gros**
for ladies, and one for gentlemen.   In passing, Madeleine notices a stout

monsieur, la figure toute couverte de savon à barbe.   **Sur l'étagère à côté**
gentleman with his face all covered with shaving soap.   On the stand at the side

il y a un blaireau et un bol à savon.   **Le barbier est en train de passer**
there is a shaving brush and a soap bowl.   The barber is just sharpening

le rasoir sur le cuir à aiguiser.   **Madeleine frissonne et pense que cela**
the razor on the strop.   Madeleine shivers, and thinks how

doit être désagréable de se faire raser!   **Dans le salon de dames la coiffeuse**
horrid it must be to be shaved!   In the ladies' saloon the assistant

demande à Mme Roberts ce qu'elle veut.
asks Mrs. Roberts what she requires.

Mme Roberts: Une coupe pour la petite, s'il vous plaît.   **Dégagez-lui bien**
        A haircut for the little girl, please.   Nice and short on

PARIS, UN QUATORZE JUILLET

C'est le 14 juillet, anniversaire de la prise de la Bastille en 1789, et Fête Nationale française. En haut, le feu d'artifice le long des quais jette ses reflets dans la Seine. En bas, on danse en pleine rue avec le premier venu, à la musique d'un orchestre champêtre.

| **Feu d'artifice** (m.) | **reflet** (m.) | **le premier venu** | **orchestre** (m.) **champêtre** |
| Fireworks | reflection | the first comer | country band |

le cou.   La raie sur le côté gauche.
the neck.   The parting on the left side.

La Coiffeuse: Faut-il lui passer le fer à friser, madame?
Shall I use the curling-tongs, madam?

Mme Roberts: Non, inutile, mais faites-lui une friction.
No, it is not necessary, but give her a head rub.

La Coiffeuse: Pas de shampooing?
No shampoo?

Mme Roberts: Non.   (à Madeleine): Sois bien sage.   Je vais dans
No.   (to Madeleine): Be very good.   I am going into

la pièce à côté me faire une mise en plis.   Viens me retrouver
the next cubicle to have a setting.   Come and find me

quand tu auras fini.
when you have finished.

(Madeleine enfile le peignoir et s'assied dans le grand fauteuil.   La
(Madeleine slips on the cape and seats herself in the big armchair.   The

coiffeuse commence par bien la peigner.   Puis elle lui passe la tondeuse
hairdresser begins by thoroughly combing her hair.   Then she passes the clippers

sur la nuque; puis elle fait cliqueter ses ciseaux.
over the back of her neck; then she clicks her scissors

Tout en travaillant, elle lui demande si elle se plaît en France,
While she is working, she asks her if she enjoys being in France,

et passe de bonnes vacances.)
and if she is spending a nice holiday.)

La Coiffeuse: Avez-vous au moins été à la Fête du 14 juillet quand
Did you at least go to the celebrations on July 14th, when

vous étiez à Paris?
you were in Paris?

Madeleine: Oh oui; nous avons été à la Revue.   C'était magnifique, et puis
Oh yes; we went to the Review.   It was splendid, and then

le soir nous nous sommes promenés dans les rues et nous
in the evening we walked about the streets and we

avons vu tous les Parisiens qui dansaient à la lumière
saw all the Parisians dancing by the light

des lampions. C'était très joli.
of the lanterns. It was very pretty.

(La coupe une fois terminée, la coiffeuse donne le miroir à Madeleine
(The haircut being finished, the assistant gives Madeleine a looking-glass

et lui demande si elle est satisfaite.)
and asks if she is satisfied.)

Madeleine: **C'est parfait.**
It is quite all right.

La Coiffeuse: **Je vais vous faire la friction maintenant. Que préférez-vous,**
I will give you a head rub now. Which do you prefer,

Eau de Cologne ou de lavande?
Eau de Cologne or Lavender Water?

Madeleine: **Eau de Cologne, s'il vous plaît. (Après la friction, la**
Eau de Cologne, please. (After the head rub, the

coiffeuse peigne soigneusement Madeleine, et donne un coup de brosse à ses vêtements.
hairdresser carefully combs Madeleine's hair, and gives her clothes a brush.

Elle va alors rejoindre sa mère; elle la trouve sous un
Then she (Madeleine) goes to rejoin her mother; she finds her under an

énorme appareil à ondulations indéfrisables. Une manucure est en train de
enormous apparatus for permanent waving. A manicurist is just

lui faire les ongles.)
doing her nails.)

Mme Roberts: **Je me suis tout de même laissé faire une indéfrisable. Cela**
I am having a permanent wave done after all. It

va durer encore pas mal de temps, aussi tu ferais bien
will take rather a long time still, so you had better

de rentrer toute seule. Montre-moi comment tes cheveux sont coupés.
go home alone. Show me how your hair is cut.

(Madeleine, après s'être fait examiner, laisse sa mère en compagnie des
(Madeleine, after having shown herself, leaves her mother in the company of the

séchoirs et des bouteilles de lotion et va retrouver ses cousins
hair-drying machines and bottles of lotion, and goes off to find her cousins

à la maison.)
at home.)

CHEZ LE COIFFEUR

Men's Side

English.—1. Hair-lotion; 2. Scent-spray; 3. Wash-basin; 4. Hairdresser's assistant; 5. Hair-clippers; 6. Men's hairdresser; 7. Towels; 8. Razor; 9. Soap-bowl; 10. Shaving-brush; 11. Powder-spray; 12. Strop.

French.—1. Lotion (f.); 2. Vaporisateur (m.); 3. Cuvette (f.); 4. Aide-coiffeur (m.); 5. Tondeuse (f.); 6. Coiffeur (m.) pour messieurs; 7. Serviettes (f.pl.); 8. Rasoir (m.); 9. Bol (m.) à savon; 10. Blaireau (m.); 11. Pulvérisateur (m.); 12. Cuir (m.) à aiguiser.

Further Useful Expressions	**La barbe, s.v.p.** Shave, please	**pas trop près** not too close	**les cheveux, s.v.p.** haircut, please	**pas trop courts** not too short

AT THE HAIRDRESSER'S

Ladies' Side

English.—1. Douche; 2. Wash-basin; 3. Nail-polisher; 4. Manicurist; 5. Permanent-wave apparatus; 6. Perfumes, creams and powders; 7. Face-packs; 8. Drying-hood; 9. Curling-irons; 10. Lipstick; 11. Comb; 12. Hand-mirror.

French.—1. Douche (f.); 2. Cuvette (f.); 3. Polissoir (m.); 4. Manucure (f.); 5. Appareil (m.) à ondulations indéfrisables; 6. Parfums, crèmes et poudres-de-riz; 7. Masques (m.) anti-rides; 8. Sèche-cheveux (m.); 9. Fer (m.) à friser; 10. Bâton (m.) de rouge; 11. Peigne (m.); 12. Glace (f.) à main.

les bouts seulement	couper	onduler	boucler	rafraîchir	une ondulation indéfrisable
a trim only	to cut	to wave	to curl	to trim	permanent wave

LES CHEVEUX ET LA BARBE—HAIR AND BEARD

la moustache   moustache
les favoris   whiskers
les côtelettes   side-whiskers *(mutton chops)*
la barbe   beard
la barbe en pointe   pointed beard

la tête chauve bald head
les cheveux bouclés   curly head
les cheveux en brosse   bristly hair
la raie médiane   parting *(in the middle)*
la raie à gauche   parting *(on the left)*

MARSEILLE: LE PORT

Notre impression du grand port d'escale montre les bassins à flot et les bassins de radoub.

Port (m.) **d'escale**
Port of call

bassin (m.) **à flot**
wet dock, flooding dock

bassin de radoub
dry dock

la perruque wig
les cheveux longs long *(loose)* hair
les cheveux courts bobbed hair
le chignon bun
la natte pig-tail
les macarons "earphones"
à la garçonne shingled
la frange fringe
la tête head
le front forehead
les tempes temples
la nuque back of the neck
le sommet crown of the head
la joue cheek

EACH, EVERY

Mettez chaque livre à sa place= Put each book in its place.
Il rit chaque fois que je le vois= He laughs every time I see him.
Donnons du chocolat à chaque enfant= Let's give chocolate to each of the children.
Donnons chacun cent francs= Let's all give a hundred francs.
Donnons cent francs à chacun= Let's give a hundred francs to everybody.
Donnons des fleurs à chacune= Let's give flowers to every one *(woman)*.
Note that **chaque** is an adjective and has the same form for both masculine and feminine.
Chacun *(masc.)* and **chacune** *(fem.)* are pronouns.

DONC

Attendez donc= Do wait
Jouez donc= Do play
Parlez-lui donc= Do speak to him
Montrez-le-lui donc= Do show it to him
Gardez-en donc= Do keep some
Restez-y donc= Do stay there
Soyez donc sérieux= Do be serious
Asseyez-vous donc= Do sit down
Donc like English "do" is used for emphasis and is often not translatable.

WHICH, WHAT

Quel homme?= Which man?
Quels hommes?= Which men?
Quelle femme?= Which woman?
Quelles femmes?= Which women?
Quel homme?= What man?

Quels hommes?= What men?
Quelle femme?= What woman?
Quelles femmes?= What women?
Lequel de ces deux?= Which one of these two *(men)*?
Laquelle de ces deux?= Which one of these two *(women)*?
Lesquels de ces hommes?= Which of these men?
Lesquelles de ces femmes?= Which of these women?
Quel homme!= What a man!
Quels hommes!= What men!
Quelle femme!= What a woman!
Quelles femmes!= What women!

Which (or what)

followed by a masculine noun, singular
quel
followed by a feminine noun, singular
quelle
followed by a masculine noun, plural
quels
followed by a feminine noun, plural
quelles

Which one

replacing a masculine noun, singular
lequel
replacing a feminine noun, singular
laquelle

Which

replacing a masculine noun, plural
lesquels
replacing a feminine noun, plural
lesquelles
In exclamation "what a . . .!"= **quel** or **quelle**.
"What" (when object of a verb)= **que** or **qu'est-ce que**.
Que faites-vous?
Qu'est-ce que vous faites?
What are you doing?
Qu'avez-vous?
Qu'est-ce que vous avez?
What have you got?
Que pensez-vous?
Qu'est-ce que vous pensez?
What do you think?

N.B.—After **de** or **à** or any other preposition or if the verb is omitted, **que** is changed to **quoi.**
De quoi parlez-vous? = What are you talking about?
À quoi cela sert-il? = What is this for?
Il n'y a pas de quoi = Don't mention it *(in answer to an apology).*
Quoi de nouveau ce matin? = What is new this morning?
Il a quelque chose contre moi. Je ne sais quoi = He has something against me. I don't know what.
Un je ne sais quoi = An indefinable something, something or other.
What (when the subject of the sentence) = **qu'est-ce qui.**
Qu'est-ce qui brûle? = What is burning?
Qu'est-ce qui vous amuse? = What is amusing you?
Qu'est-ce qui est tombé? = What has fallen?
Qu'est-ce qui est arrivé? = What has happened?
Qu'est-ce qui vous est arrivé? = What has happened to you?

OF WHICH, TO WHICH, ETC.

Auquel de ses livres pensez-vous? = Which of his books are you thinking of?
À laquelle de mes sœurs voulez-vous envoyer ces fleurs? = To which one of my sisters do you want to send these flowers?
Auxquels de ses amis écrivez-vous? = To which of his friends are you writing?
Duquel parlez-vous? = Of which one are you speaking? *(i.e. of a man)*
À laquelle pensez-vous? = Of which one are you thinking? *(i.e. of a woman)*

Desquels voulez-vous? = Which do you want? *(i.e. things which are masculine)*
Desquelles voulez-vous? = Which do you want? *(i.e. things which are feminine)*

EXERCISES

I   Translate into English

1. Veuillez servir le fromage. Duquel désirez-vous, monsieur? 2. Apportez-moi des fruits, s'il vous plaît. 3. Lesquels voulez-vous, madame? Que dire? 4. À quoi cette machine sert-elle? 5. Achetez donc une livre de chaque sorte. 6. Vendez donc une demi-livre à chacun. 7. En quoi pouvez-vous lui être utile (= useful)? 8. Qu'est-ce qui leur est arrivé? 9. Qu'est-ce qui vous intéresse? 10. Qu'est-ce qu'on peut faire? 11. Qu'avez-vous contre moi? 12. Qu'est-ce qu'ils ont? 13. Laquelle des deux est la plus belle? 14. Lequel de ces cigares voulez-vous? 15. Que pensez-vous de son opinion?

II   Translate into French

1. Do come. 2. Do take it. 3. Do write to her. 4. Do send it to him. 5. Do buy some of each sort (la sorte). 6. What are you saying? 7. What do you think of her? 8. What does he want to tell me? 9. Which of these cigars do you prefer? 10. Which of the two is the more intelligent (woman)? 11. What a beautiful woman! 12. Tell me which one (cheese) you will have. 13. What can you give us? 14. Which of these men is your brother? 15. Which of these girls will play with us? (*Key on page* 336.)

KEY TO THE EXERCISES

Lesson Twenty-seven

I

1. joliment.   2. premièrement.   3. longuement.   4. bien.   5. mal.   6. curieusement.   7. généralement.   8. complètement.   9. mieux.   10. absolument.

II

1. He is a good man. 2. He is the best man in the world. 3. This dinner is well done. 4. It is better than yesterday's. 5. Your hotel is better than mine. 6. You are doing it better than he. 7. He is my best friend. 8. He speaks French better

than I. 9. She speaks very badly. 10. He is much worse this morning. 11. He is less intelligent than his father. 12. I am extremely hungry. 13. It is terribly hot. 14. Unfortunately I could not find him (or it). 15. He is evidently seriously ill. 16. I like tennis very much, but I like golf better. 17. Yesterday she was well, but today she is much worse. 18. He speaks little, but his wife speaks much less. 19. I finished my work. So much the better for you. 20. You (I, we) have to leave at once.

III

1. J'aime beaucoup ce tableau. 2. Ils sont énormément riches. 3. Elle parle mieux que sa sœur. 4. C'est une très bonne fille; elle travaille toujours bien. 5. Malheureusement il a perdu le livre. Tant pis pour lui. 6. Ceci n'est pas son meilleur livre. 7. L'aimez-vous mieux qu'elle? 8. Avez-vous bien dormi? 9. Vous avez mal écrit cette lettre. 10. Pire que jamais. 11. Votre père va-t-il mieux? 12. Non, il va pis qu'hier. 13. J'ai terriblement soif. 14. Pouvez-vous le faire immédiatement? 15. Heureusement je suis libre à présent. 16. Généralement il est chez lui de cinq à six. 17. Veuillez parler plus distinctement. 18. Malheureusement je ne l'ai pas trouvée chez elle. 19. Il pense que vous viendrez, naturellement. 20. C'est exactement mon opinion.

Lesson Twenty-eight

I

Versailles is near Paris. It is 18 kilometres from Paris to Versailles. What is the distance from Paris to Le Havre? Le Havre is 228 kilometres from Paris. From Le Havre one can go by boat to New York. How many days does one need to go from Europe to America? About five or six days. How many hours does one need to go from Paris to Le Havre? Three to four hours. Here is a time-table. There is an express train which leaves at half past twelve. A fast train leaves Paris at seven o'clock. At five in the afternoon there is a slow train. But it is very slow; it stops at every station.

II

1. Versailles est-il loin de Paris? 2. Habitez-vous loin d'ici? 3. Notre maison est à cinq minutes d'ici; nous habitons près de l'église. 4. Quelle distance d'ici à la gare? 5. Environ trois kilomètres; une demi-heure à pied. 6. Irez-vous en bateau ou en chemin-de-fer? 7. Combien d'heures faut-il pour aller d'ici au bord de la mer? 8. Est-ce qu'il y a un train express le matin? 9. Il n'y a qu'un train omnibus. Il s'arrête à toutes les gares. 10. N'y a-t-il pas de trains rapides? 11. Le meilleur train est un rapide qui part à midi et arrive à huit heures trente-cinq du soir. 12. Il ne s'arrête que deux fois.

Lesson Twenty-nine

I

1. Oui, il y en a. 2. Il n'y en a pas autant. 3. Il n'y en a pas beaucoup, mais il y en a assez. 4. Non, il n'y en a pas assez. 5. Il n'y en a pas du tout. 6. Il en a plus que Paul. 7. Charles en a le plus. 8. Robert a le moins de glace, mais André n'en a pas. 9. André. 10. Charles en a trop.

II

1. How many persons will there be at your house? 2. Have you got as much money as Rockefeller? 3. I have not enough money. 4. Will you give this poor boy a little money? 5. There were too many people with him. 6. I drank as much as he. 7. I worked so much that I am tired. 8. You are not working enough. 9. He does not speak so much as she. 10. Don't smoke so much. 11. He does not smoke much. Yes, he does. 12. Do they drink a lot? 13. No, not much. 14. Are these mussels fresh? I should say so.

III

1. Vous ne mangez pas assez de légumes. 2. Il y aura trop de personnes. 3. Vous buvez trop de bière. 4. Vous avez donné trop de viande à mon fils. 5. Y aura-t-il assez de vin? 6. Il ne lit pas assez. 7. Je lis plus de trois heures. 8. Combien de lettres avez-vous écrites? 9. Vous n'aviez pas tant d'appétit que votre frère. 10. Vous n'avez pas travaillé? Si. 11. Elle ne fume pas beaucoup. 12. Vous n'écrivez pas assez d'exercices. 13. Si vous voulez vous coucher maintenant, je partirai. 14. S'il me paie, je vous payerai. 15. S'il vient, dites-lui que je l'attends.

Lesson Thirty

I

1. Two and three make five. 2. How much are sixteen and eleven? 3. I told him a hundred times. 4. This gentleman goes to church every day at half past ten. 5. He leaves for Paris in half an hour. 6. How many times did he write to them? 7. They leave for America in a quarter of an hour. 8. He sleeps half the time. 9. Give him half of that apple. 10. Give him a third of this. 11. How many oranges do you want? 12. Please let me have a dozen of them. 13. Charles lost his pencil. Here is one; is it his? 14. Your parents are with mine. 15. Whose cake is this? It is theirs.

II

1. Cette chaise est à lui, mais ce fauteuil est à vous. 2. Quel beau tableau! Est-ce le vôtre? 3. Notre jardin est plus petit que le vôtre. 4. À qui sont ces fleurs? Elles sont à moi; les vôtres sont dans l'autre chambre. 5. Voudriez-vous un peu de ce gâteau? Je peux vous en donner la moitié. 6. Combien de pages de ce livre avez-vous lues? J'en ai lu une vingtaine. 7. Je l'ai payé un millier de francs. 8. Quelle heure est-il? 9. Il est cinq heures et quart. 10. Il est neuf heures et demie du soir. 11. Sept et six font treize. 12.

Combien font cinq fois huit? 13. Je n'ai pas de crayons. 14. En voici une dizaine. 15. J'ai oublié ma plume. Voici la mienne. 16. Ne prenez pas le sien. 17. Vous prenez le sien. 18. Avez-vous trouvé la sienne? 19. Je n'ai pas la sienne. 20. Combien d'oranges voulez-vous? Donnez-m'en une demi-douzaine.

III

1. Six heures trente du matin. 2. Neuf heures du matin. 3. Onze heures moins le quart. 4. Midi et quart. 5. Une heure et demie de l'après-midi. 6. Sept heures moins dix du soir (dix-huit heures cinquante). 7. Huit heures cinq du soir (vingt heures cinq). 8. Minuit trois.

Lesson Thirty-one

I

1. Will you please serve the cheese. Which do you want, sir? 2. Bring me some fruit, please. 3. What kind do you want, madam? What shall I (we) say? 4. What is this machine for? 5. Do buy one pound of each sort. 6. Do sell half a pound to each. 7. In what way can you be useful to him (her)? 8. What has happened to them? 9. What interests you? 10. What can one do? 11. What have you got against me? 12. What have they got? 13. Which of the two is the more beautiful? 14. Which of these cigars do you want? 15. What do you think of his opinion?

II

1. Venez donc. 2. Prenez-le donc. 3. Écrivez-lui donc. 4. Envoyez-le-lui donc. 5. Achetez-en donc de chaque sorte. 6. Que dites-vous? 7. Que pensez-vous d'elle? 8. Que veut-il me dire? 9. Lequel de ces cigares préférez-vous? 10. Laquelle de ces deux est la plus intelligente? 11. Quelle belle femme! 12. Dites-moi lequel vous voulez. 13. Que pouvez-vous nous donner? 14. Lequel de ces hommes est votre frère? 15. Laquelle de ces jeunes filles va jouer avec nous?

SUR LA CÔTE D'AZUR

Les mimosas, les pins, les palmiers perchés sur les coteaux et une mer calme et bleue—c'est un pays de rêve où le soleil brille presque toujours dans un ciel pur.

Pin (m.)	**palmier** (m.)	**coteau** (m.)	**rêve** (m.)	**ciel** (m.)
Pine tree	palm tree	slope	dream	sky

TRENTE-DEUXIÈME LEÇON

M. LESAGE ET SON TRAVAIL—MR. LESAGE AND HIS WORK

Monsieur Lesage va au bureau par le métro. Il habite la banlieue.
Mr. Lesage goes to the office by subway. He lives in the suburbs.

Chaque matin il va à la station du métro, qui n'est pas loin de
Every morning he goes to the subway station, which is not far from

chez lui. Il prend son billet au guichet. Ensuite il descend
his house. He gets his ticket at the booking office. Then he goes down

l'escalier et va sur le quai, où il attend le train. Quand le
the stairs and goes on to the platform, where he waits for the train. When the

train arrive il monte dans un compartiment et il s'assied. Mais bien
train arrives he gets into a carriage and sits down. But quite

souvent il n'y a pas de place assise et M. Lesage est obligé de rester debout.
often there is no room to sit down and Mr. Lesage has to stand.

Pendant le voyage il lit son journal.
During the journey he reads his paper.

La politique ne l'intéresse pas. Il s'intéresse aux sports et au théâtre.
Politics do not interest him. He is interested in sport and in the theatre.

Le matin le train est toujours bondé. Quand le train arrive à sa
In the morning the train is always crowded. When the train arrives at his

gare il en descend et il monte l'escalier. Le bureau est tout près
station he gets out (of it) and goes up the stairs. The office is quite near

de la gare. Il y va à pied. Quelquefois quand
the station. He walks there (lit., goes there on foot). Sometimes when

il pleut il prend l'autobus. À neuf heures il arrive au bureau de la
it rains he takes the bus. At nine o'clock he arrives at the office of

compagnie dont il est propriétaire. Il est fabricant de jouets. Le
the company of which he is the proprietor. He is a toy manufacturer. The

bureau est au centre de la ville. L'usine n'est pas à Paris; elle est dans
office is in the centre of the town. The factory is not in Paris; it is in

la banlieue. Dans le bureau il y a beaucoup d'employés. M. Lesage est leur
the suburbs. In the office there are many employees. Mr. Lesage is their

M. LESAGE GOES TO THE OFFICE

After studying Lesson 32, make certain, before passing on, that you can name in French everything in this picture—the train itself, the subway station, the passengers seated and those standing, etc. The following words and expressions will help you:— **un compartiment de seconde classe; beaucoup de monde; le contrôleur; les voyageurs; debout; assis; le quai; sont descendus; changer de train; monter l'escalier; sortir du métro.** (The word **Correspondance** means that this is one of the stations where one can change on to other connecting lines.)

patron. Lors qu'il arrive dans le bureau il lit la correspondance.   **Ensuite il**
employer.   When he arrives in the office he reads the correspondence.   Then he

dicte quelques lettres à une sténo-dactylo.   Elle les écrit à la machine.
dictates some letters to a shorthand-typist.   She types them.

Quand la sténo a fini les lettres M. Lesage les signe.   Ensuite un
When the typist has finished the letters Mr. Lesage signs them.   Then one

des commis les met à la poste.   Voici une des lettres que M. Lesage a
of the clerks posts them.   Here is one of the letters which Mr. Lesage has

récemment dictées:—
recently dictated:—

> **Paris, le 12 juin, 195..**
> Paris, 12th June, 195..

    Messieurs,
    Dear Sirs,

Voici bientôt six mois que je n'ai reçu de commande de
It will soon be six months since I received an order from

vous.   Je ne puis m'expliquer ce silence que par la
you.   I can only explain (to myself) this silence by the

stagnation générale des affaires.   Désireux de ranimer
general business stagnation.   As I should be glad to renew

nos rapports, je vous adresse par le même courrier mon
our relations, I am sending you by the same post my

dernier catalogue, et je m'empresse d'attirer votre
latest catalogue, and I especially wish to call your

attention sur les prix exceptionnels auxquels je puis
attention to the exceptional prices at which I can

vous offrir actuellement mes articles.   Je crois donc agir
offer you my goods at present.   I do believe that I am acting

dans votre meilleur intérêt en vous conseillant de faire
in your best interests by advising you to make

dès maintenant vos achats pour la saison d'hiver.   Dans
your purchases now for the winter season.   Hoping

l'espoir d'une forte commande, je vous prie d'agréer, Messieurs,
to have the pleasure of receiving a large order, I remain, Sirs,

nos salutations distinguées.
Yours faithfully,

Paul Lesage

Quelques jours plus tard M. Lesage
A few days later Mr. Lesage

reçut la réponse suivante:—
received the following reply:—

Bordeaux, le 15 juin 195. .
Bordeaux, 15th June, 195. .

Monsieur,
Dear Sir,

Nous vous remercions de l'offre que vous nous avez faite par
We thank you for the offer which you made us in

votre lettre du 12 ct. (courant).
your letter of the 12th inst.

Nous avons examiné votre prix-courant et les échantillons, et nous
We have examined your price-list and samples, and we

sommes heureux de commander à votre maison les
have the pleasure of ordering from your firm the

marchandises énumérées sur le bon de commande ci-inclus.
goods specified in the enclosed order form.

Nous espérons que vous pourrez exécuter cette commande
We hope that it will be possible for you to execute this order

de suite. Nous serons forcés de refuser
at once. We shall be compelled to refuse

de prendre livraison de la marchandise, si elle n'est pas
acceptance of the goods, if they are not

entre nos mains le 30 ct. au plus tard.
in our hands by the 30th inst. at the latest.

Recevez, Monsieur, nos sincères salutations,
Yours faithfully,

L. Meunier

p.p. Grands Magasins de Bordeaux.

M. LESAGE IN HIS OFFICE

With the exception of M. Lesage, whom you already know to be **le patron** or employer, everybody and everything in this typical office is listed on page 343. When you have studied this list carefully, you should be able to give its French name to any object in the picture. Then, with the assistance of the following expressions, you should be able to write in French a description of the picture, telling the story in your own words. **Le patron; assis à son bureau; objets sur le bureau; appelle sa secrétaire; dicte des lettres; appelle le garçon de bureau; lui dit de mettre les lettres à la poste.**

LE BUREAU—THE OFFICE

le bureau writing-table, desk, office	**la corbeille à papier** wastepaper basket
le fauteuil easy chair	**le coffre-fort** safe
la chaise chair	**le calendrier** calendar
le bloc-notes scribbling block	**la sténo-dactylo(graphe)** shorthand-typist
la règle ruler	**la machine à écrire** typewriter
un encrier inkpot	**une étagère** bookshelf
le buvard blotting paper	**le pèse-lettres** letter balance
un ouvre-lettres letter-opener	**la lampe de table** desk-lamp
le tiroir drawer	**le garçon de bureau** office boy
les rayons shelves	**le téléphone** telephone

CE QU'IL FAUT POUR ÉCRIRE—WRITING MATERIALS

la feuille de papier sheet of paper	**le stylo(graphe)** fountain-pen
le papier carbone carbon paper	**le porte-mines** *(propelling)* pencil
la copie carbon copy	**le taille-crayon** pencil sharpener
le porte-plume penholder	**le bâton de cire à cacheter** stick of sealing
la plume nib	wax
le crayon pencil	**une enveloppe** envelope

"HAVE" AS AN IMPERATIVE

Aie ⎫
Ayez ⎭ =have . . .! **Ayons**=let us have . . .!

Aie (ayez) de la patience!=have patience!

Ayons du courage!=Let us have courage!

Il faut avoir de la patience=You *(we)* must have patience.

Il ne faut pas avoir peur=You *(we)* must not be afraid.

"BE" AS AN IMPERATIVE

Sois . . .! ⎫
Soyez . . .! ⎭ =Be . . .! **Soyons . . .!**=Let us be . . .!

Sois (Soyez) patient(e)!=Be patient!

Sois (Soyez) donc sérieux (sérieuse)!=Do be serious!

Ne sois (soyez) pas si impatient!=Don't be so impatient!

Soyons exacts (exactes)=Let us be punctual.

Ne soyons pas en retard=Don't let us be late.

Notice that the adjectives are either masculine or feminine.

WHO, WHOSE, WHOM, ETC.

Qui est-ce?=Who is it?

Qui l'a?=Who has got it?

Qui l'avait?=Who had it?

Qui l'a fait?=Who did it?

Qui avez-vous vu?=Whom did you see?

Avec qui allez-vous?=With whom are you going?

À qui l'avez-vous donné?=To whom did you give it?

À qui est ce chapeau?=Whose hat is this?

À qui sont ces gants? = Whose gloves are these?

De qui parlez-vous? = Of whom are you speaking?

Qui? = Who? *or* Whom?

À qui? = To whom?

De qui? = Of whom?

Avec qui? = With whom?

N.B.—À qui est . . .? = Whose is . . .?

À qui sont . . .? = Whose are . . .?

HOW TO TRANSLATE "IT IS" ("IT WAS")
1. c'est . . . (c'était) . . .

c'est (c'était)	it is (it was)
bon	good
facile	easy
vrai	true
amusant	amusing
là-bas	over there
mon jardin	my garden
le mien	mine

Est-ce ⎱ **votre**   Is it ⎱ your hat?
Était-ce ⎰ **chapeau?** Was it ⎰

"It is" = c'est ("it was" = c'était) if followed by a noun; or by an adjective, provided the word "it" does not refer to a previous noun.

2. il est (était); elle est (était)

Voici mon briquet. Il est joli, n'est-ce pas? = Here is my petrol-lighter. It is nice, isn't it?

Voici ma montre. Elle est petite, n'est-ce pas? = Here is my watch. It is small, isn't it?

Le jardin	The garden
Il est à moi	It is mine
Il était à moi	It was mine
Il sera à moi	It will be mine
La maison	The house
Elle est à moi	It is mine
Elle était à moi	It was mine
Elle sera à moi	It will be mine

"It" = il or elle according to the gender of the noun "it" refers to.

3. il est (il était) . . .

il est (il était)	it is (it was)
deux heures	two o'clock
tard	late
midi	noon
minuit	midnight

"It is" = il est ("it was" = il était) when speaking of time.

4. il fait (il faisait) . . .

il fait (il faisait)	it is (it was)
beau	fine
mauvais	nasty
chaud	hot
froid	cold
sec	dry
humide	wet
du vent	windy
du brouillard	foggy

"It is" = il fait ("it was" = il faisait) when speaking about the weather.

5. il . . .

il pleut	It is raining
neige	snowing
gèle	freezing
dégèle	thawing
il pleuvait	It was raining
neigeait	snowing
gelait	freezing
dégelait	thawing

EXERCISES

I   Répondez en français

1. Où est le bureau? 2. Qui est le propriétaire de la compagnie? 3. Où est l'usine? 4. Qu'est-ce qu'il y a dans le bureau? 5. Qui écrit les lettres? 6. Qui les met à la poste? 7. Avez-vous une machine à écrire? 8. Quel temps fait-il aujourd'hui? 9. Dans quel mois fait-il du brouillard? 10. Est-ce qu'il fait chaud aujourd'hui? 11. Quelle est la date? 12. À qui est ce livre?

II   Traduisez en français

1. The clerk arrives at the office at a quarter to eight. 2. The boss dictates many letters. 3. The typist types them on the machine. 4. The clerk goes to the office on foot. 5. When it rains he comes by bus. 6. He sits down in the Underground. 7. When the train arrives he gets out. 8. She lives in the suburbs. 9. Don't be late. 10. Whose typewriter is this? 11. To whom are you writing? 12. It is 5 past 7. 13. It is very late. 14. It is a nice day. 15. Whose watch is this? It is mine.

III   Traduisez en anglais

1. L'usine de M. Lesage est dans la banlieue. 2. Le patron emploie beaucoup de commis. 3. La sténo arrive à neuf heures moins cinq. 4. Le commis descend de l'autobus. 5. Il habite près d'ici. 6. Elle ne veut pas rester debout. 7. Le proprié- taire de la compagnie ne voyage pas en troisième classe. 8. La gare n'est pas loin de chez lui. 9. Elles descendent sur le quai et elles attendent le train. 10. Quand le train arrive, elles y montent.

(Key on page 369.)

ANNECY: LE VIEUX QUARTIER

Ses canaux, bordés de maisons avec balcons et contrevents, sont une caractéristique pittoresque de la ville, située parmi les montagnes de la Haute Savoie au sud du lac Léman.

Bordé(es) (p.p.)	**balcon** (m.)	**contrevent** (m.)	**parmi**	**le lac Léman**
Bordered	balcony	shutter	among	Lake of Geneva

TRENTE-TROISIÈME LEÇON

LES SPORTS

Georges Lesage est un amateur passionné de sports.   Il est membre d'une
George Lesage is an ardent sports amateur.   He is a member of a

équipe de football et il joue dans des matchs contre d'autres équipes.
football team and plays in matches against other teams.

Quelquefois il joue comme avant, et quelquefois comme demi.   Son équipe est
Sometimes he plays as a forward and sometimes as a half-back.   His team is

une des mieux connues; elle a gagné beaucoup de matchs importants contre
one of the best known; it has won many important matches against

d'autres clubs français et étrangers.   Il est aussi membre d'une association
other clubs, French and foreign.   He is also a member of a sports

sportive qui possède un grand terrain de sports; il y a un vélodrome,
club which possesses a large sports ground; there is a cycling track,

une piste, une piscine et plusieurs terrains pour le football et le
a running track, a swimming pool and several fields for Association football and

rugby, deux sports pour lesquels les Français sont très enthousiastes.
rugby, two games about which the French are very enthusiastic.

En outre il y a plusieurs rings pour les amateurs de boxe et des courts de tennis,
In addition there are several boxing rings and tennis courts,

deux sur gazon et six courts durs.   L'autre jour Georges a invité son cousin
two grass and six hard courts.   The other day George invited his English

anglais à l'accompagner à une grande matinée sportive.   Les courses à pied,
cousin to accompany him to a big sports meeting.   Running,

LES SPORTS=SPORTS

La natation swimming	**Le football** Association football
La pêche fishing	**L'athlétisme** (m.) athletics
Le canotage boating	**Le ski** ski-ing
L'aviron (m.) rowing	**Le patinage** skating
Le yachting yachting	**La chasse** hunting
Le tennis tennis	**Le tir** shooting
La boxe boxing	**Les courses de chevaux** racing
La lutte wrestling	**Le cyclisme** cycling
L'escrime (f.) fencing	**L'équitation** (f.) riding

le lancement du disque et du javelot, le saut en longueur et en hauteur,
discus and javelin throwing, long jump and high jump,

le saut à la perche, la lutte, la boxe, l'escrime, etc., y sont représentés par
pole jumping, wrestling, boxing, fencing, etc., are represented there by the

les meilleurs athlètes parisiens, dont plusieurs champions internationaux.
best Parisian athletes, among them several international champions.

Le jour de l'événement les deux cousins arrivent dans une des tribunes,
On the day of the event the two cousins arrive at one of the stands,

qui sont bondées.
which are crowded.

Charles: **Nous sommes un peu en retard.**
We are a little late.

Georges: **Nous n'avons pas perdu grand'chose. Nous n'avons manqué que**
We have not lost much. We have only missed a few

quelques épreuves éliminatoires.
trial heats.

Charles: **As-tu un programme?**
Have you a programme?

Georges: **Oui, et un crayon pour prendre des notes.**
Yes, and a pencil to take notes.

Charles: **Attention, voici l'épreuve final de la course à obstacles.**
Look, this is the final heat for the hurdle race.

Georges: **Mauvais départ.**   **Charles: C'est le petit homme portant des**
Bad start.   It is the little man wearing

lunettes qui a gagné.   **Georges: Trop facilement.**
spectacles who has won.   Too easily.

Charles: **Quel est le concours suivant?**
What is the next event?

Georges: **Le saut en longueur. Il sera suivi d'une course à pied.**
The long jump. It will be followed by a race.

Charles: **Le voilà qui saute! Bien sauté! Combien a-t-il**
There he jumps! Well jumped! What distance has he

sauté?   **Georges: Presque cinq mètres.**
jumped?   Nearly 17 feet.

Deux fameux joueurs français de tennis; une course d'obstacles au meeting inter-
universitaire; le départ d'une Course de Sept Jours de cyclisme au Vélodrôme d'Hiver;

Sportif-ive (adj.)	**départ** (m.)	**montrer**	**photomontage** (m.)
Sporting	start (of an event)	to show	montage photograph

PARIS SPORTIF
et un match de football au Parc des Princes, sont montrés dans ce photomontage
représentant la vie sportive de Paris. Ce sont les sports les plus populaires en France.

Course (f.) de Sept Jours
A favourite French cycling test which lasts day and night for seven days.

Charles:	**Pas mal du tout. Voyez cette grande coupe.**
	Not bad at all. Look at that large cup.
Georges:	**Je crois que c'est le prix pour la course de cent mètres.**
	I think that is the prize for the hundred metres race.
Charles:	**Assisterons-nous à la distribution des prix?**
	Shall we be present at the prize-giving?
Georges:	**Bien sûr, elle aura lieu à la fin des**
	Certainly, it will take place at the end of the
	concours de saut.
	jumping competitions.

VOCABULARY

une course race
un stade stadium
une partie game
une équipe team
une épreuve event; race; heat
une demi-finale semi-final
une finale final
le terrain ground
la piste track
un match amical a friendly game
un match nul a drawn game
gagner to win
perdre to lose
battre to beat
gagné won
battu beaten
perdu lost
disqualifier to disqualify
jouer au tennis to play tennis (*golf, etc.*)
une partie de tennis a game of tennis
la mi-temps half-time
la deuxième mi-temps second half
le concurrent competitor

L'ATHLÉTISME—ATHLETICS

1. **la course** running
   le départ start
   le coureur runner
   le but finish
   être léger à la course to be a swift runner
2. **la course à obstacles** hurdle-race
   la haie hurdle

3. **le saut** jumping
   le saut en hauteur high jump
   le saut en longueur long jump
   le saut à la perche pole jump
   le sauteur jumper
   la perche pole
   la latte bar
4. **le lancement du javelot** javelin throwing
   le javelot javelin
5. **le lancement du disque** discus throwing
   le disque discus

LE FOOTBALL— ASSOCIATION FOOTBALL

le terrain de jeu (le stade) field
le but goal
l'arbitre (m.) referee
la balle ball
les spectateurs (le public) spectators
la tribune stand
le gardien goalkeeper
un arrière droit a right back
un arrière gauche a left back
un demi droit a right half back
un demi centre a centre half back
un demi gauche a left half back
un ailier droit an outside right
un ailier gauche an outside left
un inter-droit an inside right
un inter-gauche an inside left
l'avant-centre the centre forward

AUCUN, AUCUNE

Je ne connais aucun de ses amis=I know none of his friends.

Je n'ai aucun ami=I have no friend.
Aucun(e) de vous n'est arrivé(e) à l'heure= None of you have arrived in time.
Ce livre m'intéresse plus qu'aucun autre= This book interests me more than any other.
Cette robe vous va mieux qu'aucune autre= This frock suits you better than any other.
Sans aucun doute=Without any doubt.
aucun(e)=any; preceded or followed by **ne**=none, no, not any

AUTRE

Si vous n'aimez pas ces couteaux je vous en montrerai d'autres=If you don't like these knives I'll show you others.
Une autre fourchette s'il vous plaît. Celle-ci n'est pas propre=Another fork please. This one is not clean.
Je l'ai rencontré l'autre jour=I met him the other day.
C'est une autre affaire=That is another matter.
Elle ne parle jamais d'autre chose=She never speaks of anything else.
Il est resté, les autres sont partis=He has stayed, the others have left.
Vous me demandez du savon et une serviette; je n'ai ni l'un ni l'autre=You ask me for some soap and a towel; I haven't got either.
L'un et l'autre sont partis ⎫
L'une et l'autre sont parties ⎬ =They have both left.
C'était bien autre chose alors=It was (things were) very different then (i.e., much better or much worse).
Nous autres Anglais=We English
Vous autres Français=You French
À d'autres!=Tell that to others; don't tell me that! (slang)
autre=other
l'un ⎫
l'une ⎬ **et l'autre**=both
ni l'un ni l'autre=neither
l'un ou l'autre=either
autrefois=formerly
autrement=otherwise

autre part=elsewhere
d'autre part=on the other hand
de temps à autre=from time to time

MÊME

Le même jour=The same day
La même année=The same year
Le jour même=The very same day
L'année même=The very same year
Il dit toujours la même chose=He always says the same (thing).
C'est la même chose qu'en anglais=It is the same as in English.
Il est toujours le même=He is always the same.
Elle est toujours la même=She is always the same.
Il ne m'a même pas repondu=He has not even answered me.
Elle ne m'a même pas remercié=She did not even thank me.
Je le ferai quand même=I'll do it all the same.
Je le ferai moi-même=I'll do it myself.
Il est fou de même que son père=He is mad like his father.

HOW TO TRANSLATE "ARE YOU"
1. Êtes-vous . . . ?

Êtes-vous (étiez-vous) are you (were you)?

le patron ici?	the boss here?
Anglais(e)?	English?
fatigué(e)?	tired?
pressé(e)?	in a hurry?
en retard?	late?

Normally "are you"=**êtes-vous** ("were you"=**étiez-vous**). Note, however, that "are you"=**avez-vous** ("were you"=**aviez-vous**) in the following cases:

2. Avez-vous . . . ?

Avez-vous (aviez-vous) are you (were you)

chaud?	hot?
froid?	cold?
faim?	hungry?
soif?	thirsty?

raison?	right?
tort?	wrong?
peur?	afraid?
honte?	ashamed?
sommeil	sleepy?
pitié de lui?	sorry for him?
besoin de cela?	in need of that?

N.B.—When speaking of *things* and not *persons* use **être chaud, être froid.**

il a froid = he is cold

il (= le vin) est froid
elle (= l'eau) est froide $\Big\}$ it is cold

3. . . . -vous?

Venez			coming?
Allez			going?
Attendez	$\Big\}$-vous?	are you	waiting?
Écoutez			listening?
Mangez			eating?

Allez-vous	are you going to
(alliez-vous)	(were you going to)
attendre?	wait?
partir?	leave?
le faire?	do it?
en manger?	eat some?

No difference is made in French between "*I come*" and "*I am coming*"; "*I wait*" and "*I am waiting*"; "*are you coming?*" and "*do you come?*"; "*are you waiting?*" and "*do you wait?*", etc.

EXERCISES

I Traduisez en anglais

1. Cette partie m'intéresse plus qu'aucune autre. 2. Il court plus vite qu'aucun de ses concurrents. 3. Aucun d'eux n'est arrivé à l'heure. 4. Aucun spectateur ne l'a vu. 5. Il y a un autre vélodrome près d'ici. 6. Il ne parle jamais d'autre chose. 7. Je suis resté seul à la maison; les autres sont allés à la piscine. 8. Il a le même handicap que moi. 9. Nous jouons dans la même équipe. 10. Si vous n'aimez pas ces épreuves nous pouvons en voir d'autres. 11. Vous me demandez si je joue au tennis et au football? Je ne joue ni à l'un ni à l'autre. 12. Assisterez-vous à la distribution des prix qui aura lieu demain?

II Traduisez en français

1. None of your friends was on the sports ground. 2. I have seen neither the one nor the other. 3. They are faster than any of their competitors. 4. Did you play with them the other day? 5. He always plays on the same tennis court. 6. This game interests him more than any other. 7. We had a game of tennis the other day. 8. Are you a member of the sports club? 9. Are you Charles's cousin? 10. Are you warm enough? 11. Are you coming? 12. Are you going to play? (*Key on pages 369 and 370.*)

HISTOIRE AMUSANTE

The words which you cannot be expected to know are translated below. With that help you should be able to read this simple tale.

Deux petites filles se promènent dans la campagne.

Au milieu d'un pré paissent deux vaches, une blanche et une noire.

Tiens, dit l'une des deux petites à sa camarade, tu vois ces deux vaches?

Oui.

Eh bien, c'est la vache blanche qui donne le lait et la vache noire qui donne le café!

___

Pré (m.), meadow; **paissent** (from **paître**), are grazing; **campagne** (f.), country.

TRENTE-QUATRIÈME LEÇON

LES SPORTS (suite)—SPORTS (continued)

Le football n'est pas le seul sport qui intéresse Georges.   Il est aussi
Football is not the only sport that interests Georges.   He is also

amateur de boxe.   L'autre jour il
fond of boxing.   The other day he

a été mis knock-out à la fin d'un
was knocked out at the end of a

match sur cinq rounds.   "Je n'étais
match of five rounds.   "I was not

pas bien entraîné," c'est ce
well trained," is what he

qu'il dit.   Mlle Lesage joue au
says.   Mlle Lesage plays

tennis.   Elle est membre d'un club,
tennis.   She belongs to a club,

et elle joue dans des matches
and plays in matches

contre d'autres clubs.   Elle est bonne joueuse et gagne beaucoup
against other clubs.   She is a good player and wins many

de ses parties.   Le sport qui intéresse M. Lesage est la course de chevaux.
of her games.   The sport that interests M. Lesage is horse-racing.

Accompagné de son beau-frère il est allé à Longchamp, l'un des champs
Accompanied by his brother-in-law he went to Longchamp, one of the

de course les plus populaires de la région parisienne.   Mme Roberts les a
most popular race-courses near Paris.   Mrs. Roberts accompanied

accompagnés aussi.   Elle a dit qu'on y voit de si jolies toilettes.
them also.   She said that one can see such beautiful dresses there.

Il y avait énormément de monde sur les pelouses.   M. Lesage et les
There was an enormous crowd on the lawns.   M. Lesage and the

Roberts se sont installés dans une des tribunes du pesage.
Roberts got seats in one of the stands of the paddock.

LONGCHAMP, UN JOUR DE GRAND PRIX

C'est le Derby des Parisiens. Et les tribunes bondées, les mannequins qui font valoir les derniers modèles, le tableau d'affichage entouré d'ardents spéculateurs, la perspective d'une fin serrée—tout nous offre l'impression d'un événement sportif des plus importants. Longchamp est dans le Bois de Boulogne à Paris.

Tribune (f.)	**bonder**	**faire valoir**	**tableau** (m.) **d'affichage**	**fin** (f.) **serrée**
Stand	to fill	show to advantage	number board	close finish

M. Lesage a risqué mille francs sur un cheval, pour lequel il avait reçu
M. Lesage risked 1,000 francs on a horse for which he had received

un bon tuyau.   Mme Roberts n'a pas fait attention aux tuyaux qu'on lui avait
a good tip.   Mrs. Roberts did not take any notice of the tips given

donnés.   Elle a mis cinq cents francs sur un cheval dont l'air lui plaisait.
to her.   She put five-hundred francs on a horse, which she liked the look of.

Elle a eu la veine de le voir gagner.   C'était bien son jour de veine.
She had the luck to see it win.   It really was her lucky day.

Quant à Madeleine, elle va devenir bonne patineuse.   Avec sa cousine
As for Madeleine, she is going to become a good skater.   With her cousin

elle va patiner trois fois par semaine dans un skating qui vient de
she goes skating three times a week at a skating rink which has

s'ouvrir dans leur quartier.   Le sport favori de Charles (malgré sa
just been opened in their district.   Charles's favourite sport (despite his

mésaventure infortunée) est toujours le cyclisme, qui est un des
unfortunate mishap) is still cycling, which is one of the

AT THE SKATING RINK

In this picture Lucie Lesage is showing Madeleine Roberts and the others how easy it is to skate! Try to describe the scene in French, introducing the following words which are new to you:—**accoudoir** (m.)=balustrade; **tricot** (m.)=jumper, knitted-vest; **patins** (m.) **à glace**=ice-skates.

sports les plus populaires en France. L'autre jour il s'est égaré en
most popular sports in France.   The other day he lost his way when

rentrant d'une randonnée aux environs de Paris.   En outre, l'un
returning from a trip into the country around Paris.   In addition, one

de ses pneus a crevé.   Heureusement un monsieur
of his tyres burst.   Fortunately a gentleman

est arrivé à qui il a pu
arrived of whom he was able

demander son chemin.
to ask his way.

Charles: **Pardon, monsieur.**
                     Excuse me, sir,

veuillez me dire où je suis—
will you please tell me where I am—

je me suis égaré.
I have lost my way.

Le monsieur: **Vous êtes près de Fontainebleau.   Au coin de la rue vous**
                 You are near Fontainebleau.   At the corner of the street

                 verrez un poteau-indicateur.
                 you will see a sign-post.

Charles: **Pourrai-je faire réparer mon pneu à Fontainebleau?**
                 Shall I be able to get my tyre repaired at Fontainebleau?

Le monsieur: **Sans doute; vous y trouverez des garages.**
                 Undoubtedly; you will find some garages there.

Charles: **Bonsoir, monsieur, je vous remercie.**
                 Good evening, sir, and thank you.

Le monsieur: **Il n'y a pas de quoi, mon ami.**
                 You are welcome (my friend).

(Charles continue son chemin, poussant son vélo, lorsqu'un sergent de ville
(Charles continues his way, pushing his bike, when a policeman

l'arrête.)   **Le sergent: Halte, mon petit, il faut allumer la lanterne.**
stops him.)   Stop, my little man, you must put your light on.

Charles: **Déjà?   Quelle heure est-il donc?**
                 Already?   What is the time then?

Le sergent: **Il est huit heures**
It is ten

moins dix.
to eight.

Charles: **Mais faut-il allumer**
But do I have to have it lit

quand je ne suis pas
when I am not

sur mon vélo?
on my bike?

Le sergent: **Parfaitement,**
Certainly,

mon petit.
my little man.

Charles: **Bien, j'allumerai.**
All right, I shall put it on.

J'ignorais le règlement.
I did not know the regulations.

LE TENNIS—TENNIS

le court tennis court
le filet net
la raquette racquet
la palette table tennis bat
une balle de tennis tennis ball
le joueur de tennis tennis player
le ramasseur de balles ball-boy
la ligne de côté side line
la ligne de service service line
la ligne médiane central line
la ligne du fond base line
l'arbitre umpire
le filet net
la balle ball

LA COURSE DE CHEVAUX—HORSE RACING

le champ de course race-course
les tribunes stands
la tribune judge's box
le juge judge

le pesage paddock
la pelouse public enclosures
la piste course (*track*)
le départ starting-point
l'arrivée finish
une haie hurdle
un cheval de course race-horse
le jockey jockey
la casquette cap
la cravache whip
un bookmaker bookmaker
le pari-mutuel totalisator
l'écurie (f.) stables

LA BOXE—BOXING

1. **le boxeur** boxer
le ring (*English pronunciation*) ring
les cordes (f.pl.) ropes
l'arbitre referee
le public public
les seconds seconds
le commencement d'un match sur 15 rounds
the beginning of a 15-round match

THE FISTIC ART

Your task here is to study the lists on pages 357 and 359 and then to describe in French everything you see in the picture—ropes, ring, seconds, the various blows exchanged by the boxers, and what is happening to the tired-looking boxers shown in the lower right-hand portion of the picture. You will note from the vocabularies that in boxing, as in other sports, many English expressions are made use of in French without any alteration, and even the English pronunciation is used in some instances. A description of the above scene in French should, therefore, give you no great difficulty.

2. **Un des boxeurs place un direct gauche, que son adversaire esquive par dessous** One of the boxers delivers a straight left, which his opponent eludes by "ducking."
3. **Un crochet du droit**   a right hook
4. **Un coup balancé**   a swing
5. **Les deux boxeurs en clinch**   The two boxers clinching
6. **L'un des boxeurs est mis knock out (est knock-outé)**   One of the boxers is knocked out.

JUST

Ils viennent d'arriver = They have just arrived.
Maman vient de sortir = Mother has just gone out.
Il venait d'envoyer le télégramme = He had just sent the telegram.
Nous venions de passer quelques jours à la campagne = We had just spent a few days in the country.
Venir de, followed by an Infinitive, expresses the immediate past.

TO BE GOING TO

Je vais écrire des lettres = I am going to write some letters.
Qu'est-ce qu'il va faire? = What is he going to do?
Nous allons le voir cet après-midi = We are going to see him this afternoon.
Il allait jouer du piano = He was going to play the piano.
Nous allions sortir = We were going out.
Aller, followed by an Infinitive, indicates the immediate future.

TO HAVE SOMETHING DONE

Elle fait faire une robe pour sa petite fille = She is having a dress made for her little girl.
Voulez-vous faire réparer cela? = Will you have this repaired?
Je le ferai travailler = I shall make him work.
Voulez-vous faire nettoyer ma chambre? = Will you have my room cleaned?

Je le lui ferai envoyer = I will get it sent to him.
Faites frire ce poisson = Have this fish fried.
Voulez-vous faire rôtir ce poulet? = Will you roast this chicken; will you have this chicken roasted?

Faire, followed by an Infinitive, means to have (or get) something done. Note also the following expressions:

faire une promenade = to take a walk
faire des emplettes = to go shopping
faire la vaisselle = to wash up
faire trente kilomètres = to walk (or drive) thirty kilometres.
quel temps fait-il? = how is the weather?
il fait beau = it is fine
il fait mauvais = it is bad
il fait chaud = it is hot
il fait froid = it is cold
il fait frais = it is cool
il fait vilain = it is nasty
il fait clair = it is light
il fait sombre = it is dark
il fait lourd = it is sultry

THE INFINITIVE AFTER VERBS AND PREPOSITIONS

Avant d'entrer dans la maison = Before entering the house.
Il avoue avoir dit cela = He admits having said this.
Je n'ai pas besoin d'y aller = I have no need to go there.
Je l'ai vu battre le chien = I saw him beating the dog.
Au lieu de sonner = Instead of ringing.
Finissons cela avant de rentrer = Let us finish that before going home.
Après avoir fait cela = After having done that.
Après avoir ouvert la fenêtre = After having opened the window.
Après avoir fini mon travail = After having finished my work.
Après être arrivé = After having arrived.
J'aime à faire cela = I like doing that.
C'est jouer un jeu dangereux = That is playing a dangerous game.

When a verb follows another verb or a preposition (except **en**) it must be in the Infinitive. Note the examples above. In English, forms in "*-ing*" are used where in French the Infinitive has to be employed. Notice that **après** takes the Past Infinitive.

Note also the following uses of the Infinitive (*in place of an English subordinate clause or personal mood*):

Je crois le connaître=I think I know him.

Il pense avoir raison=He thinks that he is right.

Nous croyions entendre un cri=We thought we heard a cry.

Comment savoir si c'est vrai?=How do I (*do we, does one*) know, if it is true?

Pourquoi manger quand on n'a pas faim?= Why eat when you are not hungry?

Que faire?=What shall I (*we, one*) do?

Qui croire?=Whom am I (*are we, is one*) to believe?

Je ne sais que faire=I don't know what to do.

Note further the use of the Infinitive in signs and general notices:

défense de fumer=smoking forbidden   **à vendre**=for sale

EXERCISES

I Translate into English

1. Venez m'aider. 2. Elle regrette de ne pas pouvoir vous rencontrer (=to meet) ce soir. 3. Je n'ai pas le temps de vous envoyer des lettres. 4. Permettez-moi de vous donner un avis (=advice). 5. Je suis heureux de vous entendre parler ainsi (=like this). 6. Veuillez me faire réveiller à six heures. 7. Je vais faire faire une robe d'après-midi chez ma couturière. 8. Comme il fait froid nous faisons allumer du feu. 9. Je vous ferai envoyer votre valise. 10. Je crois avoir vu ce monsieur. 11. Faites venir la domestique. 12. Je vais mettre ces lettres à la poste. 13. Elles vont finir (=to finish) dans une minute. 14. Il semble (=seems) avoir oublié son rendezvous. 15. Il vient de voir votre père. (*Key on page* 370.)

II Translate into French

1. He has just gone out. 2. They have just arrived. 3. I am going to open the window. 4. Are you going to play now? 5. I believe that I saw your aunt at the concert. 6. They are going to leave tonight. 7. Is it cold? 8. Was it hot yesterday? 9. Have the windows closed; it is too cold. 10. I'll make him work. 11. Have these eggs boiled. 12. I think that I know them. 13. Instead of skating we shall go swimming. 14. After having finished his work he made a trip on his bicycle into the surroundings of the town. 15. I like watching the skaters. 16. He lost his way returning from the race-course. 17. He gave me a good tip. 18. My favourite sport is cycling. 19. The other day he lost 1000 francs. 20. It was not his lucky day.

UN HÔTEL DU VIEUX PARIS

Dans ces petits hôtels bon marché, les gens peu fortunés trouvent un confort restreint.
Remarquez les volets que l'on ferme la nuit. Chaque maison en est pourvue en France.

Bon marché	**peu fortuné-e**	**confort** (m.)	**restreint-e** (adj.)	**le volet**
Cheap	of slender means	comfort	limited	shutter

TRENTE-CINQUIÈME LEÇON

À LA CAMPAGNE—IN THE COUNTRY

La France est un pays agricole.　Les petits propriétaires terriens
France is an agricultural country.　Small landed proprietors

y sont très nombreux.　Dans un village presque tous les habitants sont
are very numerous there.　In a village almost all the inhabitants are either

des cultivateurs ou des vignerons.　On y trouve aussi quelques artisans,
farmers or vine-growers.　There are also to be found some workmen,

un curé, un médecin et un instituteur.　Presque chaque maison est entourée
a priest, a doctor and a schoolmaster.　Almost every house is surrounded

d'une cour et d'un jardin.　On y voit aussi des écuries pour les chevaux,
by a courtyard and a garden.　There are also to be seen stables for the horses,

des étables pour le bétail, des granges pour le blé, des remises pour
cowsheds for the cattle, barns for the wheat, sheds for the

les voitures et les chariots.　Dans la cour on peut voir des chèvres avec leurs chevreaux,
carriages and the carts.　In the courtyard one can see goats with their kids,

des poules avec leurs poussins, des dindons, des oies et des pigeons.　Les maisons les
hens with their chicks, turkeys, geese and pigeons.　The smallest

plus petites ont seulement un rez-de-chaussée et sont couvertes de paille.　On les appelle
houses have only a ground-floor and are covered with straw.　They are called

des chaumières.　Les autres maisons ont un premier et quelquefois
"chaumières" (thatched cottages).　The other houses have a first and sometimes

aussi un deuxième étage.　Les seuls édifices du village
also a second floor.　The only (public) buildings of the village

sont l'église et l'école.　Le printemps est une saison de grand
are the church and the school.　Spring is a season of hard

travail pour le cultivateur, car il doit labourer ses terres et semer
work for the farmer, for he has to plough his lands and to sow

les différentes espèces de blé.　Dans les jardins, les jardiniers
the different kinds of grain.　In the gardens, the gardeners

aussi ont beaucoup à faire.　Ils doivent bêcher le sol pour le préparer
too have much to do.　They must dig the ground to prepare it

à recevoir les plantes qu'ils veulent y planter.   Le soleil fait croître l'herbe
to receive the plants which they want to plant there.   The sun makes the grass grow

et mûrir le blé.   Au commencement de l'été le foin est
and the wheat ripen.   In the beginning of the summer the hay is

mûr.   Il est coupé, séché et transporté à la ferme.   À la fin de juillet ou
ripe.   It is cut, dried and taken to the farm.   At the end of July or

au commencement d'août la moisson commence.   Après avoir coupé le blé,
beginning of August the harvest begins.   After the wheat has been cut,

on le met en gerbes pour le sécher.   Puis on le battra pour en sortir les
it is made into sheaves to dry.   Then it will be threshed to get out the

grains, qui seront transportés au moulin pour en faire de la farine.
grain, which will be taken to the mill to be made into flour.

En automne on récolte les pommes de terre et les betteraves; dans les
In autumn potatoes and beetroot are harvested; in the

vignobles c'est le temps des vendanges.   Dans le verger on cueille
vineyards it is the time of the grape-harvest.   In the orchard the last

les derniers fruits: les pommes, les poires et les prunes.   Les pommes poussent
fruits are picked: apples, pears and plums.   The apples grow

sur un arbre; c'est le pommier.   La poire pousse sur le poirier et la prune
on a tree; it is the apple tree.   The pear grows on the pear tree and the plum

sur le prunier.   Les cerises, qui poussent sur le cerisier, ont déjà été
on the plum tree.   The cherries, which grow on the cherry tree, were already

cueillies en juin.   L'été est la période des excursions à pied, à bicyclette ou
picked in June.   Summer is the time of excursions on foot, on a bicycle or

en auto, et des promenades dans les bois et dans les forêts.   C'est la saison
by car, and of walks in woods and forests.   It is the season

des grandes chaleurs et des orages.   Les Lesage passent presque tous les
of great heat and of thunderstorms.   The Lesages spend almost all the

dimanches à la campagne.   Ils se lèvent de bonne heure, montent dans leur
Sundays in the country.   They get up early, get into their

auto, et arrivent bientôt en pleine campagne.
car, and soon arrive in the open country.

Quand il fait chaud ils vont dans une forêt.   Ils y choisissent un bon endroit
When it is hot they go into the forest.   There they choose a good place

A FRENCH VILLAGE SCENE

You are now getting very near the end of the Course. If you have studied all the lessons carefully you should be well equipped to cope with almost any situation in which a traveller in France might find himself or herself. So far most of the Course has had a more or less urban background, but this picture shows you a very typical section of the sort of village life you may encounter if you go through France by car, by bicycle or on foot. Think of yourself, therefore, as making ready for such a tour, and study the list set out on page 365 until you feel competent to name in French any object in this picture without aid. Write a description of the picture.

à l'ombre pour faire leur pique-nique.   Mme Lesage leur a préparé
in the shade to have their picnic.   Mme Lesage has prepared them

un grand panier plein de bonnes choses.   Après le repas ils se promènent
a large basket full of good things.   After the meal they stroll about

dans la forêt.   Ainsi ils passent une journée agréable en plein air.
in the forest.   Thus they spend a pleasant day in the open air.

LE VILLAGE—VILLAGE

le poteau indicateur sign-post
une église church
le curé parish priest
le pâturage pasture land
un étang pond
une école school
la ferme farm-house
la pompe à eau water-pump
une étable cowshed
la vache cow
le veau calf
une écurie stable
le cheval horse
la herse harrow
le seau à lait milk-pail
la meule de foin hay-rick
la fourche à foin pitchfork
le poulailler chicken-house
le coq cock
la poule hen
le poussin chick
la grange barn
une oie goose
le dindon turkey
la voiture carriage
le chariot cart
le moulin à vent windmill
le pigeon pigeon
la colombe dove

TO GROW

pousser ⎫
croître ⎬ = to grow (*of plants*)

grandir = to grow (*of persons*)
devenir vieux = to grow old
cultiver = to grow, to till, to cultivate
planter = to grow, to plant
adulte = grown up
les adultes ⎫
les grands ⎬ = the grown-ups

THE FRENCH VERB

French verbs are divided into four groups, according to the ending of the Infinitive. These groups are called Conjugations.

1st Conjugation, Infinitive in **-er**,
  like **donner** = to give.
2nd Conjugation, Infinitive in **-ir**,
  like **finir** = to finish.
3rd Conjugation, Infinitive in **-re**,
  like **prendre** = to take.
4th Conjugation, Infinitive in **-oir**,
  like **recevoir** = to receive.

Verbs in -er

Most verbs terminate in **-er** and they are conjugated like **donner** (*see pages* 391-392) except **aller** (*see page* 394) and a few minor changes in other verbs (*see* page 371).

Verbs in -ir

Many verbs end in **-ir**. Some are conjugated like **finir**, others are irregular.

FINIR = TO FINISH

Present	Imperfect
je finis	**je finissais**
tu finis	**tu finissais**
il finit	**il finissait**
nous finissons	**nous finissions**
vous finissez	**vous finissiez**
ils finissent	**ils finissaient**

Future	Conditional
je finirai	**je finirais**
tu finiras	**tu finirais**
il finira	**il finirait**
nous finirons	**nous finirions**
vous finirez	**vous finiriez**
ils finiront	**ils finiraient**

(*Continued on page* 368)

English

1. Foliage; 2. Trunk (of tree); 3. Branch; 4. Twig; 5. Side-road; 6. Main road; 7. Grass; 8. Meadow; 9. Poplars; 10. Ass; 11. Pannier; 12. Hamlet; 13. Farm; 14. Ploughman; 15. Team of oxen; 16. Ploughed land; 17. Furrow; 18. "Spit" (of soil); 19. Fowls; 20. Fowl house; 21. Peasant (girl); 22. Hayricks; 23. Cattle chewing cud; 24. Hilly country; 25. Hill; 26. Mountain top; 27. Valley; 28. Vineyard; 29. Fallow land; 30. Chestnut tree; 31. Telegraph poles; 32. Spinney; 33. Man in shirtsleeves; 34. Woman knitting; 35. Thermos flask; 36. Hamper; 37. Man fishing; 38. Fishing rod; 39. Fishing-tackle; 40. Stream or brook.

French

1. Feuillage (m.); 2. Tronc (m.); 3. Branche (f.); 4. Brindille (f.); 5. Chemin

Further Useful Words	montagneux mountainous	ondulant undulating	boisé wooded

À LA CAMPAGNE

(m.) vicinal; 6. Chaussée (f.); (route (f.) nationale); 7. Herbe (f.); 8. Prairie (f.); 9. Peupliers (m.); 10. Âne (m.), bourrique (f.); 11. Panier de bât (m.); 12. Hameau (m.); 13. Ferme (f.); 14. Laboureur (m.); 15. Attelage (m.) de bœufs; 16. Terre (f.) labourée; 17. Sillon (m.); 18. Bêchée (f.) de terre; 19. Volaille (f.); 20. Poulailler (m.); 21. Paysanne (f.); 22. Meules (f.pl.) de foin (m.); 23. Bétail (m.) ruminant; 24. Terrain (m.) accidenté; 25. Colline (f.); 26. Cime (f.), sommet (m.); 27. Vallée (f.); 28. Clos (m.) de vigne (f.); 29. Terre (f.) en friche; 30. Châtaignier (m.); 31. Poteaux (m.pl.) télégraphiques; 32. Bosquet (m.); 33. Homme en bras de chemise; 34. Tricoteuse (f.); 35. Bouteille (f.) isolante (thermos); 36. Panier (m.) à provisions; 37. Pêcheur (m.); 38. Canne (f.) à pêche; 39. Attirail de pêche (m.); 40. Ruisseau (m.).

escarpé	sauvage	boueux	marécageux
steep	wild	muddy	marshy

Perfect: j'ai fini, tu as fini, il a fini, etc.
Imperative: finis, finissons, finissez
The verb choisir = to choose is conjugated like finir.
sortir is conjugated like dormir, servir, partir and sentir (see page 395).
cueillir = to pluck, to gather, to pick, is like ouvrir, to open, but Future is je cueillerai, Conditional is je cueillerais, and the Perfect is j'ai cueilli.
j'ouvre, tu ouvres, il ouvre, nous ouvrons; j'ouvrais; j'ouvrirai; j'ai ouvert, etc.
couvrir = to cover is like ouvrir.

Verbs in -re
There are a few dozen of them. Some are conjugated like vendre (see page 391), others are irregular.
Of the verbs occurring in this lesson, faire has been given on pages 105 and 149 and mettre on pages 122 and 149. New verbs are battre and croître.

BATTRE = TO BEAT, TO THRASH
Present:
je bats
tu bats
il bat
nous battons
vous battez
ils battent
Imperfect: je battais, etc.
Future: je battrai, etc.
Conditional: je battrais, etc.
Perfect: j'ai battu, etc.
Imperative: bats, battons, battez

CROÎTRE = TO GROW
Present:
je croîs
tu croîs
il croît
nous croissons
vous croissez
ils croissent
Imperfect: je croissais, etc.
Future: je croîtrai, etc.
Conditional: je croîtrais, etc.
Perfect: j'ai crû (f., crûe)
Note the circumflex which is used to distinguish it from forms of croire.

CROIRE = TO BELIEVE
Present:
je crois
tu crois
il croit
nous croyons
vous croyez
ils croient
Imperfect: je croyais, etc.
Future: je croirai, etc.
Conditional: je croirais, etc.
Perfect: j'ai cru, etc.
Imperative: crois, croyons, croyez

Verbs in -oir
There are only a few of them, but they are all irregular. Avoir = to have, voir = to see, vouloir = to wish, and pouvoir = to be able, have already been given. A new verb in this lesson is:

RECEVOIR = TO RECEIVE
Present:
je reçois
tu reçois
il reçoit
nous recevons
vous recevez
ils reçoivent
Imperfect: je recevais, etc.
Future: je recevrai, etc.
Conditional: je recevrais, etc.
Perfect: j'ai reçu, etc.
Imperative: reçois, recevez, recevons

EXERCISES

I Répondez en français aux questions suivantes

1. Fait-il chaud en été? 2. Restez-vous en ville en été? 3. Qu'y a-t-il dans les champs? 4. Qu'est-ce qui pousse dans le verger? 5. Où poussent les poires? 6. Y a-t-il des fruits aux arbres en hiver? 7. Où fait-il plus chaud, au soleil ou à l'ombre? 8. Que fait le laboureur en été? 9. Comment appelle-t-on les petits de la vache? 10. Où les Lesage vont-ils passer le dimanche? 11. Quand se lèvent-ils? 12. Qu'est-ce que Mme Lesage leur

prépare? 13. Que font-ils quand il fait chaud? 14. Que font-ils quand ils ont faim?

II Traduisez en anglais

1. Au printemps les arbres portent des fleurs; en été ils sont couverts de feuilles et ils portent des fruits; en automne les feuilles tombent. 2. Quand il fait beau on préfère être en plein air. 3. Votre mère n'est-elle pas sortie? 4. Comme le cœur me bat! 5. Ne battez pas le chien! 6. Croyez-vous ce qu'elle a dit? 7. Qui est-ce qui croit tout ce qu'il lit? 8. Il laisse croître ses cheveux. 9. Il ne sait pas ce

qu'il veut. 10. Je pourrai vous aider quand vous voudrez.

III Traduisez en français

1. I shall finish my job on Saturday. 2. Haven't they finished yet? 3. You can have an apple tree or a plum tree: choose. 4. They are fighting (beat themselves) for nothing. 5. I never believe what he says. 6. Why don't you believe me? 7. I read it, but I did not believe it. 8. We get two pints (about a litre) of milk each morning. 9. He got ten pounds of apples. 10. You will get them tomorrow. (*Key on page 370.*)

KEY TO THE EXERCISES

Lesson Thirty-two
I

1. Il est au centre de Paris. 2. M. Lesage en est le propriétaire. 3. Elle est dans la banlieue. 4. Il y a des tables, des chaises, des machines à écrire, etc. 5. La sténodactylo les écrit. 6. Le garçon de bureau. 7. J'en ai une (je n'en ai pas). 8. Il fait beau (mauvais). 9. En novembre. 10. Il (ne) fait (pas) chaud aujourd'hui. 11. C'est aujourd'hui le trois avril. 12. C'est à moi *or* c'est le mien.

II

1. Le commis arrive au bureau à huit heures moins le quart. 2. Le patron dicte beaucoup de lettres. 3. La steno les écrit à la machine. 4. Le commis va au bureau à pied. 5. Quand il pleut il vient en autobus. 6. Il s'assied dans le métro. 7. Quand le train arrive il descend. 8. Elle habite la banlieue. 9. Ne soyez pas en retard. 10. À qui est cette machine à écrire? 11. À qui écrivez-vous? 12. Il est sept heures cinq. 13. Il est très tard. 14. Il fait beau. 15. À qui est cette montre? Elle est à moi *or* c'est la mienne.

III

1. M. Lesage's factory is in the suburbs. 2. The boss employs many clerks. 3. The

typist arrives at five to nine. 4. The clerk gets out of the bus. 5. He lives near here. 6. She does not want to stand. 7. The owner of the firm does not travel third class. 8. The station is not far from his house. 9. They get out on to the platform and wait for the train. 10. When the train arrives they get in.

Lesson Thirty-three
I

1. This game interests me more than any other. 2. He runs (or is running) faster than any of his opponents. 3. None of them has arrived in time. 4. None of the spectators has seen him. 5. There is another cycling track near here. 6. He never speaks of anything else. 7. I remained in the house alone; the others went to the swimming-bath. 8. He has the same handicap as I. 9. We play in the same team. 10. If you don't like these events we can see others. 11. You are asking me if I play both tennis and football? I play neither. 12. Will you be present at the distribution of prizes, which will take place tomorrow?

II

1. Aucun de vos amis n'était sur le terrain de sports. 2. Je n'ai vu ni l'un ni

l'autre. 3. Ils sont plus rapides qu'aucun de leurs concurrents. 4. Avez-vous joué avec eux l'autre jour? 5. Il joue toujours sur le même court de tennis. 6. Cette partie l'intéresse plus qu'aucune autre. 7. Nous jouions une partie de tennis l'autre jour. 8. Êtes-vous membre de l'association sportive? 9. Êtes-vous le cousin de Charles? 10. Avez-vous assez chaud? 11. Venez-vous? 12. Allez-vous jouer?

Lesson Thirty-four

I

1. Come and help me. 2. She regrets not being able to meet you tonight. 3. I have not the time to send you letters. 4. Allow me to give you advice. 5. I am glad to hear you speaking like this. 6. Will you please have me called at six? 7. I am going to have an afternoon frock made at my dressmaker's. 8. As it is cold we have made a fire. 9. I'll have your suitcase sent to you. 10. I believe that I have seen this man. 11. Tell the maid to come. 12. I am going to post these letters. 13. They are going to finish in a minute. 14. He seems to have forgotten his appointment. 15. He has just seen your father.

II

1. Il vient de sortir. 2. Ils viennent d'arriver. 3. Je vais ouvrir la fenêtre. 4. Allez-vous jouer maintenant? 5. Je crois avoir vu votre tante au concert. 6. Ils (elles) vont partir ce soir. 7. Est-ce qu'il fait froid? 8. Est-ce qu'il faisait chaud hier? 9. Faites fermer les fenêtres; il fait trop froid. 10. Je le ferai travailler. 11. Faites bouillir ces œufs. 12. Je crois les connaître. 13. Au lieu de patiner nous irons nager. 14. Après avoir fini son travail il faisait une excursion à bicyclette dans les environs de la ville. 15. J'aime regarder les patineurs. 16. Il s'est égaré en rentrant du vélodrome. 17. Il m'a donné un bon tuyau. 18. Mon sport favori est le cyclisme. 19. L'autre jour il a perdu mille francs. 20. Ce n'était pas son jour de veine.

Lesson Thirty-five

I

1. Oui, il fait chaud en été. 2. Je n'y reste pas tout le temps. 3. Il y a du blé. 4. Des pommiers, des poiriers, des cerisiers, des pruniers, etc. 5. Elles poussent sur le poirier. 6. Il n'y en a pas. 7. Il fait plus chaud au soleil. 8. Il coupe le blé. 9. On les appelle des veaux. 10. À la campagne. 11. Ils se lèvent de bonne heure. 12. Elle leur prépare un bon déjeuner. 13. Ils vont dans la forêt. 14. Ils mangent leur déjeuner.

II

1. In spring the trees have blossom; in summer they are covered with leaves and they bear fruit; in autumn the leaves fall. 2. When it is fine one prefers to be in the open air. 3. Hasn't your mother gone out? 4. How my heart beats! 5. Don't beat the dog! 6. Do you believe what she said? 7. Who believes all that he reads? 8. He lets his hair grow. 9. He does not know what he wants. 10. I shall be able to help you when you wish.

III

1. Je finirai mon travail samedi. 2. N'ont-ils pas encore fini? 3. Vous pouvez avoir un pommier ou un prunier: choisissez! 4. Ils se battent pour rien. 5. Je ne crois jamais ce qu'il dit. 6. Pourquoi ne me croyez-vous pas? 7. Je l'ai lu, mais je ne le croyais pas. 8. Nous recevons un litre de lait chaque matin. 9. Il a reçu dix livres de pommes. 10. Vous les recevrez demain.

ANOTHER TONGUE TWISTER

Les soixante-six chemises fines de l'archiduchesse sont archi-sèches.

The sixty-six fine chemises of the archduchess are bone-dry.

ZOOLOGIE

Le maître: Citez-moi un quadrupède?
L'élève: Une table, monsieur.

Citer, to name, point out (as an example).

ROUNDING OFF YOUR KNOWLEDGE

A S the student has now reached a stage in the Course where he should be able to read French newspapers and even books, no further reading material is provided. The purpose of the present section, which is divided into 20 items, with an Appendix on Irregular Verbs and one on Correspondence, is to round off the student's knowledge, especially of French Grammar, and to leave him in a position where he can undertake adequately any ordinary problem of speaking, reading or writing, in French.

I

PECULIARITIES OF SOME VERBS IN -ER

1. envoyer = to send
Present: j'envoie, tu envoies, il envoie, nous envoyons, vous envoyez, ils envoient.
Imperfect: j'envoyais
Future: j'enverrai
Conditional: j'enverrais
Imperative: envoie, envoyons, envoyez
Perfect: j'ai envoyé

Similarly: nettoyer = to clean, il nettoie; essuyer = to wipe, il essuie. Verbs in -ayer may either make this change or keep the "y," e.g., payer, il paie or il paye.

2. manger = to eat
Present: see Lesson VIII.
Imperfect: je mangeais
Future: je mangerai
Conditional: je mangerais
Imperative: mange, mangeons, mangez
Perfect: j'ai mangé

3. appeler = to call
Present: see Lesson XXI.
Imperfect: j'appelais
Future: j'appellerai
Conditional: j'appellerais
Imperative: appelle, appelons, appelez
Perfect: j'ai appelé

4. acheter = to buy
Present: see Lesson XIV.
Imperfect: j'achetais
Future: j'achèterai
Conditional: j'achèterais
Imperative: achète, achetons, achetez
Perfect: j'ai acheté

5. espérer = to hope
Present: j'espère, tu espères, il espère, nous espérons, vous espérez, ils espèrent
Imperfect: j'espérais
Future: j'espérerai
Conditional: j'espérerais
Imperative: espère, espérons, espérez
Perfect: j'ai espéré

Note:
1. Verbs in -yer change y into i before e mute.
2. Verbs ending in -ger insert e after the g whenever the next letter is a or o. (so that the g remains soft throughout).
3. Most verbs in -ler double the l before e mute.
4. e becomes è when the next syllable has e mute and the consonant between is not doubled.
5. é becomes è when the final syllable contains e mute.

II

VERBS CONJUGATED WITH ÊTRE
Il est devenu vieux = He has become old
Elle est morte = She has died; she is dead
Ils sont restés chez nous = They have stayed with us

In addition to the verbs of motion in Lesson XVII, the following are conjugated with être:

rester = to stay (je suis resté)

devenir = to become (**je deviens, il devient, nous devenons, ils deviennent; je devenais; je deviendrai; je suis devenu**)

mourir = to die (**je meurs, il meurt, nous mourons, ils meurent; je mourrai; je suis mort**)

VERBS OF MOTION CONJUGATED WITH AVOIR

J'ai sauté = I have jumped.

Avez-vous nagé? = Have you been swimming?

Il n'a pas couru = He did not run.

Many verbs of motion are conjugated with **avoir**. The most frequent of these are:

sauter = to jump (**j'ai sauté**)

nager = to swim (**nous nageons, je nageais,** etc., like **manger**)

courir = to run (**je cours, il court, nous courons, ils courent; je courais; je courrai; j'ai couru**)

Certain verbs may be used either with **avoir** or **être**. Such verbs are:

rentrer
sortir
monter
descendre

These verbs are conjugated with **avoir** only when they have a direct object. Compare the following:

Il a monté les chaises = He took the chairs upstairs.

Il est monté = He went upstairs.

Elle a descendu vos malles = She took your trunks downstairs.

Elle est descendue = She went downstairs.

Il a sorti les enfants = He took the children out.

Il est sorti = He went out.

Ils ont rentré les enfants = They brought the children home.

Ils sont rentrés = They went (have come) home.

III

AGREEMENT OF PAST PARTICIPLE

1. When used with **avoir**:

(a)

j'ai acheté	I have bought
un chapeau	a hat
une cravate	a tie
des chapeaux	hats
des cravates	ties

When the object follows, the Past Participle is invariable.

(b) **Le chapeau que j'ai acheté** = The hat that I bought.

La cravate que j'ai achetée = The tie that I bought.

Les chapeaux que j'ai achetés = The hats that I bought.

Les cravates que j'ai achetées = The ties that I bought.

If the direct object precedes the Past Participle, the Participle must agree with that direct object in number and gender (i.e., -e is added in f.sing., -s in m.pl., -es in f.pl.).

2. Used with **être** the Participle agrees with the Subject in number and gender (except in the case of reflexive verbs—see below):

Il est arrivé = He has arrived
Elle est arrivée = She has arrived
Ils sont arrivés = They (m.) have arrived
Elles sont arrivées = They (f.) have arrived

Note:

1. This question of agreement concerns chiefly the spelling, as the forms are pronounced alike except when the past participle ends in a consonant. E.g., **allé, allée, allés, allées** are all pronounced alike (ah-lay); **dit** (dee), **dite** (deet), **dits** (dee), **dites** (deet).

2. When the object preceding a verb conjugated with **avoir** is an indirect object the Past Participle remains invariable, e.g., **je leur ai écrit** = I wrote to them.

3. When the Past Participle ends in -s, it remains unchanged in masculine plural, e.g., **pris** (pree) = taken; m.pl., **pris**; f., **prise**; f.pl., **prises**.

IV

REFLEXIVE VERBS

Va te coucher! = Go to bed!

Dites-leur de se dépêcher! = Tell them to hurry!

Elle s'est acheté une robe = She bought a dress for herself.

Est-ce que vous vous êtes blessé? = Did you hurt yourself?

Je me suis fait mal au pied = I hurt my foot.

Il s'intéresse à la musique = He is interested in music.

Il s'est marié avec une jeune Française = He got married to a young Frenchwoman.

Elle se trompe = She is making a mistake, she is mistaken.

Dites-lui de se taire! = Tell him to keep quiet!

Ils s'aiment beaucoup = They love each other very much.

Nous nous connaissons depuis longtemps = We have known each other for a long time.

Ils se sont reconnus = They recognised each other.

Nous ne nous sommes pas compris = We did not understand each other.

Nous nous manquons beaucoup = We miss each other very much.

Quand nous reverrons-nous? = When shall we see each other again?

Elle s'est couchée à neuf heures = She went to bed at nine o'clock.

Note from the above examples that some reflexives may also be reciprocal, naturally only in the plural. In that case **nous, vous** or **se** = "each other," "one another."

Compound tenses of reflexive verbs are formed with **être**. The Past Participle agrees with the reflexive object if it is direct.

V

VERBAL FORMS TERMINATING IN -ANT
(Present Participle)

The French Present Participle, corresponding to English verbal forms in "*-ing*," has the termination -ant, the same for all verbs; it can easily be formed from the 1st person plural of the Present Tense by replacing -ant for -ons; **nous parlons** =

we speak; **parlant**=speaking; **nous mangeons**=we eat; **mangeant**=eating, etc.

The only exceptions are: **ayant**=having; **étant**=being; **sachant**=knowing.

The Present Participle is often merely descriptive and therefore treated as an adjective, i.e., it agrees in gender and number with the noun it qualifies.

e.g., **le mois suivant**=next month
la semaine suivante=next week
les chapitres suivants=the following chapters
les personnes suivantes=the following persons

If the Present Participle has the function of a verb, i.e., if it expresses an action, it is invariable.

Ne voulant pas l'offenser, j'ai accepté son invitation=Not wishing to offend him, I have accepted his invitation.

Croyant que l'autre restaurant serait meilleur marché, nous y allâmes=Thinking that the other restaurant would be cheaper, we went there.

Étant fatigué, il s'est couché de bonne heure=Being tired, he went to bed early.

Ayant déjeuné très tard, je n'ai pas encore faim=Having lunched very late I am not hungry yet.

En voyageant on apprend beaucoup de choses=By travelling one learns a great many things.

En le faisant maintenant, vous gagnerez du temps=By doing it now you will save time.

En lui écrivant n'oubliez pas de le mentionner=When writing to him don't forget to mention it.

Il est tombé en traversant la rue=He fell while crossing the street.

Note in the last four examples the use of **en** to denote that one action is going on at the same time as another.

The French verbal form in **-ant** is much less frequently used in French than the corresponding form in "-ing" is in English. On the other hand the Infinitive is more widely used in French.

VI

THE INFINITIVE

In French the Infinitive is used:

(a) As Subject:

Voir c'est croire=Seeing is believing.

Il avoue avoir dit cela=He admits having said it.

Jouer n'est pas travailler=Playing is not working.

(b) After prepositions (except after **en**, which is followed by the Present Participle):

Après avoir vu le cadeau=After having seen the present.

Le plaisir de vous voir=The pleasure of seeing you.

Sans tourner la tête = Without turning his head.

Avant de commencer = Before starting.

Il passe son temps à lire = he spends his time reading.

(*c*) In public notices, posters, etc., the Infinitive is used instead of the Imperative:

Pousser—Tirer = *(on doors)* Push—Pull

Se méfier des contrefaçons = Beware of imitations

Prière de faire suivre = Please forward

Prière de ne pas marcher sur le gazon = Please do not walk on the grass

Défense d'afficher sous peine d'amende = Bill-stickers will be prosecuted

Défense de fumer = Smoking forbidden

(*d*) As in the above examples the Infinitive is very often governed by **à** or **de**:

une machine à coudre = a sewing machine

une machine à écrire = a typewriter

continuer à chanter = to continue to sing; to go on singing

refuser de payer = to refuse to pay

(*e*) The Infinitive is preferred to a subordinate clause when the subject does not change:

Je crois connaître votre cousin = I think (that) I know your cousin.

Il pense avoir raison = He thinks *(that)* he is right.

Je crois avoir vu votre femme = I think (that) I saw your wife.

(*f*) **aller chercher** = to call for, to go and fetch

envoyer chercher = to send for

VII

COMPLEMENTS OF VERBS

1. **Je l'ai rencontré hier** = I met him yesterday.

2. **Ne leur parlez pas** = Don't speak to them.

3. **Il a payé mille francs à mon père** = He paid my father a thousand francs.

4. **Dites à votre mère qu'il viendra à midi** = Tell your mother that he will come at noon.

5. **Elle a acheté une robe à sa fille** = She bought a dress for her daughter.

6. **J'ai emprunté cet argent à mon ami** = I borrowed this money from my friend.

7. **Il pense à elle** = He thinks of her.

French verbs with direct or indirect complements correspond to a great extent to English verbs with the same kind of complements (examples 1 and 2). Whereas English verbs often have the appearance of having two direct objects (example 3), in French one is direct and the other indirect. The preposition before an indirect complement cannot be omitted as in English (example 4). The preposition indicating the indirect complement is usually **à**, which not only translates "*to*" but also "*for*," "*from*," "*of*," etc. (examples 5-7).

The following are some of the most frequent verbs which take indirect complements in French but direct in English:

apprendre qch.[1] **à** qqn.[2] = to teach smn.[3] smth.[4]

conseiller à qqn. **de faire** qch. = to advise smn. to do smth.

commander à qqn. **de faire** qch. = to command smn. to do smth.

coûter à qqn. = to cost smn.

---

[1] **quelque chose**   [3] someone
[2] **quelqu'un**   [4] something

dire à qqn. **de faire** qch. = to tell smn. to do smth.

défendre à qqn. **de faire** qch. = to forbid smn. to do smth.

demander à qqn. **de faire** qch. = to ask smn. to do smth.

ouvrir à qqn. = to let smn. in

ordonner à qqn. **de faire** qch. = to order smn. to do smth.

obéir à qqn. = to obey smn.

permettre à qqn. **de faire** qch. = to allow smn. to do smth.

promettre à qqn. **de faire** qch. = to promise smn. to do smth.

pardonner à qqn. **d'avoir fait** qch. = to forgive smn. for having done smth.

plaire à qqn. = to please smn.

rappeler qch. **à** qqn. = to remind smn. of smth.

répondre à qqn. = to answer smn.

recommander à qqn. **de faire** qch. = to recommend smn. to do smth.

souhaiter qch. **à** qqn. = to wish smn. smth.

faire peur à qqn. = to frighten smn.

faire plaisir à qqn. = to please smn.

faire savoir qch. **à** qqn. = to let smn. know smth.

faire du bien à qqn. = to do smn. good

faire du mal à qqn. = to harm, hurt smn.

faire croire qch. **à** qqn. = to make smn. believe smth.

demander pardon à qqn. = to ask (to beg) smn.'s pardon

penser à qqn. = to think of smn.

Direct in French, but indirect in English, are the following:

aimer qqn. ou qch. = to be fond of smn. or smth.

attendre qqn. ou qch. = to wait for smn. or smth.

chercher qqn. ou qch. = to look for smn. or smth.

aller chercher qqn. ou qch. = to call for smn. or smth.

envoyer chercher qqn. ou qch. = to send for smn. or smth.

demander qqn. ou qch. = to ask for smn. or smth.

écouter qqn. ou qch. = to listen to smn. or smth.

regarder qqn. ou qch. = to look at smn. or smth.

sentir qch. = to smell of smth.

payer qch. = to pay for smth.

VIII

THE SUBJUNCTIVE

1. **Je sais qu'il est parti** = I know that he has left.

2. **Il est possible qu'il soit parti** = It is possible that he has (may have) left.

3. **Je doute qu'il soit parti** = I doubt if he has left.

4. **Pensez-vous qu'il soit parti?** = Do you think that he has (may have) left?

In sentence No. 1 (I know that he has left) the dependent clause expresses a plain statement of fact.

But when the statement in a dependent clause (as in sentences 2–4) is considered by the speaker as uncertain or doubtful, a different form of the verb is used in French: the Subjunctive Mood (plain statements are said to be in the Indicative Mood).

There are only two simple tenses of the Subjunctive, viz., Present and Imperfect, but the latter has become almost obsolete in modern spoken French, its place being taken by the Present Subjunctive.

The Present of the Subjunctive is formed from the Present Participle by changing the ending **-ant** into **-e, -es, -e; -ions, iez, -ent.**

	give	finish	lose	have	be
That I may	**que je donne**	**finisse**	**perde**	**aie**	**sois**
That you may	**que tu donnes**	**finisses**	**perdes**	**aies**	**sois**
That he may	**qu'il donne**	**finisse**	**perde**	**ait**	**soit**
That we may	**que nous donnions**	**finissions**	**perdions**	**ayons**	**soyons**
That you may	**que vous donniez**	**finissiez**	**perdiez**	**ayez**	**soyez**
That they may	**qu'ils donnent**	**finissent**	**perdent**	**aient**	**soient**

Note that both **avoir** and **être** have irregular Present Subjunctives which bear a close resemblance to the Imperative (see page 391).

Irregular Present Subjunctives are:

aller	**venir**	**boire**	**prendre**	**faire**
que j'aille	**vienne**	**boive**	**prenne**	**fasse**
que tu ailles	**viennes**	**boives**	**prennes**	**fasses**
qu'il aille	**vienne**	**boive**	**prenne**	**fasse**
que nous allions	**venions**	**buvions**	**prenions**	**fassions**
que vous alliez	**veniez**	**buviez**	**preniez**	**fassiez**
qu'ils aillent	**viennent**	**boivent**	**prennent**	**fassent**

	vouloir	**pouvoir**	**savoir**	**recevoir**
que je	**veuille**	**puisse**	**sache**	**reçoive**
que tu	**veuilles**	**puisses**	**saches**	**reçoives**
qu'il	**veuille**	**puisse**	**sache**	**reçoive**
que nous	**voulions**	**puissions**	**sachions**	**recevions**
que vous	**vouliez**	**puissiez**	**sachiez**	**receviez**
qu'ils	**veuillent**	**puissent**	**sachent**	**reçoivent**

The Subjunctive is used in the following cases:

(*a*) After verbs expressing some emotion, such as fear, joy, sorrow, surprise, regret, etc. Such are:

>   **craindre**=to fear
>   **avoir peur**=to be afraid
>   **être charmé**=to be delighted
>   **être surpris**=to be surprised
>   **s'étonner**=to be astonished
>   **être bien aise**=to be glad
>   **être fâché**=to be sorry
>   **se réjouir**=to rejoice
>   **c'est dommage**=it is a pity

(b) After verbs expressing a wish, will or desire, such as:

aimer = to like
désirer = to desire
vouloir = to be willing, to want
préférer = to prefer
souhaiter = to wish
avoir envie = to wish

Exception: **espérer** = to hope, which takes the Indicative.

(c) After expressions of doubt and uncertainty:

douter = to doubt
nier = to deny
il est douteux = it is doubtful
il est invraisemblable = it is unlikely
je ne crois pas = I don't believe

Il n'est pas sûr = it is not certain
There are many other such expressions.

(d) After the following:

il faut que = it is necessary that
il est possible que = it is possible that
afin que ⎱ so that
pour que ⎰
à moins que = unless
avant que = before
quoique ⎱ although
bien que ⎰
en cas que = in case that
de peur que = for fear that
il est temps que = it is time that

(e) In certain exclamations:

Vive le Président! = Long live the President!
Dieu soit loué! = God be praised!

IX

THE PASSIVE VOICE

(a) **Son père a été tué dans un accident** = His father has been killed in an accident.
Elle a été transportée à l'hôpital = She has been taken to hospital.
Ils sont très alarmés par la maladie de leur mère = They are very much alarmed by the illness of their mother.
Elles ont été reçues par votre ami = They have been received by your friend.

(b) **Comment s'appelle-t-il?** = What is he called?
Ces oranges se vendent trois cents francs la douzaine = These oranges are sold at 300 francs a dozen.
Vous vous trompez = You are mistaken.

(c) **Je n'en connais pas les détails** = I am not acquainted with the details.
On me dérange tout le temps = I am being disturbed all the time.
On appelle cela une fermeture éclair = That is called a zip fastener.
On lui a dit de partir = He was told to go.

(a) The passive voice is made up of the verb être and the Past Participle, which must agree in number and gender with the subject. In many cases the French passive

corresponds to the English passive. Note from the examples under (a) that **été** corresponds to the "*been*" of the English passive voice, and that **par** translates English "*by*" after a passive (as does **de**).

(b) Some reflexive verbs are translated into English by passives, e.g.,

se vendre = to be sold
s'appeler = to be called
se tromper = to be mistaken
s'étonner = to be astonished

(c) An active construction in French often corresponds to the English Passive (see also Lesson XXIX).

HOW TO TRANSLATE "DO," "DID'

(a) **Fume-t-elle?** = Does she smoke?
Elle ne fume pas = She does not smoke.
Si, elle fume = Yes, she does.

(b) 1. **Avez-vous commencé?** = Did you begin?
Je n'ai pas regardé = I didn't look.
L'avez-vous fait? = Did you do it?
Il n'a pas oublié = He did not forget.
Pourquoi ne l'avez-vous pas fait? = Why didn't you do it?
Lui avez-vous parlé? = Did you speak to him (*or her*)?
Y avez-vous pensé? = Did you think of it?

Je ne l'ai pas payé = I didn't pay for it.

2. **Êtes-vous sorti?** = Did you go out?
Êtes-vous parti de bonne heure? = Did you leave early?
Pourquoi n'y êtes-vous pas resté? = Why didn't you stay there?

3. **Vous êtes-vous amusé?** = Did you enjoy yourself?
Vous êtes-vous fait mal? = Did you hurt yourself?
S'est-il trompé? = Did he make a mistake?
Se sont-ils brûlés? = Did they burn themselves?

Nous ne nous sommes pas trompés = We didn't make a mistake.

(a) "*Do*" or "*does*" cannot be translated in questions or replies. "*Does she smoke?*" (the same as "*Is she smoking?*") = **Fume-t-elle?**

(b) There are three ways of translating "*Did you . . .?*" and "*I didn't . . .*"

1. **Avez-vous . . .? Je n'ai pas . . .** This is the usual translation.
2. **Êtes-vous . . .? Je ne suis pas . . .** When used with certain verbs: see Lesson XVII and p. 371.
3. **Vous êtes-vous . . .? Je ne me suis pas . . .** With all reflexive verbs.

Questions can also be made:

1. By a rising inflexion of the voice without change of word order (as in English): **Vous avez fumé?** = You have smoked *(been smoking)*?
2. By **est-ce que**, where the subject retains its place before the verb: **Est-ce qu'il a fumé?** = Did he smoke? Has he smoked *(been smoking)*?
3. When the subject of the question is a noun it precedes the verb, which must be followed by a personal pronoun of the same person, gender and number as the noun subject: **Votre frère fume-t-il?** = Does your brother smoke? Is your brother smoking?

X

MUST, OUGHT

Tu dois dire la vérité = You must tell the truth.
Tu devrais dire la vérité = You should *(ought to)* tell the truth.
Le train doit être en retard = The train must be late.
Vous devez venir me voir = You must come and see me.
Il doit tenir sa parole = He ought to keep his word.
Les enfants doivent obéir à leurs parents = Children ought to obey their parents.
Elle doit y être maintenant = She must be there now.
S'il n'est pas chez lui il a dû sortir = If he is not at home he has had to go out.

Nous devons faire ceci = We have to do this.

Il doit arriver de meilleure heure = He is to arrive earlier.

The verb **devoir** (of which the ordinary meaning is "*to owe*") is used in translating "must," "ought to," "should," "have to," "am to," "is to," "are to."

The forms of the verb **devoir** are:

Present: je dois, tu dois, il doit, nous devons, vous devez, ils doivent.
Imperfect: je devais, etc.
Preterite: je dus, etc.
Future: je devrai, etc.
Perfect: j'ai dû, f. due

The difference between **devoir** and **falloir**

(see Lesson XXII) is that **falloir** denotes absolute necessity, whereas **devoir** implies obligation or supposition. Another difference is that **devoir** can take a personal subject (**je, tu, vous, mon ami,** etc.), whereas **falloir** is always used impersonally, i.e., it can only have **il** as subject.

The forms of the verb **falloir** are:
Present: il faut
Imperfect: il fallait
Perfect: il a fallu
Preterite: il fallut
Future: il faudra
Conditional: il faudrait
Il me faut y aller＝I must go there
　(it is necessary for me to go there)

Je dois y aller＝I must go there
　(I am obliged to go there)

XI

THE ONE WHO, THOSE WHO (WHICH)
Lequel est le chef d'orchestre?＝Which one is the conductor?
Celui qui est debout en avant＝The one who is standing in front.
Lesquels sont les violonistes?＝Which are the violinists?
Ceux qui sont à gauche＝Those who are on the left.

Laquelle est la harpiste?＝Which one is the harpist?
Celle qui est assise à droite＝The one who is sitting on the right.
Lesquelles sont les cantatrices?＝Which are the singers?
Celles qui sont debout en arrière＝Those who are standing at the rear.

Celui qui conduit l'orchestre est le chef d'orchestre. Celle qui joue de la harpe est la harpiste.
Ceux qui jouent du violon sont les violonistes.　　Celles qui chantent sont les cantatrices.
Celle qui joue du piano est la pianiste.

Lequel est votre sac à main? = Which is your handbag?

Celui qui est sur la table = The one which is on the table.

Lesquels sont vos gants? = Which are your gloves?

Ceux qui sont un peu déchirés = Those which are slightly torn.

Laquelle est sa chaise? = Which is his chair?

Celle qui est au jardin = The one which is in the garden.

Celui qui = the one who, he who (referring to a masculine noun)

the one which, that which (referring to a masculine noun)

Celle qui = the one who, she who (referring to a feminine noun)

the one who, that which (referring to a feminine noun)

Ceux qui = those who *or* which (referring to a plural masculine noun)

Celles qui = those who *or* which (referring to a plural feminine noun)

Laquelle de ses peintures préférez-vous? = Which of his paintings do you prefer?

À laquelle de ses sœurs pensez-vous? = Which of his sisters are you thinking of?

Auquel de mes frères avez-vous écrit? = To which of my brothers did you write?

Duquel parlez-vous? = Of which one (masc.) are you speaking?

De laquelle parlez-vous? = Of which one (fem.) are you speaking?

Desquels parlez-vous? = Of which (masc. pl.) are you speaking?

Desquelles parlez-vous? = Of which (fem. pl.) are you speaking?

XII

QUELQUE

Ne voulez-vous pas acheter quelques fleurs? =
Won't you buy some flowers?
J'ai quelques livres pour vous =
I have got some books for you.
Il l'a trouvé quelque part =
He found it somewhere.
Quelqu'un m'a dit =
Someone told me.
Quelqu'une de ses amies =
One of his girl-friends.

Quelques-unes de ses amies =
Some (plural) of his girl friends.
Quelque jour =
Some day or other.
Ces quelques lignes =
These few lines.
Il y a quelques années =
Some years ago.
Quelques amis =
A few friends.

quelque = some, any, a few
quelqu'un, quelqu'une (plur. m. **quelques-uns**; plur. f. **quelques-unes**) =
somebody, someone, anybody, anyone
quelque chose (m.) = something
quelque part = somewhere
quelquefois = sometimes
quelconque = whatever, any

N.B.—**quelque chose de bon** = something good
rien de nouveau = nothing new
Rien and **quelque chose**, followed by an adjective, require **de**. Note that this adjective is always in the masculine.

XIII

TOUT, TOUS, TOUTE, TOUTES

1. **Tout le temps il est occupé** = All the time he is busy.

   Toute la famille est partie = All the family (the whole family) has left.

   J'ai travaillé tout le dimanche = I worked all Sunday.

   Il n'a pas travaillé toute la semaine = He did not work the whole week.

   Tous les hommes ne sont pas les mêmes = All men are not the same.

   Il a mangé tout le gâteau = He has eaten all the cake.

   Il a bu toute la bière = He has drunk all the beer.

   Il a fumé tous mes cigares = He has smoked all my cigars.

Voici toutes mes cigarettes = Here are all my cigarettes.

Elle n'a pas dormi toute la nuit = She did not sleep all night.

Je n'ai pas mangé toute la journée = I have not eaten all day.

Tout le monde est content = Everybody is pleased.

2. **Nous voulons tout voir** = We want to see everything.

Tout est perdu = All is lost.
Ils ont tout perdu = They lost everything.
J'ai vu tout cela = I have seen all that.

3. **C'est tout autre chose** = That is quite another thing.

   Je suis tout prêt = I am quite ready.

   Elle est tout heureuse = She is completely happy.

1. "All" as an adjective = **tout, toute, tous, toutes.**
2. "All" (= everything) as a pronoun = **tout.**
3. **tout** as an adverb = quite, completely.

Pronunciation:

    tout—*too* except in liaison where **t** is pronounced.

    toute, toutes—*toot.*

    tous—usually *too*, but when stressed and meaning "all of them" (etc.), *toos.*

E.g.,

Unstressed: **Où sont tous vos livres?** = Where are all your books?

Stressed: **Je les ai tous vendus** = I sold them all.

Unstressed: **J'ai vu tous vos enfants** = I have seen all your children.

Stressed: **Je les ai vus tous** = I have seen them all.

Note also the following expressions:
toute de suite=at once
tout à fait=entirely
tout à coup=suddenly
tout à l'heure=a moment ago; just now; in a moment.
tout au plus=at most
tout à vous (in closing a letter)=yours sincerely

tout de même=all the same
pas du tout or **du tout**=not at all
rien du tout=nothing at all
tout le monde=everybody

LA DAME ET LE MENDIANT
Mais vous ne me racontez pas du tout ιa même histoire qu'hier!
Naturellement, Madame: vous n'avez pas cru celle d'hier.

XIV

PEOPLE
1. **La nation**=nation
   la nation française=the French nation
2. **le peuple**=nation, the masses, the people
   le roi et son peuple=the king and his people
   la volonté du peuple=the will of the people
3. **les gens; le monde**=persons

les jeunes gens=young people (men)
les vieilles gens=old people
beaucoup de gens
beaucoup de monde }=many people
la plupart des gens
la plupart du monde }=most people
quels sont ces gens?=who are these people?
peu de monde=few people

4. **on dit**=people say, they say

XV

UN COUP DE . . . ETC.
un coup=a blow, a stroke, a knock, is very frequently used in combination with other words. Some of the most common are:
un coup de pied=a kick
un coup d'œil=a glance, a view

un coup de téléphone=a "ring"
un coup de tonnerre=a clap of thunder
un coup de poing=a blow (with the fist)
un coup de coude=a nudge
un coup de fusil=a rifle shot
un coup de bâton=a blow with a stick
un coup de brosse=a brushing
un coup de canon=a gun shot
un coup de théâtre=an unexpected incident
un coup de main=a helping hand
boire un coup=to have a drink
boire à petits coups=to sip
tout à coup=suddenly
tout d'un coup=all at once; at one blow
coup-sur-coup=in quick succession

XVI

WHO, WHOSE, WHOM, WHICH
(Relative Pronouns)
L'homme qui parle est mon père=The man who is speaking is my father.

C'est la jeune fille qui vous a écrit=It's the girl who wrote to you.
C'est la jeune fille à qui vous avez écrit=It's the girl to whom you wrote.

Les bateaux qui venaient du nord=The ships which came from the north.

L'homme que vous avez entendu parler= The man whom you heard speaking.

C'est une chose dont je ne suis pas surpris= That is a thing (something) I am not surprised at (at which I am not surprised).

Les bateaux que vous avez vus=The boats which you saw.

C'est la dame que vous avez vue l'autre jour =That is the lady whom you saw the other day.

Voici le livre que vous cherchez= Here is the book you are looking for.

Je ne connais pas le monsieur dont il parle=I don't know the man of whom he is speaking.

C'est la dame dont nous avons reçu la lettre=That is the lady from whom we have received the letter.

Le monsieur dont vous connaissez la fille=The man whose daughter you know

Qui=who, which, that—when Subject.

Que=whom, which, that— when the Direct Object.

Dont=whose, of whom, of which, from whom, from which.

Note. (1) Relative pronouns are always expressed in French, whereas in English they are frequently understood, e.g., **la dame que j'ai vue**=the lady I saw.

(2) When **dont** is used the word order must invariably be:

1.	2.	3.
Antecedent	Dont	Subject
Le monsieur	**dont**	**vous**

4.	5.
Verb	Direct Object
connaissez	**le fils**

(3) **Dont** can never be preceded by a preposition; if the relative pronoun is governed by a preposition, or depends on a noun which is itself governed by a preposition, **qui** is used when referring to persons, or some form of **lequel** (compare Lesson XXXI) when referring to things.

L'homme dans la maison de qui je demeurais =The man in whose house I lived . . .

Voilà le monsieur avec qui nous avons joué= This is the man with whom we have played.

C'est l'hôtel dans lequel nous avons demeuré =This is the hotel in which we lived.

Ce n'est pas le restaurant auquel je pense= This is not the restaurant I am thinking of.

C'est le garçon à qui j'ai payé l'addition=
This is the waiter to whom I paid the
bill.

La maison, à laquelle je vais vous conduire=
The house to which I am going to take
you.

C'est le jardin dans lequel nous étions l'année
dernière=This is the garden in which we
were last year.

Les gens avec qui nous avons joué=The
people we played with (with whom).

Les cartes avec lesquelles nous avons joué=
The cards we played with (with which).

XVII

WHO, WHOSE, WHOM, WHAT, WHICH
(Interrogative Pronouns)

Qui, que, lequel, laquelle, etc. (but not
"dont") are used as both relative pronouns
and interrogative pronouns (i.e., for asking
questions).

Qui est arrivé?
Qui est-ce qui est arrivé?
> Who has arrived?

Qu'est ce qui s'est passé?
> What has happened?

Que faites-vous?
Qu'est-ce que vous faites?
> What are you doing?

Qui voyez-vous?
Qui est-ce que vous voyez?
> Whom do you see?

Que voyez-vous?
Qu'est-ce que vous voyez?
> What do you see?

qui est-ce qui? ⎫
or qui?   ⎬ who?

qui est-ce que? ⎫
or qui?   ⎬ whom?

FRC—N

qu'est-ce qui? ⎫
or quoi?   ⎬ what? (Subject)

qu'est-ce que? ⎫
or que?   ⎬ what? (Object)

À qui parlez-vous?=Whom are you speaking to?

De qui parlez-vous?=Whom are you speaking of?

À quoi pensez-vous?=What are you thinking of?

De quoi parlez-vous?=What are you speaking of?

Note.—Prepositions are followed by qui
when referring to persons, and by quoi
when referring to things.

Quoi as the subject is used when the verb
is omitted:

Quoi de nouveau?=What is the news?

Quoi is also used as a kind of noun
equivalent in the following expressions:

Il a de quoi vivre=He has enough to live on.

Donnez-moi de quoi écrire=Give me
something to write with.

Il n'y a pas de quoi=Don't mention it (in
answer to apologies).

Un je ne sais quoi=An indefinable something.

Lequel, laquelle, lesquels, lesquelles,
auquel, à laquelle, auxquels, auxquelles,
etc., are used in the sense of which (one)?
(Compare Lesson XXXI.)

Lequel de vos livres est le plus intéressant?
=Which of your books is the most
interesting?

XVIII

USE OF DE AND À

une lanterne de papier = a paper lantern
une table de bois = a wooden table
la lune de miel = honeymoon

un cadeau de noces = a wedding present
un voyage d'agrément = a pleasure trip
une maison de campagne = a country house
un chapeau de paille = a straw hat
un timbre de vingt francs = a twenty franc stamp
le train de minuit = the midnight train
une leçon de français = a French lesson
un professeur de français = a teacher of French

(b) **un bateau à voiles** = a sailing boat
un moulin à vent = a windmill

une brosse à dents = a tooth-brush
une cuillère à thé = a teaspoon
un verre à vin = a wine-glass

Note from the above examples the use of **de** and **à** to translate English nouns used as adjectives.

(a) When the English adjective means "made of," "composed of," "belonging to," the French equivalent is a noun preceded by **de**.

(b) When the English adjective means "for the purpose of," "by means of," a noun preceded by **à** is used in French.

(c) Sometimes when definite things are referred to or are used with nouns which usually take the definite article in French (although not in English), the definite article is used in connection with **de** or **à**:

la boîte aux lettres = the letter-box
la tour de l'église = the church tower
le prix du café = the price of coffee
aller à l'église = to go to church
être à l'école = to be in school
du nord au sud = from north to south
de l'est à l'ouest = from east to west
du matin au soir = from morning to night

(d) After **rien, quoi, personne, quelqu'un** and **quelque chose**, **de** is inserted before an adjective:

e.g., **quelque chose d'intéressant** = something interesting

rien de nouveau = nothing new
il n'y avait personne d'important = there was no one important there

est-ce qu'il y avait quelqu'un de tué dans l'accident?=was anybody killed in the accident?

quoi de si pressé?=what is the hurry about?

(*e*) For **de** used after expressions of quantity see Lesson XXIX.

(*f*) **Jouer**=to play; (1) with **de** when applying to a musical instrument: **jouer du piano**=to play the piano; **jouer de la harpe**=to play the harp, etc.; (2) with **à** when referring to games; **jouer au tennis**= to play tennis; **jouer aux cartes**=to play cards, etc.

Quoi de si pressé?

XIX

DE OR À BEFORE INFINITIVE
(*a*)
Essayez de travailler un peu=Try to work a little.

Avez-vous fini de le lire?=Have you finished reading it?

Elle a oublié de me réveiller=She forgot to wake me up.

J'ai offert de le lui prêter=I offered to lend it to him (or her).

Il refuse de nous aider=He refuses to help us.

Tâchez d'être ici à neuf heures=Try to be here at nine o'clock.

Il n'a pas besoin de travailler=He does not need to work.

J'ai envie d'aller au théâtre demain=I should like to go to the theatre tomorrow.

Il a honte de ne pas l'avoir fait=He is ashamed of not having done it.

Il a peur de vous le dire=He is afraid to tell you.

Vous avez eu raison de ne pas le leur dire= You were right in not telling them.

Nous n'avons pas le temps d'aller le voir= We have not time to go and see him.

Il n'a pas l'air d'être très intelligent=He does not seem to be very intelligent.

Je suis content de vous avoir vu=I am glad to have seen you.

Il est difficile d'apprendre cette langue=It is difficult to learn that language.

C'est aimable de la part de votre sœur de me prêter son parapluie=It is kind of your sister to lend me her umbrella.

(b)

Il aime à manger des huîtres=He likes to eat oysters.

Vous a-t-il aidé à faire cela?=Did he help you to do this?

J'ai beaucoup à faire aujourd'hui=I have much to do today.

Elle apprend à chanter=She is learning to sing.

Je suis prêt à sortir=I am ready to go out.

Je n'ai rien à lui dire=I have nothing to tell him (or her).

Cherchez à le comprendre=Try to understand him.

Commençons à jouer=Let us begin to play.

Elle demande à vous parler=She wants to speak to you.

Elle demande à voir le directeur=She asks to see the director.

J'ai du travail à faire=I have some work to do.

Cette règle est facile à comprendre=This rule is easy to understand.

The usual translation of "to" before an infinitive is de. If "to" denotes the aim or end in view à is used.

Especially note the following:

With de:

il s'agit de=it is a question of

finir de=to finish

avoir besoin de=to need to

avoir envie de=to wish, want, desire

avoir honte de=to be ashamed to

avoir peur de=to be afraid to

avoir raison de=to be right to

avoir tort de=to be wrong to

avoir l'amabilité de=to have the kindness to

avoir l'air de=to seem, to appear

avoir l'obligeance de=to be good enough to

de la part de (de ma part, de sa part, etc.)= on behalf of, on the part of

With à:

prendre plaisir à=to take pleasure in

passer le temps à=to pass the time in

être habitué à=to be accustomed to

prêt à=ready to

habitué à=accustomed to

acheter à tempérament=to buy on instalments

être à la mode=to be in fashion

filer à l'anglaise=to take French leave

Note.—1. Il est, followed by an Infinitive requires de; c'est requires à.

Il est difficile de faire cela

C'est difficile à faire
    That's difficult to do

2. Verbs or adjectives take pour (i.e., in order to) before Infinitive, when cause. reason or motive is stated.

E.g. **Il fait trop chaud pour rester au soleil**
= It is too hot to remain in the sun.

Il fait trop sombre pour lire = It is too
dark to read.

3. The Infinitive is used without a
preposition after the following verbs:

pouvoir = to be able
savoir = to know how to
vouloir = to wish
falloir = to be necessary
devoir = to owe
aller = to go ⎱ and all other verbs of
venir = to come ⎰ motion
faire = to make
laisser = to let
oser = to dare
voir = to see
entendre = to hear
sentir = to feel
désirer = to desire
préférer ⎱ = to prefer
aimer mieux ⎰
croire = to believe
and other verbs of thinking,
wishing and declaring.

E.g. **Il me fallait le quitter ce matin** = I had
to leave him this morning.

Savez-vous jouer du piano? = Can you
play the piano?

Je l'ai vue sortir = I saw her go out.

Il voulut dîner tard = He wanted to
dine late.

Allez-vous me donner l'argent? = Are
you going to give me the money?

J'espère revenir bientôt = I hope to
return soon.

Nous préférons rester chez nous = We
prefer to stay at home.

XX

RULES FOR GENDERS

Unfortunately no rules can be given for
determining the gender of every noun. The
following rules, however, will be found
useful as they cover a considerable number
of nouns.

Masculine are:

1. Men and male animals—**un homme, le
   chat, le chien, le tigre.**
2. Seasons, months, days—**le printemps, le
   mois de janvier, le lundi.**
3. Winds, cardinal points—**le nord, le sud,
   l'est, l'ouest.**
4. Mountains, metals, trees—**le Mont
   Blanc, le fer, le rosier.**
5. Adjectives and infinitives used as nouns
   —**le bleu, le manger, le boire.**
6. Most nouns ending in a consonant—**le
   prix, le rat, le bras, le fort, le bout.**

7. Most nouns ending in a sounded vowel
   —**le café, un opéra, le bateau, le pneu.**
8. Nouns ending in -ment—**le département,
   le gouvernement, le régiment.** (Exception: **la jument,** mare.)
9. Nouns ending in -age—**le village, le
   langage, le garage.** (Exceptions: **la
   cage, une image, la nage, la page** (of a
   book), **la plage, la rage.**)

Feminine are:

1. Women and female animals—**la femme,
   la chatte, la chienne, la tigresse.**
2. Most countries ending in -e mute—**La
   France, La Belgique, La Russie.**
3. Words ending in -tion—**la nation, la
   révolution.** (Exception: **le bastion.**)
4. Most nouns ending in -ie, -te, tie—**la
   boulangerie, l'amitié** (friendship).
   (Exceptions: **le parapluie, le génie,
   un incendie, le foie.**)

5. Abstract nouns ending in -eur—**la peur, la chaleur, la douleur.** (Exceptions: **l'honneur, le labeur, l'heur** (luck, chance), **le bonheur, le malheur.**)

6. Abstract nouns ending in -té—**la majesté, la qualité, la liberté, l'égalité, la fraternité.**

Some nouns whether masculine or feminine apply to either sex: **le professeur** = the teacher (man or woman); **la brute** = the brute (man or animal); **la recrue** = the recruit; **la connaissance** = acquaintance; **la personne** = person.

Some nouns are either masculine or feminine according to the sex of the person referred to: **le** or **la concierge; un** or **une enfant, éleve** (pupil), **artiste.**

A few nouns have two genders with change of meaning. The most frequently used of them are:

le livre = book; **la livre** = pound
le page = page-boy; **la page** = page (of a book)
le tour = turn, trick; **la tour** = tower
le critique = critic; **la critique** = criticism
le manche = handle; **la manche** = sleeve; **La Manche** = English Channel
le poêle = stove; **la poêle** = frying pan
le mousse = cabin boy; **la mousse** = froth, moss
le voile = veil; **la voile** = sail

APPENDIX I

Synopsis of Conjugations (Regular and Irregular Verbs)

THE AUXILIARY VERBS

AVOIR (to have) ÊTRE (to be)

Present Participle

ayant = having   **étant** = being

Past Participle

eu = had   **été** = been

Compound (Perfect) Participle

ayant eu =   **ayant été** =
  having had   having been

Indicative Mood

Present

j'ai = I have	**je suis** = I am
tu as = thou hast	**tu es** = thou art
il a = he has	**il est** = he is
elle a = she has	**elle est** = she is
nous avons = we have	**nous sommes** = we are
vous avez = you have	**vous êtes** = you are
ils ont = they have	**ils sont** = they are
elles ont = they have	**elles sont** = they are

Imperfect

j'avais		**j'étais**
tu avais	I was	**tu étais**
il avait	having	**il était**
nous avions	I had,	**nous étions**
vous aviez	etc.	**vous étiez**
ils avaient		**ils étaient**

I was being I was, etc.

Preterite

j'eus		**je fus**
tu eus		**tu fus**
il eut	I had,	**il fut**
nous eûmes	etc.	**nous fûmes**
vous eûtes		**vous fûtes**
ils eurent		**ils furent**

I was, etc.

Future

j'aurai		**je serai**
tu auras	I shall	**tu seras**
il aura	have,	**il sera**
nous aurons	etc.	**nous serons**
vous aurez		**vous serez**
ils auront		**ils seront**

I shall be, etc.

Conditional

j'aurais		**je serais**
tu aurais	I	**tu serais**
il aurait	should	**il serait**
nous aurions	have,	**nous serions**
vous auriez	etc.	**vous seriez**
ils auraient		**ils seraient**

I should be, etc.

Compound Forms, see page 392

Imperative

aie	= have	**sois**	= be
ayez		**soyez**	
ayons = let us have		**soyons** = let us be	

Subjunctive Mood

Present		Imperfect	
que j'aie		que j'eusse	
que tu aies		que tu eusses	
qu'il ait	that I may	qu'il eût	that I might
que nous ayons	have, etc.	que nous eussions	have, etc.
que vous ayez		que vous eussiez	
qu'ils aient		qu'ils eussent	
que je sois		que je fusse	
que tu sois		que tu fusses	
qu'il soit	that I may	qu'il fût	that I might
que nous soyons	be, etc.	que nous fussions	be, etc.
que vous soyez		que vous fussiez	
qu'ils soient		qu'ils fussent	

THE REGULAR VERBS

I	II	III
donner = to give	finir = to finish	vendre = to sell

Present Participle

donnant = giving	finissant = finishing	vendant = selling

Past Participle

donné = given	fini = finished	vendu = sold

Compound (Perfect) Participle

ayant donné = having given   ayant fini = having finished   ayant vendu = having sold

Indicative Mood

Present

je donne		je finis		je vends	
tu donnes	I give,	tu finis	I finish,	tu vends	I sell,
il donne	I am	il finit	I am	il vend	I am
nous donnons	giving,	nous finissons	finishing,	nous vendons	selling,
vous donnez	etc.	vous finissez	etc.	vous vendez	etc.
ils donnent		ils finissent		ils vendent	

Imperfect

je donnais		je finissais		je vendais	
tu donnais	I was	tu finissais	I was	tu vendais	I was
il donnait	giving,	il finissait	finishing,	il vendait	selling,
nous donnions	etc.	nous finissions	etc.	nous vendions	etc.
vous donniez		vous finissiez		vous vendiez	
ils donnaient		ils finissaient		ils vendaient	

Preterite

je donnai		je finis		je vendis	
tu donnas		tu finis		tu vendis	
il donna	I gave,	il finit	I	il vendit	I sold,
nous donnâmes	etc.	nous finîmes	finished,	nous vendîmes	etc.
vous donnâtes		vous finîtes	etc.	vous vendîtes	
ils donnèrent		ils finirent		ils vendirent	

Future

je donnerai	} I shall give, etc.		je finirai	} I shall finish, etc.		je vendrai	} I shall sell, etc.	
tu donneras			tu finiras			tu vendras		
il donnera			il finira			il vendra		
nous donnerons			nous finirons			nous vendrons		
vous donnerez			vous finirez			vous vendrez		
ils donneront			ils finiront			ils vendront		

Conditional

je donnerais	} I should give, etc.	je finirais	} I should finish, etc.	je vendrais	} I should sell, etc.
tu donnerais		tu finirais		tu vendrais	
il donnerait		il finirait		il vendrait	
nous donnerions		nous finirions		nous vendrions	
vous donneriez		vous finiriez		vous vendriez	
ils donneraient		ils finiraient		ils vendraient	

Imperative

donne } = give
donnez
donnons = let us give

finis } = finish
finissez
finissons = let us finish

vends } = sell
vendez
vendons = let us sell

Subjunctive Mood

Present

que je donne	} that I may give, etc.	que je finisse	} that I may finish, etc.	que je vende	} that I may sell, etc.
que tu donnes		que tu finisses		que tu vendes	
qu'il donne		qu'il finisse		qu'il vende	
que nous donnions		que nous finissions		que nous vendions	
que vous donniez		que vous finissiez		que vous vendiez	
qu'ils donnent		qu'ils finissent		qu'ils vendent	

Imperfect

que je donnasse	} that I might give, etc.	que je finisse	} that I might finish, etc.	que je vendisse	} that I might sell, etc.
que tu donnasses		que tu finisses		que tu vendisses	
qu'il donnât		qu'il finît		qu'il vendît	
que nous donnassions		que nous finissions		que nous vendissions	
que vous donnassiez		que vous finissiez		que vous vendissiez	
qu'ils donnassent		qu'ils finissent		qu'ils vendissent	

Compound Forms

I have, etc.	j'ai	I shall have, etc.	j'aurai	that I may have, etc.	que j'aie	eu had été been donné given fini finished vendu sold
	tu as		tu auras		que tu aies	
	il a		il aura		qu'il ait	
	nous avons		nous aurons		que nous ayons	
	vous avez		vous aurez		que vous ayez	
	ils ont		ils auront		qu'ils aient	
I had, etc.	j'avais	I should have, etc.	j'aurais	that I might have, etc.	que j'eusse	
	tu avais		tu aurais		que tu eusses	
	il avait		il aurait		qu'il eût	
	nous avions		nous aurions		que nous eussions	
	vous aviez		vous auriez		que vous eussiez	
	ils avaient		ils auraient		qu'ils eussent	

REFLEXIVE VERBS

Reflexive verbs have two pronouns of the same person—one is the subject, the other the object. They form their compound tenses with être.

The past participle of reflexive verbs agrees in number and gender with the reflexive pronoun if it is the direct object. If this pronoun is the indirect object, the past participle does not agree with it.

Conjugation of the Reflexive Verb, se reposer = to rest.

Present Participle: se reposant = resting.
Past Participle: reposé = rested.

Indicative Mood

Present	Preterite	Imperfect
I rest, I am resting	I rested	I rested, I was resting
je me repose	je me reposai	je me reposais
tu te reposes	tu te reposas	tu te reposais
il se repose	il se reposa	il se reposait
nous nous reposons	nous nous reposâmes	nous nous reposions
vous vous reposez	vous vous reposâtes	vous vous reposiez
ils se reposent	ils se reposèrent	ils se reposaient

Future	Conditional	Imperative
I shall rest	I should rest	
je me reposerai	je me reposerais	repose-toi ⎫
tu te reposeras	tu te reposerais	reposez-vous ⎬ = have a rest
il se reposera	il se reposerait	reposons-nous = let us have a rest
nous nous reposerons	nous nous reposerions	
vous vous reposerez	vous vous reposeriez	
ils se reposeront	ils se reposeraient	

Subjunctive Mood

Present	Imperfect
that I may rest	that I might rest
que je me repose	que je me reposasse
que tu te reposes	que tu te reposasses
qu'il se repose	qu'il se reposât
que nous nous reposions	que nous nous reposassions
que vous vous reposiez	que vous vous reposassiez
qu'ils se reposent	qu'ils se reposassent

Compound Tenses

I have rested		I shall have rested	
je me suis ⎫	reposé	je me serai ⎫	reposé
tu t'es ⎬	or	tu te seras ⎬	or
il or elle s'est ⎭	reposée	il or elle se sera ⎭	reposée
nous nous sommes ⎫	reposés	nous nous serons ⎫	reposés
vous vous êtes ⎬	or	vous vous serez ⎬	or
ils or elles se sont ⎭	reposées	ils or elles se seront ⎭	reposées

I had rested		I should have rested	
je m'étais ⎫	reposé	je me serais ⎫	reposé
tu t'étais ⎬	or	tu te serais ⎬	or
il or elle s'était ⎭	reposée	il or elle se serait ⎭	reposée
nous nous étions ⎫	reposés	nous nous serions ⎫	reposés
vous vous étiez ⎬	or	vous vous seriez ⎬	or
ils or elles s'étaient ⎭	reposées	ils or elles se seraient ⎭	reposées

That I may have rested

que je me sois
que tu te sois
qu'il *or* qu'elle se soit
que nous nous soyons
que vous vous soyez
qu'ils *or* qu'elles se soient

} reposé
or
reposée
reposés
or
reposées

That I might have rested

que je me fusse
que tu te fusses
qu'il *or* qu'elle se fût
que nous nous fussions
que vous vous fussiez
qu'ils *or* qu'elles se fussent

} reposé
or
reposée
reposés
or
reposées

Conjugated Negatively

je ne me repose pas
tu ne te reposes pas
il ne se repose pas, etc.

je ne me reposais pas, etc.

je ne me suis pas reposé
tu ne t'es pas reposé
il ne s'est pas reposé

je ne me reposerai pas, etc.

Conjugated Interrogatively

est-ce que je me repose?
te reposes-tu?
se repose-t-il? etc.

me reposais-je? etc.

me suis-je reposé?
t'es-tu reposé?
s'est-il reposé? etc.

me reposerai-je? etc.

Conjugated Negatively-Interrogatively

est-ce que je ne me repose pas?
ne te reposes-tu pas?
ne se repose-t-il pas?

ne me reposais-je pas? etc.

ne me suis-je pas reposé?
ne t'es-tu pas reposé?
ne s'est-il pas reposé?

ne me reposerais-je pas? etc.

Imperative Conjugated Negatively

ne te repose pas, ne vous reposez pas, ne nous reposons pas

IRREGULAR VERBS IN COMMON USE

(*a*) The verbs are arranged in alphabetical order.

(*b*) Compound forms are not given; when nothing is said to the contrary they are formed with **avoir** + the past participle.

(*c*) The pronouns are omitted in the following tables. If you find this at first confusing write on a loose slip of paper: **je, tu, il (elle), nous, vous, ils (elles).**

(*d*) Since the endings of the Imperfect, Preterite, Future, Conditional and Subjunctive are always regular they can be ascertained from the preceding tables. Only the 1st person singular (**je** . . .) is given below.

(*e*) Only the familiar form of the Imperative is given. The other forms are identical with the plural forms of the Present Indicative ending in -ez and -ons.[1]

Infinitive	Participles	Present Indicative	Imperfect, Preterite	Future, Conditional	Imperative	Subjunctive
Aller[2] *go* (*aux.* être)	allant allé	vais, vas, va allons, -ez, vont	allais allai	irai irais	va (vas-y)	que j'aille que j'allasse
Boire *drink*	buvant bu	bois, -s, -t buvons, -ez, boivent	buvais bus	boirai boirais	bois	que je boive que je busse
Conduire *conduct*	conduisant conduit	conduis, -s, -t conduisons, -ez, -ent	conduisais conduisis	conduirai conduirais	conduis	que je conduise que je conduisisse

[1] The vous imperatives of dire, faire, and savoir are dites, faites, and sachez, respectively.

[2] Like aller is conjugated: s'en aller = to go away (je m'en vais, tu t'en vas, il s'en va, etc.).

Infinitive	Participles	Present Indicative	Imperfect, Preterite	Future, Conditional	Imperative	Subjunctive
Connaître *know*	connaissant connu	connais, -s, aît connaissons, -ez, -ent	connaissais connus	connaîtrai connaîtrais	connais	que je connaisse que je connusse
Courir *run*	courant couru	cours, -s, -t courons, -ez, -ent	courais courus	courrai courrais	cours	que je coure que je courusse
Craindre *fear*	craignant craint	crains, -s, -t craignons, -ez, -ent	craignais craignis	craindrai craindrais	crains	que je craigne que je craignisse
Croire *believe*	croyant cru	crois, -s, -t croyons, -ez, croient	croyais crus	croirai croirais	crois	que je croie que je crusse
Devoir *owe*	devan'. dû, (f.) due	dois, -s, -t devons, -ez, doivent	devais dus	devrai devrais	—	que je doive que je dusse
Dire *say*	disant dit	dis, -s, -t disons, dites, disent	disais dis	dirai dirais	dis	que je dise que je disse
Dormir[1] *sleep*	dormant dormi	dors, -s, -t dormons, -ez, -ent	dormais dormis	dormirai dormirais	dors	que je dorme que je dormisse
Écrire *write*	écrivant écrit	écris, -s, -t écrivons, -ez, -ent	écrivais écrivis	écrirai écrirais	écris	que j'écrive que j'écrivisse
Envoyer *send*	envoyant envoyé	envoie, -es, -e envoyons, -ez, envoient	envoyais envoyai	enverrai enverrais	envoie	que j'envoie que j'envoyasse
Faire *do, make*	faisant fait	fais, -s, -t faisons, faites, font	faisais fis	ferai ferais	fais	que je fasse que je fisse
Falloir *be necessary*	fallu	il faut	il fallait il fallut	il faudra il faudrait	—	qu'il faille qu'il fallût
Lire *read*	lisant lu	lis, -s, -t lisons, -ez, -ent	lisais lus	lirai lirais	lis	que je lise que je lusse
Mettre *put*	mettant mis	mets, mets, met mettons, -ez, mettent	mettais mis	mettrai mettrais	mets	que je mette que je misse
Mourir *die* (aux. être)	mourant mort	meurs, meurs, meurt mourons, -ez, meurent	mourais mourus	mourrai mourrais	meurs	que je meure que je mourusse
Ouvrir[3] *open*	ouvrant ouvert	ouvre, -s, -e ouvrons, -ez, -ent	ouvrais ouvris	ouvrirai ouvrirais	ouvre	que j'ouvre que j'ouvrisse
Pleuvoir *rain*	pleuvant plu	il pleut	il pleuvait il plut	il pleuvra il pleuvrait	—	qu'il pleuve qu'il plût
Pouvoir *be able*	pouvant pu	peux (or puis), -x, -t pouvons, -ez, peuvent	pouvais pus	pourrai pourrais	—	que je puisse que je pusse
Prendre[4] *take*	prenant pris	prends, -s, prend prenons, -ez, prennent	prenais pris	prendrai prendrais	prends	que je prenne que je prisse
Recevoir *receive*	recevant reçu	reçois, -s, -t recevons, -ez, reçoivent	recevais reçus	recevrai recevrais	reçois	que je reçoive que je reçusse
Rire[5] *laugh*	riant ri	ris, -s, -t rions, -ez, -ent	riais ris	rirai rirais	ris	que je rie que je risse
Savoir *know*	sachant su	sais, -s, -t savons, -ez, savent	savais sus	saurai saurais	sache	que je sache que je susse

[1] Like **dormir** are conjugated: **partir** = to set out, to start; **mentir** = to lie; **servir** = to serve; **sentir** = to feel.
[2] This verb changes its y into i before e mute.
[3] Like **ouvrir** are conjugated: **couvrir** = to cover; **découvrir** = to discover; **offrir** = to offer; **souffrir** = to suffer.
[4] Like **prendre** are conjugated: **apprendre** = to learn; **comprendre** = to understand; **entreprendre** = to undertake.
[5] Like **rire** is conjugated: **sourire** = to smile.

Infinitive	Participles	Present Indicative	Imperfect, Preterite	Future, Conditional	Imperative	Subjunctive
Suivre *follow*	suivant suivi	suis, -s, -t suivons, -ez, -ent	suivais suivis	suivrai suivrais	suis	que je suive que je suivisse
Tenir[1] *hold*	tenant tenu	tiens, -s, -t tenons, -ez, tiennent	tenais tins	tiendrai tiendrais	tiens	que je tienne que je tinsse
Venir[2] *come* (aux. être)	venant venu	viens, -s, -t venons, -ez, viennent	venais vins	viendrai viendrais	viens	que je vienne que je vinsse
Vivre *live*	vivant vécu	vis, -s, -t vivons, -ez, -ent	vivais vécus	vivrai vivrais	vis	que je vive que je vécusse
Voir *see*	voyant vu	vois, -s, -t voyons, -ez, voient	voyais vis	verrai verrais	vois	que je voie que je visse
Vouloir *wish*	voulant voulu	veux, x, -t voulons, -ez, veulent	voulais voulus	voudrai voudrais	veuille veuillez	que je veuille que je voulusse

[1] Like tenir are conjugated: appartenir=to belong; contenir=to contain; obtenir=to obtain; retenir=to retain.
[2] Like venir are conjugated: devenir=to become; revenir=to return; se souvenir (de)=to remember.

APPENDIX II
LA CORRESPONDANCE

1. Cartes d'invitation

Monsieur et Madame Dupont prient Madame X . . .
de leur faire le plaisir de venir dîner avec eux lundi prochain
le 23 avril à 7 heures 30.

Monsieur et Madame Dupont prient Monsieur X . . .
de leur faire l'honneur de venir passer la soirée chez eux
samedi le 4 décembre.

2. On accepte l'invitation

Madame X . . . remercie Monsieur et Madame Dupont
de leur aimable invitation à laquelle elle se rendra avec le
plus vif plaisir.

3. On décline l'invitation

(a) Monsieur X . . . remercie Monsieur et Madame
Dupont de leur aimable invitation. Il regrette vivement
qu'un engagement antérieur le prive du plaisir de s'y rendre
et les prie d'agréer ses hommages respectueux.

(b) Madame,
Je vous remercie infiniment de votre aimable invitation.
Des affaires urgentes me forçant à quitter Paris, je devrai
malheureusement me priver du plaisir de me présenter chez
vous lundi. Je vous prie, Madame, de croire à mon vif
regret.

J'ai l'honneur d'être, Madame,
votre très dévoué,
X . . .

prier=to ask
faire plaisir=to give pleasure
prochain=next
la soirée=the evening

remercier=to thank
se rendre=to go
vif=great

vivement=extremely
antérieur=previous
priver=to deprive
agréer=to receive, to accept
infiniment=infinitely
les affaires (f.pl.)= business
je devrai=I shall have to
malheureusement= unfortunately
croire=believe
l'honneur d'être=the honour of being
dévoué=devoted

4. Renseignement

Monsieur,
   Le 18 de ce mois (du mois prochain), j'arriverai à . . .
(accompagné de ma famille); je compte rester quinze jours.
   Veuillez donc m'informer si vous tenez à ma disposition
une chambre à un lit (deux lits) et à quel prix, tous frais
compris.
   Dans l'attente d'une prompte et affirmative réponse,
veuillez agréer, Monsieur, mes salutations.
                                          Jules Lambert.

le renseignement =
   enquiry
compter = to count, to
   expect
quinze jours = a fortnight
veuillez m'informer =
   please inform me
la disposition = disposal
les frais (m.pl.) = costs
dans l'attente = awaiting

5. Réponse à No. 4

Monsieur,
   En réponse à votre lettre j'ai le plaisir de vous faire savoir
que j'aurai une chambre à deux lits à votre disposition le
18 juillet.
   Le prix de la pension, chambre et taxes comprises est de
1500 frs. par personne.
   La pension comprend:
Petit déjeuner—Café au lait ou thé, pain et beurre.
Déjeuner—Poisson, plat de viande, légumes, dessert et café.
Dîner—Potage, plat de viande, légumes, dessert.
La boisson n'est pas comprise.
   Nous vous garantissons une nourriture soignée et une
belle et grande chambre avec tout confort.
   Espérant l'honneur de votre visite, veuillez agréer,
Monsieur, l'assurance de ma considération dévouée.
                                          (Mme) H. Picard

faire savoir = to let know

comprendre = to include

le potage = soup
la boisson = drinks
la nourriture = food

soigné = first-rate

espérer = to hope

6. Réponse à No. 5

Madame,
   Veuillez me réserver une grande chambre à deux lits, de
préférence avec salle de bain. Nous arriverons samedi soir
à neuf heures.
                          Sincères salutations,
                                          Jules Lambert.

de préférence = prefer-
   ably
la salle de bain = bath-
   room

7. Lettre privée

Mademoiselle,
   Vous serez sans doute surprise de recevoir cette lettre,
puisque nous ne nous connaissons pas.
   Un ami d'affaires de mon père, Monsieur Pernot de
Toulon, nous a écrit qu'une dame française avait exprimé
le désir d'entrer en correspondance avec une Anglaise.
Ayant l'intention depuis longtemps de rafraîchir mes
connaissances de français acquises à l'école, je me permets
de venir vous faire la proposition suivante:
   Nous nous écrirons tous les quinze jours—vous en anglais

puisque = since
connaître = to know
exprimer = to express
ayant = having, as I have
depuis longtemps = for a
   long time past
rafraîchir = to brush up
la connaissance = know-
   ledge
suivant = following
tous les quinze jours =
   every fortnight

et moi en français—en nous retournant chaque fois les lettres corrigées. Qu'en pensez-vous?

Je vais donc commencer par vous dire qui je suis. Mon nom est Florence May. J'ai vingt ans et j'étudie les langues modernes (français, allemand, italien) à une des écoles polytechniques à Londres.

Je suis une fervente du ski et du tennis. Le mois prochain je prendrai part à un voyage organisé par un des bureaux de voyages dans les montagnes d'Écosse pour y faire du ski. Je vous écrirai plus longuement encore à ce sujet.

J'espère recevoir bientôt de vos nouvelles et vous salue cordialement entretemps.

Votre amie inconnue,

Florence May.

corriger = to correct
le nom = name
étudier = to study
la langue = language
allemand = German
je suis une fervente de =
    I am keen on
prendre part = to take
    part
l'Écosse = Scotland
à ce sujet = about this
recevoir de vos nouvelles
    = to hear from you
bientôt = soon
entretemps = meanwhile
inconnu = unknown

8. Lettres d'affaires

Monsieur,

Ayant appris votre adresse par M. Georges Durant je me permets de vous écrire bien que je n'aie pas encore eu l'honneur de faire votre connaissance.

J'ai le vif désir d'entrer en relations avec la maison que vous représentez. Veuillez avoir l'obligeance de m'indiquer l'heure à laquelle vous pourriez me recevoir.

Agréez, Monsieur, avec mes remercîments l'expression de ma considération distinguée.

Charles Maurois.

appris = learned (from
    apprendre)
je me permets = I take
    the liberty
bien que (+ subj.) =
    although
avoir l'obligeance de = to
    be so kind as
indiquer = to indicate
recevoir = receive

Monsieur,

En possession de votre honorée du 3 ct. (= courant) je m'empresse de vous dire que j'aurai grand plaisir à faire votre connaissance et, si possible, à entrer en rapport avec votre maison si renommée. Vous me trouverez tous les jours, dans l'après-midi, entre les quatre et six heures à l'Hôtel Majestic.

Agréez, Monsieur, l'expression de toute ma considération.

M. Smith.

honorée = esteemed
    favour
courant = instant
le rapport = relation
la maison = firm
renommé = renowned

9. Demande de prix courant (carte-postale)

Messieurs,

Je vous prie de bien vouloir m'envoyer votre dernier tarif.

Agréez, Messieurs, mes salutations empressées,

Julien Herriot.

prier = to ask, to beg
de bien vouloir = to be
    kind enough to
dernier = last, latest
le tarif = price-list

10. Envoi de tarif

Monsieur,

Nous vous accusons réception de votre carte-postale d'hier. Ci-inclus vous trouverez notre dernier tarif.

Dans l'espoir d'être favorisés de vos ordres nous vous prions d'agréer, Monsieur, nos salutations empressées.

A. Legrand et Fils.

accuser = to acknowledge
ci-inclus = enclosed
trouver = to find
favoriser = to favour

The date:	**Paris, le 21 juillet 195-** **le 1ᵉʳ mars 195-** **lundi, le 17 avril, 195-**
Business Letters:	Opening: **Messieurs (Monsieur, Madame)** Ending: **Agréez, Messieurs, mes salutations empressées** or: **Veuillez agréer l'expression de mes sentiments distingués** or: **Agréez, monsieur, mes salutations les plus distinguées**
Moderately familiar:	Opening: **Cher Monsieur (Chère Madame, Chère Mademoiselle)** Ending: **Croyez à mes sentiments distingués** or: **Votre dévoué**
Familiar:	Opening: **Mon cher Dubois (Chère Madame Dubois)** Ending: **Je vous envoie mes meilleurs souvenirs** or: **Bien à vous**

Intimate:	Love Letters:
Opening: **Cher Jules (Chère Marianne)**	To him: **Mon ami** or **Chéri**
Ending: **Affectueusement à toi**	To her: **Mon amie** or **Chérie**
or: **Bien à toi**	Ending: **Ton Georges (Ta Marie)**

The address is as in English, but no abbreviations are used for **Monsieur, Madame, Mademoiselle.**

Printed Matter: **Imprimés** (pl.)

Sample Without Value: **Échantillon sans valeur**

Please forward: **Prière de faire suivre**

C/o: **aux bons soins de . . .**

(The expression **Poste Restante**, for letters addressed to a Post Office to be left till called for, is more or less international.)

EXPRESSIONS IN COMMERCIAL CORRESPONDENCE

J'ai l'avantage de vous faire savoir
J'ai l'honneur de vous informer
= I have pleasure in informing you

En réponse à votre lettre = In reply to your letter

Recevant à l'instant votre lettre du . . . = Having just received your letter of the . . .

Faire savoir = To let (someone) know

J'ai l'honneur, l'avantage = I have the honour, the pleasure

Ayez la bonté (l'obligeance) de = Be so kind as to

Dans l'attente de votre réponse = Awaiting your reply

Espérant être favorisé de votre clientèle = Hoping to be favoured with your kind orders

Je vous suis très obligé de ce service = I am much obliged to you for this (service)

Je suis redevable de votre adresse à = I am indebted to . . . for your address

Ayant appris que vous avez besoin d'un = Having been informed that you require the services of a

J'ai l'honneur de vous offrir mes services = I beg to offer my services

À votre honorée du = to your letter of

Je connais parfaitement ce genre d'affaires =I am perfectly conversant with this (kind of) business

Nous regrettons qu'il nous soit impossible de faire l'expédition le . . . =We regret that we are unable to despatch the goods by the . . .

Nous regrettons de ne pouvoir profiter de votre offre obligeante =We regret that we are unable to avail ourselves of your kind offer

Nous regrettons qu'il nous ait été impossible de répondre plus tôt =We regret that it was impossible for us to reply earlier

La livraison aura lieu le mois prochain =Delivery will be made next month

Nous vous prions d'avoir l'obligeance d'envoyer =We beg you to be good enough to forward

UNE RUE DU VIEUX MARSEILLE

Les maisons s'entretouchaient presque dans ce quartier pittoresque où la lumière du jour y pénétrait à peine. Ce quartier à été détruit pendant la guerre.

s'entretoucher	**la lumière du jour**	**à peine**	**détruire**	**guerre** (f.)
to touch together, meet	daylight	hardly	destroy	war

SEWING AND MENDING
(Key to illustration on page 106)

Aiguille (f.)	**ciseaux (m.pl.)**	**machine (f.) à coudre**	**dé (m.)**	**épingle (f.)**
needle	scissors	sewing machine	thimble	pin
épingle de sûreté	**mannequin (m.)**	**coudre**	**raccommoder**	**repriser**
safety-pin	dressmaker's dummy	to sew	to mend	to darn

RESTAURANT
(Key to illustration on page 165)

Garçon, apportez-moi . . .	**le menu**	**la carte des vins**
Waiter, bring me . . .	bill of fare	wine-list
la carte du jour	**dîner à la table d'hôte**	**l'addition, s'il vous plaît**
menu of the day	to take the set dinner	bill, please

For further expressions see page 197. Fish, page 169. Meat, pages 186–187. Vegetables, page 171. Fruit, pages 183–185. Drink, pages 70–71. Menu, page 168.

CHARACTER

Aimable	**amusant**	**bête**	**bizarre**	**entêté**	**fidèle**
kind	amusing	stupid	odd	obstinate	faithful
gai	**gentil**	**honnête**	**intelligent**	**paresseux**	**ravissant**
bright	nice	honest	clever	lazy	charming
sage[1] **sensé**	**sensible**	**sérieux**	**sympathique**	**timide**	**triste**
wise	sensible	sensitive	earnest	likeable	shy	sad

SPEECH

Parler à haute voix (à voix basse)	**faire savoir à quelqu'un**	**répéter**
to speak loudly (in a low voice)	to let someone know	to repeat
faire une gaffe	**causer avec**	**bavarder** **chuchoter**	**discuter**
to put one's foot in it;	to converse with	to chatter	to whisper	to discuss
to drop a brick				
expliquer	**raconter**	**répliquer**	**bégayer**	**zézayer**	**se taire**
to explain	to tell to, to relate	to reply	to stutter	to lisp	to be silent

AMUSEMENTS
(See also pages 282–287)

Cinéma (m.)	**cirque (m.)**	**salle (f.) de concert**	**opéra (m.)**	**opéra-comique**
cinema	circus	concert hall	opera, opera house	comic opera
revue (f.)	**casino (m.)**	**bal costumé (m.)**	**palais (m.) de danse**	**guignol**[2] **(m.)**
revue	casino	fancy dress ball	dance hall	Punch and Judy show

TREES

Bouleau (m.)	**cerisier (m.)**	**chêne (m.)**	**frêne (m.)**	**hêtre (m.)**
birch	cherry-tree	oak	ash	beech
if (m.)	**orme (m.)**	**peuplier (m.)**	**pommier (m.)**	**sapin (m.)**
yew	elm	poplar	apple tree	fir tree
saule (m.)	**verger (m.)**	**bois (m.)**	**forêt (f.)**	**bosquet (m.)**
willow	orchard	wood	forest	grove; thicket

---

[1] "Well behaved" when referring to children.   [2] Pronounced *geen-yol*.

MONT ST. MICHEL: LA GRANDE RUE

Generations of pilgrims and tourists have worn smooth the flagstones of the main
street of the little island of Mont St. Michel, historic Norman fortress-shrine which
forms the background to Roger Vercel's novel *Sous les Pieds de l'Archange*.

ALPHABETICAL GUIDE TO MAIN CONTENTS

WORD-BUILDING PICTURES AND DIAGRAMS

A CATALOG OF SELECTED
DOVER BOOKS
IN ALL FIELDS OF INTEREST

A CATALOG OF SELECTED DOVER
BOOKS IN ALL FIELDS OF INTEREST

CONCERNING THE SPIRITUAL IN ART, Wassily Kandinsky. Pioneering work by father of abstract art. Thoughts on color theory, nature of art. Analysis of earlier masters. 12 illustrations. 80pp. of text. 5⅜ x 8½. 23411-8

ANIMALS: 1,419 Copyright-Free Illustrations of Mammals, Birds, Fish, Insects, etc., Jim Harter (ed.). Clear wood engravings present, in extremely lifelike poses, over 1,000 species of animals. One of the most extensive pictorial sourcebooks of its kind. Captions. Index. 284pp. 9 x 12. 23766-4

CELTIC ART: The Methods of Construction, George Bain. Simple geometric techniques for making Celtic interlacements, spirals, Kells-type initials, animals, humans, etc. Over 500 illustrations. 160pp. 9 x 12. (Available in U.S. only.) 22923-8

AN ATLAS OF ANATOMY FOR ARTISTS, Fritz Schider. Most thorough reference work on art anatomy in the world. Hundreds of illustrations, including selections from works by Vesalius, Leonardo, Goya, Ingres, Michelangelo, others. 593 illustrations. 192pp. 7⅛ x 10¼. 20241-0

CELTIC HAND STROKE-BY-STROKE (Irish Half-Uncial from "The Book of Kells"): An Arthur Baker Calligraphy Manual, Arthur Baker. Complete guide to creating each letter of the alphabet in distinctive Celtic manner. Covers hand position, strokes, pens, inks, paper, more. Illustrated. 48pp. 8¼ x 11. 24336-2

EASY ORIGAMI, John Montroll. Charming collection of 32 projects (hat, cup, pelican, piano, swan, many more) specially designed for the novice origami hobbyist. Clearly illustrated easy-to-follow instructions insure that even beginning papercrafters will achieve successful results. 48pp. 8¼ x 11. 27298-2

THE COMPLETE BOOK OF BIRDHOUSE CONSTRUCTION FOR WOOD-WORKERS, Scott D. Campbell. Detailed instructions, illustrations, tables. Also data on bird habitat and instinct patterns. Bibliography. 3 tables. 63 illustrations in 15 figures. 48pp. 5¼ x 8½. 24407-5

BLOOMINGDALE'S ILLUSTRATED 1886 CATALOG: Fashions, Dry Goods and Housewares, Bloomingdale Brothers. Famed merchants' extremely rare catalog depicting about 1,700 products: clothing, housewares, firearms, dry goods, jewelry, more. Invaluable for dating, identifying vintage items. Also, copyright-free graphics for artists, designers. Co-published with Henry Ford Museum & Greenfield Village. 160pp. 8¼ x 11. 25780-0

HISTORIC COSTUME IN PICTURES, Braun & Schneider. Over 1,450 costumed figures in clearly detailed engravings–from dawn of civilization to end of 19th century. Captions. Many folk costumes. 256pp. 8⅜ x 11¾. 23150-X

CATALOG OF DOVER BOOKS

HOLLYWOOD GLAMOR PORTRAITS, John Kobal (ed.). 145 photos from 1926-49. Harlow, Gable, Bogart, Bacall; 94 stars in all. Full background on photographers, technical aspects. 160pp. 8⅜ x 11¼. 23352-9

FRANK LLOYD WRIGHT'S DANA HOUSE, Donald Hoffmann. Pictorial essay of residential masterpiece with over 160 interior and exterior photos, plans, elevations, sketches and studies. 128pp. 9¼ x 10¾. 29120-0

THE MALE AND FEMALE FIGURE IN MOTION: 60 Classic Photographic Sequences, Eadweard Muybridge. 60 true-action photographs of men and women walking, running, climbing, bending, turning, etc., reproduced from rare 19th-century masterpiece. vi + 121pp. 9 x 12. 24745-7

1001 QUESTIONS ANSWERED ABOUT THE SEASHORE, N. J. Berrill and Jacquelyn Berrill. Queries answered about dolphins, sea snails, sponges, starfish, fishes, shore birds, many others. Covers appearance, breeding, growth, feeding, much more. 305pp. 5¼ x 8¼. 23366-9

ATTRACTING BIRDS TO YOUR YARD, William J. Weber. Easy-to-follow guide offers advice on how to attract the greatest diversity of birds: birdhouses, feeders, water and waterers, much more. 96pp. 5³⁄₁₆ x 8¼. 28927-3

MEDICINAL AND OTHER USES OF NORTH AMERICAN PLANTS: A Historical Survey with Special Reference to the Eastern Indian Tribes, Charlotte Erichsen-Brown. Chronological historical citations document 500 years of usage of plants, trees, shrubs native to eastern Canada, northeastern U.S. Also complete identifying information. 343 illustrations. 544pp. 6½ x 9¼. 25951-X

STORYBOOK MAZES, Dave Phillips. 23 stories and mazes on two-page spreads: Wizard of Oz, Treasure Island, Robin Hood, etc. Solutions. 64pp. 8¼ x 11. 23628-5

AMERICAN NEGRO SONGS: 230 Folk Songs and Spirituals, Religious and Secular, John W. Work. This authoritative study traces the African influences of songs sung and played by black Americans at work, in church, and as entertainment. The author discusses the lyric significance of such songs as "Swing Low, Sweet Chariot," "John Henry," and others and offers the words and music for 230 songs. Bibliography. Index of Song Titles. 272pp. 6½ x 9¼. 40271-1

MOVIE-STAR PORTRAITS OF THE FORTIES, John Kobal (ed.). 163 glamor, studio photos of 106 stars of the 1940s: Rita Hayworth, Ava Gardner, Marlon Brando, Clark Gable, many more. 176pp. 8⅜ x 11¼. 23546-7

BENCHLEY LOST AND FOUND, Robert Benchley. Finest humor from early 30s, about pet peeves, child psychologists, post office and others. Mostly unavailable elsewhere. 73 illustrations by Peter Arno and others. 183pp. 5⅜ x 8½. 22410-4

YEKL and THE IMPORTED BRIDEGROOM AND OTHER STORIES OF YIDDISH NEW YORK, Abraham Cahan. Film Hester Street based on *Yekl* (1896). Novel, other stories among first about Jewish immigrants on N.Y.'s East Side. 240pp. 5⅜ x 8½. 22427-9

SELECTED POEMS, Walt Whitman. Generous sampling from *Leaves of Grass*. Twenty-four poems include "I Hear America Singing," "Song of the Open Road," "I Sing the Body Electric," "When Lilacs Last in the Dooryard Bloom'd," "O Captain! My Captain!"—all reprinted from an authoritative edition. Lists of titles and first lines. 128pp. 5³⁄₁₆ x 8¼. 26878-0

CATALOG OF DOVER BOOKS

THE BEST TALES OF HOFFMANN, E. T. A. Hoffmann. 10 of Hoffmann's most important stories: "Nutcracker and the King of Mice," "The Golden Flowerpot," etc. 458pp. 5⅜ x 8½. 21793-0

FROM FETISH TO GOD IN ANCIENT EGYPT, E. A. Wallis Budge. Rich detailed survey of Egyptian conception of "God" and gods, magic, cult of animals, Osiris, more. Also, superb English translations of hymns and legends. 240 illustrations. 545pp. 5⅜ x 8½. 25803-3

FRENCH STORIES/CONTES FRANÇAIS: A Dual-Language Book, Wallace Fowlie. Ten stories by French masters, Voltaire to Camus: "Micromegas" by Voltaire; "The Atheist's Mass" by Balzac; "Minuet" by de Maupassant; "The Guest" by Camus, six more. Excellent English translations on facing pages. Also French-English vocabulary list, exercises, more. 352pp. 5⅜ x 8½. 26443-2

CHICAGO AT THE TURN OF THE CENTURY IN PHOTOGRAPHS: 122 Historic Views from the Collections of the Chicago Historical Society, Larry A. Viskochil. Rare large-format prints offer detailed views of City Hall, State Street, the Loop, Hull House, Union Station, many other landmarks, circa 1904-1913. Introduction. Captions. Maps. 144pp. 9⅜ x 12¼. 24656-6

OLD BROOKLYN IN EARLY PHOTOGRAPHS, 1865-1929, William Lee Younger. Luna Park, Gravesend race track, construction of Grand Army Plaza, moving of Hotel Brighton, etc. 157 previously unpublished photographs. 165pp. 8⅞ x 11¾. 23587-4

THE MYTHS OF THE NORTH AMERICAN INDIANS, Lewis Spence. Rich anthology of the myths and legends of the Algonquins, Iroquois, Pawnees and Sioux, prefaced by an extensive historical and ethnological commentary. 36 illustrations. 480pp. 5⅜ x 8½. 25967-6

AN ENCYCLOPEDIA OF BATTLES: Accounts of Over 1,560 Battles from 1479 B.C. to the Present, David Eggenberger. Essential details of every major battle in recorded history from the first battle of Megiddo in 1479 B.C. to Grenada in 1984. List of Battle Maps. New Appendix covering the years 1967-1984. Index. 99 illustrations. 544pp. 6½ x 9¼. 24913-1

SAILING ALONE AROUND THE WORLD, Captain Joshua Slocum. First man to sail around the world, alone, in small boat. One of great feats of seamanship told in delightful manner. 67 illustrations. 294pp. 5⅜ x 8½. 20326-3

ANARCHISM AND OTHER ESSAYS, Emma Goldman. Powerful, penetrating, prophetic essays on direct action, role of minorities, prison reform, puritan hypocrisy, violence, etc. 271pp. 5⅜ x 8½. 22484-8

MYTHS OF THE HINDUS AND BUDDHISTS, Ananda K. Coomaraswamy and Sister Nivedita. Great stories of the epics; deeds of Krishna, Shiva, taken from puranas, Vedas, folk tales; etc. 32 illustrations. 400pp. 5⅜ x 8½. 21759-0

THE TRAUMA OF BIRTH, Otto Rank. Rank's controversial thesis that anxiety neurosis is caused by profound psychological trauma which occurs at birth. 256pp. 5⅜ x 8½. 27974-X

A THEOLOGICO-POLITICAL TREATISE, Benedict Spinoza. Also contains unfinished Political Treatise. Great classic on religious liberty, theory of government on common consent. R. Elwes translation. Total of 421pp. 5⅜ x 8½. 20249-6

PERSPECTIVE FOR ARTISTS, Rex Vicat Cole. Depth, perspective of sky and sea, shadows, much more, not usually covered. 391 diagrams, 81 reproductions of drawings and paintings. 279pp. 5⅜ x 8½. 22487-2

DRAWING THE LIVING FIGURE, Joseph Sheppard. Innovative approach to artistic anatomy focuses on specifics of surface anatomy, rather than muscles and bones. Over 170 drawings of live models in front, back and side views, and in widely varying poses. Accompanying diagrams. 177 illustrations. Introduction. Index. 144pp. 8⅜ x11¼. 26723-7

GOTHIC AND OLD ENGLISH ALPHABETS: 100 Complete Fonts, Dan X. Solo. Add power, elegance to posters, signs, other graphics with 100 stunning copyright-free alphabets: Blackstone, Dolbey, Germania, 97 more—including many lower-case, numerals, punctuation marks. 104pp. 8⅛ x 11. 24695-7

HOW TO DO BEADWORK, Mary White. Fundamental book on craft from simple projects to five-bead chains and woven works. 106 illustrations. 142pp. 5⅜ x 8. 20697-1

THE BOOK OF WOOD CARVING, Charles Marshall Sayers. Finest book for beginners discusses fundamentals and offers 34 designs. "Absolutely first rate . . . well thought out and well executed."–E. J. Tangerman. 118pp. 7¾ x 10⅝. 23654-4

ILLUSTRATED CATALOG OF CIVIL WAR MILITARY GOODS: Union Army Weapons, Insignia, Uniform Accessories, and Other Equipment, Schuyler, Hartley, and Graham. Rare, profusely illustrated 1846 catalog includes Union Army uniform and dress regulations, arms and ammunition, coats, insignia, flags, swords, rifles, etc. 226 illustrations. 160pp. 9 x 12. 24939-5

WOMEN'S FASHIONS OF THE EARLY 1900s: An Unabridged Republication of "New York Fashions, 1909," National Cloak & Suit Co. Rare catalog of mail-order fashions documents women's and children's clothing styles shortly after the turn of the century. Captions offer full descriptions, prices. Invaluable resource for fashion, costume historians. Approximately 725 illustrations. 128pp. 8⅜ x 11¼. 27276-1

THE 1912 AND 1915 GUSTAV STICKLEY FURNITURE CATALOGS, Gustav Stickley. With over 200 detailed illustrations and descriptions, these two catalogs are essential reading and reference materials and identification guides for Stickley furniture. Captions cite materials, dimensions and prices. 112pp. 6½ x 9¼. 26676-1

EARLY AMERICAN LOCOMOTIVES, John H. White, Jr. Finest locomotive engravings from early 19th century: historical (1804–74), main-line (after 1870), special, foreign, etc. 147 plates. 142pp. 11⅜ x 8¼. 22772-3

THE TALL SHIPS OF TODAY IN PHOTOGRAPHS, Frank O. Braynard. Lavishly illustrated tribute to nearly 100 majestic contemporary sailing vessels: Amerigo Vespucci, Clearwater, Constitution, Eagle, Mayflower, Sea Cloud, Victory, many more. Authoritative captions provide statistics, background on each ship. 190 black-and-white photographs and illustrations. Introduction. 128pp. 8⅞ x 11¾. 27163-3

LITTLE BOOK OF EARLY AMERICAN CRAFTS AND TRADES, Peter Stockham (ed.). 1807 children's book explains crafts and trades: baker, hatter, cooper, potter, and many others. 23 copperplate illustrations. 140pp. 4⅝ x 6. 23336-7

VICTORIAN FASHIONS AND COSTUMES FROM HARPER'S BAZAR, 1867–1898, Stella Blum (ed.). Day costumes, evening wear, sports clothes, shoes, hats, other accessories in over 1,000 detailed engravings. 320pp. 9⅜ x 12¼. 22990-4

GUSTAV STICKLEY, THE CRAFTSMAN, Mary Ann Smith. Superb study surveys broad scope of Stickley's achievement, especially in architecture. Design philosophy, rise and fall of the Craftsman empire, descriptions and floor plans for many Craftsman houses, more. 86 black-and-white halftones. 31 line illustrations. Introduction 208pp. 6½ x 9¼. 27210-9

THE LONG ISLAND RAIL ROAD IN EARLY PHOTOGRAPHS, Ron Ziel. Over 220 rare photos, informative text document origin (1844) and development of rail service on Long Island. Vintage views of early trains, locomotives, stations, passengers, crews, much more. Captions. 8⅞ x 11¾. 26301-0

VOYAGE OF THE LIBERDADE, Joshua Slocum. Great 19th-century mariner's thrilling, first-hand account of the wreck of his ship off South America, the 35-foot boat he built from the wreckage, and its remarkable voyage home. 128pp. 5⅜ x 8½. 40022-0

TEN BOOKS ON ARCHITECTURE, Vitruvius. The most important book ever written on architecture. Early Roman aesthetics, technology, classical orders, site selection, all other aspects. Morgan translation. 331pp. 5⅜ x 8½. 20645-9

THE HUMAN FIGURE IN MOTION, Eadweard Muybridge. More than 4,500 stopped-action photos, in action series, showing undraped men, women, children jumping, lying down, throwing, sitting, wrestling, carrying, etc. 390pp. 7⅞ x 10⅝. 20204-6 Clothbd.

TREES OF THE EASTERN AND CENTRAL UNITED STATES AND CANADA, William M. Harlow. Best one-volume guide to 140 trees. Full descriptions, woodlore, range, etc. Over 600 illustrations. Handy size. 288pp. 4½ x 6⅜. 20395-6

SONGS OF WESTERN BIRDS, Dr. Donald J. Borror. Complete song and call repertoire of 60 western species, including flycatchers, juncoes, cactus wrens, many more—includes fully illustrated booklet. Cassette and manual 99913-0

GROWING AND USING HERBS AND SPICES, Milo Miloradovich. Versatile handbook provides all the information needed for cultivation and use of all the herbs and spices available in North America. 4 illustrations. Index. Glossary. 236pp. 5⅜ x 8½. 25058-X

BIG BOOK OF MAZES AND LABYRINTHS, Walter Shepherd. 50 mazes and labyrinths in all—classical, solid, ripple, and more—in one great volume. Perfect inexpensive puzzler for clever youngsters. Full solutions. 112pp. 8⅛ x 11. 22951-3

ANATOMY: A Complete Guide for Artists, Joseph Sheppard. A master of figure drawing shows artists how to render human anatomy convincingly. Over 460 illustrations. 224pp. 8⅜ x 11¼. 27279-6

MEDIEVAL CALLIGRAPHY: Its History and Technique, Marc Drogin. Spirited history, comprehensive instruction manual covers 13 styles (ca. 4th century through 15th). Excellent photographs; directions for duplicating medieval techniques with modern tools. 224pp. 8⅜ x 11¼. 26142-5

DRIED FLOWERS: How to Prepare Them, Sarah Whitlock and Martha Rankin. Complete instructions on how to use silica gel, meal and borax, perlite aggregate, sand and borax, glycerine and water to create attractive permanent flower arrangements. 12 illustrations. 32pp. 5⅜ x 8½. 21802-3

EASY-TO-MAKE BIRD FEEDERS FOR WOODWORKERS, Scott D. Campbell. Detailed, simple-to-use guide for designing, constructing, caring for and using feeders. Text, illustrations for 12 classic and contemporary designs. 96pp. 5⅜ x 8½. 25847-5

SCOTTISH WONDER TALES FROM MYTH AND LEGEND, Donald A. Mackenzie. 16 lively tales tell of giants rumbling down mountainsides, of a magic wand that turns stone pillars into warriors, of gods and goddesses, evil hags, powerful forces and more. 240pp. 5⅜ x 8½. 29677-6

THE HISTORY OF UNDERCLOTHES, C. Willett Cunnington and Phyllis Cunnington. Fascinating, well-documented survey covering six centuries of English undergarments, enhanced with over 100 illustrations: 12th-century laced-up bodice, footed long drawers (1795), 19th-century bustles, 19th-century corsets for men, Victorian "bust improvers," much more. 272pp. 5⅝ x 8¼. 27124-2

ARTS AND CRAFTS FURNITURE: The Complete Brooks Catalog of 1912, Brooks Manufacturing Co. Photos and detailed descriptions of more than 150 now very collectible furniture designs from the Arts and Crafts movement depict davenports, settees, buffets, desks, tables, chairs, bedsteads, dressers and more, all built of solid, quarter-sawed oak. Invaluable for students and enthusiasts of antiques, Americana and the decorative arts. 80pp. 6½ x 9¼. 27471-3

WILBUR AND ORVILLE: A Biography of the Wright Brothers, Fred Howard. Definitive, crisply written study tells the full story of the brothers' lives and work. A vividly written biography, unparalleled in scope and color, that also captures the spirit of an extraordinary era. 560pp. 6⅛ x 9¼. 40297-5

THE ARTS OF THE SAILOR: Knotting, Splicing and Ropework, Hervey Garrett Smith. Indispensable shipboard reference covers tools, basic knots and useful hitches; handsewing and canvas work, more. Over 100 illustrations. Delightful reading for sea lovers. 256pp. 5⅜ x 8½. 26440-8

FRANK LLOYD WRIGHT'S FALLINGWATER: The House and Its History, Second, Revised Edition, Donald Hoffmann. A total revision–both in text and illustrations–of the standard document on Fallingwater, the boldest, most personal architectural statement of Wright's mature years, updated with valuable new material from the recently opened Frank Lloyd Wright Archives. "Fascinating"–*The New York Times.* 116 illustrations. 128pp. 9¼ x 10¾. 27430-6

PHOTOGRAPHIC SKETCHBOOK OF THE CIVIL WAR, Alexander Gardner. 100 photos taken on field during the Civil War. Famous shots of Manassas Harper's Ferry, Lincoln, Richmond, slave pens, etc. 244pp. 10⅝ x 8¼. 22731-6

FIVE ACRES AND INDEPENDENCE, Maurice G. Kains. Great back-to-the-land classic explains basics of self-sufficient farming. The one book to get. 95 illustrations. 397pp. 5⅜ x 8½. 20974-1

SONGS OF EASTERN BIRDS, Dr. Donald J. Borror. Songs and calls of 60 species most common to eastern U.S.: warblers, woodpeckers, flycatchers, thrushes, larks, many more in high-quality recording. Cassette and manual 99912-2

A MODERN HERBAL, Margaret Grieve. Much the fullest, most exact, most useful compilation of herbal material. Gigantic alphabetical encyclopedia, from aconite to zedoary, gives botanical information, medical properties, folklore, economic uses, much else. Indispensable to serious reader. 161 illustrations. 888pp. 6½ x 9¼. 2-vol. set. (Available in U.S. only.) Vol. I: 22798-7
Vol. II: 22799-5

HIDDEN TREASURE MAZE BOOK, Dave Phillips. Solve 34 challenging mazes accompanied by heroic tales of adventure. Evil dragons, people-eating plants, blood-thirsty giants, many more dangerous adversaries lurk at every twist and turn. 34 mazes, stories, solutions. 48pp. 8¼ x 11. 24566-7

LETTERS OF W. A. MOZART, Wolfgang A. Mozart. Remarkable letters show bawdy wit, humor, imagination, musical insights, contemporary musical world; includes some letters from Leopold Mozart. 276pp. 5⅜ x 8½. 22859-2

BASIC PRINCIPLES OF CLASSICAL BALLET, Agrippina Vaganova. Great Russian theoretician, teacher explains methods for teaching classical ballet. 118 illustrations. 175pp. 5⅜ x 8½. 22036-2

THE JUMPING FROG, Mark Twain. Revenge edition. The original story of The Celebrated Jumping Frog of Calaveras County, a hapless French translation, and Twain's hilarious "retranslation" from the French. 12 illustrations. 66pp. 5⅜ x 8½. 22686-7

BEST REMEMBERED POEMS, Martin Gardner (ed.). The 126 poems in this superb collection of 19th- and 20th-century British and American verse range from Shelley's "To a Skylark" to the impassioned "Renascence" of Edna St. Vincent Millay and to Edward Lear's whimsical "The Owl and the Pussycat." 224pp. 5⅜ x 8½. 27165-X

COMPLETE SONNETS, William Shakespeare. Over 150 exquisite poems deal with love, friendship, the tyranny of time, beauty's evanescence, death and other themes in language of remarkable power, precision and beauty. Glossary of archaic terms. 80pp. 5³⁄₁₆ x 8¼. 26686-9

THE BATTLES THAT CHANGED HISTORY, Fletcher Pratt. Eminent historian profiles 16 crucial conflicts, ancient to modern, that changed the course of civilization. 352pp. 5⅜ x 8½. 41129-X

THE WIT AND HUMOR OF OSCAR WILDE, Alvin Redman (ed.). More than 1,000 ripostes, paradoxes, wisecracks: Work is the curse of the drinking classes; I can resist everything except temptation; etc. 258pp. 5⅜ x 8½. 20602-5

SHAKESPEARE LEXICON AND QUOTATION DICTIONARY, Alexander Schmidt. Full definitions, locations, shades of meaning in every word in plays and poems. More than 50,000 exact quotations. 1,485pp. 6½ x 9¼. 2-vol. set.
Vol. 1: 22726-X
Vol. 2: 22727-8

SELECTED POEMS, Emily Dickinson. Over 100 best-known, best-loved poems by one of America's foremost poets, reprinted from authoritative early editions. No comparable edition at this price. Index of first lines. 64pp. 5³⁄₁₆ x 8¼. 26466-1

THE INSIDIOUS DR. FU-MANCHU, Sax Rohmer. The first of the popular mystery series introduces a pair of English detectives to their archnemesis, the diabolical Dr. Fu-Manchu. Flavorful atmosphere, fast-paced action, and colorful characters enliven this classic of the genre. 208pp. 5³⁄₁₆ x 8¼. 29898-1

THE MALLEUS MALEFICARUM OF KRAMER AND SPRENGER, translated by Montague Summers. Full text of most important witchhunter's "bible," used by both Catholics and Protestants. 278pp. 6⅝ x 10. 22802-9

SPANISH STORIES/CUENTOS ESPAÑOLES: A Dual-Language Book, Angel Flores (ed.). Unique format offers 13 great stories in Spanish by Cervantes, Borges, others. Faithful English translations on facing pages. 352pp. 5⅜ x 8½. 25399-6

GARDEN CITY, LONG ISLAND, IN EARLY PHOTOGRAPHS, 1869–1919, Mildred H. Smith. Handsome treasury of 118 vintage pictures, accompanied by carefully researched captions, document the Garden City Hotel fire (1899), the Vanderbilt Cup Race (1908), the first airmail flight departing from the Nassau Boulevard Aerodrome (1911), and much more. 96pp. 8⅞ x 11¾. 40669-5

OLD QUEENS, N.Y., IN EARLY PHOTOGRAPHS, Vincent F. Seyfried and William Asadorian. Over 160 rare photographs of Maspeth, Jamaica, Jackson Heights, and other areas. Vintage views of DeWitt Clinton mansion, 1939 World's Fair and more. Captions. 192pp. 8⅞ x 11. 26358-4

CAPTURED BY THE INDIANS: 15 Firsthand Accounts, 1750-1870, Frederick Drimmer. Astounding true historical accounts of grisly torture, bloody conflicts, relentless pursuits, miraculous escapes and more, by people who lived to tell the tale. 384pp. 5⅜ x 8½. 24901-8

THE WORLD'S GREAT SPEECHES (Fourth Enlarged Edition), Lewis Copeland, Lawrence W. Lamm, and Stephen J. McKenna. Nearly 300 speeches provide public speakers with a wealth of updated quotes and inspiration–from Pericles' funeral oration and William Jennings Bryan's "Cross of Gold Speech" to Malcolm X's powerful words on the Black Revolution and Earl of Spenser's tribute to his sister, Diana, Princess of Wales. 944pp. 5⅜ x 8⅜. 40903-1

THE BOOK OF THE SWORD, Sir Richard F. Burton. Great Victorian scholar/adventurer's eloquent, erudite history of the "queen of weapons"–from prehistory to early Roman Empire. Evolution and development of early swords, variations (sabre, broadsword, cutlass, scimitar, etc.), much more. 336pp. 6⅛ x 9¼. 25434-8

AUTOBIOGRAPHY: The Story of My Experiments with Truth, Mohandas K. Gandhi. Boyhood, legal studies, purification, the growth of the Satyagraha (nonviolent protest) movement. Critical, inspiring work of the man responsible for the freedom of India. 480pp. 5⅜ x 8½. (Available in U.S. only.) 24593-4

CELTIC MYTHS AND LEGENDS, T. W. Rolleston. Masterful retelling of Irish and Welsh stories and tales. Cuchulain, King Arthur, Deirdre, the Grail, many more. First paperback edition. 58 full-page illustrations. 512pp. 5⅜ x 8½. 26507-2

THE PRINCIPLES OF PSYCHOLOGY, William James. Famous long course complete, unabridged. Stream of thought, time perception, memory, experimental methods; great work decades ahead of its time. 94 figures. 1,391pp. 5⅜ x 8½. 2-vol. set.
Vol. I: 20381-6   Vol. II: 20382-4

THE WORLD AS WILL AND REPRESENTATION, Arthur Schopenhauer. Definitive English translation of Schopenhauer's life work, correcting more than 1,000 errors, omissions in earlier translations. Translated by E. F. J. Payne. Total of 1,269pp. 5⅜ x 8½. 2-vol. set.
Vol. 1: 21761-2   Vol. 2: 21762-0

MAGIC AND MYSTERY IN TIBET, Madame Alexandra David-Neel. Experiences among lamas, magicians, sages, sorcerers, Bonpa wizards. A true psychic discovery. 32 illustrations. 321pp. 5⅜ x 8½. (Available in U.S. only.) 22682-4

THE EGYPTIAN BOOK OF THE DEAD, E. A. Wallis Budge. Complete reproduction of Ani's papyrus, finest ever found. Full hieroglyphic text, interlinear transliteration, word-for-word translation, smooth translation. 533pp. 6½ x 9¼. 21866-X

MATHEMATICS FOR THE NONMATHEMATICIAN, Morris Kline. Detailed, college-level treatment of mathematics in cultural and historical context, with numerous exercises. Recommended Reading Lists. Tables. Numerous figures. 641pp. 5⅜ x 8½. 24823-2

PROBABILISTIC METHODS IN THE THEORY OF STRUCTURES, Isaac Elishakoff. Well-written introduction covers the elements of the theory of probability from two or more random variables, the reliability of such multivariable structures, the theory of random function, Monte Carlo methods of treating problems incapable of exact solution, and more. Examples. 502pp. 5⅜ x 8½. 40691-1

THE RIME OF THE ANCIENT MARINER, Gustave Doré, S. T. Coleridge. Doré's finest work; 34 plates capture moods, subtleties of poem. Flawless full-size reproductions printed on facing pages with authoritative text of poem. "Beautiful. Simply beautiful."—Publisher's Weekly. 77pp. 9¼ x 12. 22305-1

NORTH AMERICAN INDIAN DESIGNS FOR ARTISTS AND CRAFTSPEOPLE, Eva Wilson. Over 360 authentic copyright-free designs adapted from Navajo blankets, Hopi pottery, Sioux buffalo hides, more. Geometrics, symbolic figures, plant and animal motifs, etc. 128pp. 8⅜ x 11. (Not for sale in the United Kingdom.) 25341-4

SCULPTURE: Principles and Practice, Louis Slobodkin. Step-by-step approach to clay, plaster, metals, stone; classical and modern. 253 drawings, photos. 255pp. 8⅛ x 11. 22960-2

THE INFLUENCE OF SEA POWER UPON HISTORY, 1660–1783, A. T. Mahan. Influential classic of naval history and tactics still used as text in war colleges. First paperback edition. 4 maps. 24 battle plans. 640pp. 5⅜ x 8½. 25509-3

CATALOG OF DOVER BOOKS

THE STORY OF THE TITANIC AS TOLD BY ITS SURVIVORS, Jack Winocour (ed.). What it was really like. Panic, despair, shocking inefficiency, and a little heroism. More thrilling than any fictional account. 26 illustrations. 320pp. 5⅜ x 8½.
20610-6

FAIRY AND FOLK TALES OF THE IRISH PEASANTRY, William Butler Yeats (ed.). Treasury of 64 tales from the twilight world of Celtic myth and legend: "The Soul Cages," "The Kildare Pooka," "King O'Toole and his Goose," many more. Introduction and Notes by W. B. Yeats. 352pp. 5⅜ x 8½.
26941-8

BUDDHIST MAHAYANA TEXTS, E. B. Cowell and others (eds.). Superb, accurate translations of basic documents in Mahayana Buddhism, highly important in history of religions. The Buddha-karita of Asvaghosha, Larger Sukhavativyuha, more. 448pp. 5⅜ x 8½.
25552-2

ONE TWO THREE . . . INFINITY: Facts and Speculations of Science, George Gamow. Great physicist's fascinating, readable overview of contemporary science: number theory, relativity, fourth dimension, entropy, genes, atomic structure, much more. 128 illustrations. Index. 352pp. 5⅜ x 8½.
25664-2

EXPERIMENTATION AND MEASUREMENT, W. J. Youden. Introductory manual explains laws of measurement in simple terms and offers tips for achieving accuracy and minimizing errors. Mathematics of measurement, use of instruments, experimenting with machines. 1994 edition. Foreword. Preface. Introduction. Epilogue. Selected Readings. Glossary. Index. Tables and figures. 128pp. 5⅜ x 8½.
40451-X

DALÍ ON MODERN ART: The Cuckolds of Antiquated Modern Art, Salvador Dalí. Influential painter skewers modern art and its practitioners. Outrageous evaluations of Picasso, Cézanne, Turner, more. 15 renderings of paintings discussed. 44 calligraphic decorations by Dalí. 96pp. 5⅜ x 8½. (Available in U.S. only.)
29220-7

ANTIQUE PLAYING CARDS: A Pictorial History, Henry René D'Allemagne. Over 900 elaborate, decorative images from rare playing cards (14th–20th centuries): Bacchus, death, dancing dogs, hunting scenes, royal coats of arms, players cheating, much more. 96pp. 9¼ x 12¼.
29265-7

MAKING FURNITURE MASTERPIECES: 30 Projects with Measured Drawings, Franklin H. Gottshall. Step-by-step instructions, illustrations for constructing handsome, useful pieces, among them a Sheraton desk, Chippendale chair, Spanish desk, Queen Anne table and a William and Mary dressing mirror. 224pp. 8⅛ x 11¼.
29338-6

THE FOSSIL BOOK: A Record of Prehistoric Life, Patricia V. Rich et al. Profusely illustrated definitive guide covers everything from single-celled organisms and dinosaurs to birds and mammals and the interplay between climate and man. Over 1,500 illustrations. 760pp. 7½ x 10⅛.
29371-8